The Natural History of

WHALES &
DOLPHINS

The Natural History of

WHALES & DOLPHINS

PETER G. H. EVANS

Facts On File Publications
New York • Oxford

First Published in the United States of America by Facts on File, Inc.
460 Park Avenue South, New York, New York 10016.

Library of Congress Cataloging-in-Publications Data
Evans, Peter G. H.
  The natural history of whales and dolphins.
  Bibliography: p.
  Includes index.
  1. Cetacea.   I. Title.
QL737.C4E93   1987   599.5   86–24037
ISBN 0–8160–1732–8

10   9   8   7   6   5   4   3   2   1

Printed in Great Britain

Contents

Colour plates

Tables

Figures

Series editor's foreword

In recent years there has been a great upsurge of interest in wildlife and a deepening concern for nature conservation. For many there is a compelling urge to counterbalance some of the artificiality of present-day living with a more intimate involvement with the natural world. More people are coming to realise that we are all part of nature, not apart from it. There seems to be a greater desire to understand its complexities and appreciate its beauty.

This appreciation of wildlife and wild places has been greatly stimulated by the world-wide impact of natural-history television programmes. These have brought into our homes the sights and sounds both of our own countryside and of far-off places that arouse our interest and delight.

In parallel with this growth of interest there has been a great expansion of knowledge and, above all, understanding of the natural world — an understanding vital to any conservation measures that can be taken to safeguard it. More and more field workers have carried out painstaking studies of many species, analysing their intricate behaviour, relationships and the part they play in the general ecology of their habitats. To the time-honoured techniques of field observations and experimentation has been added the sophistication of radio-telemetry whereby individual animals can be followed, even in the dark and over long periods, and their activities recorded. Infra-red cameras and light-intensifying binoculars now add a new dimension to the study of nocturnal animals. Through such devices great advances have been made.

This series of volumes aims to bring this information together in an exciting and readable form so that all who are interested in wildlife may benefit from such a synthesis. Many of the titles in the series concern groups of related species such as otters, squirrels and rabbits so that readers from many parts of the world may learn about their own more familiar animals in a much wider context. Inevitably more emphasis will be given to particular species within a group as some have been more extensively studied than others. Authors too have their own special interests and experience and a text gains much in authority and vividness when there has been personal involvement.

Many natural history books have been published in recent years which have delighted the eye and fired the imagination. This is wholly good. But it is the intention of this series to take this a step further by exploring the subject in greater depth and by making available the results of recent research. In this way it is hoped to satisfy to some extent at least the curiosity and desire to know more which is such an encouraging characteristic of the keen naturalist of today.

Ernest Neal
Taunton

Preface

The 1st of September 1968 was one of those typical days of early autumn. After a cold clear night, a veil of mist lay over the sea, occasionally broken by glimpses of the shadowy cliffs of the southern Irish coast. Then as the sun rose the mist faded to reveal a perfect day — no cloud in the sky and a mirror calm sea. Our 10m sailing boat slipped from the quayside of Kinsale, and we moved at about five knots (9km per hour) along the steep cliffs of the Cork coast past the Old Head of Kinsale. We intended to make a transect southwards to a rich fishing bank, known as the Labadie Bank. We were nearing the end of two months of surveys, directed at determining the distribution of seabirds at sea. Most of the team were anxious to see the large numbers of great and Cory's shearwaters that had been seen in previous summers from the cliffs of Cape Clear bird observatory. However, such observations are favoured by periods of strong westerly or southwesterly winds and instead we were treated to anti-cyclonic weather with cloudless skies and flat calm seas. Although we saw few large movements of seabirds, we did see large numbers of dolphins. As we moved south on this September morning, I was eagerly anticipating further schools of common dolphins on the way to the fishing banks.

About 5km past the Old Head of Kinsale, we saw a distant shape above the horizon. I concluded that it was a ship many kilometres away and only glimpsed briefly being so close to the horizon. Imagine my surprise when the ship came into view again and revealed itself to be a fin whale, twice as large as our own boat. It broke the surface allowing us to see the entire back and small curved dorsal fin before sending a plume of steam into the air and descending once more in a shallow dive. That was my first introduction to whales — and one I shall never forget.

The many sightings of cetaceans we had on that cruise fired the enthusiasm of Peter Kinnear and myself and we resolved to set up a group to learn more about these creatures in the waters of Britain and Ireland. Up to that time our knowledge had come either from earlier whaling activities off the Scottish and Irish coasts, or as a result of animals being washed up on our shores. No information had been derived from live sightings.

During our two months' cruise we had battled with problems of identification and many of our sightings were unconfirmed. However, with increasing experience we were able to distinguish the closely related white-sided and white-beaked dolphins and some of the larger rorquals (members of the family that includes blue, fin, minke and humpback whales), and we became more confident that difficulties of identification could be overcome. Nowadays, there are many such cruises in different parts of the world, and a growing body of experienced observers. Once the key identification features are known, the problems though still present are made much easier. Our first task when setting up a Cetacean Group in the UK was to convince sceptics that identification was possible at sea.

In 1973, we formed a Cetacean Group within the UK Mammal Society, and now there exists a network of observers, including some professional zoologists as well as many amateurs, numbering over 300 persons, who provide sightings records from around the British Isles. This has provided us with a reasonable picture of the status and distribution of different cetacean species in our seas, complementing the information collected by the British Museum's strandings scheme. Sightings are logged on standardised recording forms, with descriptions and/or photographs to help verify identification; they are then transcribed along with environmental information onto a computer data base for future analysis. In order to overcome the problems of varying effort in different months of the year or at different locations, a number of observers operate on a regular basis and both effort and weather conditions are quantified. In this way, we have been able to follow patterns in seasonal occurrence for different species as well as changes in the numbers observed over time. Sometimes this has revealed information about breeding seasons, and aspects of ecology and behaviour. It has also pinpointed areas where particular species may concentrate, enabling us to make more intensive cruises to study the ecology and behaviour of those particular species. We are far behind our American colleagues, partly through lack of resources; but it is to be hoped that we will be able to develop these aspects further in the not too distant future.

I was a schoolboy when I saw that first whale, but in the 18 years since then I have been lucky enough to travel to many different parts of the world to see species uncommon or absent from British shores. Amongst ice floes in West Greenland, I have watched humpback whales propelling their enormous bulks fully out of the water, their long flippers beating the surface. I have stood on a scorching hot hilltop surrounded by cactus plants, observing a sperm whale basking over a Caribbean coral reef. I have sat in a small pirogue with a vast school of spinner dolphins leaping and spinning around me in the Indian Ocean. I have never ceased to be in awe of these magnificent animals. For centuries their lives have remained an almost complete mystery to us whilst we have exploited them often to near extinction. Only now are we beginning to give them the respect they deserve, as we unravel some of their fascinating secrets.

Our knowledge of the lives of whales and dolphins has burgeoned enormously in the last 15 years. With restrictions upon commercial whaling, an ever increasing number of whale researchers have concentrated their efforts upon observations at sea. To overcome some of the tremendous problems in studying animals that live most of their lives out of view under the surface of the sea, methods have been devised which were sometimes costly and often ingenious. I shall try to review some of these, but in a book of this length, it is obviously not possible to present a comprehensive account nor indeed am I the most appropriate person to write it. Instead my aim is to give the reader an introduction to whales and dolphins, particularly their ecology and behaviour, pointing to more detailed sources of information should the reader wish to follow up particular aspects.

My interest in cetaceans has often had to take second place to other research, notably in population genetics and evolutionary ecology. Sometimes these other interests will surface in this book. However, any personal viewpoints or speculations will be emphasised as such so the reader can distinguish them from others. Natural history and zoology books often do not pay sufficient attention to distinguishing well-supported fact from speculation, and books on cetaceans are certainly no exception. There have been so many myths about cetaceans propagated in this way, which have contributed more confusion than light. I hope I shall not be contributing further.

In order not to fill the text with scientific names nor too many references, I have confined the former to an extended check list of cetaceans in Chapter 3, and been selective with the references I have cited, with emphasis where possible on recent publications and those that are likely to be reasonably accessible. I am unhappy about restricting the number of references in this way but with such a vast literature it is possibly the only way to ensure that the text flows reasonably well. I have tried to make sure, wherever possible, that particular findings I quote are attributed to the appropriate persons. If one is to try to be up to date, then it becomes necessary often to present results not yet published formally. Indeed, much literature on cetaceans is available only as unpublished reports or conference abstracts and often has not been reviewed by fellow scientists. These preliminary results are nevertheless very important and I gratefully acknowledge the many friends and colleagues who have made them available. By the time this book is read, it is likely that many of these will have been published in more accessible periodicals.

In particular, I should like to thank the following for giving up their time constructively to criticise sections of this book: Alan Baker, John Bannister, Lawrence Barnes, Nigel Bonner, Sidney Brown, David Caldwell, Raymond Duguy, Bill Evans, Ray Gambell, David Gaskin, Natalie Goodall, Jonathan Gordon, Louis Herman, Toshio Kasuya, Christina Lockyer, David Macdonald, Bruce Mate, Simon Northridge, Hideo Omura, Bill Perrin, Ricardo Praderi, Randall Reeves, Graham Ross, Chris Smeenk, Bill Watkins, Howard Winn and Bernd Wursig. For the excellent line drawings, I should like to thank Michael Clark and also Euan Dunn; and for various help, I thank Stephanie Hall, Frances Haynes, Mary-Rose Lane and Gina Scanlan. Photographs were kindly provided by Tom Arnbom, Ken Balcomb, Arnoud van den Berg, Howard Braham, Steve Leatherwood, Tony Martin, Thomas Sorensen and Tim Waters, with help from Carl Kinze, Christina Lockyer, Vassili Papastavrou and Chris Smeenk. A number of friends/colleagues and their publishers are gratefully acknowledged for reproduction of figures from their work. Those sources are cited in the figure headings, and full details are then given in the bibliography. Finally I am grateful to Ernest Neal for his help and encouragement.

1 Whales and dolphins — an introduction to the order Cetacea

Whales and dolphins are the most specialised of mammals. They live their lives entirely in water, sometimes at great depths where little light penetrates yet sounds may echo hundreds of kilometres across vast undersea chasms. We can do little but marvel at adaptations of form and physiology, behaviour and ecology demanded by their specialised existence.

For most people, their first observation will be of a torpedo-shaped body streaming through the surface of the water, its curved dorsal fin catching the sun before the animal submerges again. The immediate reaction might be that this is a shark, a cold-blooded fish which it superficially resembles. Dolphins and their larger whale relatives, however, are most definitely mammals. They are warm-blooded; they breathe air with lungs and so must periodically come to the surface; and they give birth to live young which the mother suckles on milk secreted by its mammary glands.

Being warm-blooded, cetaceans must use some of their energy to maintain a stable body-core temperature. Most land mammals do this by an insulating coat of hair or fur; however, in water this would impede progress and reduce any advantage gained by their streamlined form. Cetaceans overcome this with an insulating layer of fat called blubber. This varies in thickness between species; in the bowhead whale of Arctic waters, it may be as much as 50cm thick, with a skin epidermis six to eight times thicker than any other cetacean. Within a number of species, it may also vary between seasons; many of the great whales build up fat reserves as a thick layer of blubber during their season of feeding in polar waters, in preparation for a long migration into relatively unproductive warmer waters where many will mate or calve. In this way, they can maintain a stable body temperature of 36–37°C despite living in an environment that is usually less than 25°C and may be as low as 10°C. Fat may also be laid down in other regions of the body — in organs such as the liver, tissues such as muscle, and in bone in the form of oil where it may account for as much as 50 per cent of the body total.

Not all cetaceans lack hair, however. The right whale, for example, has hairs along the chin and upper jaw, and its relative the bowhead has hair follicles on the snout, lips and chin, and behind the blowholes; the young of some species have hairs around their snout. We may speculate that these represent vestigial characters in the evolution of aquatic living by Cetacea. However, whilst they exist, they may serve as tactile organs in a social or sexual context. Other vestigial characters inherited from terrestrial ancestors include olfactory nerves (serving the sense of smell) and hindlimb bones, visible only within the body skeleton.

The thick layer of blubber is but one way that cetaceans are able to maintain their body temperature. Within that layer is a fine network of thin-walled capillaries which operate what is referred to as a counter-current system, the heat lost from outflowing blood (from the warm body core) being at least partly recovered by closely adjacent inflowing blood. Respiration rates are reduced and metabolic rate increased, both serving further to conserve heat. Finally, just as we readily lose heat through appendages such as hands and feet, cetaceans minimise this by the reduction of protruding parts which leads to a relatively large surface-to-volume ratio. In this way, the large whales are better able to live in the chill polar waters and that might help to explain the absence of small species at very high latitudes.

LOCOMOTION

It is no coincidence that the largest of all animals known to exist on this Earth is a whale (the blue whale, which may attain weights of 130–150 tonnes). Only an aqueous medium could support such a weight, for limbs would need to be so large that an animal on land could hardly be mobile. That is one of many reasons that has been put forward to account for the decline and fall of the dinosaurs at the end of the Cretaceous Period.

One of the most awesome sights there can be is that of an 18m whale breaching the surface, turning rapidly in pursuit of a shoal of fish or sparring with a competitor for a mate. Such mobility has been achieved by a number of remarkable adaptations (Fig. 1.1). The head is elongated with no obvious neck or shoulders. The skull has become telescoped so that both upper and lower jaws extend well beyond the entrance to the nasal passages (nares), and the one to two blowholes have migrated to the top of the head where they allow exchange of air whilst the animal is moving (Fig. 1.2). Unlike most mammals, cetaceans show a reduction in the number of neck vertebrae that are fused, usually to between two and seven. In some species, such as the rorquals (for example, blue, fin and humpback whales), white whales and river dolphins, these are completely separate. This allows greater flexibility of the neck. The two forelimbs have a skeletal structure similar to that of the human arm but with the 'fingers' contained within a common integument and flattened to form a pair of horizontal paddle-shaped flippers (Fig. 1.3). These are used for steering and stability although they appear to be important also in social and sexual contexts as tactile organs.

The hindlimbs have been lost, at least externally; there are still traces of their bony skeleton within the body, the vestigial remains of the pelvic girdle and in some cases of the femur. There are no external ears, only two minute openings on the side of the head which lead directly to the hearing organs. The external sexual organs also show adaptations to reduce drag through the water. The penis of the male is generally

Figure 1.1 Skeletons of toothed and baleen whales compared with terrestrial mammal. The fore- and specially the hindlimbs are much reduced; the seven neck vertebrae have become compressed and in a number of species, they are fused together; whilst the tail vertebrae are better developed to take the muscles that support the fibrous horizontally flattened tail flukes

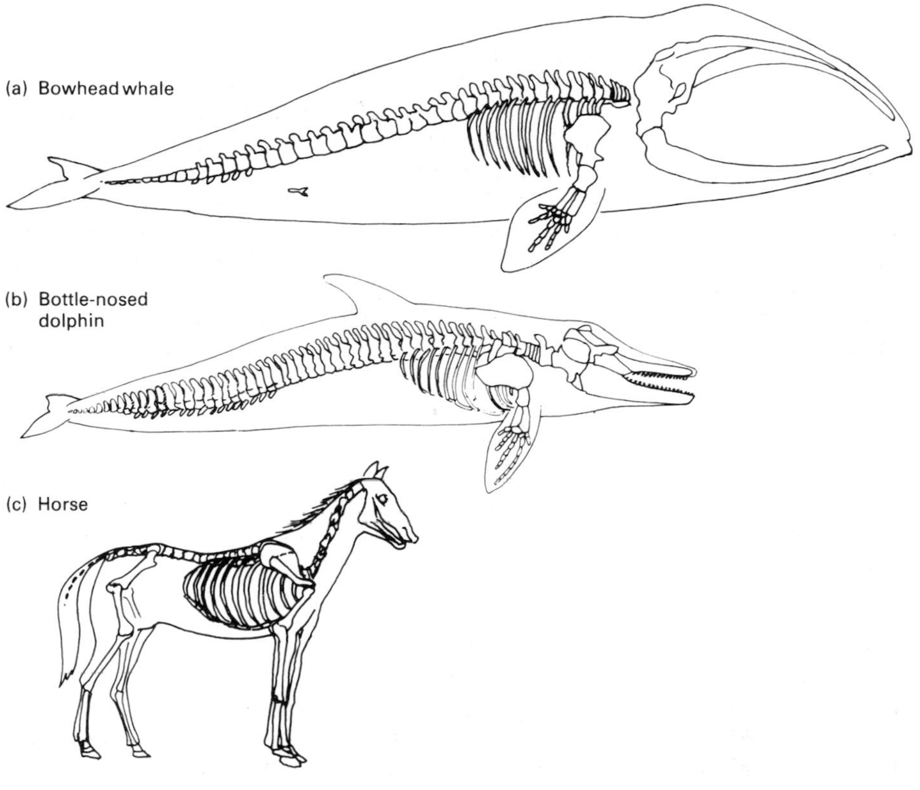

(a) Bowhead whale

(b) Bottle-nosed dolphin

(c) Horse

Figure 1.2 Nasal passages of toothed and baleen whales. Note the elongated passages necessitated by the more posterior position of the nostrils on the top of the head, compared with a land mammal. Note also the size of connective tissue cushion (the spermaceti case in the sperm whale). Although both groups have two openings to the nasal passage, these are divided internally in odontocetes so that only one blowhole is visible externally; in mysticetes, they are separated at the surface to form two external blowholes (although the two columns of vapour may merge to form a single spout)

(a) Odontocete-sperm whale

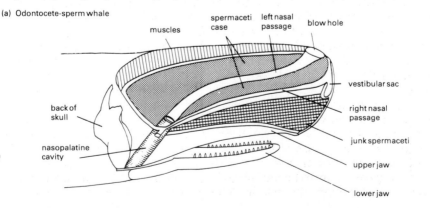

muscles — spermaceti case — left nasal passage — blow hole — vestibular sac — back of skull — right nasal passage — junk spermaceti — nasopalatine cavity — upper jaw — lower jaw

Figure 1.2 (continued)

(b) Mysticete-bowhead whale

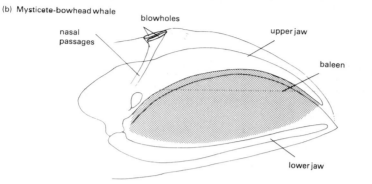

Figure 1.3 Modifications of forelimbs of cetaceans compared with human. In most cetaceans, the hindlimbs and pelvic girdles have been lost altogether, although some baleen whales have rudiments of both, freely floating in muscle tissue just in front of the anus. The forelimbs are also reduced to form paddle-shaped flippers, comprising very short humerus, radius and ulna bones, and 4–5 digits (in rorquals and some odontocetes, the thumb is lost), enclosed within a common integument

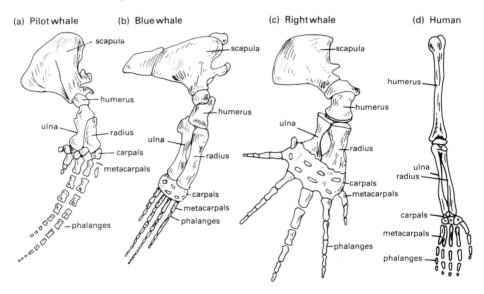

completely hidden within muscular folds, whilst the teats of the female are also concealed within slits on either side of the genital area (Fig. 1.4).

Besides a pair of flippers, the only other protruding parts are a boneless horizontal tail fluke, powered by two muscle masses, one occupying the upper region and the other the lower part of the tail stock, used to drive the animal forwards (see Arkowitz and Rommel 1985); and in most species, an upright dorsal fin made not of bone but of a fibrous and fatty material. It is thought to function as a keel, providing stability to the animal, although it may also help in temperature regulation. These may, however, be secondary functions now since a number of species, such as the bowhead, narwhal, white whale and finless porpoise, all appear to

Figure 1.4 External sex differences in cetaceans. In the male, a small slit hides the retractile penis and there is a fairly distinct umbilicus slightly anterior to it. In the female, the genitalia open much closer to the anal vent

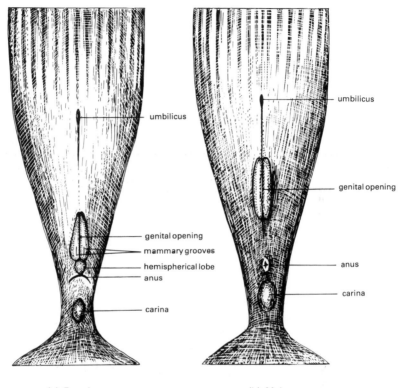

umbilicus

umbilicus

genital opening

genital opening

mammary grooves

hemispherical lobe

anus

anus

carina

carina

(a) Female   (b) Male

manage perfectly well without one, and others such as the gray whale and the sperm whale possess only an irregular ridge or hump. Evolutionary biologists tend to seek adaptive explanations for any peculiarity of anatomy or physiology, yet there may be no such explanation. The character may have evolved in a different context some time in the past or it may never have had an important selective advantage, its origin being due to coincidental linkage of those genes conferring that character with others responsible for some other character(s); it may even simply be an 'architectural' development — one part of the anatomy cannot evolve without another part supporting it. Once present, that character may serve a number of secondary functions. In many dolphin species (shown at its extreme in the killer whale), the dorsal fin of the male is larger than that of the female. Clearly, in these cases, it can serve as a means to recognise the sex of an individual, at least when it is mature. In this way it may be used in courtship for mate selection and in aggressive encounters by competing males.

Dolphins moving through the water alongside a boat have attained speeds of 39km per hour (21 knots) over short distances (Lang and Pryor 1966), whilst individually marked migrating whales have been recorded travelling distances of over 3,700km (2,000 nautical miles) at an average continuous speed of 17km per hour (nine knots) (Brown 1977). These speeds are probably unusual, and prolonged cruising speeds are probably generally between 9 and 17km per hour (5–9 knots) for dolphins (Au and Perryman 1982; Webb 1975), and 4–30km per hour (2–16 knots) for the faster-moving rorquals (Lockyer 1981a). Some of the faster speeds recorded when bow-riding may be aided by the thrust created by the hull of the boat (Hertel 1969; Scholander 1959), and the action of leaping may also improve energy saving (Au and Weihs 1980). Nevertheless, we are still a long way from understanding how cetaceans achieve some of the speeds recorded.

Unlike the rigid hull of a ship, a cetacean can reduce some of the turbulence created as it moves through the water by having a flexible body in which the blubber is not rigidly fixed to the underlying muscular tissues (Essapian 1955). There is a very well-developed system of ridges lying directly beneath the skin whilst the smooth outer layer of epidermis of the skin secretes tiny droplets of a high polymer of ethylene oxide. These droplets are thought to assist the shedding of epidermal skin cells into the water, thus reducing turbulence and drag by breaking up and dispersing the energy contained in the water particles passing over the body. When a fluid flows past a streamlined body, as when a dolphin swims through water, the particles of the fluid in the immediate vicinity of the body are held on to and retarded in their original motion. Those fluid layers nearest the body are retarded most. If the drag on these particles is reduced to a small amount, the more distant layers glide over one another creating what is termed 'laminar flow', allowing the animal to pass through the water more efficiently. For details of this complex subject, the reader should consult Harrison and Thurley (1974), Peterlin (1970), Purves (1963, 1967a), Purves and Pilleri (1978), and Sokolov *et al.* (1969). However, this is an area of research where conjecture is much in evidence, and it may turn out that some of these suggested adaptations do not function in this way nor indeed be necessary to explain fast movement through water.

DIVING AND RESPIRATION

Fish do not need to come to the surface to breathe air in the way that cetaceans do; they are able to extract oxygen dissolved in water. Cetaceans, on the other hand, must hold their breath when diving and resurface at intervals both to expel used air and to take in new fresh air. Living as they do so much of the time underwater, often at considerable depths, it is remarkable how they manage to do this. If a human dives down for longer than he or she can hold their breath, they have to take with them a cylinder of compressed air. This is because the air pressure within their lungs must equal or slightly exceed the pressure of the water around them. If it does not, their chest would be crushed. Under compression, the nitrogen in the air dissolves to full capacity in the fluids and tissues of the body. When a diver ascends, this dissolved nitrogen comes out of solution in the form of bubbles of the gas. These may occur in any part of the body and when they are present in the muscles cause the painful condition known as the 'bends'. A cetacean avoids this by taking with it rather little air, enough to fill its relatively small lungs. Since only a proportion of air contains nitrogen, the amount that could dissolve in the body fluids and tissues at any one time is also small and, instead of entering the blood or tissues, the lungs compress and drive the air into the windpipe and its branches and into the extensive nasal passages. These nasal passages also have thickened membrane linings which prevent gas exchange to the tissues. Even when the alveoli of the lungs have collapsed, oxygen may continue to be exchanged because the terminal airways of the lung are unique in having a rich network of capillaries in the epithelium. The increased respiratory surface provided by so many fine capillaries is also thought to allow rapid return to the lungs of any nitrogen absorbed during the dive. In deep-diving species, such as the sperm whale, it has been shown that expiration can take place very quickly even at low lung volumes. This is valuable in reducing the time taken for each breath and may help to prevent 'the bends' by allowing the alveoli to empty almost completely during a dive. The chest is flexible and the diaphragm set very obliquely so that the weight of the abdominal viscera against it on one side makes the lungs on the other side collapse (see Harrison and Ridgway 1976 for a review of deep diving in marine mammals; also Fig. 1.5).

When a cetacean is returning to the surface, its lungs gradually expand and the nasal plug that closes the blowholes is forced open, emitting any foul air which appears as a cloud of spray. During respiration it is estimated that 80 to 90 per cent of the air in the lung is replaced. There has been much discussion of what precisely is causing the 'blow' or spout that is so often the tell-tale sign of a whale's presence. Some consider that it is produced by water from around the blowhole being forced into the

Figure 1.5 Respiratory system of a whale in action during a deep dive. The lungs are small, elongated and highly elastic. They are situated relatively far forward so that the diaphragm is more horizontally placed than in land mammals, and the thorax is more barrel-shaped. This results in the surface of the lung facing the diaphragm being much larger, so that the diaphragm can evacuate much of the air in the lung in a short time (during surfacing), the lungs can re-fill efficiently, and, during a deep dive, they can collapse to force the air into windpipe and nasal passages and hence prevent absorption of nitrogen, or 'the bends'

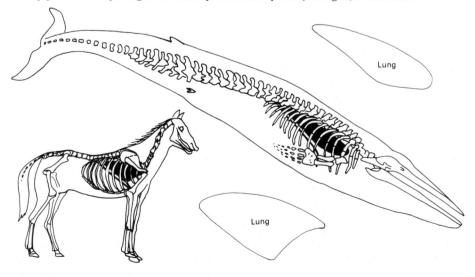

air, but recent electron microscope studies by Joseph Fanning in Australia show that, unlike other mammals, cetaceans have a very specialised absorptive epithelium lining the trachea. Glands in this region produce secretions which collect at the bottom of the junction between the larynx and the trachea. In other mammals these would be removed by cilia on the epithelium; in cetaceans it is suggested that they are removed by the violent coughing movement of the blow. As soon as the animal has exhaled, it takes in fresh air, the air sacs of the lungs return to their expanded state for maximum gas exchange, and it dives again. The duration of a blow and interval between dives typically varies between species and, of course is related to the particular behaviour of the animal at the time — whether it is about to undertake a long and deep dive, or rest awhile upon the surface, or make a short shallow dive.

The record for deep-diving is held by the sperm whale, a large toothed whale that, from stomach contents, we know will take large squid that dwell upon the deep sea bottom. They have been found entangled in submarine cables at depths of 1,000m or more, recorded by sonar at depths of 2,000m and there is even some evidence of dives of over 3,000m (Berzin 1972; Clarke 1980; Heezen 1957; Leatherwood et al. 1983: 86; Lockyer 1981b). Such dives may last an hour or more whilst another ocean-going species, the bottlenose whale, has been recorded underwater for as long as two hours (Benjaminsen and Christensen 1979: 153–4). Quite apart from problems faced by the very high pressures experienced at these depths, we may wonder at how whales manage to move around since muscles require oxygen to function and one might expect this to be used up rather quickly on a single breath of air. One important adaptation is the presence of unusually large amounts of myoglobin in the muscles, a substance which combines with oxygen to form an oxygen store. Sperm whales are particularly efficient in this respect, absorbing up to 50 per cent of the total oxygen store in the muscles (twice as much as in land mammals). During dives, cetaceans may also reduce their heart rate and limit blood flow to the heart and brain. This may not only reduce the oxygen debt but also help to prevent the animal becoming chilled in the comparatively cool waters of the deep sea.

Unlike any other cetacean, sperm whales possess a vast spermaceti organ which occupies most of the upper part of the head. Many people have speculated on its possible function. It may serve as an acoustic lens, focusing echolocation signals and hence aiding the detection of the whereabouts of agile squid prey in areas where light is virtually absent. It may function as a secondary sex organ, used in sparring by males (which have substantially larger heads than females). Or, as suggested by the British marine biologist, Malcolm Clarke (1978, 1979), it may help buoyancy control. Clarke's hypothesis is quite ingenious. The spermaceti organ comprises a network of sinuses and nasal passages, and the suggestion is that as the sperm whale dives into cooler deeper water, the flow of water in the head passages controls the temperature of the wax which solidifies (it has a constant melting point of 29°C whereas the normal body temperature is 33.5°C), shrinks and in so doing, increases the density of the head, so aiding the animal's descent. When the whale starts to ascend, the wax is warmed by increasing the blood flow in the capillaries of the head, this increases buoyancy and allows the animal to rise with the minimum of expenditure of effort. Much of this is still necessarily speculative but it may help to explain how sperm whales manage to make such fast descents and ascents (between 100 and 170m per minute; the ascent usually being slower than the descent), and how they can make quite deep dives at relatively short intervals (2–5 minutes). Of course, as noted earlier, all these possible functions of the large spermaceti organ may operate whether or not it evolved originally for that purpose.

SENSES

Perhaps one of the most important aspects of cetaceans that humans tend to overlook, when drawing parallels to themselves, is the development of different senses necessitated by an aquatic environment. We have flexible joints and an opposable thumb which have been important in the acquisition of manual skills; our vocal apparatus has allowed us to develop language, probably an important route to the evolution of culture; and vision plays an all important role in the everyday lives of most of us.

Smell and Taste

Living in water, cetaceans must rely more upon sound than vision and their powers of olfaction are also clearly reduced. Adult toothed whales, indeed, do not possess olfactory bulbs or nerves whilst these are greatly reduced in baleen whales. Anatomical studies have revealed that cetaceans do have taste buds at the base of the tongue, and common and bottle-nosed dolphins and harbour porpoises have all been shown in captivity to be able to distinguish different chemicals, even small differences in the concentration of citric acid (Nachtigall 1986). However, some tests have shown a poorly developed ability to detect salinity and an apparent inability to detect sugar. Although it may be that neither smell nor taste are important in the lives of cetaceans, more work is clearly needed. We have not properly examined the possibility of close communication by certain species using one or other of these senses, in the way that pheromones (chemical substances produced and released into the environment by animals) are used by many terrestrial mammals to indicate sex or status.

Touch

Although external protrusions such as limbs have been sacrificed for greater streamlining, those that do exist may nevertheless be important as tactile organs. This is best expressed in social or sexual contact when animals may rub against one another, touch flippers, or press the genital organs against a neighbour (which is not always a member of the opposite sex nor necessarily of the same species!). Short hairs around the snout or chin may help to glean more information about their close environment and indicate quickly when the air-water interface has been penetrated. This may be, for example, why river dolphins living in a dark and turbulent environment have whiskers around their long and sensitive snout.

Vision

Since little light exists except near the surface, we can expect vision not to be greatly developed. On the other hand, it should perhaps not be underestimated. The fact that many dolphins are patterned with distinctive markings may not be related solely to the need for camouflage from predator or prey by disruptive coloration. They may serve as important species identification cues in the same way as the sexes may recognise one another by differences in dorsal fin or head size. Of course many species live in relatively shallow coastal waters where there is a reasonable amount of light. For a review of the role of vision in the life of cetaceans, see Madsen and Herman (1980).

The position of the eyes in baleen whales and the largest of the toothed whales, the sperm whale, suggests that they do not possess stereoscopic vision. However, most other species have their eyes positioned further forwards, indicating that they can probably see stereoscopically both forwards and downwards. Tests on captive bottle-nosed dolphins have shown that they have good visual acuity both underwater and in air (Dawson 1980). This is rather surprising because one would expect dolphins to need to adjust the shape of the lens, yet cetaceans lack ciliary muscles which would normally achieve this. There have been many suggestions put forward to explain this apparent anomaly but there are problems with most of these. It is obvious that dolphins can see very accurately in air on immediate departure from underwater — the many impressive tricks of dolphins jumping through hoops testify to this. One suggestion that has been put forward, which awaits testing, is that when passing through air, dolphins preferentially use the peripheral areas of the retina to form images (Watkins and Wartzok 1985). Alternatively, it may be found that they are indeed able to modify the shape of the lens.

Underwater, it is still not clear whether cetaceans detect objects visually by recognising sensitivity differences (by backlighting the object against light from the surface) or whether they depend more upon contrasts (where the sides of the object contrast with the background). Evidence from different sources tends to present conflicting support (see Madsen and Herman 1980; Watkins and Wartzok 1985, for reviews).

In some habitats, vision can be of little value. One such example is the turbid rivers and estuaries occupied by freshwater dolphins. They often swim on their side or even upside down while they are feeding, and it is suggested that their vision is stereoscopic forwards and upwards. The boto of the Amazon and Orinoco river catchments and the baiji which occupies the Chinese Yangtze both have very limited vision; the Indus and Ganges susus are virtually blind, their eyes having become reduced to narrow slits.

Sound

We now come to the major sense used by cetaceans, that of sound. The physical properties of water allow sound to be propagated much more effectively than it can be in air. This advantage has been put to good use by cetaceans and there is a fast growing literature on the subject (see, for example, Bateson 1966; D. Caldwell and Caldwell 1972b; Evans and Bastian 1969; Herman and Tavolga 1980; Payne 1983; Popper 1980 for reviews).

Sound is used by cetaceans in two main ways — for echolocation and for communication. Mysticetes, the baleen whales, are not known to echolocate and, although short pulses resembling echolocatory clicks have been heard in the presence of certain species (for example gray and minke whales), they are certainly not typically heard from such species. Echolocation has, however, been found in about a dozen species of toothed whales (including dolphins) and may occur in others not yet investigated (see Norris 1969; Watkins and Wartzok 1985; Wood and Evans 1980 for reviews). These intense short broadband pulses of sound are in the ultrasonic range (from 0.25 to 220kHz) and function by bouncing off objects in their path, so producing echoes from which the animal is able to build up an acoustic picture of its surroundings. They are directed forwards in a narrow beam and often have discrete emphases on particular frequencies. Different species have a different characteristic range of frequencies of clicks whilst a particular species will to some extent vary its clicks according to context (Evans and Awbrey 1986).

Echolocating cetaceans have a remarkable ability to discriminate fine detail (see Au *et al.* 1982 and related papers), and it has been suggested, by the American cetologist Ken Norris, that this is achieved by the bones in the skull being arranged to form a parabolic reflector focusing sounds at the forehead. The melon, a waxy lens-shaped body in the forehead, focuses the sounds produced in the nasal passages so that they may be emitted in a narrow stream whilst returning sound waves are channelled through oil-filled sinuses in the lower jaw to the inner ear (Fig. 1.6). The channelling of sound is made more precise by the isolation of the inner ear from the skull by means of a bubbly foam. This reduces interference from extraneous resonances. There is growing evidence for this hypothesis (see Norris 1969; Norris and Harvey 1974; Popper 1980) although it is not easy to test unequivocally and it may not necessarily be generally applicable. Recent studies of the physical properties of lipids at different temperatures, by Carter Litchfield and his colleagues from Rutgers University, New Jersey, suggest that at least in the bottle-nosed dolphin

Figure 1.6 Sound propagation and reception in dolphins (adapted from Norris and Harvey 1974). Sound (both clicks and whistles) is probably produced in the region of the nasal plugs, refracted in some way (not yet fully known) to form a beam by the melon and, in the case of sonar clicks, the echoes received through the oil in the lower jaw, to the ear bulla

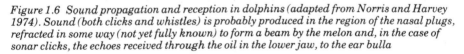
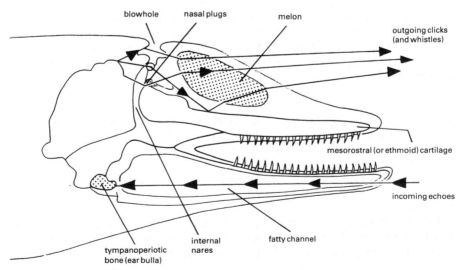

Table 1.1: Sounds made by various cetacean species

Species	Sound type	Frequency range (Hz)	Maximum energy (Hz)	Signal duration (secs)	Comments	Source
Mysticetes						
Blue whale	AM moan	12.5–200	20–32	15–38	may comprise 1–3 parts. In latter case, 1st part modulated at rate of 3.85/sec, 2nd and 3rd at 7.7/sec; brief intervals may occur between them, with 390Hz pulse of 0.5–1.0 sec duration preceding 3rd part	1–4
	click	21,000–31,000	25,000			
Fin whale	FM moan	?6–95	c.18–23	1	pulses usually increase in amplitude in first third of sound, then remain relatively constant over middle period and then decline over final third of pulse. Repeated at relatively fixed intervals varying from 6–37+ sec between pulses, sometimes as doublets but otherwise repeated over 2–20 min period, with 1–3 min pause, extending over several hours. Variants include ragged pulses around 20Hz as short bursts of <0.1sec to defined pulses of c. 1 sec; broadband rumbles of c.20Hz	1, 5–6
	FM moan		c.40–75	0.3	never repeated	
	AM click	16,000–28,000		8.8	may comprise 2–3 parts, 3–3.4msec in duration, with pulse intervals 250–336msec	
Sei whale	AM click		3000	0.7	7–10 pulses per burst, each of 4 msec duration	1

Bryde's whale	FM moan	70–245		0.4	frequency modulations of only c.15Hz upward and/or downward	1, 7
Minke whale	grunt	80–140		0.165–0.32	repeated at irregular/regular intervals at 2.1–2.3 pulses/sec	1, 8–9
	FM thump train	<100–800+	100–200	0.05–0.07	repeated at regular intervals over period of 1+ min, but with indiv. variation in frequency composition and repetition rates	
	AM click	3300–3800/ 5500–7200/ 10,200– 12,000(20,000)	4000–7500	0.5–1msec		
	ratchet pulse	850 850		1–6msec 25–30msec	(single pulsed units) (multipulsed units)	
Humpback whale	moan/groan	<4000		7–36min	'songs' organized into themes composed of repeated phrases and syllables in fixed order, usually ended with a surface ratchet includes short, long, 'elephant', 'lion' and two-part snores	1, 10–12
	snore					
	low grunt	120–250				
	chirp/whistle/ squeal	500–1650				
	click	2000–7000	1600	0.5		
Gray whale	metallic knock	90–2000	300–1000	1.8–2.8	(2)9–12(30) pulses/burst with 6(2–15) pulses/sec, each pulse of <0.05–0.1 sec duration (pulse and frequency modulated)	1, 13–14
	metallic grunt	250–300	250–300	0.3	rapid FM up-down sweep	
	tonal moan	125–1250	170–430	1–2	pulse and frequency modulated	
	belch	150–1570	225–600	0.3–0.9	pulse and frequency modulated, given singly or in pairs, sometimes at end of metallic knocks	

Table 1.1 (continued)

Species	Sound type	Frequency range (Hz)	Maximum energy (Hz)	Signal duration (secs)	Comments	Source
Grey whale	bubble blast	130–840	200–500	3.2	can be heard at up to 2.5km distance	
	subsurface bubble trail	250–850	250–700	3.3		
Bowhead whale	tonal FM moan	50–500	50–300 (100–300) (100–200)	4–5 (1–2) (0.5)	frequency modulation descending, ascending or relatively constant. Sometimes accompanied by tonal FM sound of 400–1000Hz	24–25 26–31
	pulsed tonal purr	100–800		1–3	30–75 pulses/sec (with 3–14 harmonics)	
	tonal AM call	150–375			modulation frequency between 10 and 30Hz	
	complex pulsed call	100–3500		0.3–7.2	5–30 pulses/sec each of 0.01–0.05 sec duration staccato pulse train produced in some, with a low 50 to 100Hz tonal component reproduced simultaneously	
Southern right whale	up call		50–200	0.5–1.5	low, tonal, FM upsweeps	1, 17–19
	down call		100–200	0.5–1.5	low, tonal, FM downsweeps	
	constant call		50–500	0.5–6.0	tonal, with little FM	
	high call		200–500	0.5–2.5	high, tonal, FM sweeps	
	hybrid call		50–500	0.5–2.5	complex mixtures of FM sweeps and amplitude modulation; high call pulsing at end	
	pulsed call		50–200	0.5–3.5	complex mixtures with amplitude modulation of noise and/or an FM signal	

Odontocetes

Sperm whale	pulsed clicks	<100–30,000	10,000–16,000	1–10secs to 20 mins+	1.5–3.0 pulses/burst, 2–30+msec duration, but varying from 1 per 5–10secs to 60+/sec. Clicks repeated at very regular intervals, some with characteristic repetition rates (termed codas)	20–21
Narwhal	whistle	300–10,000 (18,000)		0.5–1.0 (0.05–6.0)	some given at constant frequency but most with steadily decreasing or increasing pitch, and some fluctuating	22–23
	pulsed tones		500–5,000	0.56–1.34	repeated at intervals varying from 1.2 to 10 secs; majority comprise single unbroken signals	
	pulsed clicks	500–24,000	500–5,000	3.6(0.5–23.3)	mainly at 5–10 clicks/sec	
			12,000–24,000	0.7(0.2–1.8)	mainly at 50–60 clicks/sec	
White whale	whistle		1200–1600	2–4msec		24–25
	clicks		40,000/80,000/120,000	20–250µsec		
	clicks					
Killer whale	clicks	100–80,000	250–500	0.8–25msec		26–31
	clicks	to 35,000	14,000–40,000	0.5–1.5msec		
	clicks		12,000	0.1–0.5msec		
	whistle	1,500–18,000	6,000–12,000	0.05–10/12	frequency modulated	
	pulsed call	1,000–25,000	1,000–6,000	0.5–1.5 (<0.05–>10)	harsh 'scream'-like, may be unique to particular pod; calls may be discrete or < occasionally variable	
Long-finned pilot whale	pulsed clicks	to 35,000+		0.8–25msec	1–>300 pulses/sec	32–33
	whistle	2,800–4,700	3,400–4,700	0.65–1.0	calls produced at rate of 14.7–41.4/min	
	clicks					
Rough-toothed dolphin	whistle	100–200,000	3,000–10,000	0.1–0.9		34–35
	pulsed clicks			50–250µsec		

15

Table 1.1 (continued)

Species	Sound type	Frequency range (Hz)	Maximum energy (Hz)	Signal duration (secs)	Comments	Source
Indo-Pacific hump-backed dolphin	whistle		3,000–20,000	0.05–0.25 (1.2)	single sounds or series of 2–10	25
	scream		3,000–30,000	0.1–0.3 (0.05–1.0)	always grouped into series.	
Atlantic white-sided dolphin	clicks		10,000–30,000	100–150μsec	series of distinct single pulses, becoming a crackle at high repetition rates; also, rarely, a creak	36
	whistle	8200–12,100		0.5		
Pacific white-sided dolphin	whistle	1000–12,000		0.2–1.2		37–38
	clicks	60–80,000		0.25–1msec		
Common dolphin	whistle	4000–16,000	4,000–9,000		5 whistle types paired, with clicks and whistles at same time	32, 38–39
	clicks	200–150,000	30,000–60,000	35–350μsec		
Bottle-nosed dolphin	bark	200–16,000		0.1		38, 40–42
	whistle	4000–20,000		0.1–3.6	narrow bands, 18 contours	
	whistle	2000–20,000		0.8–0.9	signature whistles, mostly pure tones	
	clicks	200–300,000	15,000–130,000	10–200μsec		
	clicks	100–300,000+		1–10msec		
Spotted dolphin	whistle	6500–13,300		0.46		28, 34, 36
	pulses	to 150,000		0.075–0.2msec		
Spinner dolphin	whistle	8700–14,300		0.43		36
Commerson's dolphin	pulsed cry	1000–6000		0.5–2.0		43
	clicks	to 100,000+		1–3+	2–100+ clicks per sec	
	clicks	to 100,000+		0.2–0.5	50–80 clicks per sec	

Species	Sound	Frequency (Hz)	Duration	Remarks	Ref.
Heaviside's dolphin	clicks	to 2,000(5,000)	0.3–0.5	2–100+ clicks per sec	44
	click burst	to 2,000(5,000)	0.4–>2.0	50–70 clicks per sec	
	tonal cry	to 2,000(5,000)		repetition increasing to relatively constant at 300–500 pulses/sec, declining thereafter	
Harbour porpoise	pulses	41,000	0.5–5msec		45–46
	pulses	<100,000–160,000	0.1msec		
		2000			
		110,000–150,000			
Indus susu	clicks	25,000–200,000		single or multiple clicks	47
	clicks	100,000			
Boto	pulses	60,000–65,000	65msec		27, 38, 48
			15–100μsec		
Baiji	whistle	6,000	300msec	clicks usually emitted as pulse trains, occurring simultaneously or 1800 out of phase	49
	clicks	8,000–120,000	60msec		

Reference sources: 1 Thompson et al. 1979; 2 Beamish and Mitchell 1971; 3 Cummings and Thompson 1971a; 4 Edds 1982; 5 Schevill et al. 1964; 6 Watkins 1981; 7 Thompson and Cummings 1969; 8 Schevill and Watkins 1972; 9 Winn and Perkins 1976; 10 Payne and McVay 1971; 11 Winn et al. 1971; 12 Tyack 1983; 13 Dahlheim et al. 1984; 14 Moore and Ljungblad 1984; 15 Ljungblad et al. 1980, 1982; 16 Clark and Johnson 1984; 17 Payne and Payne 1971; 18 Cummings et al. 1972; 19 Clark and Clark 1980; 20 Watkins and Schevill 1977; 21 Watkins 1980; 22 Watkins et al. 1971; 23 Ford and Fisher 1978; 24 Morgan 1979; 25 Purves and Pilleri 1983; 26 Schevill and Watkins 1966; 27 Diercks et al. 1971; 28 Diercks 1972; 29 Ford and Fisher 1983; 30 Awbrey et al. 1982; 31 Dahlheim and Awbrey 1982; 32 Busnel and Dziedzic 1966; 33 Taruski 1979; 34 Evans 1967; 35 Norris 1969; 36 Steiner 1981; 37 M. Caldwell and Caldwell 1970; 38 Evans 1973; 39 Schevill and Watkins 1962; 40 Au et al. 1974; 41 M. Caldwell and Caldwell 1967; 42 Diercks et al. 1971; 43 Watkins and Schevill 1980; 44 Watkins et al. 1977; 45 Schevill et al. 1969; 46 Mohl and Anderson 1973; 47 Pilleri et al. 1971, 1976; 48 Wood and Evans 1980; 49 Youfu unpubl.

Notes: The information assembled above summarises some of the main studies on sounds produced by cetaceans. Often it is difficult to resolve data collected by different people and different sounds may be associated with particular contexts. As our knowledge improves, it is likely that the above data will be revised and for the present, it is best regarded as a general and often preliminary description of sounds produced by selected cetacean species.

AM = Amplitude modulated FM = Frequency modulated

and the pilot whale, the sound is not refracted by those lipids within the main body of the melon, but at the interface between the melon and seawater (Litchfield *et al*. 1975, and related papers).

Other sounds made by cetaceans appear to be for communication. The large baleen whales mainly use the lower frequencies, producing tonal sounds lasting between ½ and 20 seconds or more, in the frequency range 20 to 3,000Hz, depending upon the species (Table 1.1). In the rorqual whales, these sounds are usually well below 200Hz. Such low frequency sounds have the advantage of carrying great distances and it has been speculated that the great whales may be in sound contact with one another over distances of tens or even hundreds of kilometres, particularly if they make use of deep ocean channels. Differences in water densities, salinity, temperature and ocean currents produce a channel at a particular depth which tends to trap sound rather like a cylinder does. Propagation of sound via these channels could reach distances of 5,600km, although in the present century with a rather noisier ocean from motor-driven boats this is unlikely to exceed 800km (see Payne and Webb 1971 for a discussion). Of course these are theoretical estimates and it would be difficult indeed to verify that they applied in practice. Nevertheless even accounting for background sound interference, low frequency sound may be propagated up to 80km, and various stations (termed SOFAR, or sound fixing and ranging) have made use of those channels to record underwater sounds, such as from submarines.

The toothed whales produce a wide variety of sounds (Table 1.1). Members of the family Delphinidae (including the dolphins, killer whales and pilot whales) produce whistle-like calls and pulsed squeals typically in the range of 1,000 to 20,000Hz (20kHz). On the other hand, species in the families Physeteridae (the sperm whales), Phocoenidae (porpoises) and Platanistidae (river dolphins) appear to produce only clicks and bursts of clicks which may function primarily for echolocation. In the family Monodontidae, narwhals produce narrowband pulses and longer tonal whistles whilst white whales, one of the most varied of 'songsters', produce whistle-like signals as well as short broadband clicks. In the family Ziphiidae, only the northern bottlenose whale has been examined and this produces low level clicks and whistles.

We have seen that echolocating clicks may emanate at least partly from the forehead rather than from the throat, but how are whistles, squeals and the like actually produced? Cetaceans do not have vocal cords and are rarely seen to blow bubbles when making sounds. One suggestion is that the sounds are produced in the larynx, just as in other mammals, with whistles generated rather as they would be by humans except that they are blown internally (Purves 1967b). Another suggestion, which has received more recent support, is that both clicks and whistles are produced in the nasal plug region (Evans and Maderson 1973; Norris *et al*. 1971). Compressed air is thought to pass from the nasal sacs ventral to the plugs to the dorsal sacs as a series of pulsed sounds, with whistles produced from the left side and clicks from the right side (Dormer 1979). Air is then stored in the dorsal nasal sacs and recycled to the lower sacs for the next burst of sounds.

Biomagnetism

We shall return to sounds in later chapters when considering the varied ways they are used in navigation, food finding and communication. In the meantime there is one more sense which may be used by cetaceans. This is biomagnetism. Anatomical studies on a variety of animals (ranging from birds to bacteria) have revealed particles of magnetite, in birds usually in the head or neck region. There have been problems of contamination since minute particles of magnetite (which comprises ferrous and ferric oxides) may be present on dissecting instruments and it is difficult to ensure they are not present. However, experiments by the late Bill Keeton and his colleagues in the USA have shown that homing pigeons can orientate in the absence of any cues (sun, stars, etc.) but are disorientated in the presence of strong magnets. Magnetic material, and possibly magnetite, has been found recently in the brains of the bottle-nosed dolphin, Cuvier's beaked whale, Dall's porpoise and the humpback whale (Bauer *et al.* 1986). In the UK, Margaret Klinowska (1986) has found a correlation between the sites of live cetacean strandings and the presence of local magnetic field lines intersecting the coast. No such correlation was obtained for strandings of animals already dead nor for sites where magnetic field lines ran parallel to the coast. It is always difficult to interpret correlational information since various factors may be correlated with one another; in this instance, unfortunately, we often cannot be certain of the precise fate of the stranded animal (whether it actually stranded alive or dead) and other factors such as current systems affecting the distribution of strandings need to be taken into account. Still, this is an area of research clearly warranting further attention though there is no reason to suppose that even if available to an animal, biomagnetism is used regularly. As with most animals studied, it is probable that multiple sensory systems are used in navigation.

I have briefly introduced some of the adaptations of anatomy and physiology that cetaceans possess in order to live an aquatic existence. Other aspects of their biology, ecology and behaviour will be explored further in later chapters. Before looking at these, however, perhaps we should consider the possible routes taken by the different cetacean groups during the course of their evolution.

2 Evolution

THE EARLIEST CETACEANS

Fifty million years ago in a world of tropical vegetation, swamp and advancing seas, lived the first recognisable cetaceans. They were elongated aquatic mammals, some of small or moderate size, but others possibly up to 21m long, with reduced hindlimbs and long snouts, and adapted to life in shallow coastal fringes as well as open seas. Fossils of these creatures have been found in rock strata from the early Middle to Late Eocene ages and have been classified within a separate suborder called Archaeoceti (including the zeuglodonts, so named after the generic name, *Zeuglodon*, a name no longer used for one of these forms).

For many years, the most primitive family of Archaeoceti, the Protocetidae, was represented solely by two specimens, *Protocetus atavus*, based on a skull from Egypt, and *Pappocetus lugardi*, based on a lower jaw from Nigeria (*Eocetus schweinfurthi* was at one time also classified as a protocetid). Related species have now been found in India, but perhaps the most exciting discoveries were made recently in the Himalayan region of neighbouring Pakistan with the finding of the most primitive of all archaeocetes, *Pakicetus inachus* (Gingerich and Russell 1981; Gingerich *et al.* 1983) and *Pakicetus attocki* (West 1980). These have led to a re-classification of two other genera of fossil mammals (*Ichthyolestes* and *Gandakasia*) from Pakistan, once considered primitive ungulates (called mesonychid condylarths) whose only remains, the teeth, are intermediate between those of the mesonychids and protocetid whales to which they are now linked. Members of the terrestrial order Condylarthra are thought to have given rise to the archaeocetes at the end of the Paleocene, which then colonised the sea about 50 million years ago during the Early to Mid Eocene (*Pakicetus* was probably a quadrupedal animal, for example). Cetaceans thus share common ancestry (the Condylarthra) with the Artiodactyla, that gave rise to the modern ungulates. This is supported both by fossil evidence and similarities in blood composition, fetal blood sugar, chromosomes, insulin, uterine morphology, and tooth enamel microstructure from modern representatives (Barnes 1984a,c). Together with aspects of skull morphology, these point to the Mesonychidae as the most likely ancestors of the Cetacea.

Mesonychids were large-bodied creatures, and judging from their dentition, some were carnivorous, some herbivorous, and some omnivorous. Since their fossils were sometimes found in sediments deposited in estuaries and lagoons, it is thought that a variety of mesonychids were evolving towards an aquatic existence.

During the Paleocene, the Mediterranean-Arabian Gulf region formed a narrow semi-enclosed arm of the western part of the ancient Tethys Sea (Figure 2.1). It is probably here, around 50 million years ago, that populations of condylarths started to colonise coastal fringes and swamps, possibly exploiting niches vacated at the end of the Cretaceous (nearly 15 million years earlier) by the vanishing plesiosaurs, ichthyosaurs and other reptiles. It is possible that as the warm waters of the Tethys Sea expanded during the Eocene (due to the subsidence of Europe and volcanic activity in various parts of the world) giving rise to the Atlantic and Indian Oceans, selection pressures may have favoured adaptations for the capture of fast-moving and agile fish rather than the freshwater and estuarine molluscs and sluggish fish which previously formed their diet. The dentition of the archaeocetes, like their terrestrial relatives, remained heterodont (differentiated into incisors, canines and grinding teeth). Like modern Cetacea, they had dense ear bones, space around the bones for fat deposits, and air sacs to isolate the ear from the skull; a long palate; and nostrils located on top of the snout. They also had an elongated body with a long tail and short neck, reduced hindlimbs, paddle-shaped front limbs, and a point of flexion in the tail vertebrae that allowed up and down (as opposed to side to side) movement (Barnes 1984a,c).

The earliest archaeocete fossils have been found in Pakistan, India and North Africa, but other archaeocetes have been found throughout the world's oceans — in Britain, the southeastern United States, Australia and even Antarctica. Archaeocete bones were first found in the United States 150 years ago and were originally believed to represent a large fossil reptile. It was named *Basilosaurus* — 'king of the reptiles', but later recognised instead as a whale-like mammal. Archaeocetes comprise two, possibly three, families: the Protocetidae and the Basilosauridae (with two subfamilies Dorudontinae and Basilosaurinae, recognised by some as separate families). The Dorudontinae were medium-sized creatures, with generalised features compared with the more derived, giant Basilosaurinae. The latter was not serpent-like as some authors have depicted them (see Figure 2.2; Barnes and Mitchell 1978 for further details).

During the Oligocene (38–25 million years ago), the archaeocetes were replaced by members of at least four different families, the Agorophiidae and Squalodontidae, both primitive odontocetes, and the Aetiocetidae and Cetotheriidae which were primitive mysticetes. These represent clear intermediate stages between archaeocetes and the modern odontocetes and mysticetes, being similar both to each other and to archaeocetes. A progressively more aquatic mode of life in all cetacean lineages resulted in a backwards shift of the external nostrils, and the development of structures to seal them against water. The long mobile neck, functional hindlimbs and, eventually, most of the pelvic girdle were all lost, together with any pelage remaining that would indicate their terrestrial mesonychid ancestry. At the same time, the body became more torpedo-shaped for greater streamlining, a dorsal fin developed (probably shared

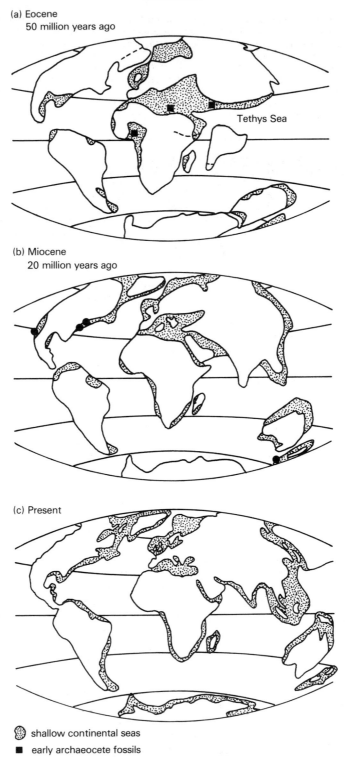

(a) Eocene
50 million years ago

Tethys Sea

(b) Miocene
20 million years ago

(c) Present

shallow continental seas

■ early archaeocete fossils

● early cetothere fossils

Figure 2.1 The world during the Eocene, Miocene and Present showing changes to the continents and seas, and sites of fossil cetacean ancestors. At the end of the Paleocene (54 million years ago), the western edge of the Tethys Sea (now the Mediterranean-Arabian Gulf region) may have provided the conditions for colonisation of the sea during the Eocene by the earliest cetaceans, the archaeocetes. Later, during the late Oligocene (24 million years ago), rich marine deposits in New Zealand and the United States possibly provided suitable conditions for the evolution and dispersal of early baleen-bearing mysticetes (cetotheres) during the Miocene. Any evolution or radiation of cetacean families since then will have occurred in a world where the distribution of continents and seas was little different from the present

Figure 2.2 The first cetaceans — the archaeocete Basilosaurus *(following Barnes 1984c). Despite its snakelike, flexible neck, the skull structure and spine (adapted for up-and-down-movement of the tail) classify this as an early whalelike mammal*

primitively by all groups but lost later by some), together with horizontal tail flukes for forward propulsion (see Gaskin 1982: 165–9 for details). The most primitive odontocetes, like the archaeocetes before them, had heterodont dentition. However, during the Late Oligocene the teeth became modified in some to form the long rows of many sharp uniform teeth with single roots and conical crowns (homodonty), typical of a number of present-day odontocetes. Some highly derived odontocetes have secondarily lost or reduced parts of their dentition, or have developed specialised teeth.

By the mid-Oligocene, the teeth of some mysticetes had given way to rows of baleen plates, the remarkable keratin feeding structures present in all modern mysticetes, which evolved suspended from the curved transverse ridges of the palate. Baleen is epidermal in origin, growing as fibres embedded in a softer matrix. As the softer material is rubbed away by the tongue, the fibres become exposed. Most present-day types of baleen whales still have teeth during the early stages of fetal development, and some very primitive fossil mysticetes had functional teeth as adults, further indications of their common ancestry with the toothed whales (supporting independent anatomical and chromosomal evidence). Many modifications of the archaeocete skull towards the odontocete and mysticete forms involved telescoping of the front of the skull (Figure 2.3). In odontocetes, the development of acoustic scanning, as a means of locating cues underwater and to aid the capture of fish, probably took place alongside the telescoping of the skull, and evolution of various specialised organs including the melon, nasal passages and, in the sperm whales, the spermaceti organ. Active echolocation may have been practised by the earliest odontocetes of the Oligocene or at least they were pre-adapted to do this, with the ear bones isolated by fat bodies and air sacs allowing directional hearing. The American cetologist, James Mead (1975b), has suggested that the asymmetry of soft tissues in and around the nares may have preceded asymmetry of the bones.

Figure 2.3 Telescoping of the skull during the evolution of cetaceans. Note the backwards migration of the nostrils and the telescoping of the cranial bones from a primitive archaeocete through to modern odontocete and mysticete

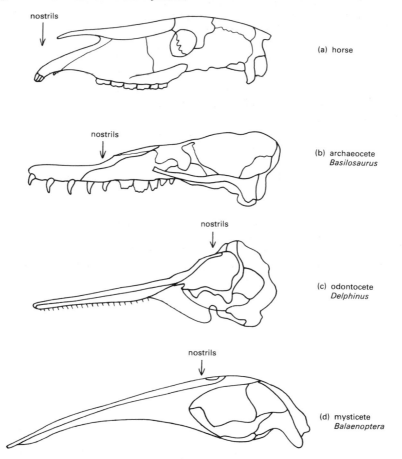

ODONTOCETES OR TOOTHED WHALES

The earliest true odontocetes were the Agorophiidae, a group of short-beaked whales with triangular shark-like teeth (Whitmore and Sanders 1977). These gave rise to the squalodonts, some of which may have somewhat resembled present-day killer whales in behaviour, though not in morphology. Most were relatively large animals with bodies 3m or more in length, and skulls almost fully telescoped (unlike their predecessor). The nares have moved to the top of the head and they had many teeth though these were still differentiated with long, pointed teeth at the front and multiple-rooted cheek teeth with accessory denticles. The squalodonts were possibly most abundant in the late Oligocene and early Miocene, dispersed throughout the southern hemisphere, although most have been found in European deposits, for example in Italy and in the lower Rhine area of West Germany (Rothausen 1968a,b).

The squalodonts gave rise to the family of extremely long-snouted primitive dolphins traditionally called Eurhinodelphidae and now generally referred to as the Rhabdosteidae. Early and Middle Miocene fossils of these have been found in various parts of the world, including Europe (Belgium and Italy), North America (Maryland, Virginia, and California), South America (Patagonia), and in freshwater deposits in Australia (Barnes 1977; Barnes *et al.* 1985; Fordyce 1983; Myrick 1979a). Most species were about 3m in body length and they appear to have been very abundant, sometimes making up the bulk of fossil cetaceans in deposits. Although they had fully telescoped skulls, and many homodont teeth, they had symmetrical skulls and are not very similar to modern delphinids. By the Middle Miocene (about 15 million years ago), they were probably being superseded by representatives of families with living relatives.

Various other dolphin-like families (and early baleen whales) flourished in the Miocene but then became extinct. These include the Squalodelphidae (tentatively placed by Barnes in the superfamily Squalodontoidea), known from two taxa, one (*Squalodelphis*) in northern Italy, and the other (*Diochotichus*) from Argentina. They are among the earliest known odontocetes with asymmetrical skulls. They were small animals, probably less than 3m long with many homodont teeth, and telescoped skulls comparable to that in the Rhabdosteidae and the derived species of Squalodontidae. Some authors consider that the beaked whales may have evolved from squalodelphids, but this requires greater evidence.

Within the superfamily Delphinoidea may be found most of the living cetacean species. These include the Delphinidae (true dolphins), Phocoenidae (porpoises) and Monodontidae (white whales and narwhals), as well as the extinct Miocene Albireonidae and the Kentriodontidae from which they are all thought to be derived. Most kentriodontids were small animals approximately 2m or less in length. They had relatively short beaks and symmetrical skulls with many homodont teeth although some species had small accessory denticles on their cheek teeth (Barnes 1978, 1984a). The family was relatively diverse in the Middle and Late Miocene, represented by species in both the Atlantic and Pacific Oceans, though none has been found that is more recent than about ten million years old. The family Albireonidae is presently known only from one Late Miocene species which appears to have evolved from a kentriodontid.

The family Delphinidae is a relatively modern group. The oldest known fossil comes from the Late Miocene, about eleven million years ago (Barnes 1978, 1984a). This is the most diverse living cetacean family, although it is not abundant in the fossil record which may relate to its pelagic habit. Most fossils are from Pliocene deposits in Europe. They appear to have had generalised diets, and possess intermediate-sized beaks. Most living members have functional teeth in both jaws, a melon with a distinct beak, and a dorsal fin. The skull shows marked asymmetry with a single crescent-shaped blowhole, the concave side of which faces forward on top of the head. Members of the family include pilot whales, killer whale, common dolphin and Risso's dolphin.

The earliest members of the families Phocoenidae and Monodontidae (now generally recognised as families separate from the Delphinidae) are now known to date also from the Late Miocene, probably sharing with the

Delphinidae a kentriodontid ancestor (Barnes 1977, 1984b). Fossil phocoenids have been found on the Pacific coasts of North and South America, suggesting that they originated in shallow waters in the temperate latitudes of the North Pacific Ocean. Pliocene fossils found in Europe and from New Zealand are now considered to be members of other groups. Two new fossil genera have recently been proposed by the American palaeontologist, Lawrence Barnes, who has also extensively reviewed the taxonomy of Phocoenidae (Barnes 1985). Living members of the family Phocoenidae are a rather uniform group. They are small, lack a beak and, with the exception of the finless porpoise, they have small, low triangular dorsal fins. The many teeth are spade-like in shape, being laterally compressed and flattened, and the skull characters include an eminence or boss on each premaxilla bone in front of the opening to the nares.

From the fossil record, we now know that monodonts (which include the narwhal and white whale confined to the Arctic) must have occupied temperate waters as far south as Baja California in the Northeast Pacific during the Late Miocene and Pliocene (Barnes 1977, 1984b). The Indo-Pacific Irrawaddy dolphin is considered by the Japanese cetologist, Toshio Kasuya (1973), to be a member of this family (on the basis of some skull characters) rather than within the family Delphinidae and if this is correct, then we might expect to find further fossil relatives in other parts of the world. Despite the superficial dissimilar appearance of the narwhal and white whale, their body forms actually have a number of features in common. Neither has a dorsal fin and the flippers turn upwards at the tips as they grow older. The narwhal has only two teeth, both of which are non-functional (at least as teeth); these are short in the female but in the male the left tooth continues to grow to form an elongated tusk. The white whale on the other hand has between eight and eleven teeth in each jaw, often curved and irregular in form.

The superfamily Platanistoidea (the so-called 'river' dolphins) is one of the most highly evolved groups of living cetaceans. The freshwater habit of many members is probably secondary since some fossil genera (*Saurodelphis*, *Anisodelphis* and *Ischyrorhynchus* in the family Iniidae) have been found in Miocene and Pliocene marine deposits, and all odontocetes are primitively marine. Other, possibly related, families are the Acrodelphidae, Pontoporiidae and Platanistidae. The relationships of living members of this superfamily are still poorly understood and it may be that new fossils will substantially clarify the picture. They seem to have evolved quite separately from the Delphinoidea, and they may have originated from some taxon within the Agorophiidae (Barnes 1984a, Barnes *et al.* 1985). One family, the Acrodelphidae, is now extinct. It occurred in the Miocene and comprises a number of long-snouted genera, possibly related to the highly derived, Recent platanistids from Asia.

Living 'river' dolphins are all small to medium sized dolphins with a long beak bearing numerous pointed teeth, a flexible neck, pronounced melon and large brain, rather broad short flippers with visible fingers, but a poorly developed dorsal fin, and reduced vision (in the Indus and Ganges dolphins, the lens has been lost altogether).

The family Iniidae includes the Recent freshwater Amazon dolphin or boto (*Inia*), although fossil marine genera (see above) from South America appear to belong to the same family. All of these are characterised by having relatively heavily built, intermediate length snouts and large teeth with wrinkled enamel. Skulls have upturned crests at the margin of the face but no large crests as in *Platanista*.

Members of the Pontoporiidae (formerly called Stenodelphinae or Stenodelphininae) are the only modern odontocetes which retain a symmetrical skull. Pliocene fossils ascribed to this family have been found in South American marine deposits and, like the only living representatives, the franciscana (*Pontoporia*), they all appear to have been coastal marine animals. Nowadays, the franciscana is not considered closely related to *Platanista*, as was previously thought (Kasuya 1973, Zhou 1982). The freshwater baiji (*Lipotes*) of China was once classified in the Iniidae until Zhou and his colleagues (1979) assigned it to the family Lipotidae. However, Barnes (1984a) suggests it may be better classified in a subfamily of Pontoporiidae in the light of discovery of Late Miocene and Pliocene marine fossils — dolphins in the family Pontoporiidae with features intermediate between *Pontoporia* and *Lipotes*.

The family Platanistidae is represented by two Asiatic freshwater dolphins, *Platanista* spp., which are small dolphins with a unique pattern of distribution of air sinuses in their skulls, including a large pneumaticised crest on each side of the skull over the eye orbit. Although they possess some primitive characters including flexible flippers and neck, they have a large number of derived cranial characters that make their skulls one of the most modified of any cetacean (Barnes 1984a).

The beaked whales form the family Ziphiidae, known from the fossil record from at least the Middle Miocene, and possibly derived from the Early Miocene Squalodelphidae (Mead 1975a; Moore 1968). They are so named because the beak-like rostrum extends free of the melon. They are moderately large-sized animals that feed mainly on squid. Most of their lives are a complete mystery to us, living as they do in the deep oceans. Indeed some are known only from stranded specimens, having never been seen alive in the wild. Most members of the family have a strongly asymmetric skull. In the past, they have usually been classified with the sperm whales in a single superfamily on the basis of this and a number of other similarities (they both have 42 chromosomes instead of the usual 44, for example, although the morphology of the chromosomes differs). However, it is now considered that the beaked whales acquired asymmetry quite independently whilst in three species (the Tasman beaked whale and the closely related Baird's and Arnoux's beaked whales) the skull is in fact nearly symmetrical. Fossils have been found in many parts of the world — Europe (e.g. Italy), North America, South America (e.g. Argentina, Peru), and even in freshwater deposits in Africa. In all living species, except the Tasman beaked whale, the teeth are very reduced in number and entirely absent from the upper jaw. On each side of the lower jaw of adult males there are only one or two teeth and these are often much enlarged, projecting from the mouth as small tusks. In young males and in females the teeth do not usually emerge so that they sometimes appear to be toothless. Most fossil and some living species retain small, conical 'dolphin-like' teeth in both upper and lower jaws, indicating that beaked whales evolved from ancestors with many homodont teeth.

Among the odontocetes, the sperm whales (family Physeteridae) show many unique features, and are one of the most ancient of living families, the fossil record indicating that they probably diverged from the main odontocete line at an early stage. The earliest sperm whales have been found in Early Miocene deposits (23 million years old) in Patagonia, whilst other Miocene fossils have been discovered elsewhere in Argentina and in various parts of North America (e.g. California and Maryland) and Europe (e.g. Belgium). Most of the remains are based upon isolated teeth and our knowledge of the relationships within the family is still inconclusive (Barnes *et al.* 1985). At present, the relationship between the sperm whale and the smaller pygmy sperm whale and dwarf sperm whale is uncertain. All three have a similar appearance with a barrel-shaped head (most pronounced in the sperm whale, and containing the spermaceti organ), long narrow underslung lower jaw with many homodont teeth, and an upper jaw without functional teeth (although in the dwarf sperm whale there may be up to three pairs of rudimentary teeth). Clearly the three species are related, but there are differences in structure of the top of the cranium between the sperm whale and the other two species, and Barnes *et al.* (1985) among others have classified the pygmy and dwarf sperm whales in a separate family, Kogiidae, within the Superfamily Physeteroidea. The oldest known kogiid comes from Miocene deposits in Mexico and has a raised and twisted sagittal crest behind the nares.

MYSTICETES OR BALEEN WHALES

We now come to the other major subdivision of cetaceans, the mysticetes or baleen whales. Soviet scientists, S.E. Kleinenberg (1958) and A.V. Yablokov (1964), considered that mysticetes had a separate origin to the odontocetes, on the basis of the rather substantial differences between living representatives of the two groups. However, the characteristics they use are not applicable to all fossils or even all living mysticetes and odontocetes. A common ancestry has been supported more recently by studies of the number and morphology of chromosomes in the nuclei of cells, and even the DNA and RNA molecules within the chromosomes are very similar (Arnason 1974; Kulu 1972).

Mysticetes are now generally thought to have evolved from a toothed ancestor (perhaps represented by the extinct family Aetiocetidae) sometime in the Oligocene (Barnes 1977, 1984a; Mchedlidze 1976; Van Valen 1968). *Aetiocetus* shows some resemblance to the present-day rorquals, having a loosely articulated lower jaw and similar air sinus system, although it has a full set of differentiated (heterodont) teeth (three incisors, one canine, four premolars and three molars). It has been found in Late Oligocene rocks in Oregon, on the west coast of North America, although remains of earlier, baleen-bearing mysticetes come from New Zealand. It has been suggested that zooplankton-rich deposits found in Oligocene strata on both the west coast of the United States and in New Zealand indicate conditions that may have favoured the evolution of baleen and the filter-feeding mode of life, so accounting for the presence of early forms in the two regions (Fordyce 1977, 1980; Gaskin 1982:219–22, 242). From here they may have dispersed eastwards towards Europe and into the Pacific and Indo-Pacific regions along lines of high productivity during the late Cenozoic (see Fordyce 1977, 1980, 1984).

While the toothed whale skull was becoming modified to contain acoustic apparatus and its jaw and dentition developing for the capture of fast-moving fish, the baleen whale skull became modified to feed upon concentrations of plankton. The upper margin of the 'forehead' of the skull became greatly extended, probably primarily to combat the stresses on the skull and jaws imposed by the wide opening and closing of the mouth. Long baleen plates developed to sieve the plankton, and throat grooves which could be distended to allow the whale to take in great gulps of seawater. The neck vertebrae were reduced since flexibility of head movement was less important than in odontocetes. The trend toward larger head size was accompanied by a similar trend for large body size, reaching its maximum in the blue whale, the largest of all known mammals.

The most primitive of truly toothless baleen whales is the extinct Cetotheriidae which range from the Late Oligocene to the Late Pliocene (Kellogg 1969). This is one of the largest families of Cetacea, fossil or living, comprising at least 60 species of moderate sized whales (3 to 10m long) with skulls showing only a limited amount of telescoping.

The living mysticetes comprise four families. The oldest of these is the family Balaenidae. It is well represented in Late Miocene and Pliocene deposits of Europe and has recently been described from rocks of similar age in California (Barnes 1977). The earliest member of the group, *Morenocetus*, is found in the same Miocene deposits in Argentina as the earliest sperm whales. There are three living balaenid representatives, the Arctic bowhead and the northern and southern right whales. They are characterised by an arched rostrum which gives a deeply curved jawline, very long slender baleen plates and no throat grooves. They are rather rotund animals with a relatively large head (about one-third of the body length), and a narrow upper jawbone quite unlike the rorquals.

The southern hemisphere pygmy right whale (*Caperea*) is now placed within a separate family Neobalaenidae (Barnes and McLeod 1984). The reason for this is its unique cranial telescoping and a highly modified lower jaw. The only known fossil member of this family, *Caperea simpsoni*, comes from South America.

The Eschrichtiidae is now represented only by the gray whale of the North Pacific. Its origins are unknown since the oldest fossils date from a Late Pleistocene deposit near Los Angeles, California, and are indistinguishable from the living species (Barnes and McLeod 1984). Because of their unique anatomy, gray whales must be assumed to have a very separate evolutionary history from other baleen whales with ancestors to be found probably in Miocene and Pliocene deposits. A North Atlantic population of the gray whale became extinct in Recent historical times (possibly in the seventeenth or early eighteenth centuries), and bones have been found along the Florida coast of the southeastern United States. The species has a relatively small head with a rather narrow, gently arched rostrum, two (rarely four) short throat grooves and no dorsal fin. The absence of fossils may relate in part to a coastal habit with beached carcasses more likely to have been scattered and broken, rather than to survive as identifiable fossils.

The family Balaenopteridae comprises the humpback whale and

various similar species, including the relatively small minke and giant blue whales. These are collectively referred to as rorquals. All are streamlined in appearance and have a rather straight jawline. They also have rather short baleen plates and many throat grooves, folds of skin extending from the chin backwards under the belly. Balaenopterids are thought to have arisen sometime in the Miocene from the Cetotheriidae, with similarities in body proportions and skull structure but longer and more complex skulls (Barnes 1977). Many fossils (from Late Miocene through Pliocene) have been found in Europe and the eastern United States.

An important review of the status of our knowledge on fossil marine mammals has been published recently by Lawrence Barnes, Daryl Domning and Clayton Ray (1985) to which the reader is referred for further details. Figure 2.4 derives from this review and presents their current view of the phylogeny of all cetacean families.

In this chapter I have attempted to present the essence of our recent knowledge of the origins of modern cetaceans, and their possible relationships. Whenever zoologists try to piece together the evolutionary history of an animal group, they are limited by the fossil record available to them. This has clearly been the case also for cetaceans, with gaps both in time (particularly from the Oligocene backwards) and in space (fossil deposits concentrated in certain regions, e.g. the eastern United States, California and Mexico, northern Italy and West Germany, and New Zealand). Thus we have a rather biased view which should be taken into account when reading this book. We can look forward to a fuller view of cetacean evolution as more finds are made and specimens examined and described (see, for example, recent reviews by Barnes 1984b; Fordyce 1982; de Muizon 1983a,b). However, we should remember that fossils need to be preserved in sedimentary rocks and such rocks have not formed everywhere over the relevant periods.

Before leaving the subject of cetacean evolution, it is worth noting that, in recent years, molecular evidence has been gathered from a variety of living animal groups so that possible evolutionary relationships can be determined, independent of paleontological evidence. Jerold Lowenstein (1985) has made such comparisons by protein sequencing and immunology. His results suggest that living representatives of pinnipeds, cetaceans and sirenians may have common ancestors much more recent than the paleontological evidence indicates. Cetaceans appear to be most closely related to the ruminant artiodactyls, for which there is no fossil record earlier than 40 million years ago. This implies that the 50-million-year-old *Pakicetus* (the earliest of whales found) actually precedes the divergence between artiodactyls and cetaceans, and so could not be a true whale. Toothed and baleen cetaceans are estimated by molecular data to have diverged about 20 to 25 million years ago, and all the dolphins and porpoises are closely related. If some of these findings are correct, they would certainly modify our present understanding of cetacean evolution. For the time being, we should regard them with some caution since we are far from knowing exactly how to translate molecular differences into real time.

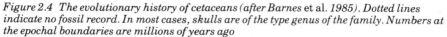

Figure 2.4 The evolutionary history of cetaceans (after Barnes et al. 1985). Dotted lines indicate no fossil record. In most cases, skulls are of the type genus of the family. Numbers at the epochal boundaries are millions of years ago

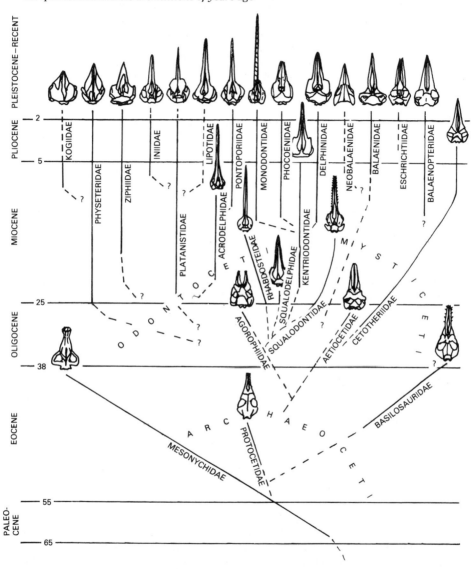

3 Classification

This chapter presents a systematic list of all living cetacean species in the world. It is provided for reference rather than to be read from start to finish. Its purpose is: (1) to enable the reader to find out basic information about any species referred to elsewhere in the book; and (2) to use as a field guide in combination with the chapter on distribution. In this way, anyone in a particular region of the world can learn what species he or she may expect to find, and then determine how to identify one from another.

The extent of our long ignorance of whales and dolphins is reflected in the fact that we still do not know how many different forms exist. A few are known only from dead specimens that have arrived on our shores; many more have been described on the basis of very limited material; and maybe half of all known species have been scarcely seen in their natural environment. Coupled with the fact that differences between forms are often very slight, it is no wonder that there is great disagreement over how to classify cetaceans. For classification at the level of the family and above, I have followed recent recommended changes reviewed by Barnes *et al.* (1985). For classification of species and genera, I have followed the lists adopted by the International Whaling Commission and the United States Marine Mammal Commission, including recent revisions. A number of species have a variety of common names which tends to add to the confusion for the general reader. Some authors (without mentioning names!) have contributed further by erecting their own somewhat idiosyncratic nomenclature. I have decided to give priority to the names that the two bodies above have adopted, but I also include some of the commoner alternative names for the benefit of the reader. Names of the authorities responsible for the classification or nomenclature at each taxonomic level are given, together with the dates these were made; if amendments then followed, the name and date for that authority is given subsequently. An authority's name is placed in parentheses if the species name has remained the same since the date of naming, but has now been assigned to a different genus.

For completeness, I list all the extinct cetacean taxa down to subfamily level. For living cetaceans, I also include a brief description of the major features used to distinguish between the different taxa, and for each species I give their distribution, status and key identification characters (including typical adult total lengths, weights, tooth/baleen counts). I have treated some closely related species together. For further details, I strongly recommend the reader refers to the excellent *Sierra Club Handbook of Whales and Dolphins* produced by Steve Leatherwood and Randall Reeves with paintings by Larry Foster (1983). The accounts below follow them, but with a number of changes, usually arising from more recent information.

ORDER CETACEA — Brisson 1762

Suborder Archaeoceti Flower 1883   Extinct
Family Protocetidae Stromer 1908

Family Basilosauridae Cope 1868

Subfamily Dorudontidae (Miller 1923) Slijper 1936
Subfamily Basilosaurinae (Cope 1868) Barnes and Mitchell 1978

Suborder Odontoceti Flower 1867

The toothed whales, teeth always being present either numerous, uniform and conical or reduced to a single tooth; asymmetrical skull (but symmetrical in fossil representatives); single nasal opening (there are two openings to nasal passage divided by an external central septum but these are internal).

SUPERFAMILY SQUALODONTOIDEA (Brandt 1872) Simpson 1945   Extinct

Family Agorophiidae Abel 1913 (includes Microzeuglodontidae — Stromer 1903)

Family Squalodontidae Brandt 1872

Subfamily Patriocetinae (Abel 1913) Rothausen 1968
Subfamily Squalodontinae (Brandt 1872) Rothausen 1968

Family Rhabdosteidae Gill 1871 (= Eurhinodelphidae — Abel 1901)

Family Squalodelphidae Dal Piaz 1916

SUPERFAMILY PLATANISTOIDEA (Gray 1863) Simpson 1945

River dolphins, virtually toothless with a long beak and rather broad short flippers; eyes variably reduced.

Family Acrodelphidae Abel 1905   Extinct

Family Platanistidae Gray 1863

Figure 3.1 The river dolphins: Indus and Ganges susus, boto, baiji and franciscana

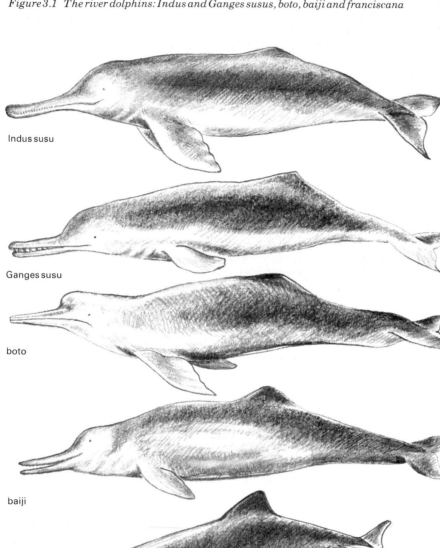

Indus susu

Ganges susu

boto

baiji

franciscana

Platanista minor (Owen 1853)   Indus Susu (Indus River Dolphin)
Length c. 2–2.5m; weight c. 80–90kg; 27–33 pairs of slender, sharp-pointed teeth in each jaw; a robust grey-brown dolphin with paler belly, with very long narrow beak, broad paddle-like flippers, blowhole a single long slit on head, eyes reduced to pinholes; almost extinct (around 500 individuals) with distribution confined to the Indus river system within the provinces of Sind and Punjab, Pakistan.

Platanista gangetica   Ganges Susu
(Roxburgh 1801)   (Ganges River Dolphin)
Length c. 2–2.5m; weight c. 80–90kg; 27–33 pairs of slender, sharp-
pointed teeth in each jaw; indistinguishable from the previous species,
differing only in skull morphology with slightly lower bony crests; more
common (c.5,000) than Indus susu, occurring in Ganges, Brahmaputra,
Kharnaphuli and Meghna river systems of western India, Bangladesh
and Nepal (possibly only c.40).

Family Pontoporiidae (Gill 1863) Kasuya 1973 (= Stenodelphinae —
True 1908)

    Subfamily Parapontoporiinae — Barnes 1984   Extinct
    Subfamily Pontoporiinae (Gill 1871) Barnes 1984

Pontoporia blainvillei   Franciscana
(Gervais and d'Orbigny 1844)   (La Plata Dolphin)
Length c. 1.5–1.7m; weight 32–52kg; 50–60 pairs of slender, finely-
pointed teeth in each jaw; very similar in appearance to the Indus and
Ganges susus, being grey-brown in colour (paler underside) with a very
long narrow beak (but with straight mouthline), and broad paddle-like
flippers; however, the forehead is more rounded (at least in adults), the
blowhole is crescent-shaped, and there is a distinct triangular (slightly
recurved) dorsal fin; estuarine/marine rather than freshwater, in the
coastal waters of South America from São Paulo, Brazil, south to
Peninsula Valdés, Argentina, but including the estuary of La Plata.
Numbers unknown probably in the low thousands.

Family Iniidae Flower 1867 (includes Pontoplanodidae — Ameghino
1892; Saurocetidae — Ameghino 1891; Saurodelphidae — Abel 1905)

Inia geoffrensis   Boto
(de Blainville 1817)   (Boutu or Amazon Dolphin)
Length uncertain but c. 2–2.5m; weight 85–160kg; 24–34 pairs of teeth
in each jaw; dentition unique with conical front teeth and molariform
rear teeth; coloration variable from pinkish (mainly underside) through
blue-grey (paler underside) to almost white (older individuals); broad
body with long beak lined with stiff hairs, an abrupt forehead,
crescent-shaped blowhole, paddle-shaped flippers, and a long low dorsal
hump; reduced, though functional, eyes. Distribution throughout the
Amazon and Orinoco river systems up to 3,000km from the coast in
several Central and northern South American countries; some size
variation between regions. Numbers unknown but probably in the
thousands or low tens of thousands.

Family Lipotidae Zhou, Qian and Li 1979

Lipotes vexillifer   Baiji
Miller 1918   (Beiji or Whitefin Dolphin)
Length c. 2–2.5m; weight c. 135–230kg; 30–35 pairs of uniform-sized
conical teeth in each jaw; coloration pale blue grey but with paler
undersides; long narrow slightly upturned beak, fairly abrupt forehead,

rectangular blowhole, and broad rounded flippers and low triangular dorsal fin; very small eyes, possibly functional. Distribution confined to the middle and lower Yangtze river system (and adjacent lakes) in China. Numbers unknown but possibly less than 1,000.

SUPERFAMILY DELPHINOIDEA (Gray 1821) Flower 1864 (includes Monodontidoidea — Fraser and Purves 1960)

The dolphins (including some small whales, for example killer, false killer whale, pilot whales, narwhal and white whale). Most forms have functional teeth in both jaws, a melon with a distinct beak, and a dorsal fin.

Family Kentriodontidae (Slijper 1936) Barnes 1978   Extinct

Subfamily Kampholophinae Barnes 1978
Subfamily Kentriodontinae Slijper 1936
Subfamily Lophocetinae Barnes 1978

Family Albireonidae Barnes 1984   Extinct

Family Monodontidae Gray 1821

Subfamily Orcaellinae (Nishiwaki 1963) Barnes 1984

Orcaella brevirostris (Gray 1886)   Irrawaddy Dolphin
Length c. 2–2.5m; c. 100kg; 12–19 pairs of small, conical teeth in upper jaw, 12–15 pairs in lower jaw; coloration blue-grey on back and flanks, lighter grey on belly; stout body with rounded head, distinct melon but no beak, broad, fairly long paddle-like flippers, and small sickle-shaped dorsal fin with rounded tip. Distribution principally coastal in tropical Indo-Pacific (Indonesia, Burma, Vietnam, India and Pakistan) extending east to New Guinea and northern Australia and west to Bay of Bengal, and including mainly brackish parts of the rivers Irrawaddy (Burma), Mahakam (Borneo), Mekong (Vietnam to Cambodia), Ganges and Brahmaputra (India). Population size unknown.

Subfamily Delphinapterinae   Gill 1871

Delphinapterus leucas   White Whale
(Pallas 1776)   (Beluga or Belukha)
Length c. 3–5m (varies between populations, and males larger than females); weight 500–1,500kg; 8–11 pairs of irregular, often curved, teeth in upper jaw, 8–9 pairs in lower jaw; white when adult but young slate-grey to reddish-brown changing to blue-grey at 2 years old; stout body with small head, well-defined neck, prominent, rounded melon (though can change shape) with short but distinct beak, short broad paddle-shaped flippers, no dorsal fin but with slightly darker narrow ridged back, broad tail flukes with deeply-notched centre. Distribution is circumpolar, mainly in Arctic but extending to subarctic, occupying mainly coastal and estuarine areas often among pack ice. Population size known only for certain regions but probably total is at least between 40,000 and 55,000 (mainly in Baffin Bay, Davis Strait, Barents, Kara and

Figure 3.2 The family Monodontidae: narwhal, white whale and Irrawaddy dolphin

Irrawaddy dolphin

Laptev Seas but numbers reduced in eastern Canada by historical over-exploitation). Present hunting rates predicted to cause further population declines in eastern Canada, Barents and White Sea.

Subfamily Monodontinae (Gray 1821) Miller and Kellogg 1955

Monodon monoceros Linnaeus 1758   Narwhal
Length c. 4–5m (+ male tusk length 1.5–3m; males larger than females); weight 800–1,600kg; 1 pair of teeth in upper jaw; in male, left tooth greatly extended as spiralled tusk; body mottled grey-green, cream and black, whitening from belly with age (young are grey, blue-grey or black); stout body with small, rounded head, bulbous forehead, very slight beak, flippers short, broad with upturned tips, no dorsal fin but ridged back, fan-shaped tail flukes with deep notch in centre. Distribution is circumpolar, mainly in High Arctic, often amongst pack ice and generally more offshore than white whale. Population size best known for High Arctic (Canada and West Greenland) where estimate is 10,000–30,000; total is unknown, but probably somewhere between 25,000 and 50,000 (mainly in Baffin Bay, Davis Strait and Greenland Sea).

Family Phocoenidae (Gray 1825) Bravard 1885

Subfamily Phocoenoidinae   Barnes 1984

Australophocaena (= *Phocoena*) *dioptrica*   Spectacled Porpoise
(Lahille 1912) Barnes 1985
Length c. 1.55–2.04m; weight c. 60–84kg; 18–23 pairs of small teeth
(laterally compressed to give spade-shape) in upper jaw, 16–19 pairs in
lower jaw; black above and white below, with black rim to eyes and lips,
and grey stripe from white flippers to jaw angle, rotund body, little
forehead, no beak, relatively small flippers with rounded tips, triangular
dorsal fin with rounded peak (larger in males). Very poorly known.
Distribution apparently in coastal waters of eastern South America from
southern Uruguay south to Tierra del Fuego, and including Falkland
Islands and South Georgia; skeletal material also found in Auckland
Islands (New Zealand), in subantarctic islands of New Zealand, and
Kerguelen Island, Indian Ocean. Population size unknown.

Phocoenoides dalli   Dall's Porpoise
(True 1885)   (or True's Porpoise)
Length c. 1.8–2.1m; weight c. 135–220kg; 19–29 pairs of small,
spade-shaped teeth in each jaw; black coloration with variable white
patch on flanks and belly, and white on tips of dorsal fin and tail flukes;
very stout body, small head without defined beak, small pointed flippers,
small fairly triangular dorsal fin often largely white, with hooked tip,
pronounced keel on tail-stock. Four forms recognised, with different
colour patterns: three forms of Dall's subspecies, one all black, one
striped, and one with white lateral patch below and posterior of dorsal
fin; and True's subspecies, resembling last but with patch extending
anteriorly to flippers (colour variants develop at fetal stage). Characteristic fast movements generating trail of spray behind dorsal fin. Distribution is confined to coastal and deep waters of northern North Pacific and
Bering Sea northwards from southern Japan in west and southern
California in east, at least in summer as far north as Pribilof Islands.
Population size estimated by strip transect to be between 0.79 and 1.738
million (particularly common in Sea of Okhotsk and southern Bering
Sea).

Subfamily Phocoeninae (Gray 1825) Barnes 1984

Phocoena phocoena (Linnaeus 1758)   Harbour Porpoise
Length 1.4–1.8m; weight 54–65kg; 19–28 pairs of small, spade-shaped
teeth in each jaw; dark grey back with paler grey patch on flanks and
white belly, grey line from flippers to jawline; small, rotund body with
small head, no forehead or beak, short slightly rounded flippers, low
triangular dorsal fin with concave trailing edge. Rarely breaches clear of
water. Distribution mainly coastal in temperate and subarctic North
Atlantic (mainly from southern Carolina north to central west
Greenland/Gulf of St Lawrence in west and southwestern Ireland north
to coast of northern Norway and Murmansk in east; now rare along
Iberian/French coasts, Mediterranean and Baltic except western
approaches) and North Pacific (mainly from northern Sea of Japan north

Figure 3.3 The family Phocoenidae: Harbour porpoise, Burmeister's porpoise, vaquita, spectacled porpoise, Dall's porpoise and finless porpoise

Harbour porpoise

Burmeister's porpoise

vaquita

spectacled porpoise

Dall's porpoise

finless porpoise

to Kamchatka peninsula, USSR, in west and from Point Conception, California, north to Gulf of Alaska in east); isolated populations in Black Sea and southern Sea of Azov. Population size unknown but recent declines noted in southern parts of North Atlantic range.

Phocoena spinipinnis Burmeister 1865   Burmeister's Porpoise
Length c. 1.4–1.8m; c. 40–70kg; 14–16 pairs of small, spade-shaped teeth in upper jaw, 17–19 pairs in lower jaw; dark grey-black above and on flanks, lighter patches on belly; small, rotund body with small head, no forehead or beak, large broad flippers tapering to blunt tip, low dorsal fin with convex trailing edge and blunt spines or tubercles at the base of front. Distribution is confined to coastal waters of temperate South America from Patagonia, Argentina, north to Uruguay on the Atlantic side and from Valdivia, Chile, north to Bahia de Paita, northern Peru; possibly also Falkland Islands. Population size unknown but apparently common in Beagle Channel and Strait of Magellan, and probably also mainly on Pacific coast.

Phocoena sinus   Vaquita
Norris and McFarland 1958   (Cochito or Gulf of California Porpoise)
Length c. 1.2–1.5m; c. 30–55kg; 20–21 pairs of small, spade-shaped teeth in upper jaw, 18 pairs in lower jaw; in appearance almost identical to the harbour porpoise though slightly darker, dorsal fin with trailing concave edge but slightly higher than the harbour porpoise. Very poorly known. Distribution confined to upper part of Gulf of California, Mexico. Population size unknown but must be very small.

Neophocaena phocaenoides   Finless Porpoise
(G. Cuvier 1829)   (Black or Black Finless Porpoise)
Length c. 1.4–1.65m (male slightly larger than female); weight c. 30–45kg; 13–22 pairs of teeth (crowns spade-shaped in some, as genus *Phocoena*) in each jaw; uniform grey (only black after death) often with bluish tinge, lips and chin lighter except for darker 'chin-strap', fairly rotund body, rounded forehead, no beak, flippers relatively long with blunt tips, no dorsal fin but ridged back with small tubercles. Distribution in coastal waters and estuaries of Indo-Pacific from Iran and Pakistan in the west, throughout the coasts of India, southeast Asia and Indonesia, and north to China (including to upper reaches of Yangtze River) and northern Japan. Some morphological variation between populations in western and eastern ends of range. Population size unknown, except around Japan where between 1,600 and 4,900 estimated.

Family Delphinidae Gray 1821 (includes Holodontidae — Brandt 1873; Hemisyntrachelidae — Slijper 1936)

   Subfamily Steninae (Fraser and Purves 1960) Mead 1975 (= Stenoninae — Rice 1984; includes Sotaliinae — Kasuya 1973)

Steno bredanensis (Lesson 1828)   Rough-toothed Dolphin
Length c. 2.2–2.4m (male slightly larger than female); weight c. 120kg; 20–27 pairs of teeth (finely wrinkled on the crown) in each jaw; coloration

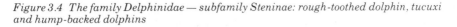

Figure 3.4 The family Delphinidae — subfamily Steninae: rough-toothed dolphin, tucuxi and hump-backed dolphins

rough-toothed dolphin

tucuxi dolphin

hump-backed dolphin

variable, often dark grey to dark purplish-grey on back and flanks, and white throat and belly, pinkish- or yellowish-white blotches on flanks round to belly, white or pinkish-white along both sides of beak, including one or both lips and tip of snout, frequently scarred with numerous white streaks; slender torpedo-shaped body with long, slender beak not clearly demarcated from forehead, relatively long flippers, centrally-placed relatively tall sickle-shaped dorsal fin, keels above and below tail stock. Distribution mainly offshore in tropical, subtropical and warm temperate seas around the world (from Virginia, USA, and Mauritania, Northwest Africa, south to Argentina and Southwest Africa in Atlantic; from northern Japan and northern California south to Australia and Peru in Pacific; and from Gulf of Aden and Bay of Bengal south to South Africa and West Australia in Indian Ocean). Some morphological variation between Atlantic and Indo-Pacific populations. Population size unknown; though widely distributed, it is apparently nowhere abundant.

Sotalia fluviatilis (Gervais 1853)   Tucuxi
Length c. 1.4–1.8m; weight c. 36–45kg; 26–35 pairs of teeth, often raggedly arranged, in each jaw; appearance similar to bottle-nosed dolphin; coloration variable geographically and with age, medium to

dark grey on back and upper flanks with brownish tinge, lighter grey sometimes with patches of yellow-ochre on lower flanks and belly, two pale grey areas sometimes extend diagonally upwards on flanks, coloration lightens with age, sometimes cream-white; small, stout torpedo-shaped body with pronounced beak, rounded forehead, relatively large spatulate flippers, small triangular centrally-placed dorsal fin. Distribution confined to Orinoco and Amazon river systems (including upper reaches) and coastal waters of northeastern South America and eastern Central America (from Panama south to Santos, Brazil). Some morphological variation such that Orinoco population in past has been recognised as separate species, *Sotalia guianensis*, being generally darker, sometimes with a brownish band extending from anal area diagonally upwards over flanks to leading edge of dorsal fin. Population size unknown, but common in most parts of its range.

Sousa chinensis (Osbeck 1765)　　　　Indo-Pacific Hump-backed Dolphin
Length c. 2–2.8m; weight c. 85kg; 29–38 pairs of peglike teeth in each jaw; coloration variable geographically and with age, dark grey-white on back and upper flanks, usually lightening on lower flanks to white belly, beak, flippers and dorsal fin may be tipped white, young uniform pale cream, adults may develop spots or speckles of yellow, pink, grey or brown; stout torpedo-shaped body with long slender beak, slight melon on forehead, rounded flippers, small but prominent centrally-placed dorsal fin, sickle-shaped in young becoming more rounded later, distinct dorsal hump in middle of back (except east of Indonesia) and similar marked keels above and below tail stocks. Characteristically makes high roll when surfacing. Wide distribution in coastal and inshore warm temperate and tropical waters of Indian and western Pacific Oceans (from Suez Canal south to southern tip of Africa (Cape Agulhas) in west along coast of India and Pakistan east to Indonesia, Borneo, New Guinea and Chinese coast from Canton River south to northern Australia); also in Red Sea, Arabian Sea and Persian Gulf. Distribution not continuous and some recognise three separate races — *S. c. plumbea* (darker), *S. c. lentiginosa* (speckled) and *S. c. chinensis* (white). Population size unknown.

Sousa teuszii (Kukenthal 1892)　　　　Atlantic Hump-backed Dolphin
Length c. 2.0m; weight c. 100kg; 26–31 pairs of peglike teeth in each jaw; indistinguishable from western populations of previous species except for having fewer teeth and more vertebrae; as with previous species, pale cream young darken as grow older. Distribution in coastal waters of West Africa (from Mauritania south to Cameroon and perhaps Angola). Population size unknown.

Subfamily Delphininae (Gray 1821) Flower 1867

Lagenorhynchus albirostris (Gray 1846)　　　　White-beaked Dolphin
Length c. 2.5–2.7m (male slightly larger than female); weight c. 180kg; 22–28 pairs small, sharp-pointed teeth in each jaw; coloration dark grey or black over most of back, but pale grey-white area over dorsal surface behind fin (less distinct in young individuals), commonly dark grey-white blaze from near dorsal surface behind eye, across flanks and downwards

to anal area, light grey or white beak mainly in Northeast Atlantic populations (but poor field identification character), white belly; very stout torpedo-shaped body, rounded snout with short beak, flippers broad at base and pointed at tip, centrally-placed, tall (particularly in adult males) sickle-shaped dorsal fin, very thick tail stock. Distribution in temperate and subpolar waters of North Atlantic (from central West Greenland, Greenland Sea and southern Barents Sea south to Newfoundland, Cape Cod and southwestern Ireland). Population size unknown but probably in tens to low hundreds of thousands.

Lagenorhynchus acutus (Gray 1828)   Atlantic White-sided Dolphin
Length c. 2.25–2.5m (male larger than female); c. 165kg; 29–40 pairs of small, sharp-pointed teeth in each jaw; coloration black on back, dark grey flanks but with long white oval blaze from below dorsal fin (not extending over back as in previous species) to area above anus, an elongated yellow-ochre band extends backwards from upper edge of white blaze towards tail, white belly; stout torpedo-shaped body, rounded snout with short black beak, pointed sickle-shaped flippers, centrally-placed sickle-shaped dorsal fin, relatively tall (particularly in adult males), pointed at tip, very thick tail stock narrowing close to tail flukes. Distribution more pelagic than previous species, in temperate and subpolar waters of North Atlantic (from central West Greenland, Iceland and southern Barents Sea south to Cape Cod and southwestern Ireland). Population size unknown but probably in tens to low hundreds of thousands.

Lagenorhynchus obscurus (Gray 1828)   Dusky Dolphin
Length c. 1.8–2.0m; weight c. 115kg; 24–36 pairs of small, pointed teeth in each jaw; coloration dark grey-black on back, large grey area (varying in intensity) on lower flanks, extending from base of beak or eye backwards and running to anus, light grey or white areas on upper flanks extending backwards from below dorsal fin as two blazes which generally meet above anal region and end at tail stock, white belly. Torpedo-shaped body, rounded snout with very short black beak, fairly long flippers distinctly curved on anterior margin with blunt tip, tall centrally-placed sickle-shaped dorsal fin. Distribution almost circumpolar (inshore in warm to cool temperate waters of southern hemisphere), incompletely known but includes South America from Argentina in Atlantic and northern Chile in Pacific south to Tierra del Fuego; southern tip of Africa; and coastal regions of South Australia, Tasmania and New Zealand, and Kerguelen Island. Probably some variation between geographically discontinuous populations. Population size unknown.

Lagenorhynchus obliquidens Gill 1865   Pacific White-sided Dolphin
Length c. 1.9–2.0m (male slightly larger than female); weight c. 150kg; 21–28 pairs of small, pointed, slightly curved teeth in each jaw; coloration dark grey or black on back, large pale grey oval area on otherwise black flanks in front of fin above flipper and extending forwards to eye which is encircled with dark grey or black, narrow pale grey stripe above eye running along length of body and curving down to anal area where it broadens out, pale grey blaze also sometimes present on posterior part of dorsal fin, white belly; fairly stout torpedo-shaped

White-beaked dolphin

Atlantic white-sided
dolphin

dusky dolphin

Pacific white-sided
dolphin

hourglass
dolphin

Peale's dolphin

Figure 3.5 The family Delphinidae — subfamily Delphininae: the genus Lagenorhynchus
*(white-beaked, Atlantic white-sided, dusky, Pacific white-sided, hourglass and Peale's
dolphins)*

body with rounded snout and very short black beak, which with black lips
demarcates it from forehead, curved flippers with blunt tip, centrally-
placed sickle-shaped dorsal fin. Distribution confined to North Pacific,
mainly temperate waters (from Kamchatka Peninsula, USSR, and
Kodiak Island, Alaska, in north to southern Japan and southern tip of
Baja California in south). Some morphological variation suggests distinct
populations in Northwest Pacific, Northeast Pacific and Baja California.
Population size unknown.

Lagenorhynchus cruciger (Quoy and Gaimard 1824) Hourglass Dolphin
Length c. 1.6–1.8m (but based on very few specimens); weight c. 100kg; c.
28 pairs of small, pointed teeth in each jaw; coloration black over back
with two large white areas on otherwise black flanks forward of dorsal fin
to black beak and backwards to tail stock, connected by narrow white
band, area of white variable in extent, white belly; torpedo-shaped body,
rounded snout with very short, well defined black beak, fairly long
pointed flippers, centrally-placed sickle-shaped dorsal fin, thick keel
above and below tail stock. Very poorly known. Distribution probably
circumpolar in cooler offshore waters of Southern Ocean (Antarctic and
subantarctic, rarely north to Chile). Population size unknown.

Lagenorhynchus australis (Peale 1848)   Peale's Dolphin
Length c. 2.0–2.2m (but based on very few specimens); weight c. 115kg; c.
30 pairs of small, pointed teeth in each jaw; coloration dark grey-black on
back, light grey area on flanks from behind eye to anus, and above this a
narrow white band behind the dorsal fin extending backwards, enlarging
to tail stock; thin black line running from leading edge of black flipper to
eye; black patch covers lower lip, chin and throat, narrowing and ending
below eyes, white belly; torpedo-shaped body, rounded snout with short
black beak, fairly long pointed flippers, centrally-placed sickle-shaped
dorsal fin. Poorly known. Distribution confined to coastal cold waters of
southern South America (southern Chile and Argentina around Tierra
del Fuego, Magellan Strait, Beagle Channel and Falkland Islands).
Population size unknown.

Lagenodelphis hosei Fraser 1956   Fraser's Dolphin
Length c. 2.3–2.5m (but based on very few specimens); weight c.
160–210kg; 34–44 pairs of slender, pointed teeth in each jaw; morpholo-
gically has features of both genera *Lagenorhynchus* and *Delphinus*;
coloration medium to dark blue-grey on back and flanks, two parallel
stripes on flanks, the upper one cream-white beginning above and in
front of eye, moving back and narrowing to tail stock, and lower one more
distinct, dark grey-black from eye to anus; sometimes also a black band
from mouth to flipper; white throat and chin but tip of lower jaw usually
black; fairly robust torpedo-shaped body, very short rounded snout with
short beak, relatively small tapering flippers, small slender centrally-
placed slightly sickle-shaped dorsal fin, pointed at tip, marked keels

Figure 3.6 The family Delphinidae — subfamily Delphininae: genera Lagenodelphis *and* Delphinus *(Fraser's and common dolphins)*

Fraser's dolphin

common dolphin

above and below tail stock. Poorly known. Distribution probably offshore warm waters of all oceans (including many parts of tropical Pacific, off eastern Australia, Malaysia, Taiwan and Japan; in Indian Ocean particularly off Natal coast, Southern Africa; and in Lesser Antilles in tropical Atlantic). Population size unknown.

Delphinus delphis Linnaeus 1758   Common Dolphin
Length 1.7–2.4m (male slightly larger than female); weight c. 75–85kg; 40–55(58) pairs of small, sharp-pointed teeth in each jaw; coloration (and beak length) variable geographically, black or brownish-black on back and upper flanks, chest and belly creamy white to white; on flanks, distinctive hourglass pattern of tan or yellowish-tan forward becoming paler grey behind dorsal fin where it may reach dorsal surface; black stripe from flipper to middle of lower jaw, and from eye to base of beak; in North Pacific, one or two grey lines running longitudinally on lower flanks; dorsal fin varies from black (often with grey central spot) to mostly white but with dark border; flippers black to light grey or white (particularly in Atlantic); slender torpedo-shaped body, long, slender beak (black, but may be tipped white), tapering flippers, slender, sickle-shaped to erect dorsal fin, centrally-placed. Distribution cosmopolitan in mainly offshore waters of all tropical, subtropical and warm temperate seas (including Mediterranean and Black Seas, Red Sea and Persian Gulf). Northern limits to distribution in Atlantic — around Nova Scotia and Iceland; in Pacific — around Japan and northern California; in Indian Ocean — rarely in Arabian and Red Seas. Southern limits in Atlantic — around Peninsula Valdés, Argentina, and southern tip of

Africa; in Pacific — South Australia, New Zealand and southern Chile; in Indian Ocean — not well known, but probably southern tip of Africa to South Australia. Some morphological variation between populations in Northwest and Northeast Pacific, North and South Atlantic, Indian Ocean and Black Sea. Population size unknown but must be one of the commonest of the world's dolphins.

Tursiops truncatus   Bottle-nosed Dolphin
(Montagu 1821)   (or Bottlenose Dolphin)
Length c. 2.3–3.1m (male larger than female, and varies geographically); weight c. 150–275kg; 18–26 pairs of teeth in each jaw; coloration also variable, usually dark grey on back, lighter grey on flanks (variable in extent), grading to white or pink on belly with some spotting on belly of some older individuals; temperate North Pacific population often more brown than grey on back, and has distinct pink area around anus, populations in Indo-Pacific and Red Sea sometimes darker than Atlantic population; stout torpedo-shaped body, robust head with distinct short beak (often with white patch on tip of lower jaw), fairly long pointed flippers, centrally-placed, tall, slender, sickle-shaped dorsal fin, moderately keeled tail stock. Distribution cosmopolitan in mainly coastal waters of all but possibly polar seas, including Mediterranean and Black Seas, Red Sea and Persian Gulf. In Pacific, range from northern Japan and southern California to southern Australia, New Zealand and Chile; in Atlantic, from Nova Scotia and northern Norway to Patagonia and southern tip of South Africa; in Indian Ocean, south probably to southern tip of South Africa; in Indian Ocean, south probably to southern tip of South Africa and South Australia. Two ecotypes (separated on morphology as well as ecology) — a coastal and an offshore form — apparently exist in at least tropical and warm temperate regions; otherwise, three separate populations have been recognised, one larger form in Atlantic (*T. t. truncatus*) and two smaller forms, one in temperate North Pacific (*T. t. gilli*) and another in Indo-Pacific and Red Sea (*T. t. aduncus*). Population size unknown but declines observed in northern Europe, Mediterranean and Black Sea.

Stenella attenuata (Gray 1846)   Spotted (or Bridled) Dolphins
Stenella frontalis (G. Cuvier 1829)   (taxonomic relationship between
Stenella plagiodon (Cope 1866)   forms uncertain, but different
Stenella dubia (G. Cuvier 1829)   named forms probably represent
                                              only the first two species)
Length c. 1.9–2.3m (in Pacific, males slightly larger than females and coastal slightly larger than offshore forms); weight c. 110kg; 29–34 pairs of small sharp-pointed teeth in upper jaw, 33–36 pairs in lower jaw; coloration and markings variable geographically and with age; dark grey on back and upper flanks, lighter grey on lower flanks and belly, white spots on upper flanks, dark spots on lower flanks and belly absent at birth but enlarging with age, spotting also decreases away from both Pacific and Atlantic coasts of North America; dark grey area (cape) on head to dorsal fin distinctly separated (though less distinct in *S. frontalis*) from light grey flanks; pronounced pale blaze on flanks, slanting up on to back behind dorsal fin; in *S. attenuata*, black circle around eye, extending to junction of beak and melon, and broad black stripe from origin of flipper

47

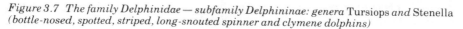

Figure 3.7 The family Delphinidae — subfamily Delphininae: genera Tursiops and Stenella
(bottle-nosed, spotted, striped, long-snouted spinner and clymene dolphins)

bottle-nosed dolphin

spotted dolphin

striped dolphin

long-snouted spinner dolphin

clymene dolphin

to corner of mouth (which tends to fade as spotting increases) together
give banded or bridled appearance to light grey sides of head (absent from
S. frontalis). Slender, to relatively stout (in coastal populations) torpedo-
shaped body, distinct forehead, and long slender beak (in East Pacific,
possibly elsewhere, longer in females) with upper and lower lips white,
pale grey or pinkish, tapering flippers, and slender sickle-shaped
centrally placed dorsal fin, fairly marked keel (except possibly large
adult males) below, and sometimes above tail stock. Distribution mainly
offshore, in tropical and some warm temperate waters throughout world.
S. attenuata applied to one form in tropical Pacific and Atlantic; *S.
frontalis* (previously considered *S. plagiodon*) only to subtropical and
warm temperate Atlantic; *S. dubia* previously applied to form of *S.
attenuata* lacking flipper stripe. Range in Pacific extends from Japan and
South China Sea east to central Gulf of California and south to New
Zealand across to Peru; in Atlantic from New Jersey and Northwest
Africa south to southern Brazil and Angola; in Red Sea and Indian Ocean
from Aldabra and Seychelles east and south to Australia and New
Zealand. Population unknown but one of the commonest of all the world's
cetaceans, with c. 3.5 million estimated in eastern tropical Pacific.
Declines due to tuna purse-seine fishery recorded in tropical Pacific.

Stenella coeruleoalba   Striped Dolphin
(Meyen 1833)   (Euphrosyne or Blue-white Dolphin)
Length c. 2.1–2.4m (male slightly larger than female); weight c. 100kg; 45–50 pairs of sharp, slightly incurved teeth in each jaw; coloration variable, dark grey to brown or bluish-grey on back, lighter grey flanks, and white belly; two distinct black bands on flanks, one from near eye down side of body to anal area (with short secondary stripe originating with this band, turning downwards towards flippers) and second from eye to flippers; distinctive white or light grey V-shaped blaze originating above and behind eye with one finger narrowing to a point below the dorsal fin and the lower one extending backwards towards tail (sometimes upwards over dorsal surface of tail stock); black flippers; slender torpedo-shaped body with distinct forehead, slender, long beak (though shorter than common dolphin), tapering flippers, and slender sickle-shaped centrally-placed dorsal fin, narrow tail stock with no obvious keel. Distribution mainly offshore in all tropical, subtropical and warm temperate seas. In Pacific, range extends from Japan and northern California south to Australia, New Zealand and Chile; in Atlantic, from Nova Scotia and France south to northern Argentina and southern tip of South Africa; in Indian Ocean south to southern tip of South Africa and Australia/New Zealand. Occasionally in Red Sea. Morphological variation noted between forms in Northwest and Northeast Pacific, and off South Africa. Population size unknown but along with common, spinner and spotted dolphins, must be among the commonest of all the world's cetaceans, with numbers certainly exceeding a million. Population around Japan estimated at between 0.4–0.6 million, and in eastern tropical Pacific at c. 250,000. Large numbers taken annually off Japan but effects on status undetermined.

Stenella longirostris (Gray 1828)   Long-snouted Spinner Dolphin
Stenella clymene   Clymene Dolphin (or Short-snouted Spinner
(Gray 1850)   Dolphin)
Length c. 1.7–2.1m (male slightly larger than female and varies geographically); weight c. 75kg; 45–65 pairs of sharp-pointed teeth in each jaw in *S. longirostris*, 38–49 pairs in *S. clymene*; coloration varies geographically and with age. Five forms recognised (four forms of *S. longirostris* and one of *S. clymene*). Largest Costa Rican form slender, all grey, males having a triangular or slightly forward-pointing dorsal fin; eastern Pacific form shorter, distinguished on skull characters; more offshore whitebelly form larger, more robust with sharper colour differentiation, some white on belly, and more sickle-shaped dorsal fin; Hawaiian form similar to previous one but larger with band of intermediate pale grey separating dark back and white belly, and sickle-shaped dorsal fin; fifth form, *S. clymene*, recognised as separate species; otherwise most similar to previous one but with short beak. Otherwise all have distinct but sloping forehead to torpedo-shaped body, relatively large (longer than spotted dolphins) black–light grey flippers; marked keel may exist below, sometimes above, tail stock. Species so named for its habit of spinning longitudinally on or above surface of water. Distribution mainly in offshore waters of all tropical, subtropical and warm temperate seas. In *S. longirostris*, Costa Rican form mainly within 150km of shore from Guatemala, through Costa Rica and Panama

south to Colombia; eastern spinner from southwest coast of Baja California south to equator and west to about 126°W; whitebelly spinner well offshore throughout most of Pacific from near Hawaii east towards Mexico and south to 14°S, west of Peru, overlapping in range with previous form; also in Atlantic, offshore of Virginia across to Mauritania and south to Brazil and Gulf of Guinea; in Indian Ocean south possibly to southern tip of Africa and Southwest Australia. Also common in southern Red Sea. *S. clymene* is known only from Atlantic, from New Jersey across to Northwest Africa and south possibly to Brazil across to Angola (though limits of distribution poorly known). Population size unknown but probably exceeds striped dolphin. Three eastern tropical Pacific populations, exploited by tuna fishery, after severe depletion, now estimated at more than 1.8 million.

Subfamily Lissodelphinae Fraser and Purves 1960 (= Lissodelphininae — Rice 1984)

Lissodelphis peronii (Lacépède 1804)   Southern Right Whale Dolphin Length c. 1.8–2.3m (but based on very few specimens); weight c. 60kg; 44–49 pairs of small, pointed teeth in each jaw; very distinctive coloration (though amounts and intensity of black or white may vary), black on back and flanks, white belly extends upwards conspicuously to lower flanks behind flippers and forwards across forehead in front of eyes so that entire beak is white, amount of white on flippers variable to all-white; small, very slender torpedo-shaped body, with underside of tail fluke white, rounded snout with short but distinct beak, tapering flippers, no dorsal fin. Distribution is circumpolar in temperate waters of southern hemisphere. Range from around Antarctic Convergence north to Southeast Australia and New Zealand across to northern Chile in Pacific, southern Brazil and Southwest Africa in Atlantic, and around 23°S in Indian Ocean (though northerly limits to distribution in latter two oceans poorly known). Usually in offshore waters, but also near Chilean coast. Population size unknown.

Figure 3.8 The family Delphinidae — subfamily Lissodelphinae: northern and southern right whale dolphins

northern right whale dolphin

southern right whale dolphin

Lissodelphis borealis (Peale 1848)   Northern Right Whale Dolphin
Length c. 2.1–3.1m (but based on very few specimens; males possibly
larger than females); weight c. 70kg; 36–49 pairs of small, pointed teeth
in each jaw; coloration black on back and flanks, extending down to navel
so that at sea gives appearance of being all black, white belly mainly
around flippers where may sometimes extend upwards; otherwise
flippers all black; characteristic small white mark at tip of lower jaw;
newborn are cream or light grey until one year old; small, very slender
torpedo-shaped body, rounded snout with short but distinct beak, slender
tapering flippers, no dorsal fin, marked keel above tail stock with narrow
curved tail flukes. Distribution confined to mainly offshore temperate
waters of North Pacific, from Kamchatka, USSR, southeastwards to
British Columbia, south to Japan across to Baja California. Population
size unknown but apparently common.

Subfamily Cephalorhynchinae Fraser and Purves 1960

Cephalorhynchus heavisidii (Gray 1828)   Heaviside's Dolphin
Length c. 1.2–1.4m (but based on very few specimens); weight c. 40kg;
25–30 pairs of small, pointed teeth in each jaw; coloration black on back
and flanks, white belly extending upwards as three lobes, two on either
side of the flipper, and one from anal region up along flanks towards tail
stock; small fairly stout torpedo-shaped body, short rounded snout with
no melon and no distinct beak, small oval-shaped black flippers, centrally
placed low triangular dorsal fin, and deeply notched tail flukes. Very
poorly known. Distribution confined to coastal waters of southwestern
Africa from Namibia south to southern tip of South Africa. Population
size unknown, but probably not very large.

Cephalorhynchus hectori (van Beneden 1881)   Hector's Dolphin
Length c. 1.2–1.4m; weight c. 40kg; 26–32 pairs of small teeth in each
jaw; coloration grey but with black mask from tip of beak (including
lower jaw) over sides of face above eyes and backward down to and
including flippers, dorsal fin black extending around base, and black tail
flukes; thin black line behind blowhole and grey forehead, small white
patch behind flipper, and narrow band of white from near genital region
upwards to lower flanks and back towards tail; small, stout torpedo-
shaped body narrowing at tail stock, short rounded snout with no melon
and a short beak, rounded black flippers, centrally placed low rounded
dorsal fin with convex rear margin. Distribution confined to coastal
waters around most of New Zealand (mainly in Tasman Bay and Cook
Strait on north and northeast coast of South Island). Population size
unknown, but possibly in low thousands.

Cephalorhynchus eutropia   Black Dolphin
(Gray 1846)   (or White-bellied Dolphin)
Length c. 1.6m (but based on very few specimens); weight c. 45kg; 30–31
pairs of teeth in each jaw; coloration black on back, flanks and part of
belly but with three small areas of white, variable in size, extending from
white belly around anal area, spot behind flippers and on throat; pale
grey area over forehead from blowhole to tip of snout; sometimes pale
grey area around blowhole. Small stout torpedo-shaped body with short

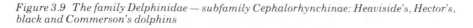

Figure 3.9 The family Delphinidae — subfamily Cephalorhynchinae: Heaviside's, Hector's, black and Commerson's dolphins

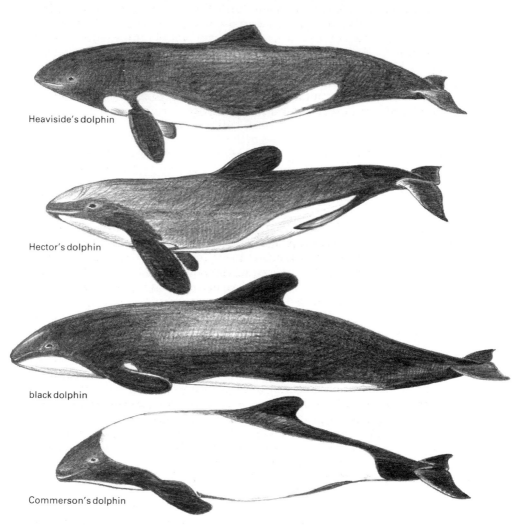

Heaviside's dolphin

Hector's dolphin

black dolphin

Commerson's dolphin

rounded snout, no melon or beak; rounded flippers, low rounded dorsal fin, centrally placed with longer leading edge and blunt apex. Poorly known. Distribution confined to coastal waters of Chile from Concepción south to Tierra del Fuego and Cape Horn. Population size unknown, but apparently not common.

Cephalorhynchus commersonii (Lacépède 1804)   Commerson's Dolphin Length c. 1.3–1.4m; weight c. 50kg; 29–30 pairs of small, pointed teeth in each jaw; coloration very striking, head and flippers black with white chevron on throat, white or pale grey cape extends up flanks and over back to neckline, black band under belly connecting flippers, dorsal fin and surrounding upper surface also black extending backwards to tail flukes and downwards to ventral surface of tail stock, small black area around anus. Form of genital patch varies between sexes. Newborn all brown. Small stout torpedo-shaped body, short rounded snout with no melon and very short beak, rounded black flippers, ridged along leading edge (often only lefthand flipper); centrally placed low rounded dorsal fin. Distribution limited to cool mainly coastal waters of eastern South America and Falkland Islands possibly east across Southern Ocean (including South Georgia) to Kerguelen Island in southern Indian Ocean. Known mainly from South American coast from Peninsula Valdés south to Tierra del Fuego. Population size unknown but very common in Magellan Strait and around the Falklands.

Subfamily Globicephalinae (Gray 1866) Gill 1872 (including Orcininae (Brandt 1873) Slijper 1936 = Orcinae — Fraser and Purves 1960); Grampidae — Nishiwaki 1964; and Globidelphinidae — Nishiwaki 1963)

Peponocephala electra (Gray 1846)   Melon-headed Whale
Length c. 2.3–2.7m (male slightly larger than female); weight c. 160kg; 21–25 pairs of small, sharply pointed teeth in each jaw; coloration black on back and flanks, slightly lighter on belly, mainly around anus and genital region; lips often white; indistinct light grey anchor-shaped throat patch, and sometimes indistinct downward-pointing darker triangle below dorsal fin, and in the face tapering towards eyes; slender torpedo-shaped body with triangular-shaped head and rounded forehead (though slightly more pointed snout than similar pygmy killer whale), slightly underslung jaw presenting very indistinct beak, long slender, pointed flippers, tall centrally placed sickle-shaped dorsal fin, slender tail stock. Distribution poorly known but apparently in offshore tropical and subtropical waters of all seas. In Pacific, reported from Japan and Hawaii south to Australia, Marquesas Islands and west coast of South America; in Atlantic, from Lesser Antilles and Gulf of Guinea in Atlantic; and from Aldabra and Maldive Islands in Indian Ocean. Population size unknown but herds up to 1,500 recorded; greatest numbers reported from Philippines.

Feresa attenuata Gray 1874   Pygmy Killer Whale
Length c. 2.2–2.5m (but based on few specimens; male slightly larger than female); weight c.150–170kg; 8–11 pairs of relatively small teeth in upper jaw, 11–13 pairs in lower jaw; coloration dark grey or black on back, often lighter on flanks giving impression of darker greyish brown cape on back, extending down flanks below dorsal fin, small but conspicuous zone of white or light grey on underside (from anus to tail stock) and around lips, and lips may be entirely white; slender torpedo-shaped body, slender, tapered head, slightly underslung jaw, flippers slightly rounded at tips, relatively tall almost centrally placed sickle-shaped dorsal fin. Distribution poorly known but apparently in offshore waters of tropical and subtropical Pacific, Atlantic and Indian Oceans. In Pacific, reported from Japan, Hawaii, Mexico and Costa Rica; in Atlantic, from Florida and Mediterranean south to Lesser Antilles and Southwest Africa; also in central Indian Ocean. Population size unknown but relatively common around Japan and Hawaii.

melon-heading whale

pygmy killer whale

false killer whale

killer whale

Risso's dolphin

long-finned pilot
whale

short-finned pilot whale

Figure 3.10 The family Delphinidae — subfamily Globicephalinae: melon-headed, pygmy killer, false killer, killer, Risso's and long-finned/short-finned pilot whales

---

Pseudorca crassidens (Owen 1846)   False Killer Whale
Length c. 4.0–5.5m (males larger than females); weight c. 1,200–2,000kg; 8–11 pairs of large teeth (circular in cross section) in each jaw; coloration all black except for a blaze of grey (variable from indistinct to nearly white) on belly between flippers, which have a broad hump on front margin near middle of flipper. Sometimes also light grey area on sides of face. Long slender body with small slender, tapered head, underslung jaw, narrow tapered flippers, tall, sickle-shaped (rounded to sharply pointed) dorsal fin, just behind midpoint of back. Distribution in offshore waters of tropical and warm temperate Pacific, Atlantic and Indian Oceans. Range in Pacific from Japan and Alaska (though rare north of southern California) south to New Zealand and Peru; in Atlantic mainly on west side, from Maryland and Norway (though rare north of southwestern British approaches) south to northern Argentina and south of tip of Southern Africa; in Indian Ocean from Red Sea south to southern tip of South Africa and New Zealand. Population size unknown but probably relatively common.

Orcinus orca (Linnaeus 1758)   Killer Whale (Orca)
Length: male 6.7–7.0 (9.5)m; female 5.5–6.5 (7.0)m; weight 4,000–5,000kg in male, 2,500–3,000kg in female; 10–12 pairs of large conical teeth in each jaw; coloration very striking black on back and sides, white belly extending as a rear-pointing lobe up the flanks and less markedly at head end around throat, chin and undersides of flippers, and a distinctive, conspicuous white oval patch above and behind eye; regional variation in exact position and extent of white patches; indistinct grey saddle over back behind dorsal fin, stout torpedo-shaped body with conical-shaped head, indistinct beak, large rounded paddle-shaped flippers and centrally-placed conspicuous dorsal fin, sickle-shaped in adult female and immatures, but very tall and erect (triangular, sometimes tilted forwards) in adult male; tail flukes have concave trailing edge and are notched in centre. Distribution worldwide in all seas (including western Mediterranean, Arabian Sea and Gulf of Aden) from tropics to both Arctic and Antarctic. Variation in morphology between regional populations but vocal dialects vary more between pods than geographically. Population size unknown, but despite cosmopolitan distribution unlikely to compare with *Delphinus* or *Stenella* species. Largest numbers apparently in Antarctic where population of more than 160,000 suggested.

Grampus griseus (G. Cuvier 1812)   Risso's Dolphin (or Grampus)
Length c. 3.3–3.8m (male slightly larger than female); weight 3.5–4.0kg; 7 pairs of peglike teeth in lower jaw only; coloration dark to light grey on back and flanks, palest in older individuals so that head may be pure white; many scars on flanks of adults; white belly enlarging to oval or anchor-shaped patch on chest and chin, flippers and tail flukes usually dark but dorsal fin may lighten with age, particularly along leading edge; newborn overall light grey changing to chocolate brown; stout torpedo-

55

shaped body narrowing behind dorsal fin to quite narrow tail stock, blunt snout, rounded with slight melon, no beak, long pointed flippers, tall centrally-placed sickle-shaped dorsal fin (taller, more erect in adult males), tail flukes have concave trailing edge and are notched in centre. Distribution tropical to temperate waters of all seas. In Pacific, range from Kurile Islands and southeastern Alaska south to New Zealand and Chile; in Atlantic, from Newfoundland and Shetland Islands, Scotland, south to Argentina and South Africa; in Indian Ocean south to southern tip of South Africa and South Australia, Tasmania and New Zealand; also recorded commonly in Red Sea. Generally offshore although widely distributed in small herds in coastal Atlantic waters of British Isles and Ireland. Population size unknown, but probably lower than *Delphinus* and *Stenella* species.

Globicephala melaena (Traill 1809) Long-finned Pilot Whale (Blackfish) Length: male 5.5–6.2 (8.5)m; female 3.8–5.4 (6.0)m; weight c. 3,000–3,500kg male, 1,800–2,500kg in female; 8–12 pairs of peglike teeth in each jaw; coloration black or dark grey on back and flanks with anchor-shaped patch of greyish-white on chin and grey area on belly, both variable in extent and intensity (lighter in younger individuals); some have grey dorsal fin (otherwise black); pale stripe along midline of underside that widens out at rear end; other lighter areas may be present (mainly in southern hemisphere populations) — grey saddle behind dorsal fin and short grey streak extending back and upwards from behind eye. Robust body with square bulbous head, particularly in old males, with slightly protruding upper lip, long, pointed and sickle-shaped flippers, and fairly low dorsal fin, slightly forwards of midpoint, with long base, sickle-shaped (in adult females and immatures) to flag-shaped (in adult males), thick keel on tail stock, tail flukes have concave trailing edge and are deeply notched in centre. Morphological variation between populations resulted in recognition of races *G. m. melaena* distributed in temperate and subarctic North Atlantic and *G. m. edwardi* in all temperate and subantarctic southern hemisphere seas, but detailed examination of taxonomic status of the two races not yet made. In North Atlantic, ranges from central West Greenland, Iceland and Barents Sea south to Cape Hatteras and northwest Africa; in South Pacific from southeastern Australia to Colombia south to around Auckland Island, New Zealand, across to Tierra del Fuego; in South Atlantic, from Brazil across to Angola south to Tierra del Fuego across to around 50°S, due south of South Africa; and in Indian Ocean, from Mozambique across to western Australia south to a line around 50°S (limits to southern hemisphere populations poorly known and here set around limits of cold Humboldt, Falkland and Benguela Currents together with West Wind Drift which seems to determine its distribution). Usually in offshore waters but in some regions will occur close to coast. Population size unknown, but in North Atlantic possibly in high tens, or even low hundreds, of thousands.

Globicephala macrorhynchus Gray 1846   Short-finned Pilot Whale Length: male 4.5–5.0 (5.5)m; female 3.3–3.6 (5.0)m; weight c. 2,500kg in male, c. 1,300kg in female; 7–9 pairs of peglike teeth in each jaw; coloration and appearance very similar to preceding species; black on back, flanks and most of belly, with anchor-shaped patch of grey on chin, and grey area of varying extent and intensity on belly (lighter in younger animals; otherwise less conspicuous and extensive than preceding species); grey saddle over back behind dorsal fin also more conspicuous; however, light grey blaze behind eye inconspicuous. Robust body, with square bulbous head particularly in old males (slightly more robust than in preceding species), slightly protruding upper lip; long sickle-shaped flippers (but proportionately shorter than preceding species), fairly low dorsal fin, slightly forward of midpoint, with long base, sickle-shaped to flag-shaped; tail flukes have concave trailing edge and deeply notched in centre. Distribution throughout tropical and warm temperate waters of all seas. In Pacific, ranges from Japan and central California (uncommonly Gulf of Alaska) in north to northeast Australia and Peru in south; in Atlantic, from about Virginia and Northwest Africa south to Venezuela and Senegal; limits in Indian Ocean from Gulf of Aden and Sri Lanka south to Southern Africa, Western Australia and New Zealand. Distribution in warmer waters overlaps with long-finned pilot whale. Population size unknown, but in eastern tropical Pacific estimated at c. 60,000.

SUPERFAMILY ZIPHIOIDEA (Gray 1865) Fraser and Purves 1960

The beaked whales, medium-sized whales with a distinct beak extending from skull; in all but Tasman and Gray's beaked whales, teeth very reduced in number and entirely absent from upper jaw; on each side of lower jaw of adult males, one or two comparatively large teeth projecting from mouth as small tusks (usually not erupted in females and juveniles); under throat, two characteristic V-shaped grooves; no notch in middle of tail flukes.

Family Ziphiidae Gray 1865 (including Choneziphiidae — Cope 1895; Hyperoodontidae — Gray 1866)

Berardius bairdii Stejneger 1883   Baird's Beaked Whale
Length c. 10.7–11.8m (male); c. 11.0–12.8m (female); weight c. 13.5 tonnes in male, c. 15 tonnes in female; two pairs of strongly laterally compressed functional teeth near tip of lower jaw, front pair larger and exposed (both pairs erupting with age); coloration bluish-dark grey, often with brown tinge; paler underside with white blotches on throat, between flippers, and around navel and anus; linear white scars (particularly in males) may also occur over back and flanks; long, slender cylindrical body with prominent bulbous forehead and relatively long tube-like beak with slightly protruding lower jaw; blowhole is crescent shaped, backward pointing, on top of head; relatively short, slightly rounded flippers; relatively small, triangular dorsal fin, slightly more than two-thirds along back; tail flukes have concave or almost straight trailing edge. Distribution confined to North Pacific, usually in offshore deep waters (but may be coastal off Japan). Range from Kamchatka and Pribilof Islands south to southeastern Japan and Baja California. Population size unknown.

Figure 3.11 Beaked whales of the family Ziphiidae: Baird's, Arnoux's, northern and southern bottlenose whale, Cuvier's and Tasman beaked whales

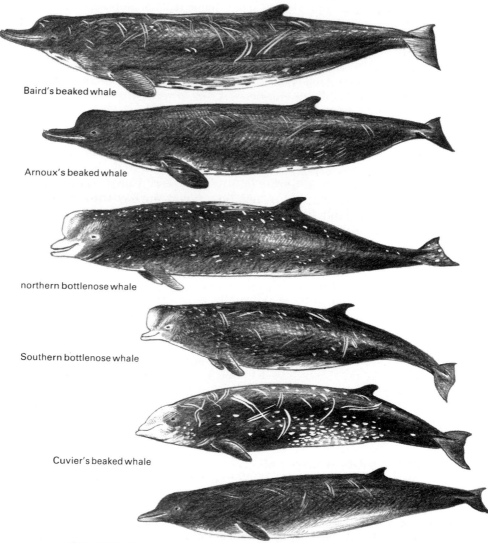

Baird's beaked whale

Arnoux's beaked whale

northern bottlenose whale

Southern bottlenose whale

Cuvier's beaked whale

Tasman's beaked whale

Berardius arnuxii Duvernoy 1851   Arnoux's Beaked Whale
Length c. 9.0–9.8m (but based on very few specimens); weight c. 9.8–10.6 tonnes; two pairs of strongly laterally compressed functional teeth near tip of lower jaw, front pair larger and exposed (both pairs erupting with age); very similar to preceding species, being primarily smaller (taxonomic distinction possibly undeserved); coloration blue-grey sometimes with a brownish tint, and darker back and flippers; old males dirty white from head to dorsal fin; paler underside with white blotches on throat,

between flippers, and around navel and anus; linear white scars (particularly in males) may also occur over back and flanks; long, slender cylindrical body with prominent bulbous forehead and relatively long tubelike beak with slightly pronounced lower jaw; blowhole is crescent-shaped, backward-pointing, on top of head; relatively short, slightly rounded flippers; relatively small sometimes distinctly sickle-shaped dorsal fin, slightly more than two-thirds along back; tail flukes have concave or almost straight trailing edge. Distribution poorly known (based on little more than 30 specimens) but apparently confined to southern hemisphere deep waters from Antarctica north to around New Zealand and central Chile in Pacific, north to Argentina and South Africa in Atlantic, and probably into southern Indian Ocean. Population size unknown.

Hyperoodon ampullatus (Forster 1770)   Northern Bottlenose Whale
Length: male 9.0–9.5m, female 7.0–8.5m; weight c. 7.5 tonnes in male, c. 5.8 tonnes in female; older males have single pair of pear-shaped teeth erupting at tip of lower jaw (in females, rarely appear through gum); coloration very variable from chocolate brown to greenish-brown above, often lighter on flanks and belly, and with irregular patches or blotches of greyish-white; lightens to buff or cream all over with age; calves uniform chocolate brown; long, relatively robust cylindrical body with bulbous forehead (more pronounced in older individuals, particularly males) and distinct dolphin-like beak; single forward-pointing crescent-shaped blow-hole in depression behind forehead giving single low (to 2m) bushy blow, slightly forward-pointing; short tapering flippers, moderate sized (c. 30cm) hooked dorsal fin, two-thirds along back; broad tail flukes have deeply concave trailing edge. Distribution confined to temperate and arctic North Atlantic, mainly in deep waters. Range from Davis Strait, Norwegian and Greenland Seas (where mainly summer) south to offshore from New York and Cape Verde Islands (where mainly winter); north-south seasonal migration takes place (except possibly residents occupying temperate seas). Population size unknown but apparently declined in last half century.

Hyperoodon planifrons Flower 1882   Southern Bottlenose Whale
Length: male 6.0–6.5m, female 7.0–7.5m; slightly smaller, but otherwise very similar to preceding species; weight c. 6.2 tonnes in male, c. 7.9 tonnes in female; older males have single pair of pear-shaped teeth erupting at tip of lower jaw (in females, rarely appear through gum); coloration variable from pale grey or brown to blue-black on back, lightening to bluish- or pale brown on flanks, usually paler on belly; some have small white spots on sides and belly, and older individuals may have extensive scarring on back and flanks, and pale grey or white head (particularly males); flippers and undersides of tail flukes grey or brown; appearance very similar to preceding species — long, relatively robust cylindrical body with bulbous forehead (more pronounced in older individuals, particularly males) and distinct dolphin-like beak; moderate sized (c. 30cm) hooked dorsal fin, about two-thirds along back; single forward-pointing crescent shaped blowhole in depression behind forehead giving single low (to 2m) bushy blow, slightly forward-pointing; short tapering flippers, broad tail flukes have deeply concave trailing edge.

Distribution poorly known but apparently circumpolar in southern hemisphere. Range from Antarctic north to around Australia, New Zealand and Chile in South Pacific, to Brazil and South Africa in South Atlantic, and north to Sri Lanka in Indian Ocean. Population size unknown.

Ziphius cavirostris   Cuvier's Beaked Whale
G. Cuvier 1823   (Cuvier's or Goosebeaked Whale)
Length: male c. 6.7m, female c. 7.0m (but based on few specimens); weight c. 5.6 tonnes in male, c. 6.5 tonnes in female; single pair of conical teeth at tip of lower jaw (usually erupt only in males); coloration very variable; grey or blue-grey in Atlantic, mustard to dark rust brown in Pacific; white or cream oval patches on belly and lower flanks (caused by parasites); paler grey or white head (particularly in older males); linear light scars often on back and sides; long stout body with small slightly concave head (likened to goose beak), beak indistinct (particularly in older individuals), slightly protruding lower jaw; low blow, slightly forward-pointing and to left; small rounded flippers but with pointed tip (inconspicuous since may be folded back within depressions or 'flipper pockets'); dorsal fin variable from small, triangular to relatively tall, sickle-shaped, about two-thirds along back; tail flukes have fairly concave trailing edge. Distribution still not clearly known but probably cosmopolitan in all except polar seas. Range in Pacific from southern Bering Sea south to Australia, New Zealand and Tierra del Fuego; in Atlantic, from Gulf of Maine and north Scotland south to Tierra del Fuego and southern tip of South Africa; in Indian Ocean, from Sri Lanka south to southern tip of South Africa and Southwest Australia. Mainly in offshore waters. Population size unknown but probably under-recorded.

Tasmacetus shepherdi   Tasman Beaked Whale
Oliver 1937   (or Shepherd's Beaked Whale)
Length c. 6–7m (based on c. 10 specimens). Weight possibly c. 5.6 tonnes; two larger teeth at tip of lower jaw (erupted only in males) but unique among beaked whales in having many (17–29) small, conical teeth lining both upper and lower jaws; very poorly known, and not yet definitely observed alive; uniform dark grey-brown on back, lighter flanks, belly almost white (at least, in dead specimens); long stout body with small head but distinct long, narrow beak, straight mouthline; crescent-shaped blowhole on top of head, asymmetric and oriented towards left; short narrow flippers; relatively small moderately sickle-shaped dorsal fin, more than two-thirds along back. Distribution possibly circumpolar in temperate waters of southern hemisphere with only c. 12 specimens from South Australia, New Zealand, Brazil, Argentina, Tierra del Fuego, Tristan da Cunha and the Galapagos Islands. Population size unknown.

Genus *Mesoplodon*

Very poorly known with forms extremely similar so that taxonomy still very uncertain. Position, shape and size of teeth used to distinguish species. All forms are uniform dark grey to black (though descriptions often based only on dead animals), long slender tapering body, small head with well-defined beak, often protruding lower jaw, single pair of generally laterally compressed teeth (which erupt only in older males); in

60

females and younger males, small sharp denticle may also be present upon teeth; broad semicircular blowhole, facing backwards and occasionally asymmetric; relatively small narrow flippers often tucked into 'flipper pockets', and triangular or sickle-shaped dorsal fin almost two-thirds along back; tail flukes have trailing edge straight or slightly concave. Any deviations from above description detailed by species below.

Mesoplodon densirostris   Blainville's Beaked Whale
(de Blainville 1817)
Length c. 4.7–5.2m; weight c. 3.6 tonnes; with exaggerated extruding tooth in adult male; black or dark grey coloration, slightly paler on belly, with grey white or pink blotches on flanks, scars and scratches over body, often on head (particularly in males), paler flippers and underside of tail flukes; head flattened directly in front of blowhole; mouthline upcurved at base. Distribution in tropical and warm temperate deep waters of all seas. Range in Pacific from Taiwan, Japan, across to northern California, south to Queensland, Tasmania and Tasman Sea (but not yet recorded from coast of South America); in Atlantic, from Nova Scotia and Madeira south to Bahamas and Gulf of Mexico (no records yet from South Atlantic); in Indian Ocean, recorded from Seychelles, Mauritius, Nicobar and southern tip of South Africa. Population size unknown but may be the commonest species of this genus.

Mesoplodon bidens   Sowerby's Beaked Whale
(Sowerby 1804)   (or North Sea Beaked Whale)
Length c. 5m; weight c. 3.4 tonnes; pair of teeth extruding from middle of beak in adult males, projecting backwards then slightly forwards; dark grey coloration, possibly slightly paler on belly, light spots scattered over back, flanks; fewer spots and lighter belly in young individuals; prominent bulge may be present in front of blowhole, slightly concave forehead, relatively long beak in some specimens; flippers slightly longer than other members of genus. Distribution restricted to temperate and subarctic deep waters of North Atlantic. Range possibly from Labrador, Iceland and central Norway south to Massachusetts (no records yet further south) and Madeira. Population size unknown but apparently more common in Northeast than Northwest Atlantic.

Mesoplodon europaeus   Gervais' Beaked Whale
Gervais 1855   (or Antillean Beaked Whale)
Length c. 4.5–5.0m; weight c. 5.6 tonnes; 1 pair of teeth in lower jaw, extruding about two-thirds from tip of beak in adult males, fitting into grooves in skin of outer upper jaw; coloration dark grey on back and flanks, paler on belly with white markings particularly around genital region; relatively small head with narrow beak. Distribution apparently confined to deep waters of warm temperate and subtropical Atlantic (mainly north of Equator). Range from New York and English Channel south to Gulf of Mexico, Trinidad and Caribbean Sea across to Ascension Island and West Africa; possibly associated with Gulf Stream. Population size unknown.

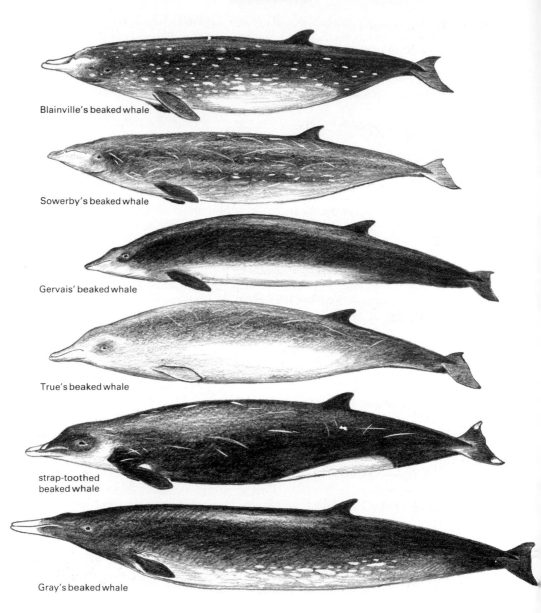

Blainville's beaked whale

Sowerby's beaked whale

Gervais' beaked whale

True's beaked whale

strap-toothed
beaked whale

Gray's beaked whale

Mesoplodon mirus True 1913   True's Beaked Whale
Length c. 4.9–5.5m; weight c. 3.2 tonnes; pair of slightly forward pointing
teeth in lower jaw (extruding from mouth in male); coloration dark grey
to grey-black on back, lighter slate grey on flanks, lighter grey on belly,
with scratches and light spots usually present, particularly in anal and
genital regions; body shape more robust, resembling Cuvier's beaked
whale; slight bulge on forehead, and slight depression in area of
blowhole; pronounced beak. Distribution so far known from temperate
waters of North and South Atlantic (mainly north and south of range of
M. densirostris), and in southwest Indian Ocean. Range very poorly

Figure 3.12 Beaked whales of the family Ziphiidae: the genus Mesoplodon *(Blainville's, Sowerby's, Gervais', True's, strap-toothed, Gray's, Andrews', Hector's, ginkgo-toothed, Stejneger's and Hubbs' beaked whales. Longman's beaked whale not depicted as known only from skull material)*

Andrews' beaked whale

Hector's beaked whale

ginkgo-toothed beaked whale

Stejneger's beaked whale

Hubb's beaked whale

known but strandings mainly from coast of northeastern United States and southeastern Canada, but also from British Isles, Ireland, France, and east coast of South Africa. Population size unknown.

Mesoplodon layardii   Strap-toothed Beaked Whale
(Gray 1865)   (or Strap-toothed Whale)
Length c. 5.0–6.0m; weight c. 3.4 tonnes; distinctive strap-shaped pair of teeth, in males extruded upwards and backwards from middle of lower jaw and curling up over upper jaw (preventing its complete opening); coloration dark purplish-brown, dark grey or black on back and flanks,

lightening to white (sometimes with yellowish tinge) on belly and to light grey over back in front of dorsal fin; white areas around dark face, below and behind flippers, and around genital slit; large white patches may occur over back. Distribution poorly known (based on c. 65 records) but apparently circumpolar in southern hemisphere, with strandings reported from Southeast Australia, New Zealand, Uruguay, Tierra del Fuego, Falkland Islands and South Africa. Population size unknown.

Mesoplodon grayi   Gray's Beaked Whale
von Haast 1896   (or Scamperdown Whale)
Length c. 5.5–6.0m; weight c. 4.8 tonnes; 1 pair of moderate-sized triangular-shaped teeth (upright, and erupting only in adult males) in lower jaw, towards back of mouth, and usually 17–22 small teeth on each side of upper jaw; coloration dark brownish-grey to black on back, grey (often mottled) on flanks, and light grey to white on belly; long very slender beak often white or with white flecks (may extend to throat); conspicuous white markings around navel, genital region and anus; conspicuous white beak may frequently be projected above water when surfacing. Distribution poorly known (based on little more than 50 records) but apparently circumpolar in southern hemisphere with strandings particularly off New Zealand, but also in South Australia, South Africa, Tierra del Fuego and Patagonia south of 30°S; sightings particularly in southern Indian Ocean; possibly exists in northern hemisphere with one stranding on Dutch coast. Population size unknown.

Mesoplodon bowdoini Andrews 1908   Andrews' Beaked Whale
Length c. 4.4–4.5m; weight c. 2.6 tonnes; 1 pair of teeth in middle of lower jaw, possibly protruding outside mouth only in adult males; teeth larger than in *M. grayi*; coloration apparently fairly uniform dark grey on back, lightening on flanks to pale grey on belly (but very poorly known and may need revision with further details). Distribution poorly known (only c. 11 specimens), with records so far only from temperate Indian and Pacific Oceans (strandings mainly from New Zealand, Australia, Tasmania and Kerguelen Island, but also Japan). Population size unknown.

Mesoplodon pacificus Longman 1926   Longman's Beaked Whale
Known only from two skulls, one a specimen stranded in Queensland, Australia in 1822, and the other found in 1955 in Somalia, on east coast of Africa. Regarded as separate species on basis of pair of very small teeth at tip of lower jaw, and unusual hoodlike formation of cheek bones, but taxonomic status still unresolved; skull size suggests a relatively large animal of c. 7m length.

Mesoplodon hectori (Gray 1871)   Hector's Beaked Whale
Length c. 3.7–4.5m (but based on very few specimens); weight c. 2 tonnes; 1 pair of relatively small triangular, flattened teeth near tip of lower jaw of adult male; coloration greyish brown on back, lightening to pale grey on lower flanks and belly, including lower jaw and chin; may have linear or oval scars on flanks; white area may be present around umbilicus. Distribution poorly known (based on 14 specimens), but apparently circumpolar in all temperate waters of southern hemisphere and temperate eastern North Pacific. Strandings recorded from Tasmania,

New Zealand, South Africa, Tierra del Fuego, Falkland Islands and southern California. Population size unknown.

Mesoplodon ginkgodens   Ginkgo-toothed Beaked Whale
Nishiwaki and Kamiya 1958   (or Japanese Beaked Whale)
Length c. 5.2m; weight c. 3.6 tonnes; 1 pair of large teeth in adult male, about two-thirds towards front of lower jaw, shaped like leaf of ginkgo tree (base of tooth being very broad); teeth almost enveloped by flap of skin from rear half of lower jaw; coloration based on dead specimens but apparently dark grey, blue-grey or black on back, lightening to pale grey on belly; many oval white scars on flanks and belly. Distribution apparently confined to warm waters of Indo-Pacific from Sri Lanka, Japan and across to California. Population size unknown, but possibly more common in western North Pacific.

Mesoplodon stejnegeri   Stejneger's Beaked Whale
True 1885   (or Bering Sea Beaked Whale)
Length c. 5.0–6.0m; weight c. 4.8 tonnes; 1 pair of very large teeth in adult male, about two-thirds towards front of lower jaw, slightly forward-pointing; coloration based mainly upon dead specimens but apparently grey-brown on back, lightening to pale grey on belly; very conspicuous light off-white areas on flanks behind head, at neck, and around mouth; as in preceding species, rear half of lower jaw raised (though mouthline straighter in females, and possibly young males) with tooth projecting from anterior edge; pair of teeth may converge towards one another. Based on strandings, distribution apparently confined to cold temperate and subarctic North Pacific, with strandings from southern Bering Sea south to Japan and central California. Population size unknown but may be most common in vicinity of Aleutian Islands where strandings commonest.

Mesoplodon carlhubbsi   Hubbs' Beaked Whale
Moore 1963   (or Arch Beaked Whale)
Length c. 5.0–5.3m (but based on very few specimens); weight c. 3.4 tonnes; 1 pair of large flattened teeth in adult male, about two-thirds towards front of lower jaw; rear half of lower jaw raised (though mouthline straighter in females and young males) with tooth projecting from anterior edge; pair of teeth may converge towards one another; as with previous species, coloration based mainly upon dead specimens but apparently dark grey to black on back, lightening at least in females on flanks and belly; distinctive white raised area or 'cap' on forehead, in front of blowhole; tip of beak white in adult males, also pale around lower jaw of females and immatures; long linear pale scratches and oval spots over back and flanks (particularly in males). Based on strandings, distribution apparently confined to cold temperate North Pacific, with strandings in Japan, Washington and southern California. Population size unknown.

SUPERFAMILY PHYSETEROIDEA (Gray 1821) Gill 1872

Robust small to very large whales, with body tapering abruptly at tail stock; small underslung lower jaw bearing numerous teeth (though may be reduced in female); teeth in upper jaw if present rarely erupt; blowhole displaced to left side, and nasal bones asymmetrical.

Family Kogiidae (Gill 1871) Miller 1923

Kogia breviceps   Pygmy Sperm Whale
(de Blainville 1838)   (or Lesser Cachalot)

Length 2.7–3.4m; weight 318–408kg; no functional teeth in upper jaw but (10)12–16 pairs of narrow inward-curving pointed teeth in lower jaw; coloration dark blue-grey on back (and outer margin of flippers, upper surface of tail flukes), shading to pale grey on flanks and dull white belly (sometimes with pinkish tinge); in appearance, rather sharklike; conical head becomes more rectangular or squarish with age; pale grey or white crescentic or bracket-shaped mark on side of head behind eye, resembling gill slits of fish; body may appear wrinkled; low, strongly sickle-shaped dorsal fin, nearly two-thirds along back; tail has concave trailing edge with distinct notch between flukes; sometimes seen basking on surface with head and back exposed; blow is inconspicuous and low. Distribution apparently cosmopolitan in deep waters of most (if not all) temperate, subtropical and tropical seas (not yet recorded from South Atlantic); known mainly from strandings which are commonest along east coast of North America from Nova Scotia to Texas; also recorded from Peru, England, Holland, France, tip of South Africa, East Africa, Arabia, India, Sri Lanka, Southeast Australia, Tasman Sea, New Zealand, and west coast of North America from Washington to Baja California. Population size unknown, but apparently not common.

Figure 3.13 The superfamily Physeteroidea: pygmy sperm, dwarf sperm and sperm whales

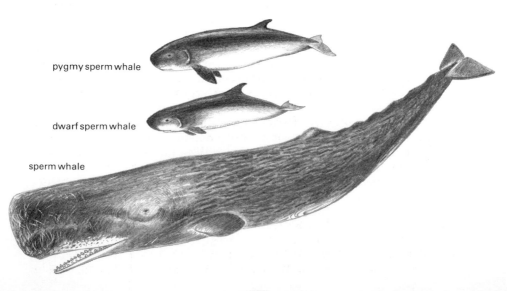

pygmy sperm whale

dwarf sperm whale

sperm whale

Kogia simus Owen 1866   Dwarf Sperm Whale
Length 2.1–2.7m; weight 136–272kg; 7–12(13) pairs of short, slender
teeth in lower jaw, but may have additionally up to three pairs of small
teeth in upper jaw; only recently recognised as distinct species; appearance and coloration very similar to preceding species; differences are
slightly smaller size, shorter (i.e. flatter) snout, taller sickle-shaped fin
(with longer base) near centre of back (resembling bottle-nosed dolphin).
Distribution poorly known but apparently cosmopolitan, possibly in
waters of continental edge. Recorded in Pacific from Japan, Indonesia,
Hawaii, California, South Australia and New Zealand; in Atlantic
mainly from Virginia to Lesser Antilles (not yet recorded from South
Atlantic); in Indian Ocean from India, Sri Lanka and South Africa.
Population size unknown, but apparently not common.

Family Physeteridae Gray 1821 (= Catodontidae, including Physodon-
tidae – Lydekker 1894)

   Subfamily Hoplocetinae Cabrera 1926   Extinct
   Subfamily Physeterinae (Gray 1821) Flower 1867

Physeter macrocephalus (= *catodon*)   Sperm Whale
Linnaeus 1758   (or Cachalot)
Length: male 15.8–18.5m, female 10.9–12.0m; weight c. 45–70 tonnes in
male, 15–20 tonnes in female; in lower jaw, (18)20–25 large conical
functional teeth (unpaired) in males, fewer and smaller teeth in female;
in upper jaw, up to 10 frequently curved teeth in male; teeth often erupt
only at sexual maturity and then, in males, only in lower jaw; coloration
dark grey or brownish grey, paler at front of head and on belly, with
white fringes to mouth, particularly at corners; juveniles are much
lighter grey overall; robust body with corrugations to skin giving
shrivelled appearance, huge square head occupying at least one-third of
body (proportion highest in adult males) projecting well beyond lower
jaw; single blowhole giving bushy blow (to height of c. 1.5m) projected
forwards at sharp angle to left; no dorsal fin but distinct triangular or
rounded hump two-thirds along body followed by spinal ridge to broad
triangular and deeply notched tail flukes; keel along underside of tail
stock; when diving deep, tail flukes thrown high into air. Distribution is
cosmopolitan in deep waters of all seas, except close to ice edge; females
undergo less extensive seasonal migrations than males, usually only to
40°north and south of Equator; males regularly to be found to 65°north
and 70°south. Probable favoured areas for feeding and breeding may
exist; feeding areas include deeper waters around Aleutians in North
Pacific; off New Zealand, Peru and Chile in South Pacific; Newfoundland
Grand Banks and continental slope west of British Isles north towards
Iceland in North Atlantic; along east coast of South America from
Argentina to Falkland Islands and around Tristan da Cunha in South
Atlantic. Mating and calving areas include waters off New Guinea and
around Hawaii in North Pacific; deep waters off East Australia,
Galapagos and Ecuador in South Pacific; around Bahamas, Azores and
Madeira in North Atlantic; off Brazil, Angola and Southwest Africa in
South Atlantic; off western Australia, around Madagascar, and west and
north of Seychelles to coasts of India, Sri Lanka and Arabian peninsula in

Indian Ocean. Separate geographical populations may exist. Population size possibly reduced in some areas by whaling, presently estimated at around 2 million.

Suborder Mysticeti Flower 1864 (= Mystacoceti)

The 'moustached', baleen or whalebone whales so named for their feeding apparatus – a series of transverse plates of comb-like baleen (keratin) which descend from roof of mouth into the buccal cavity and serve to strain plankton; the lower jaws are loosely articulated at the symphysis and the mouth cavity is expandable to accommodate the gulping method of feeding; other distinctive characters include a symmetrical skull with no melon, and a pair of nasal openings. Some fossil mysticetes have teeth.

Family Aetiocetidae Emlong 1966   Extinct

Family Balaenidae Gray 1825 (the right whales)

Large very robust whales with a proportionately large head, an arched narrow rostrum giving a deeply curved jawline in profile, narrow upper jawbone, long slender baleen plates and few or no throat grooves; all seven neck vertebrae fused.

Balaena mysticetus   Bowhead Whale
Linnaeus 1758   (or Greenland Right Whale)
Length 15.0–18.5m (female larger than male); weight c. 60–80 tonnes; 230–360 long, narrow baleen plates on each side of upper jaw; coloration black (occasionally brown or greyish-black) all over body except for white or ochreous chin patch (often with beadlike string of dark grey or black spots); sometimes also a light grey band on undersurface of tail stock; very large head, about 40 per cent length of body with enormous mouth containing very long dark grey or black baleen (longest of all cetacean species); baleen may have whitish edge and appear iridescent green; head usually without callosities; blowholes widely separated, giving V-shaped blow; in profile, older animals have broad triangular head separated by deep depression from rounded back; no dorsal fin or ridge. Distribution is circumpolar confined to Arctic, associated with ice. Short distance seasonal migration south to winter along ice edge. Five separate populations suggested with bulk of total population concentrated in Bering, Chukchi and Beaufort Seas; another population exists in Sea of Okhotsk; a third in Davis Strait and Baffin Bay; a fourth around Hudson Bay; and a relict population in Greenland and Barents Seas. One of the most seriously endangered of all the large whales with populations depleted by hunting; present population size very uncertain, but possibly c. 3,000–5,000 individuals.

Eubalaena (= *Balaena*) *glacialis*   Northern Right Whale
(Muller 1776)   (North Atlantic/Pacific Right Whale,
                                              Black Right Whale, Biscayan Right
                                                     Whale, or Nordcaper)
Eubalaena (= *Balaena*) *australis*   Southern Right Whale
Desmoulins 1822

Length 15.0–18.0m (female larger than male); weight 50–56(90) tonnes; 220–260 long, narrow baleen plates in each side of upper jaw; northern and southern hemisphere forms identical externally, and probably should not justify separate specific status; coloration black (occasionally brown), sometimes mottled, with white patches on chin and belly; area around blowholes, and both head and jaws characteristically have several large white, grey or yellowish skin callosities (infested with parasites); numerous hairs on chin and upper jaw; large head about 30 per cent length of body; long narrow baleen, usually dark brown, dark grey or black but may be pale grey or white; blowholes widely separated, giving bushy V-shaped blow, typically made once a minute during surface cruising for 5–10 minutes followed by a dive lasting 10–20 minutes, sometimes longer; large broad flippers with angular outer edge; no dorsal fin or ridge; broad tail flukes deeply notched with concave trailing edge, often lifted into air before dive. Distribution of *E. glacialis* is confined to North Atlantic and North Pacific (sometimes considered separate subspecies or even species), ranging from southern Greenland and Spitsbergen south to Florida, Gulf of Mexico, Azores and Northwest Africa in Atlantic; and Kamchatka and Gulf of Alaska south to Taiwan and Gulf of California in Pacific. Distribution of *E. australis* ranges from Brazil and South Africa south to Tristan da Cunha, Patagonia and South Georgia in Atlantic/Southern Oceans; and from Australia and Chile south to Auckland and Chatham Islands and elsewhere in subantarctic; south of Indian Ocean, recorded around Kerguelen and Crozet Islands. Seasonal migrations take place but mating/calving areas not sharply differentiated from feeding grounds. Present coastal concentrations include Bay of Fundy and Gulf of Maine to Cape Cod (in northern summer) where feeding and mating take place, and Peninsula Valdés, Patagonia (in southern winter) where mainly calving and mating take place. Populations seriously depleted after commercial human exploitation, with those in Northeast Atlantic and North Pacific particularly endangered. Some possible signs of recovery in Northwest Atlantic, and in South Pacific (off Campbell Island, New Zealand and off southern and western Australia). Present population size estimated for *E. glacialis* at 200–500 in North Pacific and 200–500(?) in North Atlantic; for *E. australis*, population larger, estimated at c. 3,000 (possibly up to 5,000).

Family Neobalaenidae (Gray 1874) Miller 1923

Small fairly streamlined whale with unique type of cranial telescoping and a highly modified lower jaw, bowed and slightly projecting beyond arched upper jaw; proportionately smaller head than balaenid whales.

Caperea marginata (Gray 1846)   Pygmy Right Whale
Length c. 5.0–6.4m (female slightly larger than male); weight 3.0–3.5 tonnes; c. 230 baleen plates on each side of upper jaw; coloration grey or dark grey on back and flanks (and flippers) lightening to white on belly and lower jaw; pale grey or white baleen plates with dark outer borders; baleen gum exposed as white band when mouth open; variable pale streaks on back and shoulders, and dark streaks from eye to flipper; body more slender than previous two species, with smaller head (about 25 per cent of body length); arched upper jaw, bowed lower jaw which projects

Figure 3.14 The right whales (families Balaenidae and Neobalaenidae): bowhead, northern/southern right and pygmy right whales

bowhead whale

northern/southern
right whale

pygmy right whale

slightly, and line of mouth extending behind and below eye; two indistinct longitudinal furrows on throat; blow is small and very indistinct; small narrow flippers with slightly rounded tips; small sickle-shaped dorsal fin about two-thirds along back; broad distinctly notched tail flukes. Distribution not clearly known since easily confused with minke whale, but apparently circumpolar mainly offshore, in temperate and subantarctic waters of all southern hemisphere seas but not extending to Antarctic (i.e. south of Antarctic Convergence). Population size unknown but most records come from South Australia, Tasmania and New Zealand, and South Africa.

Family Eschrichtiidae Ellerman and Morrison-Scott 1951 (= Rhachianectidae — Weber 1904)

Moderately robust large whale with many encrustations over back, many short baleen plates, jaws relatively short and broad, rostrum (upper jaw) narrow, gently arched; two short throat grooves; no dorsal fin.

Eschrichtius robustus   Gray Whale
(Lilljeborg 1861)   (or California Gray Whale)
Length: male 11.1–14.3m, female 11.7–15.2m; weight c. 16 tonnes in

Figure 3.15 The family Eschrichtiidae: gray whale

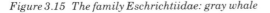

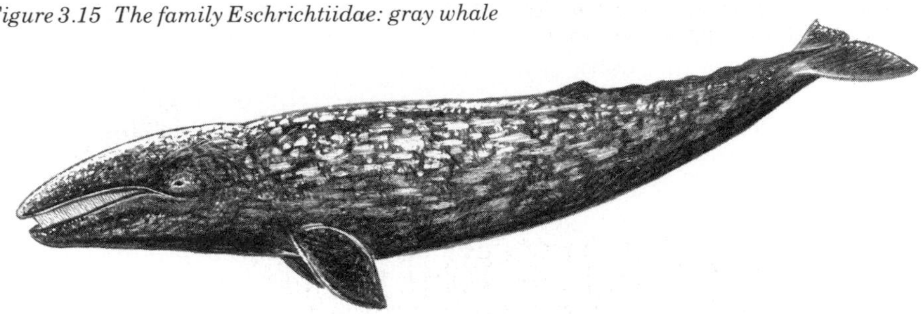

male, 30–35 tonnes in female; 130–180 relatively small baleen plates from each side of upper jaw; coloration mottled grey over entire body including flippers and tail flukes (though albino individuals not uncommon); usually covered with white, yellow or orange patches of barnacles and associated parasites (whale lice), particularly on top of head, around blowhole and on anterior part of back; fairly robust body with narrow head, arched along upper surface giving conical shape; mouth contains small hairs along upper jaw and many short coarse yellowish-white baleen plates; two (to five) short, deep longitudinal throat grooves; blow is low and heart-shaped (being indistinctly forked), typically made 3–5 times at intervals of 3–4 minutes during steady movement; broad angular flippers with pointed tips; no dorsal fin but a low hump two-thirds along the back followed by 6–12 knobs ('knuckles') along top of tail stock; large, broad tail flukes distinctly notched and often thrown into the air before a dive. Three populations once existed: one in the North Atlantic was hunted to extinction around early 1700s; a Korean population in Northwest Pacific was hunted until 1966 and is now rare; the third, Californian, population in Northeast Pacific still exists in moderate numbers, despite earlier overexploitation. Strongly migratory with Korean population moving from feeding grounds in Okhotsk Sea south to breeding grounds off South Korean coast; Californian population migrates from feeding grounds in northern Bering and Chukchi Seas south to breeding grounds in Baja California, Mexico (see Figure 8.2). Coastal habit of the species and different responses to exploitation suggest that the Northwest and Northeast 'stocks' do indeed represent discrete geographical populations. Northeast Pacific population size estimated at 17,000 to 18,000 and presently increasing; Northwest Pacific population size unknown, but in the order of 200–300.

Family Balaenopteridae Gray 1864

The rorquals, slender and streamlined in appearance, with a series of many throat grooves (fewer in humpback whale), relatively broad gently curved rostrum, with short baleen plates; dorsal fin always present (though reduced in humpback whale).

Subfamily Megapterinae Gray 1864

Megaptera novaeangliae (Borowski 1781)   Humpback Whale
Length: male 11.0–15.0m, female 11.4–15.0m; weight c. 65 tonnes;

270–400 relatively short baleen plates on each side of upper jaw; coloration grey or black on back and flanks with area of white (of variable extent) on throat and belly; flippers white underneath (sometimes also on upper surface); undersides of tail flukes partially or completely white; body more robust than other rorquals but with slender head, top of which is flattened and covered by a number of fleshy knobs or tubercles; these extend over lower jaw which also has a rounded protuberance near the tip; ridge along midline of top of head is indistinct (unlike other rorquals); very many short black or dark grey baleen plates; 14–35 broad throat grooves extending to navel; single blow is usually bushy to 3m height, typically made 4–8 times at intervals of 15–30 seconds after long dive (often only 2–4 times before long dive, in tropics); flippers very long (almost one-third total body length) and scalloped with knobs at least along trailing edge; dorsal fin variable in shape and size from small triangular knob to larger distinctly sickle-shaped, placed nearly two thirds along back; very broad distinctly notched tail flukes, commonly scalloped with knobs along trailing edge; back typically humped and tail flukes raised into air before a dive (at least in deeper waters). Distribution cosmopolitan in both hemispheres, but with apparent geographical segregation between at least ten populations. Strongly migratory from feeding grounds in polar seas (but rarely to ice edge) to tropical or subtropical coastal breeding areas (see Figure 8.1), although a population may be resident in northern Indian Ocean. Population size c. 10,000, c. 7,000 in northern hemisphere (mainly in North Atlantic) and c. 3,000 in southern oceans. Much reduced from earlier overexploitation and showing little signs of recovery except in western North Atlantic.

Subfamily Balaenopterinae (Gray 1864) Brandt 1872

Balaenoptera musculus (Linnaeus 1758)   Blue Whale
Length c. 24.0–28.0m (slightly larger in females and in southern hemisphere); weight c. 150 tonnes; 260–400 relatively short baleen plates on each side of upper jaw; coloration pale bluish-grey over most of body, mottled with grey or greyish-white; some yellow or mustard coloration may be present, mainly on belly (caused by diatoms); undersides and tips of flippers light greyish-blue or white; very broad long body with broad, flat U-shaped head with single ridge extending from raised area forwards of blowholes towards tip of snout; many short, stiff baleen plates, blue-black or black in colour; vertical slender blow (to 9m height); breathing patterns vary greatly with activity but typically make several (up to 20) shallow dives at intervals of c. 20 seconds; flippers long, slim with pointed tips; very small dorsal fin, variable in shape from nearly triangular to moderately sickle-shaped, distinctly more than two thirds along back so that seen only just prior to a dive, sometime after blow; tail flukes broad, triangular with slight median notch, lifted only slightly before diving. Portions of southern hemisphere populations (particularly in southern Indian Ocean) are recognised as separate subspecies *B. m. brevicauda* (pygmy blue whale) on basis of differences in growth patterns, shorter tail region (but extra tail vertebra), a longer trunk, and larger baleen plates. Distribution cosmopolitan, particularly along edge of continental shelves, with three major populations recognised, in North Pacific, North Atlantic and

Figure 3.16 The rorquals (family Balaenopteridae): humpback, blue, fin, sei, Bryde's and minke whales

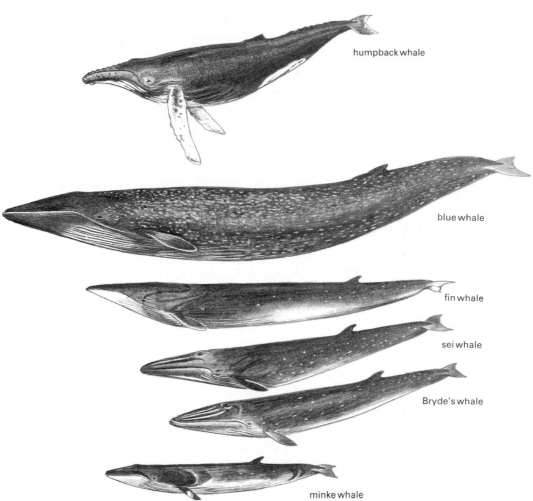

humpback whale

blue whale

fin whale

sei whale

Bryde's whale

minke whale

southern hemisphere. Strong seasonal migrations from polar feeding areas (but not in Bering Sea) to warm temperate, subtropical and tropical breeding grounds (see Figure 8.1). There may be a resident population in northern Indian Ocean (possibly of *B. m. brevicauda*). One of the most severely overexploited whale species with numbers showing some signs of slow recovery. Present population size estimated at c. 14,000 (c. 11,000, but variously estimated 2,000–20,000 in southern hemisphere; c. 2,500 in North Pacific; and 300–500 in North Atlantic).

Balaenoptera physalus   Fin Whale
(Linnaeus 1758)   (Finback, Finner or Common Rorqual)
Length: c. 18.0–25.0m (slightly larger in females and in southern hemisphere populations); weight c. 80 tonnes; 260–480 relatively short baleen plates on each side of upper jaw; coloration uniform dark grey or brown on back and flanks, but frequently with grey-white chevron

pointing forwards on back behind head; white on belly, and undersides of flippers and tail flukes; characteristic extension of white (sometimes yellowish tinged) on right side to include front baleen plates, mouth cavity and lower lip on that side; sometimes a light grey streak extends from here onto top of neck; rest of baleen (on both sides) striped with alternate bands of yellowish-white and bluish-grey, and fringed brownish-grey to greyish-white; long relatively slender head and body, narrower and more V-shaped head than blue whale; prominent ridge along middle of top of head which is not quite so flat as preceding species; many longitudinal throat grooves extending to navel, and many small baleen plates; fairly slender pointed flippers; tall blow (4–6m height) shaped like inverted cone, followed by long shallow roll showing fin, repeated 4–5 times at intervals of 10–20 seconds before dive which commonly lasts 5–15 minutes (though pattern varies with activity); triangular dorsal fin, though small, is taller than blue whale, much more obvious and backward-pointing, placed one-third along body; behind fin, the back is ridged to tail flukes, which are broad, triangular with slight median notch. Distribution cosmopolitan, though less prevalent in lower latitudes; less distinct latitudinal seasonal migrations than most other rorquals, although tendency to occupy cooler waters in summer and warmer waters in winter; low latitude populations may be resident. Several stocks recognised, with total population size estimated at c. 120,000 (c. 20,000 in northern hemisphere, mainly in North Pacific; and c. 100,000 in southern oceans).

Balaenoptera borealis Lesson 1828   Sei Whale
Length: male 12.0–17.5m, female 12.7–21.0m (slightly larger in southern hemisphere populations); weight c. 30 tonnes; 300–410 short baleen plates on each side of upper jaw; coloration dark steely grey on back, flanks and rear part of belly; throat grooves white or pale grey on anterior portion of belly; grey or white scars may occur over body, caused by lamprey bites; grey-black baleen plates fringed with white; relatively slim long body, slender head with slightly arched forehead, though not as rounded as blue whale; single prominent ridge along middle of top of head; many longitudinal throat grooves extending to navel, and many small baleen plates; fairly slender, pointed uniform grey flippers; moderately tall blow (c. 3m height) shaped like inverted cone, with almost simultaneous showing of fin; both remain in view for relatively long periods before typically shallow dive, may blow 2–3 times at 20 second intervals followed by dive of 5–6 minutes, or 5–6 times at 30–40 second intervals before longer dive of 15–30 minutes; nearly erect strongly sickle-shaped dorsal fin, tall relative to other large rorquals, placed slightly less than two thirds along back; tail flukes broad, triangular with slight median notch. Distribution cosmopolitan, mainly offshore. Seasonal migrations from polar and cold temperate feeding grounds to tropical to warm temperate breeding grounds, but not very well known. Population size estimated at c. 54,000 (c. 17,000 in northern hemisphere, possibly mainly in North Pacific; and c. 37,000, possibly less, in southern oceans).

Balaenoptera edeni Anderson 1878   Bryde's Whale
Length c. 12.5–14.0m (females larger than males; offshore form

apparently slightly larger); weight c. 26 tonnes; 250–410 short baleen plates on each side of upper jaw; very similar to sei whale but slightly smaller and has three usually prominent ridges on top of head forwards of blowhole; dorsal fin is relatively tall (though slightly smaller than sei whale), strongly sickle-shaped, about two thirds along back; although usually dark grey in colour, some have lighter grey area between head and dorsal fin over back, occasionally as band down flanks; chin and belly said to be white. Offshore form thought to be larger with longer, broader baleen plates. Distribution not well known, but particularly in coastal areas of tropical and subtropical waters of all seas. Range in Pacific from Japan and southern California south to northern New Zealand and Chile; in Atlantic, southeastern United States and Strait of Gibraltar south to Brazil and beyond southern tip of South Africa; and throughout most of Indian Ocean. Some tropical populations possibly sedentary; otherwise probably migratory. Population size estimated at c. 90,000 (c. 30,000 in southern, c. 60,000 in northern hemispheres), depleted by overexploitation.

Balaenopera acutorostrata   Minke Whale
Lacépède 1804   (Lesser Rorqual or Piked Whale)
Length: male 7.0–9.8m, female 7.5–11.0m (slightly larger in southern hemisphere populations); weight c. 10 tonnes; 230–360 short baleen plates on each side of upper jaw; coloration dark grey to black on back lightening to white on belly and undersides of flippers; individuals in northern (occasionally southern) hemisphere populations have diagonal white band on upper surface of each flipper; areas of light grey often present on flanks, one just above and behind flippers and other in front of and below dorsal fin; occasionally light chevron on back behind head; slender streamlined body with pointed, triangular head, single prominent ridge along top of head forward of blowhole; low (2m height) often inconspicuous blow, with fin often appearing simultaneously; typical breathing sequence is 5–8 blows at intervals of less than one minute; many throat grooves extending not as far as navel; slender pointed flippers; relatively tall, sickle-shaped dorsal fin, nearly two thirds along back; relatively broad notched tail flukes. Distribution cosmopolitan in polar, temperate and tropical waters of all seas. Seasonal migration from polar feeding grounds to warm temperate to tropical breeding grounds. At least three geographically isolated populations recognised, in North Pacific, in North Atlantic and in southern hemisphere. Populations thought to have benefited from overexploitation of larger relatives (by relaxation of competition for food). Present population size estimated at c. 505,000 (c. 125,000 in northern hemisphere, mainly in North Atlantic; and c. 380,000 in southern oceans).

Some 75 to 80 species of whales and dolphins occupy our seas; about 85 per cent of these are odontocetes (toothed whales), although the mysticetes (baleen whales) more than make up for the paucity of species by their generally vast size. Differences between the two suborders in their feeding apparatus have doubtless played an important part in these size differences. They have also moulded very different life styles, which have in turn determined social organisation and behaviour. We shall examine these more closely in later chapters.

4 Systematics and zoogeography

The reader, on glancing through the catalogue of species summarised in the previous chapter, should notice two patterns. First, many species are very similar to one another, to the extent that it is often difficult to tell them apart in the field. Secondly, related species often have disjunct distributions; each occupies a range geographically distinct from the other. What are the possible reasons for these patterns?

Criteria used in Classification

In order to address the first question, it is useful to look again at the classification system and examine some of its strengths and weaknesses. Classification is the ordering of animals according to their inferred relatedness. The unit in which we place them is determined by the number of shared characters and their nature. For example, sperm whales and bottle-nosed dolphins are not very similar to one another but they share some characters that we consider are rather basic, such as the presence of teeth, an asymmetrical skull and a single nasal opening. We therefore place them in the same suborder Odontoceti, but not within the same family or genus or other 'higher order' category. Bottle-nosed dolphins and white-beaked dolphins have many more characters in common so we place them in the same family Delphinidae; we believe that they are relatively closely related. However, we do not consider them as closely related as white-beaked dolphins are to white-sided dolphins; those are placed within the same genus *Lagenorhynchus*. All of the 'lower' order categories (particularly those broader than the genus) have somewhat arbitrary limits and they represent a reconstruction of how we think the different groupings evolved.

The concept of the species is rather different. We view it as a more fundamental unit of evolution. The generally accepted criterion for species is not morphological degree of difference (i.e. degrees of difference in appearance which may include bone structure, patterns of coloration, or a wide variety of other characters), but evidence that the two forms do not interbreed in nature — groups of actually or potentially interbreeding natural populations, which are reproductively isolated from other such groups (Mayr 1942). Unfortunately, it is usually not feasible to obtain genetic evidence for reproductive barriers. Bringing species into captivity and testing whether they will interbreed tells us little more than the extent to which certain types of isolating mechanisms have developed. Bottle-nosed dolphins have bred successfully with false killer whales, with a rough-toothed dolphin, Risso's dolphin and even a short-finned pilot whale (though in the latter case it was stillborn) (Dohl *et al.* 1974; Nishiwaki and Tobayama 1982; Leatherwood *et al.* 1983:6). We have no instance yet of a hybrid offspring reproducing successfully, but matings of these kinds whether successful or not would hardly constitute evidence for those animals being put under the umbrella of a single species. Some of them are clearly distantly related to one another. The important question is whether they are likely to interbreed, more than just exceptionally, in the wild.

Since genetic evidence is usually not available, systematists rely upon morphological differences, taken as evidence of genetic distinctness. In practice, this method probably works quite well. Morphological differences probably do reflect the presence of a reproductive barrier of some sort, and are probably used by the animals themselves prior to mating attempts. However, they do have some limitations. The most important one is that evolution is being viewed at a single point in time, and populations the world over are likely to be at different stages of speciation. Populations of a species may actually be reproductively isolated from one another but the process of formation of a new species be at an early stage.

We now recognise that individuals possess a great deal of genetic variation, and this forms the basis for evolutionary change to take place. Once reproductive isolation has occurred, changes probably arise by a combination of chance (the population may have an assemblage of genes that differs slightly from other populations) and selection (certain genes may be favoured in that environment over others).

Isolation and Selection

I have introduced in some detail the rationale for classifying into different groupings, and the strengths and weaknesses of such a scheme, because it may help to explain some of the taxonomic problems that are faced with cetaceans. Unlike many land-living animals, modern whales and dolphins probably encounter fewer isolating barriers. They can range over great areas of ocean, unlike a terrestrial mammal living on an island which perhaps cannot interbreed with members of another island population because it cannot swim to them. This means that at present we should not expect the same degree of geographical isolation between populations (see Figure 4.1 for an example of the overlapping distributions of similar, closely related rorqual species). Where there are apparently isolated populations despite no obvious geographical barrier, these probably reflect historical events. Animals are creatures of habit and may occupy the same breeding and feeding areas, following the same migratory routes that previous generations have done when geographical barriers did exist. This may help to explain the presence of apparently isolated populations of various otherwise far ranging species (for example humpback whales — see Figure 8.1). However, we must not assume that they are genetically isolated, even if there are morphological differences. This brings us to a second factor that may have a lesser influence than among land animals, that of selection pressures. One of the major

Figure 4.1 *Range of latitudes occupied by different rorqual whale species on feeding grounds in the southern hemisphere (from Allen 1980, after Laws 1977; Ohsumi 1978, 1979). Diagonal hatching indicates the main latitudes over which each species ranges during summer*

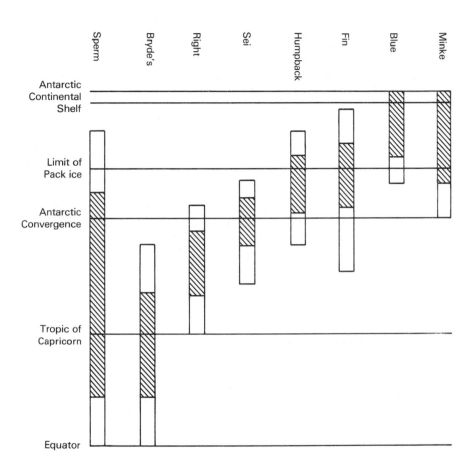

differences between land and the sea is the amount of variation in the environment that can take place. On land, climate has a big influence: temperatures may vary considerably from one region to another, and in some regions there may be strong seasonal changes in the environment. In the sea, these differences are clearly much smaller. That is not to say that they do not exist. Indeed, in the past, we have probably underestimated spatial and temporal variation in the marine environment. Nevertheless, such variation is almost certainly smaller than is present in the terrestrial environment.

If differences in selection pressures on different populations are relatively small, this may also account for the presence of rather small morphological differences. Sowerby's and Andrews' beaked whales are of very similar appearance, being distinguished mainly by small differences in dentition, yet the former occurs only in the temperate North Atlantic and the latter in the temperate Indian and Pacific Oceans. They are clearly separated geographically. We do not know precisely when isolation events took place but it is thought that they occurred sometime during the Pliocene, between two and seven million years ago (Gaskin 1982:234, Moore 1968). That is quite a long time ago and we can see many species among terrestrial animals that must have speciated more recently than this, yet which show greater morphological differences. As noted above, isolating barriers do exist in the sea even when there are no apparent physical barriers. For example, the Pacific white-sided dolphin and dusky dolphin are also very similar, but the former is confined to the temperate North Pacific and the latter to the temperate southern hemisphere. They appear to be separated by unsuitable habitat in the form of warmer seas in tropical and subtropical latitudes.

We are still a long way from knowing whether particular kinds of characters are more susceptible to selection than others, but the evidence so far would suggest so. Many populations show differences in morphology which can be translated in terms of size differences. For the purposes of human exploitation, whale species have been subdivided into stocks. Although in theory these are not taken as necessarily equivalent to genetically isolated populations, in practice this assumption is often made. Support for the presence of distinct populations among various whale species has been suggested by size differences, related differences in growth and maturation rates, and different population responses to exploitation. In the North Atlantic, six distinct fin whale populations have been identified on the basis of features such as these (Rorvik and Jonsgard 1981); a number of rorqual whale species including fin whales have southern hemisphere populations comprising larger individuals on average than those in the North Atlantic or North Pacific. Other examples may be found amongst coastal and offshore forms, where one or the other tends to be larger (for example spinner dolphins in the eastern Pacific, and Bryde's whales in the tropics). Whilst these differences may reflect limited mixing between populations, there is increasing evidence that selection pressures (for example those favouring large size) can maintain such differences despite a relatively large amount of mixing of populations in genetic terms.

When we see variations in body size between different populations, these may reflect differences in the amount and quality of food available. Where it is greater, individuals can be expected to grow better. Other selection pressures may of course also operate. In some situations, it might be advantageous to be small, and what favours one sex may not favour the other. However, even when differences in body size or growth rates are consistent from year to year between different groups of whales, they simply indicate that those groups may occupy traditional areas; some individuals, however, might cross from one group to another and it may only take a few of these for the two groups to be similar genetically. We should, therefore, not use these morphological criteria to distinguish between populations at least in genetic terms.

Some characters of morphology have clear functions. The different shaped jaws and teeth of Risso's dolphins, feeding mainly on cephalopods, compared with common dolphins, feeding on schooling pelagic fish, are one such example. The different sized baleen plates of different species of large whales feeding on various types of plankton or small fish would be another. However, once geographical isolation has occurred, the formation of a new species may result not so much from selection for a particular mode of life, but the presence of a character which may have arisen by chance but which serves for species recognition rather than for any adaptive value. The differences in markings on the flanks of different species of dolphins probably resulted in this way, and in the wild may provide behavioural barriers to reproduction between those species. In an aquatic environment, particularly at any depth, there is little light so that coloration and markings have limited opportunities to develop in different ways as features for species recognition; this would apply particularly to species like the beaked whales. If we look at the assemblages of whale and dolphin species often of very similar appearance, I would speculate that the reason for their similarity is not so much that the species have been formed only very recently, but that there is limited scope for the evolution of such morphological features that would serve as reproductive barriers. If we humans did not rely so heavily on vision, we might by using criteria such as vocalisations see much clearer differences between forms.

Antitropical Distributions

The mechanisms suggested for the evolution of different forms of cetaceans may, with an attempted reconstruction of historical events, help explain some of the interesting distribution patterns that we see between related species. A number of similar species can be grouped as pairs with what has been termed 'antitropical' distributions (Davies 1963). In other words, one member of the species pair occupies the temperate or polar region of the northern hemisphere and the other that of the southern hemisphere. The northern and southern bottlenose whales fit this pattern; so do the northern and southern right whale dolphins, and further antitropical distributions are shown in Figures 4.2 and 4.3. Sometimes, the distinction is rather small so that the pair is considered by some to comprise members of the same species. An example of this would be the temperate northern and southern hemisphere populations of the bottle-nosed dolphin which appear to be separated by smaller tropical and subtropical forms that differ also slightly in colour and morphology. At other times, the differences are larger, possibly reflecting the different timing of isolation events. An example of this has been suggested by Lawrence Barnes who considers the southern hemisphere counterpart of the North Pacific Dall's porpoise to be the more distantly related spectacled porpoise (Barnes 1985). The related species do not necessarily form pairs; there may be three or four similar species. The Pacific white-sided dolphin has two relatives, the Atlantic white-sided and white-beaked dolphins, both in the North Atlantic, with the closely similar dusky dolphin in the southern hemisphere.

It is common for there to be differences between one form of cetacean in the southern hemisphere and one each in the North Atlantic and North Pacific. These are usually smaller differences, below the level of the species, and they suggest that there is still some exchange of genes between populations (or has been until very recently). The northern and southern right whales and a number of the rorqual species appear to have this pattern of differentiation, favoured by the seasonal migrations they typically make. Northern hemisphere populations tend to spend the northern summer (April-September) feeding at high latitudes at the same time as southern hemisphere populations are on their breeding

Figure 4.2 Map of the distribution of members of genus Lagenorhynchus. *Note the species pairing, with antitropical distributions of Atlantic and Pacific white-sided, white-beaked and dusky dolphins*

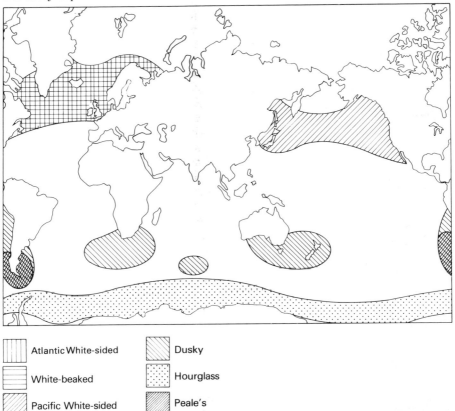

▥ Atlantic White-sided	▧ Dusky
▤ White-beaked	⠿ Hourglass
▨ Pacific White-sided	▨ Peale's

grounds close to the Equator (i.e. during the southern winter). When the northern hemisphere populations are themselves near the Equator, their southern hemisphere counterparts are in the Antarctic. This annual cycle helps to keep the two populations separate. The continent of America separates Atlantic and Pacific populations in the northern hemisphere but the Southern Ocean may allow easier exchange between the two oceans in the southern hemisphere, with movement in a westwards direction being facilitated by the West Wind Drift. Although most rorqual species have distributions that include both tropical and polar regions, the nature of the seasonal migrations described above indicate that they have a form of antitropical distribution, perhaps a relict of earlier times. Indeed, it may be that the migrations are no longer necessary but are a throwback from earlier times (see Chapter 8 for a further discussion of this suggestion). In some regions (for example the North Atlantic) fin and minke whales may not make extensive latitudinal migrations, whilst the Bryde's whale spends its entire year in tropical or subtropical seas.

We have seen that a number of related forms have so-called antitropical distributions. These discontinuous populations occupy cooler waters. They are thought to have arisen from a single population close to

Figure 4.3 Map of the distribution of members of genus Cephalorhynchus. *Members of this genus have distinct antitropically distributed populations, centred on the southern oceans*

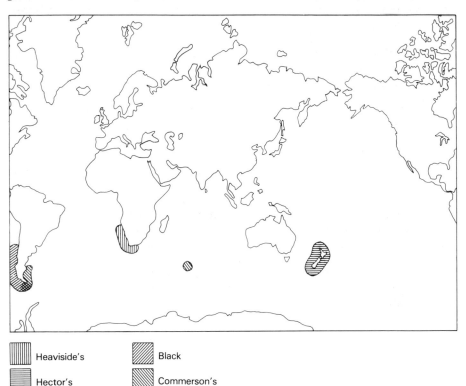

Heaviside's

Hector's

Black

Commerson's

the Equator during cool Pleistocene glacial periods which then retreated into higher latitudes at the onset of warmer interglacials, such as we are living in at the present. It has been suggested that the degree of differentiation that we can see now (into subspecies, species or genera) reflects the timing of isolation events during the long sequence of temperature oscillations between glacial and interglacial periods in the Pleistocene (see Davies 1963; Gaskin 1976, 1982).

Circumpolar and Pantropical Distributions

A few species occur only in polar or subpolar regions. These include the bowhead, narwhal and white whales of the Arctic pack ice. There do not appear to be any living counterparts to these in the southern hemisphere, although it has been suggested that the Irrawaddy dolphin which lives in warm, tropical coastal waters throughout the Indo-Pacific, may be the equatorial equivalent of the white whale.

Many species have essentially tropical or subtropical distributions in both the Atlantic and Indo-Pacific Oceans. These may represent related species such as the Atlantic hump-backed dolphin and the Indo-Pacific hump-backed dolphin; or separate populations within a species, such as the rough-toothed dolphin and different forms of spinner dolphin and spotted dolphins, both of which still present taxonomists with nightmares, so close are the different forms (see Perrin 1975 for a review of some of the taxonomic difficulties). Some species show little morphological differentiation between Atlantic and Indo-Pacific populations but have pantropical distributions. They are pelagic species which probably have fewer habitat restrictions on their distributions and so show little sign of differentiation. Examples of these include the pygmy and dwarf sperm whales, the pygmy killer whale, the melon-headed whale and the Fraser's dolphin. During glacial periods these species were probably little affected (assuming they occupied similar distributions at that time).

Freshwater and Estuarine Distributions (Figure 4.4)

In the tropical Indo-Pacific there are a number of freshwater, estuarine and coastal species. These include the blind river dolphins, the Indus and Ganges susus of India and Pakistan, and the baiji of the Yangtze River in China. Other moderately similar forms exist in the rivers, estuaries and coastal waters of eastern South America. These include the boto or boutu, a river dolphin of the Amazon and Orinoco basins, and the franciscana, a river dolphin of the La Plata estuary which has extended its range along the coast southwards into the cooler waters of Argentina. Their taxonomic relationships are still poorly understood and, though highly evolved, they are thought to have diverged early from the main odontocete line. The fossil record indicates that this occurred during the Late Oligocene or Early Miocene, and possibly their ancestors occupied the shallow coastal fringes of the ancient Tethys Sea, some forms

Figure 4.4 Map of the distribution of river dolphins and the franciscana

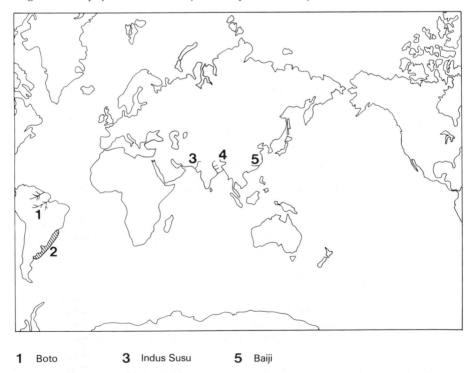

1	Boto	**3**	Indus Susu	**5**	Baiji
2	Franciscana	**4**	Ganges Susu		

returning to freshwater. During that time the Tethys Sea occupied what is now the Indian Ocean and western portion of the tropical Pacific (see Figure 2.1). David Gaskin (1982: chapter 6) has suggested that the tropical South American forms may have lived on the western edge of the Tethys Sea, but this seems unlikely since the Atlantic formed between the South American and African continents long before, during the late Cretaceous (75 million years ago). Instead I suggest that the Asian and American forms may be much more distantly related, if related at all. They could have occupied shallow epicontinental seas, returning quite independently to freshwater, with some convergent evolution of particular characters in response to selection pressures for similar habitats. It is likely that the fossil record is very incomplete and one might expect to find new forms, for example, in coastal West Africa.

Odontocete Colonisations

The more pelagic dolphins may have dispersed westwards into the Atlantic from the Indo-Pacific, aided by current systems flowing in that direction, equivalent to the present Agulhas and Benguela Currents (Perrin, Mitchell and Van Bree 1978). Some of these forms have then penetrated into cooler waters extending their distribution to temperate regions. Examples of these are the common and striped dolphins, the bottle-nosed dolphin, Risso's dolphin, false killer whale, pygmy and dwarf sperm whales, and Cuvier's beaked whale, all of which occur in the three major oceans in both hemispheres. Finally, one species, the killer whale, has become cosmopolitan occurring from the tropics to polar regions at all seasons (though it does appear to favour cooler waters). The sperm whale is also cosmopolitan but females and young rarely come into high latitudes, and the migrations of the male are seasonal.

Delphinid Speciation: Pigmentation Patterns and Camouflage

Most of the odontocete species with pantropical distributions exhibit characters that suggest they have evolved very recently. The common dolphin with its complex pigmentation patterns (and also the spinner, spotted and striped dolphins) is probably derived from a form with much simpler countershading. Edward Mitchell (1970) has suggested that dolphins (including killer whales) escape detection from both predators and prey by having a dark back and light belly. These species tend to feed in the brighter upper layers where lighting from above would make them conspicuous unless the shadow cast by their undersurface was offset by a pale belly. This he regarded as the primitive condition and other forms with extensions of white forward or aft were considered derivatives of it. In this way, pale blazes and dark stripes produce disruptive coloration, breaking up the body contours so helping to conceal the animal from its prey (or perhaps also predator). The variations on the basic theme were considered adaptive to the local conditions prevailing. The basic saddled pattern could serve for concealment through countershading in the manner described above; the striped pattern for disguise through disruptive pigmentation and camouflage; the spotted pattern for camouflage by resemblance to the background; and the crisscross pattern a composite of these, serving for disguise through disruptive pigmentation, camouflage by countershading and shadow mimicry (see Figure 4.5). This hypothesis may be used to interpret the possible courses of evolution in these different dolphins. The northern and southern right whale dolphins show the basic saddled patterns; from these types may have arisen the more complicated striped and crisscross patterns of members of the genus *Lagenorhynchus*. Likewise the saddled pattern of the spinner dolphin

Figure 4.5 Possible evolutionary development of pigmentation patterns in the family Delphinidae (from Mitchell 1970). Suggested progressive evolution from simple countershading as in northern right whale dolphin, through striped pattern of striped dolphin, crisscross pattern of common dolphin, saddled pattern of long-snouted spinner dolphin, to most complex spotted pattern of spotted dolphin

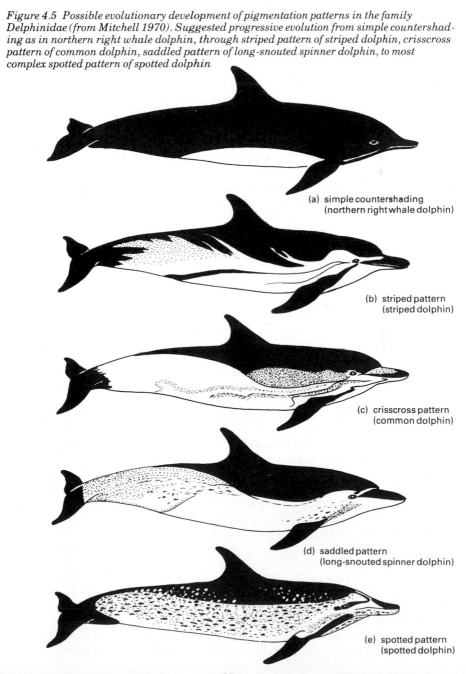

(a) simple countershading
(northern right whale dolphin)

(b) striped pattern
(striped dolphin)

(c) crisscross pattern
(common dolphin)

(d) saddled pattern
(long-snouted spinner dolphin)

(e) spotted pattern
(spotted dolphin)

may have been the basis for the development of more complex spotted and striped forms of other members of the genus *Stenella* and of the common dolphin.

Whether or not the four basic patterns evolved through adaptation to the local conditions in which those species lived, many of the further developments may have occurred by chance. Once present in locally inbred populations, they have served as species recognition features — prerequisites to successful courtship and mating.

Factors Influencing Speciation and Dispersal

Piecing together the changes that may have taken place over the last ten million years is a rather speculative exercise. We can assume that the earlier drifting of continental land masses during the early Caenozoic and before probably had important consequences on the history and dispersal of cetaceans. Most important may have been the retreat of the Tethys Sea, and the opening of dispersal routes between North and South America from the Atlantic via the shallow Caribbean into the Pacific, and around the southern hemisphere via the Southern Ocean (see Fordyce 1977, 1980; Gaskin 1976, 1982:208–47; also Figure 2.1). Fluctuations in taxonomic diversity during this period have been linked to paleotemperature fluctuations (Orr and Faulhaber 1975) and to inferred changes in marine primary productivity due to nutrient upwelling (Lipps and Mitchell 1976).

The recent evolution, that we glimpse through variation in the living cetacean groups, presumably results from fluctuations in ocean temperature accompanying glacial advances and retreats in the Pleistocene. Different major groupings of cetacea probably have different centres of origin from which speciation then occurred. Some may have radiated in tropical or subtropical regions, for example the genus *Stenella*; others (such as members of the genus *Lagenorhynchus*) may have evolved in more temperate seas. One species, the gray whale, is now limited to the North Pacific, although it formerly occurred in the North Atlantic (possibly as late as the seventeenth or early eighteenth centuries), and bones have been found on the coast of Florida (Mead and Mitchell 1984). Fossils from Late Pleistocene deposits in California suggest that the species may have had a coastal distribution.

Phocoenid Speciation and Dispersal

Another group of cetaceans that may have originated in temperate regions are the porpoises. The fossil record suggests that they originated in the North Pacific sometime in the late Miocene to early Pliocene. Barnes (1985) in his recent review of the evolution and taxonomy of the family suggests that the Dall's porpoise has a counterpart, the spectacled porpoise, in the cold temperate and subantarctic regions of the southern hemisphere. Because there are a number of morphological differences between them, he considers that the two forms must have separated before other species of porpoises split off from one another, certainly before the Pleistocene and maybe before the Pliocene. The distribution of other related species or populations of porpoises suggest more recent separation during the glacial-interglacial climatic oscillations. Examples of these are the harbour porpoise of the cold temperate North Atlantic and Pacific and vaquita of the warm temperate North Pacific, and their southern hemisphere counterpart, the Burmeister's porpoise of the temperate west coast of South America (Figure 4.6).

Paedomorphosis

A feature that a number of cetaceans appear to show is that of paedomorphosis, the persistence of fetal or juvenile characters in adults. Barnes (1985) has shown that this phenomenon may account for some apparently juvenile characters of the skull of various living porpoises when compared with their fossil ancestors. Other cetaceans also appear to show this phenomenon, and it may be that small forms such as pygmy and dwarf sperm whales, pygmy killer whale, pygmy right whale, and the smaller race of blue whale, termed pygmy blue whale, may all have arisen in this way. An interesting mechanism by which paedomorphosis might take place is indicated by the responses of the great whales in the Antarctic to overexploitation by man. During this century, fin, sei and minke whales have all reached sexual maturity at an earlier age, presumably because of the relaxation of competition with the decline in numbers of the largest species, the blue and fin whales (see pages 244–8).

Figure 4.6 Map of the distribution of members of the family Phocoenidae. Note the disjunct distributions of species groups such as harbour porpoise, vaquita and Burmeister's porpoise; and possibly the Dall's and spectacled porpoise

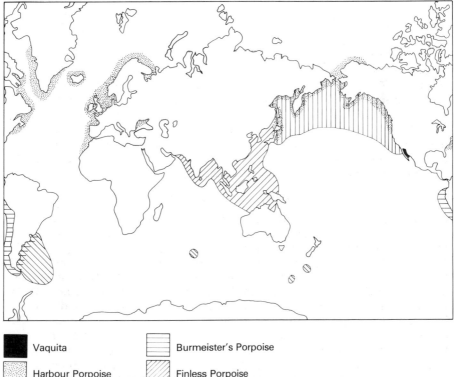

Vaquita

Harbour Porpoise

Dall's Porpoise

Burmeister's Porpoise

Finless Porpoise

Spectacled Porpoise

Beaked Whale Speciation

One major cetacean group has yet to be considered. These are the beaked whales, little known creatures of the great ocean depths, poorly differentiated, with many species forming fairly discrete populations (so far as we can tell) in different parts of the world (Figure 4.7). Although the oceans present fewer physical barriers to movement, they do include a variety of habitats, and different cetaceans appear to have become adapted to particular ones. We have seen how members of the porpoise family and the hump-backed dolphins of the genus *Sousa* inhabit primarily coastal waters; the river and estuarine dolphins live mainly in those habitats; and within certain species (for example, spinner dolphins)

Figure 4.7 Map of the distribution of members of the genus Mesoplodon. *These indicate often disjunct distributions in various oceans, with pantropical, circumpolar and antitropical distributions all represented. Note, however, that for most species the distributions are poorly known, being based primarily upon stranded specimens which may have drifted far from their place of origin. Boundaries are therefore very tentative and may not extend as broadly as indicated. Longman's beaked whale is excluded since it is known only from 2 skulls, whilst Hector's beaked whales and Tasman's distributions may extend northwards in the Pacific and Atlantic in the case of the latter*

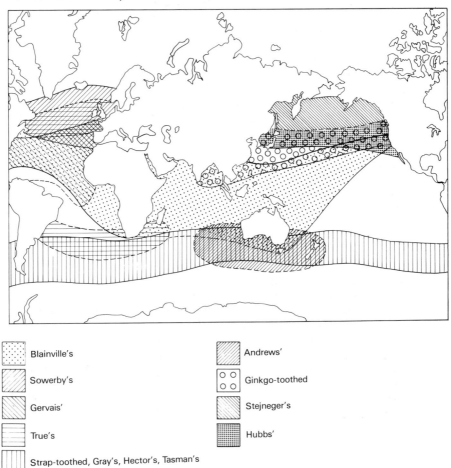

Blainville's

Sowerby's

Gervais'

True's

Strap-toothed, Gray's, Hector's, Tasman's

Andrews'

Ginkgo-toothed

Stejneger's

Hubbs'

there appear to be coastal and offshore forms differing in morphology and ecology. The beaked whales are particularly species of deep waters. Evidence from anatomical studies and of stomach contents of the better known species suggest that they feed at great depths, probably often on the sea bottom where their flexible almost toothless beaks may be adapted to the capture of agile prey, such as squid. The bottlenose whales and Cuvier's beaked whale, which are the best known members of the group, feed upon squid and also various deepwater fish, but their beaks are amongst the least developed and so they may rely less upon feeding on the sea bottom than some of their relatives in the genus *Mesoplodon*. This may explain their much wider distribution.

Within the genus *Mesoplodon*, differences between species appear to be very small, and usually relate to the shape and position of the single pair of teeth that they possess in the lower jaw. These erupt only in adult males where they may grow to relatively massive proportions. Since they are functional only in the male sex, we may speculate that they have evolved by sexual selection (the evolution of characters that enhance the chances of mating success). The presence of scars on their backs, particularly pronounced in older males, provide further support for their use in fights between males, presumably for access to females.

If populations of *Mesoplodon* occupy discrete abyssal depth regions which have become isolated from one another during the late Pliocene or Pleistocene, most of the subtle differences that we see may have arisen by genetic drift: essentially random changes in the genes which in small isolated populations may by chance become fixed in the population. The environmental conditions for the different populations are probably rather similar since we know that there is very little geographical or seasonal variation in temperature or salinity at these depths. Opportunities for local adaptation are therefore likely to be small, and the only character which seems to have diverged to any extent may result primarily from sexual selection.

Some beaked whale species have broader distributions. The northern and southern bottlenose whales occupy northern and southern hemispheres respectively, though with the former confined to the North Atlantic. The two members of the genus *Berardius* have similar distributions, with one of these, the Baird's beaked whale being confined to the North Pacific whilst its relative the Arnoux's beaked whale occurs throughout the southern oceans. Other species are circumpolar at a particular range of latitudes. Three species apparently occupy the southern oceans, mainly at temperate latitudes; they are the Gray's, strap-toothed and Hector's beaked whales, although the last may also occur in the North Pacific. Two species, the Blainville's beaked whale and Cuvier's whale, are cosmopolitan avoiding only polar waters.

I have presented a possible scenario for how some of the beaked whales, particularly within the genus *Mesoplodon*, may have evolved. However, one should be cautious before accepting such speculation. Many of those species are extremely poorly known and, in the course of time, we may find that their distributions are much larger than is known at present.

5 Present distribution

The previous chapter was rather speculative, necessitated by the nature and extent of our knowledge. Moving to a firmer footing, we are beginning to gain a clearer picture of the distribution, relative abundance and seasonal occurrence of different whale and dolphin species in a number of regions of the world. Since it is these patterns that will be of most interest to the reader wishing to see the different species, I review below some of the better known areas and what one might expect to find there. I shall start with the region I know best.

NORTHEAST ATLANTIC
(including North Sea, Baltic and Barents Sea)

Baleen Whales

The European continental shelf seas are rich for cetaceans, particularly the smaller species. Whaling operations in the early years of this century and before suggest that most of the great whales were much more abundant than they are now. In particular, the northern right whale once occurred (though probably never in very large numbers), west of the Hebrides in Scotland, in the Bay of Biscay and the North Sea. Now it is extremely rare and does not occur in either of the latter two regions. Fin and sei whales are probably the commonest of the great whales, and a portion of their populations is thought to migrate particularly along the edge of the shelf northwards in spring and south again in the autumn. Some fin whales undergo less extensive migrations and others are probably resident, occurring throughout the year west of the Iberian Peninsula (though not close to Madeira). The main wintering grounds are not known precisely but are thought to be in the region of the Canaries and Cape Verdes. In summer, fin whales are to be seen south and west of Ireland, and west of the Hebrides, sometimes coming into the Minches close to West Scotland. They probably travel mainly via the deep Faroe Channel. Sei whales may follow a similar route but are less frequently seen. The main feeding areas for both species are around Iceland (particularly off the west coast), the Denmark Strait (between Iceland and Greenland) and the Greenland Sea east to Svalbard and the western

Barents Sea. The blue whale probably has a similar distribution though perhaps occurring further offshore; it is almost certainly very rare in the Northeast Atlantic, after overexploitation by man around the turn of this century though numbers were probably never large. The same applies to the humpback whale although, possibly because of a more coastal distribution, it is occasionally seen off the west coast of Ireland and northwest Scotland in summer, en route from wintering grounds in the vicinity of the Cape Verdes off Northwest Africa to feeding grounds centred around Iceland and the Greenland Sea. It is possible that some of the western Atlantic population summers in this region since a whale tagged off Iceland was later re-sighted in the Caribbean.

The smaller relatives of the blue and fin whales are the Bryde's and minke whales. The Bryde's whale is a warm water species and though probably overlooked (or confused with the sei whale) it appears to be rare further north than Madeira and the Azores. The minke whale, however, is the commonest of all the rorquals and the one most likely to be seen from the European coast. Many headlands and offshore islands in western Britain and Ireland have one or two minkes present during the summer months, and numbers occur at this time around the Faroes, Iceland, west Norwegian coast (particularly the Lofoten Islands northwards to the Barents Sea) and concentrated around Svalbard. The species also regularly comes into the North Sea and may be seen occasionally as far south as the Northumberland coast. Most other whale species are offshore in their distribution.

Sperm Whale and Medium-sized Toothed Whales

Sperm whales wintering around the Azores and Madeira move northwards, probably following the deep ocean basins west of the Iberian Peninsula and via the Rockall Trough (west of the British Isles) into deep waters south of Iceland and east into the Norwegian and Greenland Seas. A few individuals (usually males) or small herds move onto the continental shelf and are seen off northern Scotland, Shetland and Orkney, and the Faroes, but otherwise are often seen in deep waters off the coasts of western France, Spain and Portugal. The northern bottlenose whale is another deepwater species and probably follows a similar route. There is evidence that it has declined in recent years. Only small numbers are seen in coastal waters of the British Isles, mainly around the Outer Hebrides and southwest of Ireland. Its main summering areas are between Iceland and Jan Mayen, west of Svalbard, and the Norwegian Channel west of Ålesund in Norway. Other beaked whales are very poorly known with our knowledge based primarily upon strandings which may involve individuals carried great distances by ocean currents (thus explaining records from the North Sea, for example). They probably occupy the great ocean depths used by sperm whales and northern bottlenose whales. Sowerby's beaked whales occur in the cold temperate to subarctic North Atlantic, mainly in European waters around the North Sea, but also northwards to northern Norway and Iceland, and as far south as Madeira. Cuvier's whales have a widespread distribution, though apparently less common at high latitudes. There has been a recent increase in the number of strandings around the British Isles (mainly the Atlantic coasts), but the species may be more common off the Iberian Peninsula. Other beaked whales recorded include True's beaked, Gervais' beaked and Gray's beaked whales, but together they make up only a handful of records and, with the possible exception of the first, are probably not normally distributed in European seas.

The smaller, toothed whales and dolphins do not undergo extensive latitudinal migrations but, rather, appear to make seasonal onshore-offshore movements. Long-finned pilot whales commonly come into coastal waters, particularly in late summer and autumn. They may be seen in two main regions at comparable times: in the Bay of Biscay, the western approaches to the English Channel and southwest of Ireland; and around the Faroes, Shetland and north of the Hebrides in Scotland. Probably they enter these regions from neighbouring deep ocean basins. Stranding records from the Atlantic coast of France indicate that they may have a wintering area in the Bay of Biscay. Its close relative, the short-finned pilot whale, has a tropical to warm temperate distribution, with records from Madeira and the coast of Northwest Africa. The killer whale enters coastal waters in early or midsummer ranging over wide areas but with numbers concentrated in colder waters, around Iceland, Jan Mayen, Svalbard and off the coast of northern Norway (for example, the Lofoten Islands). The species may be seen in coastal waters of Britain and Ireland, mainly along the west coast although it does enter the northern and central North Sea, usually in small numbers. The false killer whale and pygmy sperm whale are two species with their distributions generally in warmer deep waters of the North Atlantic, though less commonly on the eastern side judging by strandings records. Such records that there are may be the result of a dispersal through the North Atlantic Drift. At the other extreme, two species have almost exclusively Arctic distributions. The first is the narwhal which may be found from East Greenland across the Greenland Sea to Svalbard, and in the Barents and White Seas where a population of several thousand occurs east to Franz Josef Land and Novaya Zemlya. Between 2,000 and 4,000 white whales occupy the same region but commonly occur further south. Occasionally, wandering white whales and narwhals are recorded from the North Sea coasts, and there are, for example, recent sightings of one or more white whales off the Dutch coast.

Dolphins and Porpoises

The smaller dolphins are the species most frequently seen by the ordinary person who goes to the coast or takes a boat a short distance offshore. All species seem to undergo inshore movements in summer. The white-beaked dolphin is the commonest species in summer in coastal waters of northwest and northern Scotland, around the Faroes, Iceland and West Norway. It also occurs in the northern and central North Sea and along the west coast of Ireland, though further south in the Atlantic it is replaced by the common dolphin. The Atlantic white-sided dolphin has a similar distribution to its relative the white-beaked dolphin though it tends to occur more offshore and in a number of ways is the ecological equivalent of the generally pelagic common dolphin. The latter is the commonest species off southwest England, southern Ireland, Brittany and the Bay of Biscay, though it does follow the Gulf Stream northwards off the edge of the continental shelf. Overlapping with the common dolphin off the Atlantic coasts of France, Spain and Portugal, is the striped dolphin, which at least north of the Straits of Gibraltar, appears to be the less common species. The common dolphin is by far the most common species around the Azores. The rough-toothed dolphin, on the other hand, is apparently absent or rare from around the Azores, but may be seen in the vicinity of the Cape Verdes, and presumably south of there. It has been seen off the coast of Mauritania but generally occurs offshore. The Atlantic hump-backed dolphin, on the other hand, is much more coastal and may be found on the Banc d'Arguin, Mauritania, north to about 20°N. This region provides the northern limit for the long-snouted spinner dolphin.

The Risso's dolphin is a relatively coastal species which ranges from the coasts of West Africa (and Atlantic islands of Cape Verdes, Canaries and Azores), Portugal and the Bay of Biscay north along the west coast of Ireland, and in the Irish Sea, into west and north Scottish waters (particularly around the Hebrides and Shetland). It does not usually penetrate far into the North Sea or English Channel. The bottle-nosed dolphin once the 'common' dolphin for summer visitors to coastal holiday resorts, is now comparatively rare. Although separate offshore populations may exist, the species is primarily coastal occupying bays and estuaries and inshore channels between islands. It once occurred regularly but only in small numbers at scattered sites along the coasts of France, southern England and Wales, Belgium and Holland, but is now rare or absent from most of this region. Pollution, disturbance and lack of food have all been implicated, and most of the remaining herds occur in the north and west (for example, the Moray Firth, Minches, Galway and Clew Bays in Western Ireland). The harbour porpoise occupies similar regions and has undergone similar declines. Nevertheless, it is still probably the commonest small cetacean with concentrations off south-west and western Ireland, the Hebrides and Minches, and Shetland and Orkney. It also occurs north to northern Norway, the Faroes and Iceland, and in the northern North Sea it occurs east into the Kattegat and Skaggerak, though no longer deep into the Baltic. South of the British Isles, porpoises are rare in the Bay of Biscay and along the Iberian Peninsula but they become common again along the coast of Mauritania. Both bottle-nosed dolphin and harbour porpoise may be more or less resident in certain areas. For one reason or another, the English Channel, southern North Sea and the Baltic are comparative deserts and most cetaceans occur along Atlantic coasts and islands. This has certainly not always been the case for smaller cetaceans.

Reference Sources: Aguilar *et al.* (1983, 1984), Allen *et al.* (1980), Benjaminsen and Christensen (1979), van Bree (1977), Casinos and Vericad (1976), Christensen (1977, 1978, 1980, 1982), Duguy (1977, 1983), Duguy and Robineau (1982), Evans (1980, 1981), Evans *et al.* (1986), Fraser (1974), Kinze (1985), Maigret (1977), Maigret *et al.* (1976), Martin (1983), Martin *et al.* (1984a), Maul and Sergeant (1977), Sanpera *et al.* (1984, 1985), Schultz (1970), Sheldrick (1979), Sigurjonsson (1984, 1985), de Smet (1974) and Teixeira (1979).

MEDITERRANEAN AND BLACK SEAS

Further south, the semi-enclosed relatively warm and sheltered waters of the Mediterranean provide suitable conditions for a number of cetaceans in winter as well as summer. The western Mediterranean is much better known than the eastern portion.

Baleen Whales

The fin whale is the commonest of the baleen whales in the Mediterranean and although there may be some seasonal movements between there and the Atlantic, with sightings in the Straits of Gibraltar, it has been recorded throughout the year in the western basin; it is most often seen in summer (particularly July) between Corsica and the French Riviera and around the Italian coasts, rarely occurring further east. There is some evidence to suggest they calve in the region during late autumn, with a probable wintering area occurring around Corsica. The minke whale is rather rare, mainly in the western Mediterranean reaching as far as Tunisia, and exceptionally entering the Black Sea.

Sperm Whale, and Medium-sized Toothed Whales

One of the commoner whales in the Mediterranean is the sperm whale which is thought to breed in winter or early spring. It rarely occurs further east than Tunisia, and is commonest there and off the coast of Algeria towards the Italian coast. Both killer and false killer whales appear to be very rare in the Mediterranean except in the extreme western part (Sea of Alboran), but the long-finned pilot whale though restricted to the western basin is common in summer between Corsica and the coasts of France and Italy. Numbers build up in July and both mating and calving have been observed in this region in late September. There are a number of deepwater basins in the Mediterranean (for example in the Tyrrhenian Sea between Italy and Sardinia) and it is possibly these that are favoured in summer by the Cuvier's beaked whale which appears to be comparatively common, both in the western and eastern portions. In winter the species is thought to move to shallow areas close to the European coasts.

Dolphins and Porpoises

Among smaller cetaceans, by far the commonest is the striped dolphin, particularly off the southern European coasts of the western basin. In contrast, the species appears to be rare in the eastern Mediterranean with the exception of the Aegean Sea where it is relatively common. The common dolphin is almost certainly less abundant than the previous species, and may be declining. It is still common south of 38°N in the Alboran Sea, Gibraltar Strait and northern coast of Africa and has been observed in the eastern Mediterranean where it may occur in moderate numbers. The species is thought by some to migrate in spring through the Marmara Sea and the Bosphorus into the Black Sea returning again in the autumn. In Turkish waters of the Black Sea, very large numbers have been hunted and the species was thought to have declined considerably by 1967 when the multinational fishery ceased. It is estimated that about 200,000 animals of three species (but mainly this species) live in the Black Sea (and Sea of Azov). The Risso's dolphin is known only from the western Mediterranean. Though scarce along the Spanish coast and exceptional in the Golfe du Lion, it occurs mainly in the Ligurian Sea, especially near the French Riviera, with calving in summer. The bottle-nosed dolphin is common throughout the Mediterranean and Black/Azov Seas, and is said to be the most abundant species in Israeli waters and probably along the Egyptian coast. The harbour porpoise is now confined to the Black and Azov Seas. It occurred along the European coasts of the western basin until the beginning of the present century but is now apparently absent from the entire Mediterranean Sea. Finally the subtropical/tropical rough-toothed and Indo-Pacific hump-backed dolphins may be recorded occasionally, the former in the western basin presumably from the Atlantic, and the latter at the entrance to Port Said harbour presumably from the Suez Canal. The Mediterranean Sea has in recent years suffered from chemical pollution, but the only species here that shows signs of population decline is the common dolphin.

Reference Sources: Aguilar (1986), Casinos and Vericad (1976), Di Natale (1979a, b), Duguy *et al.* (1980, 1983), Giordano (1981), Marchessaux (1980), Marchessaux and Duguy (1978), Pilleri and Pilleri (1982).

NORTHWEST ATLANTIC
(including Caribbean Sea, Hudson Bay and Baffin Bay)

Many of the same species that are found in the Northeast Atlantic occur off the coasts of North America. However, a combination of greater population sizes and possibly deeper waters close to the coasts provides much better opportunities to see reasonable numbers of some of the great whales. Our knowledge is also much greater as a result of many detailed ship and aerial surveys.

Baleen Whales

Around the Caribbean basin there are a number of banks that are important breeding areas for humpback whales. Although the species may be seen throughout the West Indies, the majority appear to occur on the Silver, Navidad and Mouchoir Banks north of Hispaniola. Here, a population of around 2,000 has been estimated in the month of February. Different breeding populations gradually move west and north between January and April as the breeding and calving season progresses. They then migrate northwards visiting the Bermuda banks and then onwards to spend the summer in three possibly discrete concentrations: in Massachusetts Bay and Cape Cod Bay (particularly on Stellwagen Bank); in Newfoundland waters, the Gulf of St Lawrence and the Gulf of Maine; and in the Davis Strait off the coast of southwest Greenland. Other rorqual species may take similar migratory routes, although their winter breeding grounds are not precisely known. At least some spend the winter offshore in the Gulf of Mexico and around the Antilles. In summer, the same continental shelf regions as occupied by humpbacks are feeding areas for blue, fin and minke whales, although blue whales may have a more northerly distribution from the Gulf of St Lawrence, where they are regularly seen in small numbers, northwards to the ice edge. Fin whales probably make less extensive latitudinal movements and mating has been observed on the feeding grounds. They are also to be found in numbers in the New York bight. In Baffin Bay, blue, fin, sei and minke whales occur off the west coast of Greenland north into Melville Bay. Feeding concentrations of about 1,000 sei whales also occur in the

Hudson Strait, and 1,000–2,000 on the Nova Scotian shelf. The Bryde's whale occurs in small numbers mainly offshore from Florida southwards, with resident populations in the Gulf of Mexico and in the southeastern Caribbean. These areas may once have formed the wintering grounds of the now extinct Atlantic gray whale since bones of this species have been found on the Florida coast.

Another species, the numbers of which were seriously depleted by overexploitation, is the northern right whale. It is presently more common on the western side of the Atlantic and may be seen from November to March in the southeastern and southwestern Gulf of Mexico, and in Florida, apparently calving off its northeast coast and off southeastern Georgia. It occurs rarely in the central Bahamas and near Bequia, in the southern Lesser Antilles. The species migrates in spring north at least to Labrador. Concentrations of feeding and mating individuals occur around Cape Cod; in the lower Bay of Fundy (near Grand Manan Island) and northern Gulf of Maine (c. 50 individuals) and Brown's Bank region off Nova Scotia (c. 50 individuals); and in the Gulf of St Lawrence and northern coasts of Newfoundland. Its Arctic relative, the bowhead, also occurs in relict numbers with populations totalling a few hundred, in Baffin Bay and the Davis Strait, and wintering in West Hudson Strait, north of Digges Sound.

Sperm Whale, and Medium-sized Toothed Whales

In summer sperm whales (mainly males) may range from deep waters east of the southern United States north to the Davis Strait, off southwest Greenland. Their wintering grounds are probably around the Bahamas and east of the Caribbean. In the past whaling for the species was concentrated in the vicinity of the Newfoundland Grand Bank, off the Carolinas and around the Bahamas.

Sharing the Arctic waters of Baffin Bay are narwhal and white whale. At least 20,000 narwhals and 10,000 white whales spend the summer in and around Lancaster Sound, and both species are to be found in the Hudson Strait, northern Hudson Bay and Foxe Basin. At least 11,000 white whales and probably rather fewer narwhals occur in these three latter regions. It is thought that one stock of narwhals occurs from Baffin Bay to Lancaster Sound and West Greenland. On the west coast of Greenland the two species summer in Melville Bay and Thule district, moving southwards in autumn with the white whale moving further south than the narwhal, wintering in Disko Bay or further south. Population sizes are not known for either species but white whales are more abundant with several thousand breeding in the region. White whales also occur further south off the coast of eastern Canada, with about 500 individuals resident in the Gulf of St Lawrence.

The distribution of other whales is less well known. Long-finned pilot whales make regular seasonal movements into Newfoundland waters in association with movements of their squid prey. Here they have been traditionally hunted, with numbers greatly depleted though now apparently recovering. The species ranges from West Greenland to Bermuda and the Carolina coast, usually offshore although it comes into the Gulf of St Lawrence and the Gulf of Maine. As with Northeast Atlantic populations, pilot whales appear to make onshore-offshore movements rather than more protracted migrations, occurring near the coast mainly between July and October. South of Bermuda it is replaced by the short-finned pilot whale which is common in the Gulf of Mexico and throughout the Caribbean. The killer whale appears to be relatively uncommon although it can be seen from the Caribbean north to Baffin Bay, and is possibly more frequent in the Labrador Sea and off the west coasts of southern and central Greenland. The northern Labrador Sea near the entrance to Hudson Strait and southeast of Sable Island are areas of concentration for the northern bottlenose whale which may be resident in that region. The species also occurs off eastern Newfoundland and in deep channels in the Gulf of St Lawrence; there may be a northwards migration in spring to the Davis Strait. Other beaked whales are rarely recorded because of their offshore habit but strandings indicate that the Sowerby's and True's beaked whales probably occur generally in temperate waters and the Cuvier's and Gervais' beaked whales in the Gulf of Mexico and the Caribbean. Blainville's beaked whales have been stranded from Nova Scotia south to Florida, and in the Bahamas and northern Gulf of Mexico. It is in the deeper waters of the latter region and Caribbean that one can expect to see dwarf and pygmy sperm whales, false killer and pygmy killer whales, although they may range north-wards to North Carolina, perhaps associated with the Gulf Stream north of Florida. The false killer whale has been recorded further north at least to Maryland. Both dwarf and pygmy sperm whales may occur also in inshore waters during the calving season, occurring at least off Florida, where they appear to be relatively common. Another offshore and mainly tropical species, the melon-headed whale, is poorly known. It has been reported from deep waters near St Vincent in the southern Lesser Antilles.

Dolphins and Porpoises

Among dolphins, the white-beaked dolphin is relatively uncommon close to the coast, occurring mainly in cold temperate waters off the coasts of Labrador and Newfoundland and in the Davis Strait off the coast of southwest Greenland. It is found in the Gulf of Maine and is relatively common off Cape Cod, but it is rare south of here. The Atlantic white-sided dolphin is more common, usually on or along the edge of the continental shelf. Otherwise it has a similar distribution, occurring off the Labrador coast, in Davis Strait and off the west coast of Greenland (north to about Umanaq). Further south, along and above the Nova Scotia shelf the striped dolphin is common although from Cape Cod to Cape Hatteras, the common dolphin is the most frequently recorded dolphin species. The distribution of spotted dolphins is centred around the Gulf of Mexico, Sargasso Sea and Caribbean, but with one form, *Stenella attenuata* found mainly on the Caribbean side of the West Indies and another, *Stenella frontalis*, in the Gulf of Mexico and along the Atlantic US coast to Cape Hatteras. Both long-snouted spinner and clymene dolphins are very common in these regions whilst further offshore occurs the rough-toothed dolphin. In autumn 1981, there was a mass stranding of 17 Fraser's dolphins in the Marquesas Keys, Florida. This tropical pelagic species is very poorly known although it has been recorded in the Lesser Antilles.

A relatively uncommon but widespread species is the Risso's dolphin which ranges from the Lesser Antilles in the Caribbean to the coast of

Newfoundland. Also widespread is the bottle-nosed dolphin which is relatively abundant in coastal waters of Florida and the Gulf of Mexico, though possibly less common in Chesapeake Bay and along the coast of Virginia. It is rare in the Gulf of Maine and north of here. An offshore form may exist, associated with herds of more pelagic cetaceans such as the long- and short-finned pilot whales. The tucuxi occurs in the tropical North Atlantic, along the northeastern coast of South America, in Lake Maracaibo and rivers in that region and from Trinidad. The harbour porpoise is another inshore species. It was common off the coast of Southwest Greenland but large numbers have been killed incidentally in salmon nets there. Porpoises are common in summer off the Labrador coast and southern Baffin Island, in the Gulf of St Lawrence, the approaches to the Bay of Fundy (c. 4,000 individuals) and in the Gulf of Maine (which has a further sizeable summer population of 8,000–15,000). Seasonal movements clearly take place although where different populations winter is not known. The species has been recorded along the United States coast south to the coasts of Carolina and central Florida but may have declined in the southern limits of its range; it is generally uncommon in winter south of Long Island, New York.

Reference Sources: Boschung *et al.* (1983), Braham (1984), Caldwell and Caldwell (1983), Davis *et al.* (1980), Gaskin (1977a, 1979, 1984), Gaskin and Watson (1985), Jennings (1982), Kapel (1975, 1977a,b, 1979), Leatherwood *et al.* (1976), Mead (1979), Perrin *et al.* (1981), Reeves *et al.* (1983), Sorensen *et al.* (1984), Watkins and Moore (1982).

NORTHEAST PACIFIC
(including Baja California, and east Bering Sea)

This region is probably the best known of all for cetaceans, with intensive shipboard and aerial surveys particularly from Mexico and California, and in the waters off Alaska.

Baleen Whales

The wintering grounds of the blue whale are not known. Some may migrate to spend the winter from temperate latitudes south at least to 20°N, with others possibly resident in tropical waters, between 10°N and the Equator. In summer, migrating blue whales move northwards and eastwards towards the coast, where they occur in deep coastal canyons off southern and central California (for example, Monterey Bay) through the Gulf of Alaska to the Aleutian Islands, and into the Bering Sea. Although some southern populations of fin whales may also be resident, for example in the Gulf of California, a migratory movement occurs from winter breeding grounds west of central California and Mexico, towards the coast of central California and northwards to the Chukchi Sea. Concentrations occur in the Gulf of Alaska, in Prince William Sound, and along the Aleutian Islands. The minke whale occurs broadly over the North Pacific in summer. In winter, sightings tend to be at lower latitudes, mainly 20–25°N, although they are recorded further north, for example in Puget Sound. There may be three populations of sei whales in the North Pacific, an east, central and western population. Wintering

98

grounds of the sei whale extend from Piedras Blancas, California south to around the Revillagigedo Islands, off Mexico. Marking has shown that at least some migrate north to spend the summer in the waters off British Columbia. The more tropical Bryde's whale occurs from southern California southwards.

Humpbacks are more coastal, wintering from central Baja California to Cabo San Lucas and from southern Sonora to Jalisco, Mexico including Bahia de Banderas and the offshore Revillagigedo Islands, where breeding takes place. There is also a breeding population during winter and spring around the Hawaiian Islands, particularly in the Four Island Group (Maui, Molokai, Lanai and Kahoolawe) to the Penguin Bank area, but also off northwestern Hawaii and in the Kauai-Nishau area. Recent population estimates suggest that there are at least 500 ± 90 individuals here. Originally thought to be a separate population, recognisable individuals have now been identified in both Alaska (summer) and Hawaii (winter) and even wintering in different breeding grounds (Hawaii, and 4,800km due east, Socorro Island, one of the Revillagigedo Islands off Mexico). Together with similarities in the songs between the two breeding areas, these results suggest that, in the eastern North Pacific, separate populations may not exist, or at least may exhibit some genetic mixing.

The generally sheltered lagoons (for example Laguna Ojo de Liebre (Scammon's lagoon), Laguna Guerrero Negro and Laguna San Ignacio) around Baja California and the Gulf of California, Mexico, afford suitable conditions for a number of whale species. Perhaps most well known of these is the gray whale, which mates and calves in the region between early December and early March. Peak conceptions apparently occur in the late autumn as the whales move south into the area, with first births in late December and most occurring in mid January (after a gestation period of 13.75 months). There are apparently two phases or 'waves' of migration. The first occurs in March and April and includes mainly non-breeding adults and immatures followed about a month later mainly by cows and calves of that year. During much of the northwards migration they swim parallel to the coast, often staying within 2km of shore. In some regions (notably the Californian Channel Islands) where there are coastal indentations, they often cut across up to 200km offshore, taking the most direct route. The precise route taken from southeast Alaska to Nunivak Island in the eastern Bering Sea, is not yet clear. From Nunivak Island, they migrate offshore to St Lawrence Island and major feeding grounds in the northern Bering Sea and southern Chukchi Sea. Migration of the first phase peaks at Cape St Elias in the Gulf of Alaska in mid April, and at Unimak Pass (west of the Alaskan Peninsula) in late April and early May. Summer sightings further south of the feeding grounds, in the Gulf of Alaska and southeastern Bering Sea may be of gray whales making up the second phase of migration, and/or summer residents. Feeding occurs until early October, when the southward migration probably begins. The whales travel from the northern to southeastern Bering Sea and intersect the southwestern end of the Alaska Peninsula before leaving the Bering Sea through the Unimak Pass, from late October to January. The migration apparently continues along the coast and the Gulf of Alaska and on to Baja California. A portion of the population does not undergo a complete migration, and small groups may be seen off the coasts of California (e.g. near the Farallon Islands), Oregon and British Columbia (off Vancouver and Prince Charlotte Islands) during most of the year. The population in the Northeast Pacific has been estimated (for 1980) at c. 15,600.

As in the North Atlantic, the northern right whale now has only a relict population, numbering perhaps 200–250 individuals. There is one winter sighting from Hawaii and a few sightings have been made in winter and spring from the coasts of northwestern Baja California, southern California, Oregon and Washington. Further north the species has been observed in the Gulf of Alaska and Bering Sea during summer. In Arctic waters lives its relative, the bowhead. An estimated 4,400 (± 2,400!) occur in the Bering, Chukchi and Beaufort Seas. With the southwards spread of ice in the autumn, bowheads move west and south out of the Beaufort and Chukchi Seas, to winter in the Bering Sea, probably mainly off Siberia but also around the St Lawrence and St Matthew Islands. Some bowheads probably also winter in the Sea of Okhotsk. Mating and calving occurs in spring and early summer during the early stages of the migration northeast. This migration occurs in three or four pulses, and follows ice leads close to the coast through the Bering Strait into the Chukchi Sea and then past Point Barrow, Alaska, into the Beaufort Sea. Bowheads reach Cape Bathurst and the Amundsen Gulf as early as May, but elsewhere the late break up of the ice prevents bowheads from using the Mackenzie Delta and the coast of Yukon until late July.

Sperm Whale, and Medium-sized Toothed Whales

The sperm whale ranges over a considerable area of the North Pacific, mainly in deep waters. Calves are born sometime between February and June, in warm temperate to tropical latitudes, with sightings (and past whaling grounds) particularly around Hawaii, Galapagos and many locations along the equatorial belt (including, for example, off the Oregon coast). In summer sperm whales (mainly males) may occur as far north as St Lawrence Island in the Bering Strait. Its smaller relatives, the pygmy and dwarf sperm whales, are confined to warm temperate and tropical latitudes, rarely seen but occasionally stranded, the former between the Washington coast and the Gulf of California, and the latter possibly mainly further south, between central California and Baja California, Mexico, although it has been stranded at Vancouver Island, British Columbia.

In the icy waters of the Beaufort, Chukchi and Bering Seas lives the white whale. Between 7,000 and 11,500 summer in the Mackenzie River delta in the Beaufort Sea. These are thought to move westwards to winter in the Bering Sea, or in Alaska (notably in Bristol Bay and Cook Inlet, southwestern Alaska, and perhaps also the Soviet Union: Anadyr Gulf and Chukchi Sea). In spring, they return, often with bowheads, following the north coasts of Alaska and Yukon into the eastern Beaufort Sea. There are also summering populations off Alaska, and in the Beaufort, Bering and Chukchi Seas, but together these number only a few thousand. Since mating apparently occurs from April to June, prior to the time that most have migrated, it is likely that there is gene exchange between at least some of those summering populations.

The beaked whales are less well known though some species have been seen off the coasts of North America in recent years. The Baird's beaked whale usually occurs in waters greater than 1,000m depth from the Pribilof Islands south to about 20°N, but it has been seen seasonally off northern California (June-October) and off British Columbia (May-September). The Cuvier's beaked whale has a similar wide distribution including Hawaii, the Midway Islands and subtropical waters of the eastern Pacific. Other beaked whales have very occasionally been recorded as strandings on the west coast, mainly in California, and also, in the case of more temperate species, in British Columbia. These include the Blainville's and Ginkgo-toothed beaked whales in subtropical or warm temperate waters and Stejneger's and Hubbs' beaked whales in cold temperate or even subarctic waters. Other pelagic species include the melon-headed whale, pygmy killer whale and false killer whale which occur in mid Pacific, including the vicinity of Hawaii, though the latter has a more cool temperate distribution and has been seen occasionally as far north as the Gulf of Alaska. The short-finned pilot whale ranges over the same area but mainly occurs from central California (for example, around Santa Catalina Island) southwards. Although killer whales also occupy a wide area of the North Pacific, resident herds occur in various coastal regions, notably Puget Sound (Washington State), between Vancouver Island and the British Columbian coast. Transient herds are found along the Oregon coast and also at Islas Cedros and Benitos off central Baja California, Mexico.

Dolphins and Porpoises

Northern right whale dolphins live in the temperate waters off the coasts of British Columbia, Washington State, Oregon and California, occasionally occurring further south. They appear to undergo slight latitudinal movements northwards and inshore in spring, and southwards offshore in autumn. Pacific white-sided dolphins have a similar range though they tend to favour the continental slope and extend further north, from the Bay of La Paz, Mexico to the Aleutian Islands and waters south of the Alaska Peninsula. They are the most abundant cetacean off central and northern California, where surveys indicate that they make onshore movements in autumn. Overlapping with them but occurring mainly further south is the common dolphin, a pelagic species which nevertheless is the most common dolphin species in the Gulf of California (particularly the central region), after inshore seasonal movements mainly in autumn and winter. The striped dolphin occurs offshore in deep tropical and warm temperate waters. The eastern tropical Pacific also holds very large numbers of spotted dolphins (several million) and long-snouted spinner dolphins (a few hundred thousand), both of which (particularly the former) fall victim to the tuna purse-seine fishery where up to half a million died annually in the mid 1970s. Both may readily be seen around Hawaii, near Galapagos, and in the vicinity of Baja California. Both species apparently have coastal and offshore forms, whilst spinner dolphins which have received particular attention, are considered to have separate geographical forms, one close to the coast off Costa Rica, another coastal eastern form from southwestern Baja California south to the equator, a third offshore whitebelly form from

101

Mexico south across the Equator, and a fourth similar but larger form around Hawaii.

In the Northeast Pacific, Risso's dolphins tend to occupy deep waters in temperate and tropical waters, often close to the coast but rare around the coast of Mexico (20°N) and southern Oregon (42°N). Bottle-nosed dolphins are distributed from the Equator north to San Pedro, California although they have been observed 600km further north off the coast of northern California. The size of the coastal population from the Mexican border to San Pedro has been estimated at c. 240 animals.

Far offshore, the rough-toothed dolphin probably occurs over a large area of the tropical Pacific from northern California southwards across the Equator. Its range may be shared with the Fraser's dolphin, another little known species, which may associate with spotted dolphins in the tuna purse-seine fishery. Fraser's dolphins also associate with melon-headed whales.

Three species of porpoises (of the family Phocoenidae) occur in the Northeast Pacific. Two of these, the harbour and Dall's porpoise, broadly overlap in range but the former has a predominantly coastal distribution and the latter an offshore and more northern one. Dall's porpoise is apparently resident although northwards movements may be made in summer into the Bering Sea to the Pribilof Islands. In some areas they may come closer inshore, for example around the Aleutian Islands, coastal Alaska, British Columbia and Washington State, but they are still generally in deepwater channels or straits. There are also populations off the coast of southern California which build up in autumn and winter, but this is close to the southern limit of its range. Movements appear to be in association with movement of their preferred prey species. Dall's porpoises are often found in association with Pacific white-sided dolphins (from 50°N southwards) and pilot whales (from 40°N southwards). The harbour porpoise occurs along the entire Pacific coast from Point Conception, southern California to the Gulf of Alaska (and rarely along the north coast of Alaska and the Mackenzie estuary, Yukon). Seasonal onshore-offshore movements occur in Humboldt Bay, California, but along the Washington State coast it is considered to be resident. The third species, the vaquita or cochito, has a very limited distribution, confined to the northern part of the Gulf of California. In the past, the species was known mainly only from skeletal material but in March 1985, seven were incidentally caught in gill nets near El Golfo de Santa Clara, Sonora, Mexico, which continues to threaten this clearly very rare species.

Reference Sources: Braham (1984), Bryant *et al.* (1982), Darling and Jurasz (1983), Darling and McSweeney (1985), Everitt *et al.* (1979), Fay (1981), Fraker (1980), Haley (1978), Herman and Antinoja (1977), Huber *et al.* (1982), Jackson (1980), Leatherwood and Walker (1979, 1982), Leatherwood *et al.* (1980, 1982, 1984a), Ljungblad *et al.* (in press), Loughlin *et al.* (1982), Mate (1981), Mead (1981), Nagorsen (1985), Perrin *et al.* (1982, 1985), Pike and MacAskie (1969), Reilly (1984a), Rice (1974, 1978), Seaman and Burns (1981).

NORTHWEST PACIFIC
(including East China Sea, Sea of Japan, Sea of Okhotsk and West Bering Sea)

Baleen Whales

The large rorquals winter in the vicinity of Polynesia and Micronesia to the Philippines, undergoing northwards migrations in summer to feeding grounds at high latitudes. Although fin and humpback whales enter the Bering Sea, blue and sei whales do not, and none of the four species enters the Sea of Okhotsk. Some species are probably more migratory than others. Blue whales and fin whales winter to about 10°N, although the breeding grounds of the former are poorly known; fin whales winter in particular in the East China Sea, the Yellow Sea and Sea of Japan and along the Pacific coast of Japan. The East China Sea population is thought to be resident and may represent a distinct population (the Yellow Sea population may possibly also be distinct). In summer both blue and fin whales are to be found from a line east of Japan north to the Chukchi Sea and Aleutian Islands, with the latter entering the Bering Sea. Sei whales and minke whales occupy a similar area from the Sea of Japan and offshore (where they probably mainly winter) northwards to the southwestern edge of the Bering Sea; a portion of the populations of both species is possibly resident in temperate latitudes. The Ryukyu Islands, Formosa and Bonin Islands are the wintering grounds of humpbacks, which then migrate north to summer in the Bering Sea and around the Aleutian Islands. The gray whale winters in the East and South China Seas, in the vicinity of Korea, and summers in the Sea of Okhotsk. Their population size is small after overexploitation, with numbers estimated at no more than 2–300 individuals. Bryde's whales occupy generally warm temperate to tropical waters from northern Japan south to the Equator. There appears to be an offshore form (from Sanriku, Wakayama and around the Bonin Islands) and a smaller coastal form (off the west coast of Kyushu, Japan). The inshore form resembles the sei whale with relatively narrow baleen plates and a more curved rostrum of the skull.

As elsewhere, the northern right whale has been hunted to near extinction, but a population of a few hundred still occurs off the coast of Japan (at Hokkaido), and further north, off the Kurile Islands, the Kamchatka Peninsula, and in the Sea of Okhotsk. Its Arctic relative, the bowhead, has a relict population in the Sea of Okhotsk and part of the Beaufort Sea population comes into the western Bering Sea and Chukchi Sea in winter.

Sperm Whale, and Medium-Sized Toothed Whales

During summer, a few sperm whales come into the southwestern Bering Sea and off the Kamchatka Peninsula, usually in deep waters. Their breeding grounds are not well known but include the mid-Pacific around the Polynesian Islands. Both pygmy and dwarf sperm whales are probably also mainly oceanic in the warm temperate to tropical Pacific although both have been recorded from the coast of Japan, Taiwan and the Philippines. Further north in Arctic waters occurs the white whale with summering populations of c. 2,000–3,000 in the Bering Sea-Anadyr

Gulf region, c. 1,000–2,000 in eastern Siberian-Chukchi Seas, and up to 10,000 in the Okhotsk Sea. There may be exchange of individuals between these regions so they do not necessarily represent separate biological populations. Narwhal populations are poorly known but exist in East Siberian Sea, Bering Strait and northern Bering Sea (south to Kamchatka).

A number of species of beaked whales occur in the Northwest Pacific. The distribution of Baird's beaked whale is best known, partly because it has been hunted. There appear to be at least three separate populations: one in the deep channels east of the Kamchatka Peninsula, in the Sea of Okhotsk (off Abashiri but also in more shallow waters north of Sakhalin), and off the Kurile Islands; one in the Sea of Japan (Toyama Bay and west coast of southern Hokkaido); and a third in the coastal waters of the Pacific coast of Japan (mainly between 144° and 140°E). Recent studies suggest that the latter population at least makes a seasonal northwards movement in summer, arriving off the Pacific coast of Hokkaido in October-November. The continental slope (at depths of 1,000–3,000m) north of 34°N appears to be favoured, and the movement is probably associated with the subsurface Oyashio Current off Japan where several hundred were hunted each year in the 1950s. Cuvier's beaked whale is relatively common in the Sea of Japan and off the Pacific coast of Japan, and the Blainville's beaked whale occurs from Japan eastwards towards Hawaii. The North Pacific appears to be the centre of speciation for the beaked whales and three other species have been recorded. Furthest north occurs the Stejneger's beaked whale, in the southern Bering Sea south to the northern Sea of Japan. In cold temperate waters, the Hubbs' beaked whale appears to be confined to the southern Sea of Japan in the vicinity of Honshu where the cold Oyashio and warm Kuroshio Currents meet. Further south, the ginkgo-toothed beaked whale has been recorded from Southeast Japan, Taiwan and pelagic waters of the tropical Indo-Pacific. Northern bottlenose whales do not appear to occur in temperate and subarctic waters of Japan, although unconfirmed sightings in the tropical western North Pacific suggest that the species (or a similar one) may exist in that region.

Other small whales which occur in the Northwest Pacific include the melon-headed whale, pygmy killer and false killer whales, and short-finned pilot whale. All four are generally deep water species, often far offshore, mainly in warm temperate to tropical waters. However, melon-headed whales are common in the Philippine Sea, particularly near Cebu Island. Pygmy killer whales are often seen off the Pacific coast of Japan (where false killer whales also occur) and may be driven ashore by Japanese fishermen. The killer whale occurs over a much wider area extending from the Equator to the Bering Sea. In the Northwest Pacific, the short-finned pilot whale occurs in waters with surface temperatures above 15–16°C, under the influence of the Kuroshio Current and its tributaries. Thus it occurs during summer along the Pacific coast of northern Japan and in the Sea of Japan, generally retreating south in winter. However, a larger form with a more pronounced saddle mark, has recently been recognised in November, also off the Pacific coast of Japan (off Ayukawa, 38°20′N). Its close relative, the long-finned pilot whale, has not yet been confirmed in the North Pacific.

Dolphins and Porpoises

A number of dolphins have coastal or riverine distributions. The Irrawaddy dolphin lives in the brackish waters of the Irrawaddy in Burma, the Mahakam in Borneo, the Mekong delta right up to the border with Cambodia, and various other estuaries and coastal areas of Malaysia, Indonesia and Indo-China. Sharing the same range in the South China Sea and waters of Malaysia and Indonesia, is the Indo-Pacific hump-backed dolphin. This species also occurs from Borneo northwards along the Indo-Chinese coast to the Canton River and, though not recorded, it may occur in the Philippines. East of Indonesia, hump-backed dolphins lack the characteristic dorsal hump and instead have a more pronounced dorsal fin, rather similar to the bottle-nosed dolphin which they superficially resemble. Bottle-nosed dolphins are present throughout coastal regions of the Indo-Pacific, ranging north to northern Japan, where they appear to be fairly common.

One of the rarest of dolphins, the baiji, has a very restricted range, apparently confined to the Yangtze River in China. At most, only a few hundred remain, mainly in the lower Yangtze (Hubei and Anhui Provinces) although it also occurs in associated lakes such as Lake Poyang.

There are three species of porpoises in the Northwest Pacific, two of which occur also off the North American coast. The exception is the finless porpoise which occupies coastal Indo-China from northern Japan south through Japan, China, Korea, and Indonesia, and west to distant Pakistan. Finless porpoises also live in river systems and are found far up the Yangtze River, as far as Wuhan. The harbour porpoise and Dall's porpoise have more northerly distributions. Both occur from the northern Sea of Japan and northern Japanese islands (particularly Hokkaido and the northern part of Honshu) north along the Soviet coast and islands to the Sea of Okhotsk and Bering Sea. However, whilst the harbour porpoise is coastal and usually occurs in relatively shallow waters, the Dall's porpoise is also thought to occur in the vicinity of deep canyons and far offshore. The latter is particularly common in the Sea of Okhotsk and southern Bering Sea, occurring in summer as far north as the Pribilof Islands. Elsewhere, it appears to be resident although inshore-offshore movements may take place seasonally. Different populations may exist along the Pacific coast of Japan, in the Sea of Japan, and the Sea of Okhotsk. One of these, called the True's porpoise, is recognised as a separate form on the basis of coloration, with the prominent white area on the flanks and belly extending anteriorly to the flippers; it occurs off the Pacific coast of northern Japan and off the Kurile Islands, although here it overlaps with the normal form of Dall's porpoise.

Around 30,000 Dall's porpoises are killed annually by Japanese fishermen, either harpooned for food or taken incidentally in salmon gill nets. A drive fishery took 20,000 striped dolphins annually in the 1960s but this number is now much reduced, being confined to the villages of Taiji, Kawana and Futo. In most areas of the world, the striped dolphin occurs mainly offshore, but in Japan the species approaches the coast in September and October, and moves south along the coast apparently dispersing into the East China Sea for the winter, returning offshore in April for the summer. The population off Japan has been estimated at

400,000. Sharing tropical and warm temperate waters with the striped dolphin are several other species. These include the spotted dolphin which occurs primarily offshore but is also present in the South China Sea and near Japan; the long-snouted spinner dolphin, common dolphin and Fraser's dolphin, all of which are mainly pelagic. The last of these species was first discovered as a specimen stranded on the shores of Sarawak in the 1950s. Rough-toothed dolphins are said to be rare off the coast of Japan although they occur far offshore in deep waters of the warm temperate and tropical mid-Pacific. With a more northerly distribution, the Pacific white-sided dolphin occurs mainly in temperate regions from the Sea of Japan and Pacific coast of Japan north to the Kamchatka Peninsula offshore to the subarctic convergence. It is often in company with northern right whale dolphins whose distribution overlaps broadly with it. The latter species occurs from northern Honshu and Cape Inubo, off Japan north to about 51°N, and east-northeast across the Pacific to its northern limit in British Columbia. It is apparently common particularly off the northeastern coast of Japan and also in the northern part of the Sea of Japan. Like the northern right whale dolphin, Risso's dolphins occur mainly offshore, though numbers are taken in coastal fisheries. Their distribution ranges further north than the previous species, in cooler waters north of Japan to the Kurile Islands.

Reference Sources: Berzin and Vladimirov (1981), Blokhin *et al.* (1985), Brownell and Chun (1977), Chen *et al.* (1979), Hammond and Leatherwood (1984), Kasuya (1971, 1978, 1985b, 1986), Kasuya and Kureha (1979), Kasuya and Marsh (1984), Kawamura and Satake (1976), Leatherwood *et al.* (1983), Miyazaki and Wada (1978a,b), Miyazaki *et al.* (1974, 1984), Nemoto (1978), Nishiwaki (1967), Omura (1950b, 1977), Omura *et al.* (1969), Peilie (1978, 1981), Pilleri and Gihr (1974), Pilleri *et al.* (1980), Sleptsov (1955), Tomilin (1967), Yablokov *et al.* (1972), Zhou *et al.* (1977, 1980, 1982).

SOUTH ATLANTIC
(including Atlantic portion of Antarctica)

The distribution of whales and dolphins in the southern hemisphere is generally much less well known than north of the Equator. This is partly due to the much larger expanses of ocean present in the region, and partly due to the relatively low human population sizes (particularly of zoologists) there. Our picture, therefore, is very incomplete and some areas are rather better known than others.

Baleen Whales

As well as the southern African coast, one of the best known coastal regions of the South Atlantic for cetaceans lies in northern Patagonia at Peninsula Valdés. Here amongst the sheltered bays of this peninsula, several hundred southern right whales court and calve during the southern winter and spring that spans July to November. Other regions visited for mating and calving include elsewhere along the Argentinian coast, off Uruguay, southern Brazil, around Tristan da Cunha, and in the vicinity of the Cape of Good Hope in South Africa. It is in the latter region, particularly between False Bay and Algoa Bay, that its relative

106

the pygmy right whale occurs during the southern winter. Summer feeding grounds of the southern right whale are not well known although historically they were found in the Southern Ocean around subantarctic islands such as South Georgia.

With the exception of Bryde's whale, all the rorqual species undergo similar migrations, summering in subantarctic or Antarctic waters where rich feeding grounds of krill and other planktonic euphausiids or copepods exist. Some species may penetrate further south than others (Figure 4.1). Blue whales usually stay south of 40°S in summer, with concentrations around the East Scotia Basin, including South Georgia where a fishery for this species and its smaller relatives has taken place until very recently. Another population is thought to winter in Antarctic seas due south of South Africa. Like the blue whale, minke whales (particularly older males) occur right up to the ice-edge, but the fin whale does not penetrate so far south, and the sei whale is much more subantarctic in its distribution. Bryde's whales, on the other hand, remain within temperate and tropical waters. In the southeastern Caribbean and off the coast of Venezuela, the species is apparently resident but further south off the coasts of Brazil in the Western Atlantic and South Africa in the Eastern Atlantic there may be limited migratory movements. As elsewhere, two forms of Bryde's whale have been recognised from the Brazilian coast, and from the west coast of the Cape Province of South Africa (particularly from Donkergat). One form occurs inshore, is smaller, less scarred and with shorter, narrower baleen plates than the other, more offshore form. The inshore form may also be more sedentary. In the southern winter, the other rorqual species make extensive migrations northwards into warm temperate, subtropical or tropical waters. In the case of the blue whale, these may be primarily offshore but fin, sei and minke whales may move northwards closer to the coast (usually as far north as Brazil in the west and offshore west of Natal, South Africa, in the eastern Atlantic). The humpback whale is also coastal during its migration between Antarctic feeding areas and breeding grounds off the coasts of Brazil and West Africa, but populations in the South Atlantic are now reduced to only a few hundred.

Sperm Whale, and Medium-sized Toothed Whales

The commonest of the large whales is the sperm whale which spends the southern winter in lower latitudes. In the South Atlantic, the most important historical whaling grounds were around Tristan da Cunha, off the southwestern tip of South Africa, off Angola in West Africa; and in almost contiguous areas along eastern South America from Brazil to near the Falkland Islands. Most females and young do not undergo any seasonal migration, but instead are resident in warmer waters. Young bachelor pods and older males, however, may move south to areas like the Weddell Sea, though usually north of the pack ice.

In mid-Atlantic mainly at tropical latitudes both the pygmy sperm whale and dwarf sperm whale are resident. Since they are pelagic species preferring deep waters they are not commonly seen alive although they are probably quite abundant. Most records are of strandings. On the western side, pygmy sperm whales have been recorded from Santos (Brazil), Montevideo (Uruguay) and Provincia Buenos Aires (Argentina), but dwarf sperm whales only from Rio Grande do Sul (Brazil). On the eastern side, records occur particularly from the vicinity of the Cape of Good Hope in South Africa (where stomach analyses suggest an association with the continental slope). However, this distribution may better reflect the distribution of interested observers. The same applies to the ocean-going beaked whales. The better-watched areas such as the Patagonian coast, Tierra del Fuego, and the Falkland Islands off South America, South Georgia, South Shetlands and Orkneys in the Antarctic, and in Cape Province, South Africa tend to accumulate the handful of strandings of some of these poorly known species. From this we can piece together a probable wide distribution but with little idea where concentrations may occur; the few sightings that have been made and our knowledge of diet from stomach contents lead us to believe that they associate with very deep canyons. Ten species have been recorded from the South Atlantic, some more commonly than others. The commonest and most widely distributed species is the Cuvier's beaked whale, recorded from the tropics to Tierra del Fuego. The Gervais' beaked whale occurs in tropical to warm temperate waters as does the Blainville's beaked whale although the latter may extend further south. Seven beaked whale species have distributions centred on temperate to subantarctic seas; these include southern bottlenose, Tasman, Arnoux's, strap-toothed, Gray's beaked and Hector's beaked whales. Southern bottlenose whales have been recorded from southern Brazil and Rio de la Plata (Uruguay) south to Patagonia and Tierra del Fuego, from southern Africa, and subantarctic islands of the South Atlantic. The other species probably have wide distributions off southern continents, although Tasman beaked whale has not yet been found off South Africa or in the Antarctic. There have only been a dozen records of Tasman beaked whales, the southernmost being at 55°S in the Beagle Channel. The remaining four species have been recorded from Tierra del Fuego, the Falkland Islands and South Africa. Only about ten records of Hector's beaked whale exist but the other species have been recorded more frequently, with specimens also from Uruguay (strap-toothed), and Argentina (Gray's and Arnoux's). Arnoux's beaked whale occurs as far south as the ice edge, where it has been recorded from Graham Land (Antarctic Peninsula) as well as the South Shetlands.

There are a number of other species of small whales that the traveller offshore might expect to see in the tropical South Atlantic. Large herds of fast-swimming melon-headed whale and smaller herds of the rather similar pygmy killer whale probably occur throughout tropical pelagic waters, to which they are more or less confined. They share the same distribution as larger whales, the false killer whale and possibly the short-finned pilot whale, although the distribution of the former extends into temperate waters whilst that of the latter south of the Equator is poorly known. The killer whale is cosmopolitan and may be seen from the Equator to the ice floes of Antarctica. It has frequently been seen off the Patagonian coast where it poses a threat particularly to southern elephant seals and sea lions (see Plate 12).

Dolphins and Porpoises

The status and distribution of other smaller pelagic dolphins are also poorly known. Herds of rough-toothed dolphins probably occur far offshore in tropical and warm temperate waters, although they have only occasionally been recorded. In the same area, spotted dolphins and long-snouted (and possibly short-snouted) spinner dolphins appear to be much more abundant. The latter is particularly common off the coast of Fernando de Norunha Island, Brazil. Striped and spotted dolphins also occur offshore in tropical waters but their range extends south into the temperate zone; the distribution of the slightly larger Risso's dolphin is poorly known, though probably mainly temperate, with few records from the Southwest Atlantic (31 specimens known from south of 30°S, including subantarctic). Striped and spotted dolphins also range near the coast but they are less inclined to be inshore than the bottle-nosed dolphin, the distribution of which otherwise overlaps considerably. Sharing those waters in warm temperate and tropical West Africa is the Atlantic hump-backed dolphin. Its distribution is poorly known since the coasts of Angola and Southwest Africa have been little visited by zoologists, but it almost certainly does not occur in the latter region where the water is too cold. Its relative, the Indo-Pacific hump-backed dolphin, extends its distribution down the east coast as far as Cape Agulhas, reflecting warmer inshore conditions as a result of the influence of the Agulhas Current. In the Benguela Current, that sweeps around the southwestern coast of Africa, lives another coastal species, Heaviside's dolphin. It has a restricted distribution which may not extend as far north as Angola, and so might not actually overlap with the previous species. It is a small dolphin closely resembling a porpoise but about which very little indeed is known.

Across the Atlantic along the tropical shores of South America, the tucuxi (possibly comprising more than one species of the genus *Sotalia*) occurs alongside the rather similar, but larger, boto. The tucuxi is locally common between Santos in Brazil northwards across the Equator to the coasts of Venezuela, Colombia and Panama. It not only inhabits sheltered inshore waters such as the bay at Rio de Janeiro where it is said to be common, but occurs far upriver in the Amazon and its tributaries (and north of the Equator, in the river Orinoco). Much of the same riverine habitat is shared by the more solitary boto or boutu, a river dolphin that occupies not only the main river systems of the Amazon and Orinoco but, particularly during the rainy season, may be found in flooded jungles and temporary lakes. Both the tucuxi and botu show some variation between different populations, possibly isolated from one another in areas far upstream (both occur more than 2,000km from the coast). Bottle-nosed dolphins also occur in some of the coastal and estuarine habitat of the tucuxi, but, except for juveniles, can be readily distinguished by their larger size and taller, broader-based, more recurved dorsal fin.

Further south, and overlapping slightly with the tucuxi, is the franciscana. It has a long slender beak and shares many characters with the river dolphins, but it is not usually seen far up rivers. Instead it occurs mainly in coastal waters from Regencia, Espirito Santo (Brazil), and is common in the estuarine Rio de la Plata; otherwise its distribution extends south through Uruguay, occasionally to Peninsula Valdés in Patagonia, Argentina.

Two porpoises live in temperate coastal waters of South America. These are the Burmeister's porpoise and the spectacled porpoise. The range of both extends from Uruguay south to Patagonia, including around Tierra del Fuego where both are apparently common in the Beagle Channel and Strait of Magellan. However, only the spectacled porpoise has been recorded around offshore islands, such as the Falklands and South Georgia. A very similar range is occupied by the dusky dolphin (the southern counterpart of the Pacific white-sided dolphin). It occurs in inshore waters along the Argentinian coast (including Peninsula Valdés where it has been studied intensively) from Mar del Plato south occasionally to Tierra del Fuego. It also occurs on the other side of the South Atlantic, around the Cape of Good Hope, South Africa. Largely overlapping its range in southern South America are two similar and related *Lagenorhynchus* species. These are the Peale's dolphin and the hourglass dolphin. The former occurs from Peninsula Valdés to Cape Horn and Chiloe, being found annually along the south coast of Tierra del Fuego, the Beagle Channel and Magellan Strait, and around the Falkland Islands; the latter occupies the same range but is a much more pelagic species and also penetrates much further south into Antarctic waters. Southern right whale dolphins are often associated with dusky dolphins, far offshore from South Africa and in the Falkland Current between Patagonia and the Falklands. They have not been recorded north of Tierra del Fuego. Finally, the strikingly black and white Commerson's dolphin occurs from Peninsula Valdés to Cape Horn, with some isolated sightings in the Drake Passage. It is primarily coastal and is very common in the Magellan Strait and around the Falklands.

Reference Sources: Best (1971), Best and Ross (1984), Brown (1982), Brownell (1974), Brownell and Praderi (1985), Casinos (1981), Gianuca and Castello (1976), Goodall (1978), Goodall and Galeazzi (1985), Leatherwood *et al.* (1983), Lichter and Hooper (1984), Ross (1984), Saayman and Tayler (1979), Smithers (1983), Wursig (1978), Wursig and Wursig (1977, 1979, 1980).

SOUTH PACIFIC
(including Pacific portion of Antarctica)

Baleen Whales

If our knowledge of cetaceans in the South Atlantic is poor, it is poorer still in many parts of the South Pacific. Many of the great whales have had their populations greatly reduced so that our knowledge of favoured areas depends in part upon historical whaling records. The southern right whale is one such example. In the past it was hunted during the southern summer in subantarctic areas such as around the New Zealand islands of Chatham, Auckland and Campbell and off the south and southeastern coasts of Australia. While very much reduced by that hunting, and with no recovery seen earlier this century, there are now signs of population increase, for example off Campbell Island (also off South and western Australia), and also along the coast of Chile. They approach temperate coasts in spring, mainly to give birth, but their summering grounds are not well-defined, though apparently in somewhat cooler waters. Its smaller relative, the pygmy right whale, is rather poorly known but has been recorded from the coasts of South Australia, Tasmania and New Zealand.

The seasonal movements of the southern right whale are probably not very extensive; those of the large rorquals are much more so. The blue whale spends the winter in tropical and subtropical regions, migrating to spend the summer in Antarctic waters. Sharing the same feeding and wintering areas is the minke whale, but the fin whale tends not to migrate quite so deeply into Antarctic waters, and the sei whale is much more subantarctic in its distribution. Both species migrate east of New Zealand and Australia, wintering in that region and around Polynesia and Micronesia. Other migration routes taken by the fin whale are into the central South Pacific and along the west coast of South America north to Peru. The humpback whale takes similar routes but those are more discrete, often following the continental shelf. They summer in distinct areas in the Antarctic mainly in the Ross and Amundsen Seas (see Figure 8.1), then migrate to the northeast coast of Australia past New Zealand to around the islands of Samoa and Tonga; others migrate along the coasts of Chile, Peru and Ecuador to the Galapagos Islands. Bryde's whale, on the other hand, is largely resident in tropical and subtropical waters. It probably ranges throughout the equatorial Pacific and has been recorded off southeastern Australia and northern New Zealand. The species also occurs at least to 20°S, off the coast of northern Chile.

Sperm Whale, and Medium-sized Toothed Whales

Sperm whales are usually associated with deep waters. They calve in warm seas and have been recorded from around the islands of Polynesia, Micronesia and New Guinea; off the coasts of eastern Australia and New Zealand; and off the continental shelf of South America west of Chile, Peru and Ecuador, including the Galapagos Islands. Although female sperm whales and their calves are virtually restricted to tropical and temperate seas, older males move into colder waters (for example Antarctic) during the southern summer. The smaller relatives, the pygmy and dwarf sperm whales, are probably resident in tropical to warm temperate seas. The former has been recorded stranded along the coasts of southeastern Australia, Tasmania and New Zealand, and in Peru. The latter species is less well known, partly through earlier confusion with the pygmy sperm whale, but has been recorded from South Australia and New Zealand. Both species are very similar to one another, but confusion with other small species at sea may also occur. Three species which might cause confusion and which range the open sea are the melon-headed whale, the pygmy killer whale and the false killer whale. All three occur mainly in tropical or subtropical waters, widely distributed but comparatively rarely seen. The melon-headed whale has been recorded from the central South Pacific (Tuamotu Archipelago and Marquesas Islands), off the coast of Ecuador, and around Australia. The pygmy killer whale and substantially larger false killer whale have been seen in the central and eastern tropical Pacific, with the latter recorded as far south as New Zealand and Peru. Occupying the same seas but extending deep into Antarctic waters is the distinctively marked killer whale.

The short-finned pilot whale occurs along the north coast of Australia and New Zealand, in the central Pacific around the Polynesian Islands, and in the tropical eastern Pacific around Galapagos. Further south in the cold Humboldt Current that runs north along the coast of Chile and

Peru, it is replaced by the very similar, closely related long-finned pilot whale. The latter has a much more cold temperate distribution, being recorded from Auckland Island, south of New Zealand, and extending towards Tierra del Fuego on the South American continent. Since both species may occur far offshore, their distribution in the South Pacific is poorly known.

Ten species of beaked whales may occupy the deep waters of the South Pacific. Most records come from strandings so that our knowledge of the natural range of many of the species is rather incomplete. Most are very difficult, if not impossible, to identify specifically when seen at sea. One species, the Longman's beaked whale, is known only from two skulls, one of which was on the shores of Queensland, northeastern Australia. Also very poorly known is Hector's beaked whale, where the few specimens found indicate a pan Pacific and circumpolar distribution in temperate latitudes, including Tierra del Fuego, Tasmania and New Zealand in the South Pacific (and extending up to California). Other species with a similar apparently circumpolar temperate distribution include Gray's beaked whale, strap-toothed whale and Tasman beaked whale. The first of these may be commonest in the vicinity of New Zealand since most stranding records are from there. It has also been recorded from South Australia and the Chatham Islands. The strap-toothed whale has also been recorded mainly from New Zealand, but strandings have also taken place on the coast of southeastern Australia, Tasmania and Tierra del Fuego in South America. The Tasman beaked whale has never been seen with certainty alive, but strandings have been reported from South Australia, New Zealand and from the Galapagos Islands.

One species whose distribution appears to be centred on Australasian waters is Andrew's beaked whale with strandings mainly from Australia (southeast coast), Tasmania and New Zealand. Other records come from Chatham Island and Campbell Island (New Zealand). Arnoux's beaked whale is one of the few beaked whales to have been sighted at sea. It has a wide temperate southern hemisphere distribution but a large number of strandings records come from New Zealand (with some also from South Australia) suggesting that the species may at least be relatively abundant there. Finally, three beaked whales are probably both common and widely distributed, and are most likely to be identifiable at sea. These include the southern bottlenose whale, recorded from the tropical Pacific, temperate waters of Australia, New Zealand, Chile and, in summer, south to Antarctic waters; the Cuvier's beaked whale recorded in the same regions from the tropical Pacific, but mainly in temperate regions (Australia, New Zealand and Chile) south to Tierra del Fuego and rarely into subantarctic waters; and Blainville's beaked whale which is distributed mainly in tropical and warm temperate waters, and has been recorded from northeastern Australia, Tasmania, and between Australia and New Zealand in the Tasman Sea.

Dolphins and Porpoises

The tropical pelagic waters of the central South Pacific are frequented by a number of smaller dolphin species. Two species, the rough-toothed dolphin and Fraser's dolphin, occur primarily in tropical and warm temperate seas. Neither appears to be very common, though they may occur in large herds and are widely distributed. The rough-toothed dolphin has been recorded from Melanesia and Australia, and off the coasts of Ecuador and Peru. Fraser's dolphin whose existence has only been known to scientists for the last 30 years, has been reported from eastern Australia, and from the Central Pacific, but its distribution is still poorly known. Superficially it is rather similar to the striped dolphin, a much more abundant species which probably occurs mainly offshore throughout tropical to warm temperate seas. Sharing the same range (as they do in all the major oceans) are the common dolphin, spotted dolphin and long-snouted spinner dolphin, though the latter may be rather more restricted to tropical waters, rarely occurring south of Peru and northern Australia. The range of all four species is predominantly well offshore, although in New Zealand, the common dolphin makes an apparently inshore movement during summer (November-April), being seen mainly off the east coast. In certain regions off the north and east coasts of North Island, and the Cook Strait, the species may be resident or at least semi-resident. Another species, the Risso's dolphin, is more likely to be seen in continental shelf waters, around Australia and New Zealand, and along the coasts of Peru and northern Chile.

The inshore waters of the Western Pacific are frequented by the Indo-Pacific hump-backed dolphin. It occurs commonly in New Guinea and around the northern coasts of Australia. In this region, the species does not have the distinctive hump that it has farther west in the Indo-Pacific, and instead of a small almost triangular dorsal fin it has a more sickle-shaped fin. This leads to confusion with the bottle-nosed dolphin which shares the same range, though the latter is darker and does not have the obvious long beak that hump-backed dolphins have. Bottle-nosed dolphins also occur in coastal waters of South America, extending to the temperate coast of Chile. They may also occur offshore, often associated with pilot whales particularly in warmer waters.

As one moves south into temperate seas, two pelagic species are likely to be more frequently seen. These are the southern right whale dolphin and the hourglass dolphin. In western South America, the southern right whale dolphin extends its distribution via the cold Humboldt current to subtropical latitudes, off Peru, but elsewhere it is most commonly reported along the coast and far offshore from Chile, and off the continental shelf east of New Zealand. With a more restricted cold temperate and polar distribution, the hourglass dolphin may be seen usually far offshore west of Chile (mainly south of 45°S), east of New Zealand and its subantarctic islands, and in Antarctic waters.

Several dolphin species occur in coastal temperate waters. Off the coasts of eastern New Zealand (but not Australia), Chatham Island, subantarctic islands such as Campbell Island, and the coasts of Chile and Peru, the dusky dolphin may commonly be seen. The same region (except at high latitudes) is shared with the bottle-nosed dolphin. From central Chile southwards also occurs the Peale's dolphin, a species very similar to the dusky dolphin, best distinguished by the pattern of black and white markings on the flanks. The Peale's dolphin appears to be relatively common around Tierra del Fuego, the Beagle Channel and Magellan Strait but does not reach as far west as New Zealand.

Two small porpoise-sized dolphins have restricted distributions. The Hector's dolphin occurs in shallow coastal waters and bays of New

Zealand (except the extreme north and south). It is a rather local species, present in small numbers around Tasman Bay, Cook Strait and Banks Peninsula on the east coast, and along the west coast of South Island north of Milford. Across the Pacific close to the coasts of southern Chile, is its uniformly dark relative, the black dolphin. This shy species occurs from Concepción south to Navarino Island, near Cape Horn, including the Magellan Strait and channels of Tierra del Fuego. At the southern tip of South America also occurs the distinctively marked Commerson's dolphin. It is particularly common in the Magellan Strait and around southern Tierra del Fuego. The same region is occupied by two species of porpoises, the spectacled porpoise and Burmeister's porpoise. The former has been reported from subantarctic islands of New Zealand and south of Tasmania. The range of the Burmeister's porpoise probably extends from Tierra del Fuego north to the northern tip of Peru. The species has not been recorded in southern Chile (except in Tierra del Fuego) but it may occur there, in which case its uniformly dark appearance and similar size is likely to cause confusion with the black dolphin (best separated on dorsal fin shape).

Reference Sources: Baker (1972, 1977, 1978, 1981, 1983, 1985), Cawthorn (1978, 1979), Donovan (1984a,b), Fordyce *et al.* (1979, 1984), Gaskin (1968, 1972, 1973, 1977b), Leatherwood *et al.*(1983), Mead (1981), Sielfeld (1983), Soegiarto and Polunin (1982), Torres *et al.* (1979).

INDIAN OCEAN
(including Red Sea, Persian Gulf, Arabian Sea, Bay of Bengal, Antarctic and subantarctic portions)

To most people, the Indian Ocean lies between the continents of Africa, Asia and Australasia, whose northern limits are set by the coasts of Oman, Pakistan, India, Burma and Thailand between 5° and 25°N, and a line drawn at about 35°S, from the southern coasts of Australia to those of South Africa. Most of this region is therefore tropical or subtropical. In this section I will extend the southern limit to include the islands Prince Edward, Crozet, Kerguelen and Heard in the Southern Ocean, and that portion of Antarctica lying due south of the Indian Ocean. In 1979, the International Whaling Commission adopted a proposal by the Seychelles for the entire Indian Ocean north of 55°S to be recognised as a sanctuary for cetaceans, prohibiting their commercial hunting for at least ten years. Unlike other oceans, the Indian Ocean has no northern polar waters, and the status of whale stocks in the northern portion is particularly poorly known.

Baleen Whales

The southern right whale was once hunted on its wintering grounds south of the Cape of Good Hope in South Africa, and off the south and west coasts of Australia. These possibly have represented separate populations, as might summer feeding concentrations around the islands of Crozet and Kerguelen. Until recently, very much reduced in numbers, the species can still be seen in these areas, and in some is now recovering (for example off South Africa, mainly east of Cape Agulhas). Its smaller relative, the pygmy right whale, is apparently confined to temperate waters, including the coasts of South Africa and southern Australia (particularly off Tasmania), and in the southern Indian Ocean between. It is probably frequently overlooked since it is difficult to distinguish from the minke whale and in the past has probably been frequently mistaken for it.

The largest of all whales, the blue whale, spends the southern summer feeding close to the ice edge of Antarctica. It then migrates north into the Indian Ocean, but the exact whereabouts of its breeding grounds are not known. Recent ship surveys have found a breeding population resident close to the coast of Sri Lanka. They have been observed recently feeding in Trincomalee Bay, and seem to breed at the same time as those in the Antarctic, and so are unlikely to be of the same population. However, its relationship to other blue whales in the Indian Ocean is not clear. The population may refer to a smaller form of the blue whale, called the pygmy blue whale. This was once thought to concentrate in a restricted zone of the Antarctic during summer (between 30° and 80°E, and north of 54°S), and in autumn, migrate to breed in the temperate Indian Ocean. Since then, the form has been recorded from the east coast of South Africa and western Australia, and also further east off the coast of Chile. Fin whales move from summering grounds in the Antarctic (usually not as far south as blue whales) to winter in the southern Indian Ocean between the subantarctic islands such as Kerguelen and Crozet and around 20°S. They appear to be rare in the northern half of the Indian Ocean. A similar pattern of distribution apparently exists for the sei whale although its latitudinal migration is thought to be less extensive. Minke whales, on the other hand, may summer right up to the Antarctic pack ice. The extent of their northerly movements is not well known but they are certainly to be found in the southern Indian Ocean, and were recently fished extensively off Durban, South Africa. The Bryde's whale is essentially a tropical to cool temperate resident in the Indian Ocean, occurring quite commonly in the eastern Cape, and is found north to the coast of Sri Lanka and into the Persian Gulf. Humpbacks feed during summer in Antarctic waters south of the Indian Ocean, and then one population moves to the coast of western Australia and the other to eastern South Africa and the south coast of Madagascar (see Figure 8.1). Humpbacks are seen frequently moving past northern Natal, at Cape Vidal. Those may be part of a population moving up into the tropics through the Mozambique channel. Recently humpbacks have been heard singing the same unique song off Oman and Sri Lanka during the time that southern hemisphere humpbacks should be feeding in the Antarctic. Thus a population may remain in the northern Indian Ocean throughout the year.

Sperm Whale, and Medium-sized Toothed Whales

The Indian Ocean is an important region for sperm whales. In the latter part of the last century a Yankee whaling industry for the species operated from the Seychelles. In recent years there have also been some large Soviet catches. A Natal fishery was active from about 1912 and developed into the mainstay of the industry. Though now protected, this stock is apparently in good state, and must be one of the most important anywhere. Concentrations of sperm whales, mainly cows and juveniles, or groups of bachelor bulls, in such warmer waters, occur on the Mahé Banks, north of the Seychelles; around Madagascar; in the Arabian Sea and Gulf of Aden, and around the coasts of India and Sri Lanka; off eastern South Africa; and off western Australia. Its smaller relatives, the pygmy sperm whale and dwarf sperm whale, though rarely identified at sea, have been recorded stranded on the coasts of western Australia, East and South Africa, Arabia (e.g. Oman) and India, and they also form part of the bycatch in Sri Lanka. *Kogia* is in fact the genus that strands most commonly after *Tursiops* along the eastern Cape coast, South Africa. Both pygmy and dwarf sperm whales are probably widely distributed throughout the Indian Ocean.

Most of the beaked whales are even less well known. Some have been recorded from the coast of South Africa, Arabia and Sri Lanka, and so probably occur in the Indian Ocean. These include Hector's and strap-toothed beaked whales. Another species, the Longman's beaked whale, is known only from two skulls, one of which was found at Danane, on the coast of Somalia, Northeast Africa. The ginkgo-toothed beaked whale probably occurs at least in the northern Indian Ocean since it has been recorded from Sri Lanka. A number of species of beaked whales occupy the temperate or subantarctic zone of the Indian Ocean. These include the southern bottlenose whale, recorded off Sri Lanka as well as the southern Indian Ocean; Andrews' beaked whale recorded from Kerguelen Island and Western Australia; and Arnoux's beaked whale which has been recorded from South Africa and Australia and so presumably occurs between these regions. True's beaked whale has been reported regularly from the coasts of Southern Africa, and twice from southern Australia (Perth and Victoria), and so may exist as an isolated population in the southern Indian Ocean. Three species of beaked whales are probably common in the Indian Ocean. These are Cuvier's beaked whale (sighted commonly off Sri Lanka, for example), Gray's beaked whale (which has been sighted relatively frequently in deep waters south and east of Madagascar), and Blainville's beaked whale (recorded commonly from the Natal coast of South Africa, and from the islands of Mauritius, Seychelles and Nicobar).

Three small whales, melon-headed whale, pygmy killer and false killer whales, occur offshore, judging from the distribution of records, probably throughout the Indian Ocean, though the first two are typically tropical species. The last of these has also been recorded in the Red Sea, which otherwise is apparently frequented only by smaller dolphin species. The killer whale may occasionally come into the Red Sea; it has been recorded from the Arabian Sea and Gulf of Aden, and is widely distributed in the Indian Ocean in small numbers. The distribution of the short-finned pilot whale in the Indian Ocean is poorly known but is thought to extend throughout tropical and subtropical waters. It has been recorded off the coasts of East and Southern Africa, the Seychelles, Sri Lanka, Gulf of Aden, and western Australia. Further south in temperate seas, it is probably replaced by the long-finned pilot whale, although there is some strandings evidence that the two species overlap at least occasionally on the eastern Cape coast between Moscal Bay and East London.

Dolphins and Porpoises

The rough-toothed dolphin occurs in small numbers in tropical and subtropical open waters of the Indian Ocean. It has been recorded quite close to the coast of Natal, Sri Lanka, in the Gulf of Aden and even into the southern Red Sea. Sharing its range are the long-snouted spinner dolphin, spotted dolphin, striped dolphin and common dolphin, although the last may be rare in the Arabian and Red Seas. The spinner dolphin appears to be the most abundant, at least in tropical and subtropical waters (occurring, for example, to northern Natal), and is the species most frequently seen around the Seychelles. It also occurs commonly in the southern Red Sea. The spotted dolphin is common in the same waters; its range extends into the Red Sea where it has been seen even in the Gulf of Eilat. It has also been recorded off western Australia. The striped dolphin likewise occurs in warm temperate seas (including, at least occasionally, the Red Sea). The species may be seen particularly off the coasts of East and South Africa (down to 40°S in the Agulhas current system), where it can be confused with the similarly marked Fraser's dolphin. The latter is primarily a pelagic tropical species, probably ranging across the Indian Ocean though its distribution is poorly known. It has been observed off the coast of Sri Lanka and may be seen regularly in very large herds (commonly bow-riding) off the Natal coast of Southern Africa. Commonly seen in small herds both offshore and close to the coast are Risso's dolphin and bottle-nosed dolphin. Both species occur through-out the Indian Ocean, off the coasts of East and South Africa, India and Sri Lanka, and Western Australia. Both are also relatively common residents in the Red Sea north into the Gulf of Eilat. A separate form of the bottle-nosed dolphin in the Red Sea is recognised by some authorities, and occupies mainly shallow waters including the Gulf of Suez.

The shallow waters of the Red Sea and Gulf of Suez are also occupied by the Indo-Pacific hump-backed dolphin (locally referred to as the plum-beous dolphin). This species is widely distributed in inshore waters of the Indian Ocean, extending down the west side to Cape Agulhas at the southern tip of South Africa; in the Arabian Sea and Persian Gulf; along the coasts of Pakistan and India; throughout much of Indonesia, Borneo and New Guinea; and off northwestern Australia. Close inshore from the Bay of Bengal eastwards, its range is shared with the rather smaller Irrawaddy dolphin. The diminutive finless porpoise occurs over much of the same area, with a range extending from Pakistan, along the entire Indian coast, and throughout Southeast Asia and Indonesia. It prefers inshore waters, mangrove swamps and the deltas and lower reaches of rivers, such as the Indus. Two endangered small river dolphins, the Indus susu and Ganges susu, are restricted to the drainage systems of those two rivers or adjacent ones. The Ganges susu is the more common and widely distributed and it occurs not only in the Ganges but also Brahmaputra and Meghna river systems, and in Bangladesh and Nepal, mainly in the delta region and lower reaches of these rivers. The Indus susu, on the other hand, is rare and critically endangered, with 400–500 restricted to Sind and Punjab provinces of Pakistan. Most of the population occurs along a 130km stretch of the river Indus, between the barrages of Sukkur and Guddu.

Moving far offshore into temperate waters of the southern Indian Ocean, two dolphin species are most likely to be seen. One of these, the dusky dolphin, occurs commonly off the coasts of Southern Africa and has been recorded from Kerguelen Island. The other, the southern right whale dolphin, has also been reported offshore from the coast of southern Australia, and off the southern coast of South Africa; it presumably ranges across the southern Indian Ocean following the West Wind Drift. Finally, two species, the spectacled porpoise and Commerson's dolphin, may occur in the same region since they have been recorded from Kerguelen Island. Their distribution, however, is principally to the west, on the eastern seaboard of southern South America.

Reference Sources: Alling *et al.* (1984), Condy (1977), Evans (1986), Frazier (1983), Jones (1982), Keller *et al.* (1982), Leatherwood *et al.* (1984b), Mead (1981), Racey and Nicoll (1984), Robineau (1982), Rorvik (1980), Ross (1984), Smeenk (unpublished), Shrestha (1982).

We have taken a quick tour around the world to see what species one might expect to see in the different regions. In conjunction with Chapter 3, this should also help the reader determine which species he or she is observing. However, it should be borne in mind that for many species, particularly the oceanic ones, we are still far from knowing precisely their ranges. In many cases, we can see that species have particular ecological preferences. These may relate to a particular type of habitat — a river, or shallow bay or deep ocean canyon; or to a particular water mass, often associated with temperature. A few species are cosmopolitan, but many have preferences for a tropical zone, temperate or polar region either throughout the year or at least seasonally. In the next chapter, we shall examine one of the factors associated with the distribution of a species, that of its diet.

6 Food and feeding

Like all animals, whales and dolphins need energy to carry out life processes, and they obtain this from food. It is, therefore, not surprising that much of their life is geared towards this activity and many adaptations that have arisen during their evolution are related to feeding.

The most important taxonomic division of Cetacea into Mysticeti (baleen whales) and Odontoceti (toothed whales) relates to their method of feeding. Baleen whales feed by straining large quantities of water containing plankton and other larger organisms through a series of horny plates or baleen that grow down from the sides of the upper jaw (Figure 6.1). The jaws are also adapted for wide opening and, in the humpback whale, for example, it has been shown that the jaw will temporarily dislocate to increase its size during feeding. Toothed whales, on the other hand, have a set of teeth (though these may be very reduced in certain groups such as the beaked whales) which are used for grasping generally larger prey than that taken by baleen whales. Although they may vary in size and slightly in shape, such teeth are all similar in appearance (termed homodont), unlike most other mammals where they are clearly differentiated into incisors, canines, pre-molars and molars. Only one set of teeth is produced in the lifetime of the animal (termed monophyodont); odontocetes do not have milk teeth in the way that we humans do. The teeth always have a single root so that they appear as simple or slightly recurved pegs set in single sockets.

VARIATION IN FEEDING APPARATUS

Mysticetes or Baleen Whales

The size and shape of the skull and baleen plates determines the type of prey taken by Mysticete whales and the method of capture. The right and bowhead whales have very large heads which may approach one-third the total length of the body. They have a long narrow upper jaw or rostrum which arches upwards to accommodate the long slender baleen plates (2–3m long in the right whale and 4m or greater in the bowhead). There may be 200–400 plates on each side of the jaw, lined with long fine

Figure 6.1 How baleen works. (a) Cross section of head of baleen whale. (b) In rorquals such as the sei whale, the broad, gently curved rostrum and expandable throat grooves allow the mouth to open widely to engulf food organisms in a large quantity of water. The water is then sieved through the spaces between the baleen plates as the mouth closes, the throat grooves tighten up and the tongue is raised. Food material such as plankton is retained on the bristles lining the inner edges of the baleen plates before being swallowed. (c) The right whales represent the opposite extreme, with a long narrow rostrum and much longer baleen plates. They feed by skimming the surface, collecting food organisms on their baleen, and then dislodging the food with the tongue. Nevertheless, the principles of filter-feeding through baleen are similar (see (d))

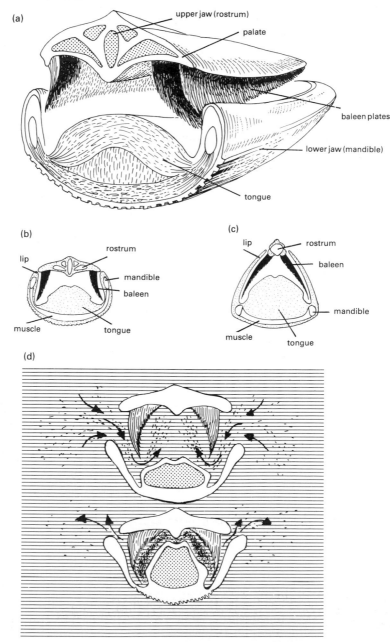

bristles. They feed by skimming the surface with their mouths open, collecting food organisms and dislodging them into the mouth with the tongue. The diet of right whales is primarily copepod crustaceans, although krill larvae may also be taken by the North Atlantic right whale and in the Southern Ocean, much larger krill (55–65mm length) may also be taken regularly (Gaskin 1982:64).

In rorqual whales, the rostrum is broader and only gently curved, and the baleen plates much shorter although they vary somewhat in size between species. Pivorunas (1976) made a special study of the function of baleen plates and their fringes in relation to diet. He suggested that it was not so much the number of baleen fringes that was important, but more the fineness of those fringes, and this was affected by the angle formed between the inner margin of the baleen plate and the longitudinal axes of the baleen tubules from which the fibres arise. In the fin whale, there are two types of fringe: a fine fringe that occurs primarily from the middle of each plate and helps to form a further seal after intake of water; and a set of stiff, coarse fringes which occur at the apex of each plate and forms a further seal at the sides, towards the back (being trapped against the inner surface of the lower jaw and the tongue during feeding). The consequence of having these two fringe types is that there is only a small semi-ovoid area in the central and posterior portion of the baleen that actually filters water from the food mass that has been gulped in. Figure 6.2 shows the range of shapes and sizes of baleen plates between species.

On each side of the jaw, sei whales have 300–400 relatively short baleen plates but with fine fringes and, like the right whales, they feed mainly upon copepods, though they also take krill and other crustaceans. They may also feed by skimming the surface with the mouth half open, taking in food organisms from patches of water concentrated with plankton. When feeding in this manner, one can often see the head raised slightly above the surface, the whale closing its mouth periodically to

Figure 6.2 Variation in baleen in the mysticete whales. Baleen plates from (a) minke, (b) sei, (c) Bryde's, (d) pygmy right, (e) gray, (f) humpback, (g), fin, (h) blue, (i) right and (j) bowhead whales

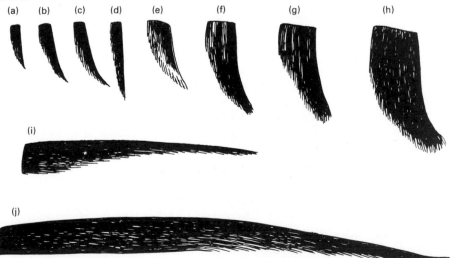

(a) (b) (c) (d) (e) (f) (g) (h)

(i)

(j)

swallow food collected upon its baleen plates. Sei whales may also feed in the way that most rorquals do, by opening the mouth widely for a short period, to engulf food in a large quantity of water. As the mouth closes, the water is forced through the spaces between the baleen plates; the throat pleats which were previously expanded (to increase the volume within the mouth) contract and the tongue is raised to force the water back out of the sides of the mouth. The food remains on the bristles which line the inner edges of the baleen plates, and is then swallowed. Such 'gulping' feeding behaviour is typical of most rorqual species.

Of the rorquals, the blue whale has the longest baleen (maximum dimensions 90cm long by 50cm wide) and the finest bristles. There are between 260 and 400 plates on each side, and these filter out the shrimps (particularly krill) upon which the species almost exclusively feeds. Fin whales have between 260 and 480 baleen plates (maximum dimensions 72cm long by 30cm wide) but these are coarser than the previous species. This allows the species to retain larger planktonic organisms. They feed not only upon krill and copepods, but also on various shoaling fish species such as herring and capelin (particularly in the northern hemisphere). Humpback whales have a similar number of baleen plates (270–400 on each side), but they are relatively narrow (maximum dimensions 60cm long by 15cm wide). They also feed on fish as well as planktonic organisms, their diet being more varied and including more fish in the northern hemisphere. The smallest rorqual is the minke whale with approximately 250 to 350 short (c. 20cm length, 10cm width) baleen plates. Its diet is similar to the humpback whale and, like that species, feeding on shoaling fish may additionally involve various breaching activities (Evans personal observations; Gaskin 1982:44–5). Although traditionally thought of as plankton feeders, we have seen that a number of species have quite catholic diets. The tropical Bryde's whale which rarely enters higher latitudes (where plankton is seasonally concentrated) feeds primarily upon fish. It has between 250 and 370 baleen plates. Like the minke whale, they are short (40cm long by 20cm wide) and fringed with fine bristles.

The gray whale is a bottom feeder. It has shorter and thicker jaws than other baleen whales, and short (5–25cm length), stiff plates (numbering between 130 and 180). The species ploughs the sea bottom mainly for benthic amphipod crustaceans, although on migration off the Californian coast it will also feed at the surface on both small fish and shrimp-like mysids that live in the kelp beds.

We have seen how the variation in the size and shape of baleen plates and the coarseness of their fringes can be attributed to the differences in size and variety of plankton upon which they feed. Clearly these adaptations do not apply to the larger sized fish which may be captured by alternative means (see section on feeding methods below). We may speculate that these baleen whales evolved in an environment where plankton was dominant in their diet and that various fish species have entered their diet secondarily since then.

Odontocetes or Toothed Whales

The toothed whales typically have a long row of even, conical teeth, suitable for grasping quick-moving prey. They feed either upon fish or squid, although the killer whale, with fewer teeth, will feed also on marine mammals and birds. The shape of the odontocete skull and jaw is closely related to the method of food capture.

A careful study of the jaw apparatus and associated muscles has been carried out recently on six delphinid species by Dana Seagars (1983) from California. Those taxa (including *Delphinus* and *Lagenorhynchus*) with long narrow jaws and relatively numerous (usually 20–65 pairs in upper and lower jaws) small, sharp teeth also have powerful muscles to the rear portion of the lower jaw. These help in grasping relatively small fish. The Risso's dolphin (genus *Grampus*) and pilot whales (genus *Globicephala*), on the other hand, have broader jaws and fewer teeth (seven pairs in the former and 7–12 pairs in the latter, concentrated towards the front of each jaw); and the more powerful muscles are those to the cheek bones and the rear part of the upper jaw. They capture mainly squid which presumably tend to be less manageable than small fish. The bottle-nosed dolphin (genus *Tursiops*) has a conservative jaw anatomy, thought to be adapted to a more catholic diet. Killer whales have broad jaws with relatively few large conical teeth (10–12 pairs in each jaw) and very powerful muscles to the rear of the upper jaw. These almost certainly aid the retainment of large prey that are likely to resist capture.

Those species that feed on squid tend to have a reduced number of teeth. In the sperm whale there are no functional teeth in the lower jaw, whilst amongst beaked whales the dentition has been reduced still further, generally to a single pair of teeth protruding from the lower jaw, and often confined to males only. Instead, they have a ribbed palate, which helps to hold their slippery-bodied squid prey.

The white whale and narwhal both have reduced dentition, with 8–11 pairs of teeth in each jaw in the case of the former, whilst in the case of the latter there are only two teeth in the upper jaw, one of which is extruded in the male (occasionally in the female) to form a spiralled tusk (probably unimportant in feeding). They have varied diets, both feeding upon squid, fish and crustaceans, whilst white whales will also feed upon worms and occasionally molluscs. Having few functional teeth, both species must use alternative means of food capture. These involve suction and the emission of a jet of water to dislodge prey such as bottom-living fish and molluscs. The highly flexible neck aids the scanning of a broader area of sea bottom and the capture of mobile prey.

Most porpoises (of the family Phocoenidae) have a number of spade-shaped teeth (though less than in Delphinidae — ranging from 13 to 28 pairs in each jaw), as well as fused neck vertebrae. The teeth of phocoenids are set at an acute angle to the line of the jaw, facilitating a shearing action during feeding although they may also employ suction when feeding (D. Gaskin personal communication). They too have a varied diet feeding upon mainly pelagic fish, some squid and, in the case of the finless porpoise, also crustaceans, particularly prawns. The Dall's porpoise is an exception with virtually non-functional teeth and a ribbed palate for capture of squid, whilst the finless porpoise has at least some of its neck vertebrae unfused for greater mobility.

Rather specialised in their feeding habits are the primitive river dolphins. They have poor eyesight, relying instead upon echo-location for food-finding in the turbid conditions that often prevail in these habitats. They possess numerous (ranging from 24 to 60 pairs in each jaw) conical pointed teeth, thickened at the base near the back. With a number of unfused neck vertebrae, the neck is flexible and together with the long slender beak these help the capture of fish, shrimps and, in certain coastal regions, octopus and squid (Myrick 1979b; Yablokov *et al.* 1972). Franciscanas have a growth of diatoms over their skin which emits bioluminescence and may help them to find their prey at night (Nemoto *et al.* 1977).

We can see that various whale and dolphin species have evolved different adaptations to feeding. In some cases different routes have been taken to achieve the same end; the varied diets of the narwhal and the white whale are not dissimilar to those of some delphinids, yet the former have few teeth and unfused neck vertebrae whereas the latter have many teeth and fused neck vertebrae.

OCEANOGRAPHIC RELATIONSHIPS TO FEEDING

If one makes a series of boat transects across a sea area, the cetaceans that are observed are likely to be clumped in their distribution. Such a distribution is probably determined primarily by that of their food prey, and to understand their association we need to examine those oceanographic factors that may be important.

We have seen in the preceding chapter that the distributions of different species are determined largely by water masses of different temperature and salinity. Some areas of the ocean have much higher productivity than others. These are concentrated towards the poles and along the boundaries of certain cool currents in otherwise warm water areas. Figure 6.3 provides a generalised map of areas of such concentration, and it is not surprising to find that these regions coincide with concentrations of marine life — fish, squid, seabirds, seals and cetaceans. The great whales require enormous quantities of plankton and other marine organisms to sustain periods of the year when food is scarce. They do this by undertaking often long migrations towards and into polar regions. In these areas in springtime, the longer days with greater hours of sunshine, warmer water temperatures and calmer seas allow phytoplankton to build up, so providing abundant food for predators ranging from zooplankton to marine mammals and to man himself. A seasonal thermocline becomes established during summer in which a middle layer forms between surface and bottom layers of different temperature and specific gravity. Nutrients stirred up from the sea bottom (by tides, etc.) may be trapped within this thermocline. Here they form a food source for planktonic plants that require the light and warmth provided by the surface layers. Such concentrations are referred to as plankton fronts and they may be induced by tides, the meeting of water masses (currents) of different temperature, and changes in the undersea topography either along coasts or along the edge of continental shelves and other deeper water canyons.

Although our understanding of how plankton fronts are formed and maintained is still far from complete, our knowledge has been increased greatly by the new-found ability to identify areas of different water temperature by satellite photography using infra-red techniques (see Holligan 1981; Pingree and Mardell 1981; Pingree *et al.* 1978 for details). Figure 6.4 shows very clearly how upwellings of cold water are revealed, in this case along the shelf break of northwest Europe and where tidally

Figure 6.3 Productive ocean regions of the world (derived from FAO, 1981; and, for Southern Ocean, from Mackintosh, 1973). Note that areas marked as productive are not necessarily of equal productivity. Nevertheless, they indicate regions where cetaceans might concentrate for feeding

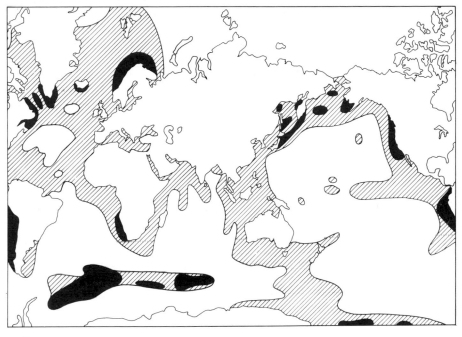

 moderate — high primary productivity

high zooplankton productivity

mixed coastal water meets stratified water north of Ushant. Studies by Patrick Holligan and his colleagues from the Marine Labs in Plymouth have shown that these areas coincide more or less with gradients of surface water temperature and of chlorophyll (a useful index of phytoplankton concentration). In some cases the area of highest productivity may be displaced into the adjacent stratified water, in others it may be concentrated in the mixed waters. The exact positioning of the plankton front is affected by many different factors — winds, tides, and so on, and we are not yet able to predict precisely where it will form or how long it will last.

Concentrations of plankton, if they are reasonably predictable in space and time, might be expected to form focal points for fish predators and, in turn, for seabirds and cetaceans feeding either directly upon the plankton or upon the associated fish. A number of recent studies have shown this both for seabirds (see, for example, Brown 1980) and cetaceans (see Dustan *et al.* 1981). Whaling operations in the Antarctic have identified regions where whales are concentrated and these correspond well to known areas of high krill concentration (see Figure 6.5). Similarly, whaling activities off northwestern Britain in the early part of the present century indicate that whales were concentrated along the shelf edge, usually in the deep waters adjacent to the shelf (Brown 1976). In

Figure 6.4 Satellite imagery of plankton fronts: (a) surface temperature; (b) surface chlorophyll-a (mg/cu. m.); (c) surface nitrate (μg at $1^{-1}N$); (d) infra-red satellite image, August 1976 (the dotted line indicates the continental shelf edge) (from Pingree et ai., 1978). Infra-red satellite photographs have been used recently to detect surface temperature variation. Paler areas indicate lower water temperatures, caused here by upwelling at the continental shelf edge, and in cooler coastal waters. Where those waters meet warmer Atlantic water from the Gulf stream, nutrients come to the surface and a plankton front develops (indicated here by high concentrations of chlorophyll produced by planktonic plants)

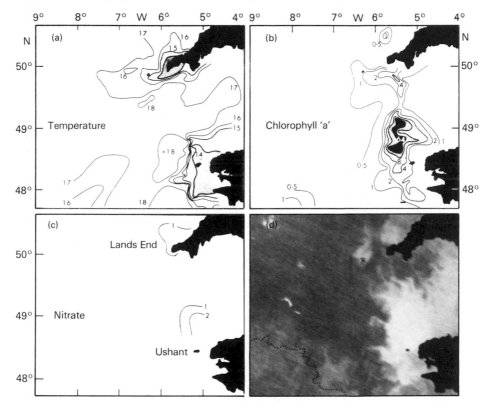

the summer of 1980, we carried out a cruise along the Atlantic seaboard of Britain and Ireland, making transects across the shelf edge and sampling apparent upwelling areas identified by infra-red satellite photography. Almost invariably those areas which were topographically flat had very few cetaceans but where there were discontinuities such as sea mounts, coastal headlands or along the continental shelf edge, cetaceans were most likely to be seen. Figure 6.6 illustrates this for the area where the shelf edge slopes most steeply, off the northwest coast of France. The surface waters at the shelf edge showed much greater variation in temperature, echo-traces showed the steepness of the shelf edge and associated plankton and fish shoals, whilst above water, both seabirds and dolphins were concentrated and observed feeding there. The picture is obviously more complicated than this and we cannot expect a perfect concordance between plankton fronts and concentrations of feeding cetaceans. Nevertheless, we are now some way towards understanding why these animals are not distributed evenly or at random

Figure 6.5 Coincidence of plankton and whale concentrations in Antarctica (adapted from Laws 1985; Mackintosh 1965, 1973). The distribution of whales within the Antarctic ecosystem (as indicated by earlier information from whale catches) is apparently related not only to major environmental boundaries such as the Antarctic Convergence but also the distribution of krill concentrations

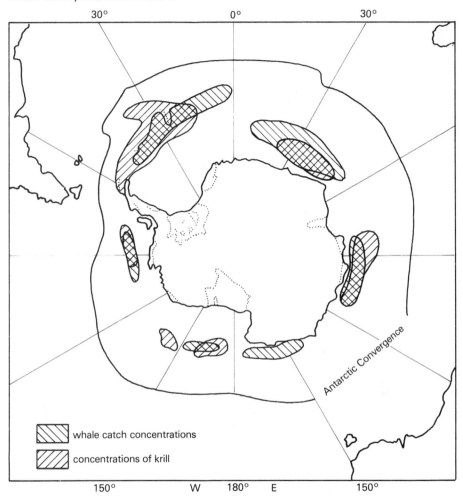

through the sea, and we can make some limited predictions of where they can be expected to be found.

FOOD FINDING

How do whales and dolphins find their food? Movement costs energy and we might expect evolution to have selected for ways to minimise the amount of energy expended. The ways different animals do this are related very much to the type of food they prey upon and its own behaviour.

Whales and dolphins feed mainly upon schooling prey. Often, at least

Figure 6.6 Temperature variation, plankton fronts and dolphin distribution on the continental shelf edge, southwest of Britain (from Evans in press). Changes in sea surface temperature occur at the edge of the continental shelf due to upwelling, which also results in nutrients coming to the surface. These provide conditions for plankton concentrations termed fronts to develop, and this provides food for fish, and other marine animals such as dolphins and seabirds. Cetacean sightings (a), water depth (b), water temperature (c) and echo sounder trace (d), derive from data collected simultaneously during a research cruise southwest of Britain, and west of Brittany, in July 1980

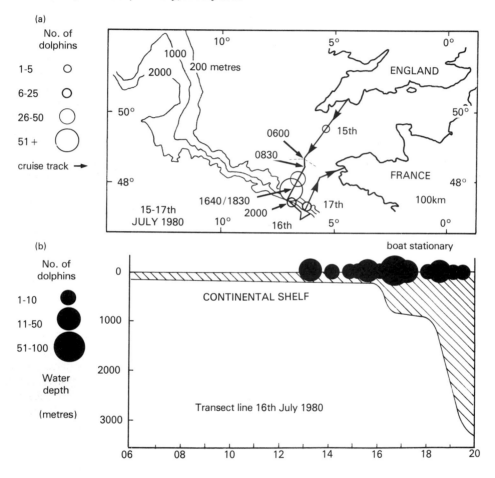

among dolphins, the number of prey individuals is greater than a single animal requires at any one time. Because it is distributed in a clumped manner, for reasons given in the previous section, the main requirement is to find those clumps. This is best achieved by searching in a group since not only can the group members cover a wider area but they can combine their collective experience to assist in finding food. This assumes that the animals will communicate this information to one another (it need not be actively; the mere presence of a vigorously feeding individual may serve to attract its neighbours) and often implies some form of co-operation. Most dolphins and fish- or squid-feeding small whales travel in schools that are broader than they are long (see Plates 8 and 16). In this way they are able to scan acoustically a greater area than would otherwise be

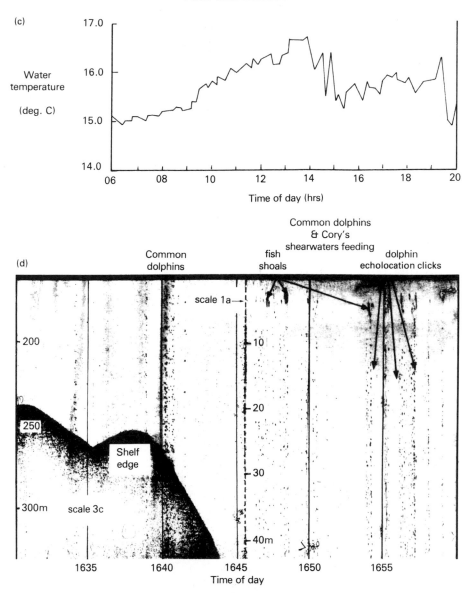

(c)

Water temperature (deg. C)

Time of day (hrs)

(d)

Common dolphins

Common dolphins & Cory's shearwaters feeding

fish shoals

dolphin echolocation clicks

scale 1a

Shelf edge

scale 3c

Time of day

possible. The size of the school is probably determined by the number of individuals that can be sustained by the prey concentration. This could explain why the great whales tend to feed singly or in twos. Their food intake is such that plankton concentrations may rarely be sufficiently large to support a number of animals at any one time. It is probable also that squid rarely exist in sufficient concentrations to support many animals in a small area, and herds of sperm whales, pilot whales and beaked whales usually number less than 100 individuals. In contrast, those dolphins such as common, spinner and spotted dolphins which feed on shoaling fish often number in the hundreds, and occasionally into the thousands. River dolphins generally live in a much more turbid environment, where their small eyes, short-range echolocating system and emphasis on tactility reflect the near-zero visibility. They are unstreamlined in form, swim relatively slowly but are highly manoeuvrable, enabling them to feed semi-solitarily on single prey items living on the bottom (Myrick 1979b).

Various cues may help in food finding. Just as topographical features of the sea bottom may aid the concentration of plankton and fish (as noted above), so they are also likely to be easier to locate. Furthermore, Bill Evans (1971, 1974) from California has demonstrated, through radio-tracking studies, how common dolphins may associate with undersea escarpments which may be as much as 2,000m below the surface and hence beyond the normal diving depths of the dolphins (see Figure 6.7; also Hui 1979). It is thought that the dolphins detect these areas by the increase in ambient sea noise created by an increased density of marine organisms. Presumably echolocation plays an important part for dolphins and other toothed whales, the emission of trains of ultrasonic clicks being used to provide an acoustic picture of the surroundings by their reflection off solid surfaces. Baleen whales tend to dive deeper and, presumably by touch and limited vision, they follow undersea contours, perhaps in contact with one another even over great distances by low frequency repeated sound signals. Even when spread over a wide area of sea as smaller subgroups during food-searching, dolphin schools may dive synchronously and therefore are also likely to be in some form of acoustic contact with one another.

There are a number of cases of cetaceans of different species associating together, and of cetaceans associating with fish (for example in the tuna purse-seine fishery) or seabirds. Although we cannot be certain how these associations are formed and the extent to which they are more than simply coincidental, it does appear that one or both members of the association may derive some benefit. In the eastern tropical Pacific, schools of spotted and spinner dolphins and yellowfin tuna feed on fishes, squid and crabs. Tuna and spotted dolphins feed mainly in the upper layers during the daytime whereas spinner dolphins may feed at lower depths mainly at night. The tuna apparently follow the spotted dolphin schools, possibly benefiting from the echolocation abilities of the dolphins. Both seabirds (such as frigate-birds) and fishermen take advantage of this association, the latter setting a net around the school, knowing that it will at the same time capture the tuna swimming close below or behind (Perrin et al. 1973). In most cases it is likely to be the seabird that makes use of cetacean schools as a cue for finding food, since it has to rely upon only the vicinity of the sea surface for food detection and capture whereas cetaceans are able to dive well below the surface. Often dolphins will pursue fish actually to the surface since it is easier to trap them at the air-sea interface, and this further helps seabirds in their attempts to capture food (see Evans 1982 for a review).

If animals were to remain in one small area, it is likely that before long they would exhaust their food supplies. Thus it is often the case that they visit an area periodically, allowing their prey to recover in the interim. We do not yet have much evidence for whether cetaceans do likewise although it would obviously make good sense if they did. Bernd and Melany Wursig (1977, 1979, 1980) from California have carried out some of the most detailed of all field studies on dolphins (bottle-nosed, dusky and spinner dolphins). They have shown, for example, that dusky dolphins in southern Argentina have bouts of feeding on southern anchovy, mainly in the afternoon hours, interspersed with periods of rest. We have observed similar behaviour in the white-beaked dolphin off the west coast of Scotland. Here they feed primarily in the morning on shoals of mackerel and whiting, with bouts of vigorous feeding activity between periods of rest, followed by regrouping. Diurnal patterns of activity vary between species, and within species between areas depending upon tides, etc. (see Chapter 7). However, its occurrence in bouts and the wide-ranging behaviour of such foraging groups (as determined by recognisably marked individuals) could enable food prey to be replenished. For an excellent general review of foraging strategies by dolphins, the reader should consult Wursig (1986).

Figure 6.7 Movements of radio-tagged common dolphin in association with undersea escarpments, southern California bight (from W.E. Evans, 1971). Note that the movement of radio-tagged individuals and most sightings of feeding schools are concentrated over escarpments and seamounts with relatively fewer sightings in intervening areas of low bottom relief.

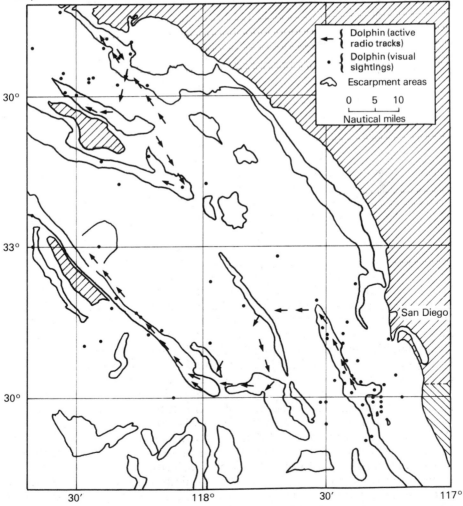

DIET

The actual food of a particular cetacean species depends partly upon its feeding apparatus and partly on aspects of distribution, ecology and feeding behaviour. We have seen earlier, for example, how different sizes and texture of baleen plates will determine the sizes and types of plankton taken by the great whales. I shall now review cetacean diets in relation to their ecology. For further details and sources of reference, the reader should consult Tables 6.1 and 6.2.

Mysticetes or Baleen Whales

In the Antarctic waters of the Southern Ocean, zooplankton exists at very high concentrations (averaging around 105 mg/cu m standing crop — Laws 1985). One species, the Antarctic krill, *Euphausia superba*, is thought to represent one half of this total and is, therefore, the key organism in the Antarctic marine ecosystem (Everson 1984). In those areas all the great whales feed primarily upon this krill species. However, as we have seen in an earlier chapter, whereas those species such as the blue whale which feed almost exclusively upon euphausiids occur right up to the pack ice edge, others such as the sei whale tend not to penetrate so far south and they feed upon a variety of crustaceans including copepods and amphipods. The more tropical Bryde's whale takes only a relatively small amount of plankton, feeding instead primarily upon anchovy and other schooling fish.

In the northern hemisphere, the diets of most baleen whales are more varied, including also copepods and even fish and squid (Table 6.1). There are not only geographical variations in diet for baleen whales, but also seasonal ones. Sometimes of course these are interrelated since some species undergo long distance latitudinal migrations. However, those that make less extensive movements also vary their diet seasonally since outside the summer there is little plankton available to them; at this time, species such as fin and sei whales have to depend upon fish or squid.

Figure 6.8 Plankton food of baleen whales: (a) Thysanoessa *(euphausiid); (b)* Euphausia *(euphausiid); (c)* Calanus *(copepod); (d)* Ampelisca *(amphipod); (e)* Mysis *(mysid)*

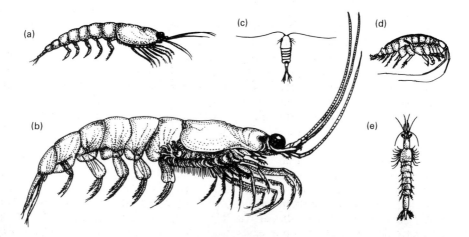

During migration in spring and autumn, gray whales feed at the surface on small fish and shrimp-like mysids (*Acanthomysis sculpta*) instead of upon gammarid amphipods which form their main prey in the Bering and Chukchi Seas in summer; off British Columbia, tubeworms and sessile polychaetes were the most important prey for summering gray whales (Darling 1977, Nerini 1984).

Some species have rather similar diets whatever ocean they are in. The northern and southern right whales, for example, feed particularly upon copepod crustaceans of the genus *Calanus* (as does their Arctic relative, the bowhead). As noted above, the blue whale feeds almost exclusively upon euphausiids. In the Southern Ocean, these are of the genus *Euphausia*, whereas in the North Pacific and North Atlantic they are primarily *Meganyctiphanes* or *Thysanoessa*.

Odontocetes or Toothed Whales

The diet of odontocetes is centred upon fish and/or squid (Table 6.2). Some species eat squid almost exclusively. These include the largest of all the toothed whales, the sperm whale, which in turn may feed upon the largest of all squid, deepwater architeuthids of 12m length or more (Roe 1969). Although offshore feeding appears to be devoted to squid, inshore sperm whales feed more upon fish; animals caught close to the coast of Iceland were found to have fed primarily upon deep-sea fish such as lumpsuckers, red-fish and angler fish that may be found down to 500m depth or more. Pygmy sperm whales and dwarf sperm whales also feed mainly on squid (and octopus), but will take fish and crustaceans such as crabs. Little is known of the diet of most beaked whales although squid, octopus and deep-sea fish appear to be important for those species examined. The diet of the northern bottlenose whale is perhaps the best known. It feeds mainly upon the squid *Gonatus fabricii*, and *Loligo*, and cuttlefish (*Sepia* sp.), though in some areas herring and cod are also important. Both the bottlenose whale and sperm whale need to be deep divers and they can remain below the surface for periods of one hour or more. Adaptations for protracted diving have been described in an earlier chapter.

Both the pilot whales and the false killer whale also prey mainly upon squid, though this may be supplemented in certain areas with fish such as cod or herring. Seasonal movements of long-finned pilot whales towards the coast of Newfoundland have been related to inshore movements of the short-finned squid, *Illex illecobrosus*, and to longer-term fluctuations in numbers (Mercer 1975). Similar population fluctuations are reflected in the Faroese pilot whale catches over the last four centuries which peaked at similar times to when herring spawned on the Faroese coast (herring may not have been fed upon directly by pilot whales but formed the prey of short-finned squid) (Evans and Nettleship 1985), and a similar relationship with squid catches has been shown over a shorter time period (Hoydal 1985).

The white whale and the narwhal both have varied diets. In the St Lawrence Estuary, Canada, the white whale feeds mainly upon capelin and sandeel, although it will also take squid, crustaceans, and possibly nereid worms and gastropod molluscs. Elsewhere in the Barents, White and Kara Seas, white fish such as haddock, cod, arctic cod and herring, Atlantic salmon, arctic char and smelt have all been taken, suggesting

Table 6.1: Diet of mysticetes

Species	Location	Main prey	Source
Blue whale	Northern hemisphere	Euphausiids (*Thysanoessa, Nematoscelis, Meganyctiphanes*) Copepods (*Temora*)	1–5
	Southern hemisphere	Euphausiids (*Euphausia*)	3–7
Fin whale	Northern hemisphere	Euphausiids (*Thysanoessa, Meganyctiphanes, Euphausia*) Copepods (*Calanus*) Fish (*Clupea, Mallotus, Ammodytes, Gadus, Pollachius, Sardinella, Theragra*, various myctophids)	1–5, 8–10
	Southern hemisphere	Euphausiids (*Euphausia, Thysanoessa*)	1, 3–8, 11
Sei whale	Northern hemisphere	Copepods (*Calanus, Eucalanus, Metridia, Temora*) Euphausiids (*Thysanoessa, Euphausia, Meganyctiphanes*) Amphipods (*Parathemisto*) Fish (*Engraulis, Mallotus, Sardinops, Boreogadus, Cololabis, Trachurus, Sardinella, Scomber, Myctophum*) Squid (*Ommastrephes, Loligo, Gonatius*)	1–5, 9, 12–14
	Southern hemisphere	Copepods (*Calanus, Clausocalanus*) Amphipods (*Parathemisto*) Euphausiids (*Euphausia*)	3, 15–17
Bryde's whale	Northern hemisphere	Euphausiids (*Euphausia, Thysanoessa, Nematoscelis*) Fish (*Engraulis, Yarrella, Vinciguerria, Maurolicus, Sardinops*)	12–13, 18–19
	Southern hemisphere	Euphausiids (*Euphausia, Thysanoessa, Pseudoeuphausia, Nyctiphanes*) Fish (*Engraulis, Sardinops, Trachurus, Maurolicus, Lestidium, Clupea, Scomber*)	1–2, 19–20
Minke whale	Northern hemisphere	Fish (*Clupea, Gadus, Mallotus, Eleginus, Boreogadus, Pollachius, Ammodytes*) Euphausiids (*Meganyctiphanes*) Pteropods	1–2, 4, 11, 21–22
	Southern hemisphere	Euphausiids (*Euphausia*)	1–3, 8, 11, 23

Humpback whale	Northern hemisphere	Fish (*Clupea, Mallotus, Gadus, Ammodytes, Osmerus, Pollachius, Engraulis, Sardina, Salmo*) Euphausiids (*Meganyctiphanes, Thysanoessa, Euphausia, Pseudoeuphausia*) Pteropods Mysids (*Mysis*) Decapods (*Pandalus*)	1–2, 4, 9, 24–26
	Southern hemisphere	Euphausiids (*Euphausia, Thysanoessa, Nyctiphanes*)	1–3, 15, 26–27
Gray whale	Northern hemisphere	Amphipods (*Ampelisca, Photis, Anonyx, Atylus, Pontoporeia*) Decapods (*Pachycheles, Fabia, Pleuroncodes, Nephrops*) Polychaetes (*Travisia, Onuphis*) Mysids (*Holmesimysis*) (mainly off Vancouver) Plant material (kelp such as *Laminaria*, and other algae) Clupeid fish	3–4, 28–30
Bowhead whale	Northern hemisphere	Copepods (*Calanus*) Euphausiids (*Thysanoessa*) Mysids (*Mysis, Neomysis*) Amphipods (*Parathemisto*, various gammarids) Isopods (*Saduria*) Pteropods (*Clione, Limacina*)	1–2, 31
Northern right whale	Northern hemisphere	Copepods (*Calanus*) Euphausiids (*Meganyctiphanes, Thysanoessa*)	1–2, 9, 32
Southern right whale	Southern hemisphere	Copepods (*Calanus*) Euphausiids (*Euphausia*)	1–2, 6–7
Pygmy right whale	Southern hemisphere	Copepods (*Calanus*)	33

Reference sources: 1 Gaskin 1976; 2 Gaskin 1982; 3 Nemoto 1959, 1962; 4 Tomilin 1967; 5 Kawamura 1980b; 6 Mackintosh 1965; 7 Mackintosh 1974; 8 Kawamura 1978; 9 Watkins and Schevill 1979; 10 Jonsgard 1966; 11 Ohsumi *et al.* 1970; 12 Nemoto and Kawamura 1977; 13 Rice 1977; 14 Jonsgard and Darling 1977; 15 Kawamura 1970; 16 Kawamura 1974; 17 Best 1967; 18 Kawamura and Satake 1976; 19 Kawamura 1977, 1980a; 20 Best 1977; 21 Evans 1980; 22 Evans 1982; 23 Nemoto 1970; 24 Nishiwaki 1959; 25 Jurasz and Jurasz 1979; 26 Winn and Winn 1985; 27 Chittleborough 1965; 28 Darling 1977a; 29 Nerini 1984; 30 Oliver *et al.* 1984; 31 Lowry and Frost 1984; 32 Watkins and Schevill 1976; 33 Ross *et al.* 1975

Note: There is not space to give an exhaustive list of prey items, but those given above are the major items recorded. They are arranged by group generally in descending order of importance. Reference sources are also not exhaustive but priority is given to more recent reviews to which the reader is referred for the earlier literature. For the common names of some of the more important fishes, see note to Table 6.2.

Table 6.2: Diet of odontocetes

Species	Location	Main prey	Source
Sperm whale	Northern hemisphere	Squid (Histioteuthidae, Onychoteuthidae, Octopoteuthidae Gonatidae, Cranchiidae, Ommastrephidae) and octopus Fish (*Sebastes, Raja, Lophius, Aptocyclus, Cyclopterus, Gadus, Icosteus, Acrotus*)	1–8
	Southern hemisphere	Squid (Histioteuthidae, Onychoteuthidae, Octopoteuthidae, Cranchiidae, Architeuthidae) Fish (*Genypterus, Hoplostethus, Polyprion, Jordanidia, Congridae*)	1–4, 6, 8–9
Pygmy sperm whale	North Atlantic/ Southern Africa	Squid (Neoteuthidae, Octopoteuthidae, Cranchiidae, Ommastrephidae, Histioteuthidae, Loliginidae, Sepiolidae, Sepiidae) and octopus Fish (deep-water, e.g. *Micromesistius*) Decapod crustaceans	10–13
Dwarf sperm whale	North Atlantic/ Southern Africa	Squid (Sepiidae, Octopoteuthidae, Neoteuthidae, Loliginidae, Ommastrephidae, Histioteuthidae) and octopus Fish (deep-water) Decapod crustaceans	10, 12–13
Narwhal	Arctic	Squid Fish (*Raja, Platichthys, Gadus, Boreogadus, Hippoglossus, Reinhardtius, Salmo, Clupea*) Crustaceans (Decapods, Euphausiids)	4, 14
White whale	Arctic	Squid (Ommastrephidae, Loliginidae) Fish (*Cyclopterus, Eleginus, Oncorhynchus, Mallotus, Ammodytes, Melanogrammus, Osmerus, Boreogadus, Salmo, Salvelinus, Coregonus*) Crustaceans (Decapods, Euphausiids) Annelids (Nereis)	1–2, 4, 15

Species	Region	Food	References
Irrawaddy dolphin	North Pacific/Indian Ocean	Fish (e.g. Anarynchidae, Cyprinidae) Crustaceans	16–17
Baird's beaked whale	North Pacific	Fish (*Eleginus, Sebastes, Scomber, Sardinella, Clupea*) Squid (Gonatidae, Onychoteuthidae, Octopoteuthidae) Crustaceans Sea cucumbers (Holothuroidea)	4, 18–19
Northern bottlenose whale	North Atlantic	Squid (Gonatidae, Sepiidae, Loliginidae, Enoploteuthidae, Cranchiidae, Myopsidae, Oegopsidae) Fish (*Clupea, Gadus, Brosmius, Cyclopterus, Sebastes, Reinhardtius, Chimaera, Squalus, Molva, Raja*) Sea stars (Asteroidea) Sea cucumbers (Holothuroidea) Gammarid and decapod crustaceans	1, 2, 4, 13, 20
Southern bottlenose whale	South Atlantic	Small squid (Cranchiidae, Neoteuthidae) Euphausiids	12–13, 21
Tasman beaked whale	Southern hemisphere	Small squid, euphausiids, decapod crustaceans, and fish (*Mercuscius, Serranus, Brotulus*)	21–22
Cuvier's beaked whale	Both hemispheres	Squid (Cranchiidae, Onychoteuthidae, Brachioteuthidae, Enoploteuthidae, Octopoteuthidae, Histioteuthidae) Deep-sea fish	12–13, 21, 23
Mesoplodon beaked whales	Both hemispheres	Squid (Ommastrephidae, Octopoteuthidae, Enoploteuthidae, Neoteuthidae) Deep-sea and mesopelagic fish (e.g. *Lampanyctus, Scopelogadus, Cepola?*)	12–13, 21, 24–26
Melon-headed whale	Both hemispheres	Squid and small fish	25
False killer whale	Both hemispheres	Squid and large fish (e.g. *Seriola, Thunnus*), sometimes dolphins (*Stenella, Delphinus*)	2, 4, 25, 27–28

Table 6.2 (continued)

Species	Location	Main prey	Source
Killer whale	Both hemispheres	Fish (*Salmo, Clupea, Gadus, Scomber, Pleurogrammus, Sardinella, Sarda, Thunnus, Hippoglossus, Myliobatis*) Pinnipeds (*Phoca, Halichoerus, Zalophus, Mirounga, Eumetopias*) Cetaceans (*Phocoenoides, Phocoena, Balaenoptera, Megaptera, Stenella*) Leatherback turtles Squid	2, 4, 29–34
Long-finned pilot whale	Atlantic	Squid (Loliginidae, Ommastrephidae, Histioteuthidae, Onychoteuthidae, Gonatidae, Cranchiidae, Brachioteuthidae, Chiroteuthidae, Sepiidae) and octopus Fish (*Gadus, Scomber, Pollachius, Molva, Dicentrarchus, Sprattus, Conger, Anguilla, Merluccius, Trisopterus, Trachurus, Reinhardtius, Caranx*)	2, 4, 11, 13, 31, 35–6
Short-finned pilot whale	South Africa; Indonesia	Squid (Loliginidae, Cranchiidae, Enoploteuthidae, Octopoteuthidae) and fish	12–13, 24
Rough-toothed dolphin	Tropics	Fish, pelagic octopus, squid, molluscs	37–38
Tucuxi	South Atlantic	Fish (e.g. armoured catfish), decapod and gammarid crustaceans	25, 27
Indo-Pacific/ Atlantic humpbacked dolphins	Both hemispheres	Fish (*Ethmalosa, Mugil, Sardina*) Gammarid crustaceans	39–42

White-beaked dolphin	North Atlantic	Fish (*Clupea, Gadus, Scomber, Merlangius, Mallotus, Trisopterus, Melanogrammus, Pleuronectes, Limanda, Eleginus, Wyperoplus*) Squid and octopus, benthic crustaceans	2, 25, 31
Atlantic white-sided dolphin	North Atlantic	Fish (*Micromesistius, Clupea, Gadus, Scomber, Osmerus, Merluccius*) Squid, gammarid crustaceans	2, 11, 25, 31
Dusky dolphin	South Atlantic	Fish (particularly *Engraulis*) Squid (Onychoteuthidae, Enoploteuthidae)	13, 25, 43
Pacific white-sided dolphin	North Pacific	Fish (*Engraulis, Merluccius, Sardina, Salmo, Cololabis, Trachurus*) Small squid (particularly Loliginidae)	4, 10, 25, 27, 44
Hourglass dolphin	Southern hemisphere	Small fish and small squid	21
Peale's dolphin	Southern hemisphere	Fish, squid (*Loligo*) and octopus, hydroids and algae	21
Fraser's dolphin	Both hemispheres	Fish (*Micromesistius, Trisopterus, Merlangius*) Small squid (*Sepia*) Crustaceans	11, 25, 45
Common dolphin	Both hemispheres	Fish (*Micromesistius, Trisopterus, Merluccius, Trachurus, Sardina, Engraulis, Merlangius, Clupea, Myctophus, Osmerus*) Squid (Loliginidae, Sepiolidae, Sepiidae, Gonatidae, Histioteuthidae)	10–11, 25, 31
Bottle-nosed dolphin	Both hemispheres	Fish (*Mugil, Anguilla, Engraulis, Phoxinus, Micromesistius, Trisopterus, Clupea, Gadus, Scomber, Corvina, Brevoortia*) Squid (Ommastrephidae, Loliginidae, Sepiidae, Lycoteuthidae)	4, 10–13, 21, 41
Risso's dolphin	Both hemispheres	Squid (Ommastrephidae, Sepiidae, Histioteuthidae, Loliginidae) and octopus Fish (at least occasionally)	4, 11–13, 27

Table 6.2 (continued)

Species	Location	Main prey	Source
Spotted dolphin	Both hemispheres	Fish (*Engraulis, Anguilla, Decapterus, Selar, Clupea, Trachurus,* Exocoetidae) Squid (Onychoteuthidae, Ommastrephidae, Enoploteuthidae)	10, 13, 46
Striped dolphin	Both hemispheres	Fish (*Diaphus, Erythocles, Micromesistius, Trisopterus, Gadiculus, Merluccius, Merlangius, Trachurus, Atherina*) Squid (Ommastrephidae, Chiroteuthidae, Loliginidae, Histioteuthidae) Decapod crustaceans (*Bentheogennema*)	10–11, 47
Spinner/clymene dolphins	Both hemispheres	Fish (Myctophidae, Exocoetidae) Squid (Enoploteuthidae, Ommastrephidae, Onychoteuthidae)	10, 13, 45, 48
Southern right-whale dolphin	Southern hemisphere	Fish (Myctophidae, *Macruronus*) Squid (Loliginidae, Gonatidae, *Nototodaris*)	21, 49–50
Northern right-whale dolphin	North Pacific	Fish (*Leuroglossus, Diaphus, Tryphoturus, Ceratoscopelus, Tarletonbeania, Lampanyctus, Cololabis*) Squid	10, 51
Heaviside's dolphin	Southern Africa	Bottom-dwelling fish Squid	11, 26
Hector's dolphin	New Zealand	Fish (*Physiculus, Engraulis, Trachurus, Crepatalus*) Squid	52–53
Black dolphin	South Pacific	Fish (*Engraulis, Sardina,* probably many other species) Squid	21
Commerson's dolphin	South Atlantic	Fish (*Sprattus, Engraulis,* Atherinidae) Squid (Loliginidae) and octopus Mysids, Isopods, Tunicates	13, 21

Harbour porpoise	Northern hemisphere	Fish (*Clupea, Ammodytes, Sprattus, Scomber, Sardina, Micromesistius, Trisopterus, Merluccius, Trachurus, Pollachius, Merlangius*) Squid (Loliginidae, Ommastrephidae)	11, 31, 54–55
Burmeister's porpoise	South Atlantic	Fish (*Merluccius, Pagrus*) Squid, Mysids, Euphausiids	21, 56
Vaquita	Gulf of California	Fish (*Orthopristis, Bairdiella*) Squid	57
Dall's porpoise	North Pacific	Fish (Myctophidae, *Cololabis, Merluccius, Clupea, Trachurus*) Squid	58–59
Finless porpoise	North Pacific	Small fish and squid, decapod crustaceans	25
Indus/ Ganges susu	Indo-Pakistan	Fish (catfish), molluscs and decapod crustaceans	60
Boto	South America	Fish (catfish, characins, cichlids) Possibly crustaceans and molluscs	25
Baiji	China	Fish (catfish, and large-scaled fish)	25
Franciscana	South America	Fish (*Engraulis, Cynoscion, Porichthys, Trachurus, Polyclemus*) Squid, octopus and decapod crustaceans	61

Reference sources: 1 Gaskin 1976; 2 Gaskin 1982; 3 Berzin 1972; 4 Tomilin 1967; 5 R. Clarke 1956; 6 M.R. Clarke 1980; 7 Roe 1969; 8 Kawakami 1980; 9 Best *et al.* 1984; 10 Fitch and Brownell 1968; 11 Desportes 1985; 12 Ross 1984; 13 M.R. Clarke 1986; 14 Finley and Gibb 1982; 15 Gurevich 1980; 16 Tin Thein 1977; 17 Leatherwood *et al.* 1984b; 18 Kasuya 1986; 19 Nishiwaki and Oguro 1971; 20 Benjaminsen and Christensen 1979; 21 Goodall and Galeazzi 1985; 22 Mead and Payne 1975; 23 Nishiwaki and Oguro 1972; 24 Leatherwood *et al.* 1976; 25 Leatherwood *et al.* 1983; 26 Mead 1981; 27 Mitchell 1975a,b; 28 Kasuya 1985b; 29 Nishiwaki and Handa 1958; 30 Condy *et al.* 1978; 31 Evans 1980; 32 Lopez and Lopez 1985; 33 Handcock 1965; 34 Whitehead and Glass 1985; 35 Sergeant 1962; 36 Mercer 1975; 37 Perrin and Walker 1975; 38 Layne 1965; 39 Busnel 1973; 40 Cadenat 1959; 41 Saayman and Tayler 1973; 42 Northridge and Pilleri 1985; 43 Wursig and Wursig 1980; 44 Walker *et al.* 1986; 45 Robinson and Craddock 1983; 46 Perrin *et al.* 1973; 47 Miyazaki *et al.* 1973; 48 Perrin *et al.* 1981; 49 Baker 1981; 50 Torres *et al.* 1979; 51 Leatherwood and Walker 1979; 52 Baker 1978; 53 Baker 1983; 54 Rae 1965; 55 Smith and Gaskin 1974; 56 Brownell and Praderi 1982; 57 Brownell 1983; 58 Wilke and Nicholson 1958; 59 McAlister 1981; 60 Jones 1982; 61 Fitch and Brownell 1971

Table 6.2 (continued)

Note: Details of prey items are given for those species that have been examined in some detail. If a cetacean species is absent from the above list, it is because the diet of that species has not been examined. The list of prey is given generally in descending order of importance. However, it should be noted that many odontocetes are probably opportunistic feeders with catholic diets so that information collected to date, on the variety and importance of particular food species, is dependent on the sampling location and the season.

To help the reader, a list of common names of the more important fish prey of cetaceans is given below:

Family:

Squalidae (spiny sharks) *Squalus*, spurdog
Rajidae (skates and rays) *Raja*, skate
Myliobatidae (stingrays) *Myliobatis*, eagle ray
Chimaeridae (rat-fishes) *Chimaera*, rat-fish
Clupeidae (herrings) *Clupea*, herring; *Sprattus*, sprat; *Sardina*, pilchard; *Sardinops*, *Sardinella*, sardine; *Brevoortia*, menhaden
Engraulidae (anchovies) *Engraulis*, anchovy
Salmonidae (salmon) *Salmo*, *Oncorhynchus*, salmon; *Salvelinus*, arctic char
Osmeridae (smelts) *Osmerus*, smelt; *Mallotus*, capelin
Cyprinidae (carps) *Phoxinus*, minnow
Myctophidae (lantern fish) *Myctophus*, *Diaphus*, *Tarletonbeania*, lantern fish
Congridae (eels) *Anguilla*, eel; *Conger*, conger eel
Scombresocidae (sauries) *Cololabis*, saury
Atherinidae (sand-smelts/silversides) *Atherina*, sand-smelt
Trachichthidae (berycoids) *Hoplostethus*, rough-fish
Carangidae (horse/Jack mackerels) *Trachurus*, *Decapterus*, scads
Sparidae (sea-breams) *Pagrus*, red porgy
Mullidae (red mullets) *Mullus*, red mullet
Mugilidae (grey mullets) *Liza*, *Mugil*, mullet
Cepolidae (band-fish) *Cepola*, band-fish
Ammodytidae (sandeels) *Ammodytes*, *Hyperoplus*, sandeel
Scombridae (mackerels) *Scomber*, mackerel

Thunnidae (tunnies) *Thunnus*, albacore, yellow fin, and blackfish tuna; *Sarda*, bonito
Acinaceidae (king-fish) *Jordanidia*, king-fish
Serranidae (sea perches) *Polyprion*, groper; *Serranus*, comber
Percichthyidae (sea basses) *Dicentrarchus*, bass
Ophidiidae (cusk eels) *Genypterus*, cusk eel
Scorpaenidae (rock-fish or red-fish) *Sebastes*, rock-fish
Sciaenidae (drums/croakers) *Bairdiella*, gulf croaker; *Cynoscion*, weakfish
Hexagrammidae (greenlings) *Pleurogrammus*, atka mackerel; *Ophiodon*, ling cod
Cottidae (gobies) *Myoxocephalus*, goby
Cyclopteridae (lumpsuckers) *Cyclopterus*, lumpsucker
Gadidae (cod fishes) *Gadus*, cod; *Boreogadus*, polar cod; *Trisopterus*, poor cod, Norway pout; *Pollachius*, saithe/pollack; *Theragra*, walleye/Alaska pollack; *Molva*, ling; *Eleginus*, navaga; *Gadiculus*, silvery pout; *Micromesistius*, blue whiting/poutassou; *Melanogrammus*, haddock; *Merlangius*, whiting
Merlucciidae (hakes) *Merluccius*, hake
Icosteidae (ragfish) *Acrotus*, brown ragfish
Lophiidae (angler fish) *Lophius*, angler fish
Pleuronectidae (flatfishes) *Pleuronectes*, plaice; *Platichthys*, flounder; *Limanda*, sole/dab; *Hippostromus*, halibut; *Reinhardtius*, Greenland halibut

that the species has a catholic diet, feeding mainly on shallow water fish (Gaskin 1982: 33–5). The narwhal also feeds on bottom-living shallow water organisms, including flounder, arctic cod and crustaceans, as well as squid.

The killer whale is the only species which regularly will feed upon other warm-blooded animals. Although observed feeding upon marine birds such as penguins and marine mammals such as Californian and southern sea-lions, elephant seals, Dall's and harbour porpoise, and large baleen whales, their reputation for doing so is probably exaggerated. For most populations, the diet appears to be primarily fish such as salmon and cod, and also squid, although doubtless their food varies between regions depending upon local availability.

Some small odontocetes are confined more or less to coastal regions and this influences the prey types that they feed upon. Thus the phocoenids (true porpoises) take small schooling fish that often spawn in coastal waters. In the case of the harbour porpoise, these include sprats, sandeel, cod, herring, whiting, mackerel, pollack, capelin and sardines (usually 10–30cm length). They will also take squid such as *Loligo* and *Illex* when available. They may also feed at some depth, having been taken in gill nets at 45–50 fathoms in the Bay of Fundy (D. Gaskin personal communication). Dall's porpoise are less closely associated with the coast, being found sometimes 100km offshore. They probably can dive to quite great depths, and feed upon squid, and fish from a variety of water depths, including herring, Jack mackerel, saury, hake and various other pelagic and deep-water benthic fish. The finless porpoise of the coastal Indo-Pacific feeds on prawns and shrimps, small squid and fish.

River dolphins obviously have a diet restricted to those forms that occur in a riverine (or estuarine) habitat. The boto of the Amazon and Orinoco is thought to feed on armoured or heavily scaled fish which it seizes with the front part of the beak and then moves backwards to the rear of the mouth where they are crushed with the help of its large somewhat molar shaped rear teeth. Cichlids, armoured catfish and characins have been obtained from their stomachs, and molluscs and crustaceans may also be taken. The franciscana or La Plata dolphin is less restricted to a riverine habitat and may be found along coastal waters in South America. Its diet is consequently more varied and includes squid, octopus, shrimp, and a variety of fish. Other river dolphins such as the Indus and Ganges susus are poorly known but their diet is thought to consist primarily of fish, molluscs and crustaceans.

The pelagic dolphins, for example of the genera *Delphinus* and *Stenella*, are wide-ranging in most warm temperate to tropical regions of the world. It is therefore not surprising to find that they are very opportunistic feeders and their diets can vary greatly between regions and at different seasons of the year. In many cases, lantern fish of the family Myctophidae are important and these are thought to be taken mainly at night when they move upwards towards the surface. Squid may also be taken, particularly at night, and have been found to be important for both spotted and spinner dolphins in the tropical Atlantic and eastern Pacific. Off southern California, common dolphins feed particularly upon squid and anchovy during winter, but during spring and summer they apparently switch to lantern fish and smelt (Leatherhead *et al.* 1983). In the Northeast Atlantic, common dolphins feed upon fish and squid throughout the year, but squid (of the genus *Loligo*) were more important in winter. Fish were mainly gadoids, particularly blue whiting, hake and codfish of the genus *Trisopterus*, and horse mackerel, captured mainly at 100–200m depth (Collet 1981, Desportes 1985). Shrimp may also be important in the diet of some delphinids, particularly the striped dolphin off the coast of Japan where the semi-pelagic species *Bentheogennema borealis* appears to be taken in considerable numbers (Miyazaki *et al.* 1973).

Dolphin species of the genus *Lagenorhynchus* have more temperate distributions and so their prey are also cooler water forms. Thus the white-beaked dolphin feeds upon pelagic fish such as cod, herring, whiting, mackerel, capelin and haddock, as well as octopus and squid, and sometimes also benthic crustaceans. Atlantic white-sided dolphins whose distribution almost completely overlaps the previous species, have a similar diet including herring, mackerel and squid, but take generally more offshore forms such as blue whiting. The Pacific white-sided dolphin also feed on a variety of fish, including anchovy and hake, and squid. Its southern hemisphere counterpart, the dusky dolphin, also takes anchovy (the southern form) and squid. The diets of the hourglass and Peale's dolphins are little known, but the Fraser's dolphin feeds upon squid, crustaceans and deep-sea fish that are captured near the surface at night.

As further studies are carried out, it is likely that the number of species of fish and squid found in the diet of many delphinid species will be extended considerably. Some prey species will have greater energy and nutrient contents than others and it is possible that dolphins select for these when available. They may also have different energy requirements at different times of the year, associated for example with breeding. However, on the whole, we may expect those species to have generalist diets upon pelagic fish and squid within a certain size range, captured in the middle or upper layers of the water column.

Bottle-nosed dolphins also feed on a wide variety of prey. In offshore regions these include pelagic fish (such as blue whiting and codfish in the Northeast Atlantic) and squid. In coastal waters, they feed upon various shallow water benthic fish (in the North Atlantic these include mullet, catfish and eels) as well as upon shrimps and other crustaceans. Since they have a wide distribution around the world, their diet will obviously vary from region to region. In the coastal waters of the Indian Ocean, for example, various benthic and coral reef-dwelling fish are taken, although in areas where species of mullet occur, they appear to be important prey. The two species of hump-backed dolphin have similar habitat preferences, being coastal in shallow waters. They have rather similar diets to the bottle-nosed dolphin, feeding upon mullet and various clupeid fish, often over coral reefs. The tucuxi also has a coastal range, in South and Central America. It feeds upon various fish (for example armoured catfish, in Surinam), prawns and crabs. In a similar coastal habitat in the Indo-Pacific, the Irrawaddy dolphin takes demersal or benthic fish and crustaceans.

Risso's dolphins are primarily squid feeders although they probably also take pelagic and demersal fish. Similar diets are suggested for other poorly known pelagic dolphins, such as the rough-toothed dolphin and melon-headed whale. The few stomachs that have been examined indicate that they feed mainly upon squid, octopus and pelagic fish.

FEEDING METHODS

In an earlier section we saw how the feeding apparatus of baleen and toothed whales determines the type of food and methods of capture that they adopt. We shall now examine feeding methods of different species in more detail.

Mysticetes or Baleen Whales

As noted earlier, baleen whales capture food by two basic methods — gulping (used by most rorqual species) and skimming (used by right whales and the sei whale). However, there are a number of elaborations upon these basic patterns. The gray whale, which feeds primarily upon the ocean floor, turns on its side (usually the right side) and swims forwards with the head forced through the top layer of the sediment. In this position it is able to scoop or suck up mud or gravel containing invertebrate prey (Figure 6.9). The whale then surfaces and, straining these sediments through its stiff baleen plates, it collects and swallows the gammarid amphipods upon which it feeds. The mud plumes that trail behind the feeding whales are often spotted by seabirds such as horned puffins, arctic terns and glaucous gulls and they feed upon those crustaceans that have escaped the baleen during the straining process. During feeding, the gray whale makes a scrape of 1–5m depth in the ocean floor which persists for some time. It has been suggested that by making these scrapes, the whale may actually be increasing the productivity of these areas and hence is effectively 'ploughing' the ocean. For a general review of gray whale feeding, the reader should consult Nerini (1984); other important recent publications include Bogoslovskaya et al. (1981), Darling (1977a), Hudnall (1981), Murison et al. (1984), Nerini and Oliver (1983), Oliver et al. (1984), Wursig, Wells and Croll, (1986).

Humpback whales use a variety of feeding methods (see Jurasz and Jurasz 1979 for a review; also Dolphin and McSweeney 1981; Hain et al. 1982). One method, referred to as bubble-net feeding, is used when the species encounters swarms of krill. One or two animals spiral upwards and emit air in the form of a train of bubbles from the blowhole (Figure 6.10; also Winn and Winn 1985:39). These bubbles form a circular net or curtain that may serve to herd the crustaceans into the centre of the ring (which may be as great as 30m in diameter though usually less than 10m). That this form of feeding actually concentrates krill has been suggested by Sylvia Earle (1979) in Alaska where she found that krill numbers within the bubble-nets during 15-second plankton tows ranged between 850 and 1,100 krill; this contrasted with 0–4 krill in surface tows adjacent and further away from the bubble-nets. One difficulty is to distinguish this from the possibility that higher concentrations within bubble-nets may simply reflect the selection by humpbacks of areas with higher prey density. Either way, this method of feeding is clearly successful at containing large numbers of krill, and different methods have been shown to be used under different conditions of prey type, density and water depth (see Dolphin and McSweeney 1981).

Other methods of humpback feeding are also thought to serve to concentrate or panic their prey. In the method referred to as flick-feeding,

Figure 6.9 Gray whale mud-skimming. Top: gray whales are believed to roll onto their sides and skim the muddy bottom of the sea, sucking up benthic gammarid amphipods. Bottom: they can also feed by surface skimming when capturing fish or squid, and by engulfing plankton swarms such as mysids, sometimes making use of tidal rips (shown from above)

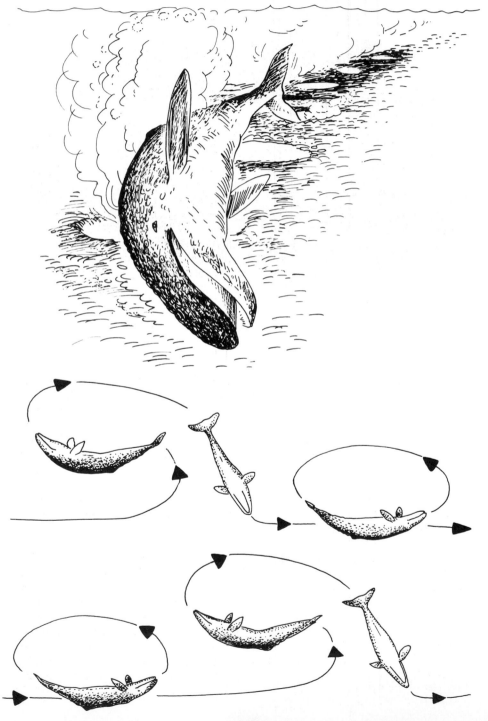

Figure 6.10 Bubble-net feeding by humpback whale. The whale blows a series of bubbles by releasing air underwater. These form a circular net, in the centre of which it surfaces, with mouth open to scoop up entrapped prey

the humpback dives but as it does so, it flicks the massive tail forwards generating a wave above it which it then passes through with mouth open. The production of this wave appears to concentrate the euphausiids. Particularly when feeding upon shoaling fish such as herring and capelin, humpbacks engage in a third method, termed lunge-feeding. Two or more may engage in this activity, apparently co-operatively since they do so in unison. Each animal lunges towards and through the surface with greatly distended throats and open jaws, landing on its belly, sides, or even on its back. If the shoals are not very large, as may be the case with herring, humpbacks may synchronously make long vertical dives in a linear fashion, herding the fish before engaging in lunging behaviour.

Fin whales also vary their feeding behaviour depending upon the nature and density of prey species. David Gaskin (1976, 1982) in Canada has described how fin whales may herd swarming euphausiids and schools of mackerel and herring. In those circumstances, they typically ascend gradually and just before breaking the surface, roll usually to the right with the mouth open. Turning sharply the whale appears to drive the euphausiids and fish across its path so enabling it to scoop them up with a final feeding lunge. At other times, fin whales may simply approach the fish school from behind, then just below the surface and at the last moment, open the mouth wide with distended throat to engulf their prey (Watkins and Schevill 1979).

Side- and lunge-feeding are also adopted by other rorqual species including blue, sei and minke whales, using similar methods to those described above (Watkins and Schevill 1979). Often the surface is used to trap the fish or plankton with lateral rolls or sudden lunges. When feeding upon dispersed shoals, minke and Bryde's whales often quarter the area back and forth forcing their prey close to the surface and then taking them with open mouth.

Bowhead and right whales feed primarily by skimming with their mouths open through surface concentrations of plankton (Lowry and Frost 1984; Watkins and Schevill 1976). These feeding bouts are short, the whales frequently stopping to clean debris such as weed from the baleen with the tongue. In right whales, a characteristic rattling sound is apparently produced by the lapping of water over the partially sub-merged baleen plates (Watkins and Schevill 1976). Subsurface feeding has also been observed, with whales swimming with open mouths up to 10m (possibly more) below the surface (see also Pivorunas 1979). Usually feeding occurs singly but if the concentration is sufficiently great they may feed alongside one another. Observations in the Beaufort Sea by Mark Fraker and Bernd Wursig (1981) have shown up to 14 bowhead whales moving in V-formation. Occasionally during these feeding actions, bowheads have beeen seen to swim on their sides with their mouths open wide near the sea surface. Bowheads also adopt other modes of feeding (see Wursig et al. 1984a,b, 1986a). These include feeding on or close to the bottom, stirring up clouds of mud like gray whales do, and then forcing this through their mouths as they come to the surface. Water column feeding also takes place in which whales dive and surface in almost the same place, either singly or in groups numbering up to ten individuals. As is the case for other species, these dives are often very synchronous even over a large area. Finally, bowheads have been seen swimming in straight tracks in shallow water, stirring the muddy bottom with their large tails. Fraker and Wursig term this 'mud tracking'.

Odontocetes or Toothed Whales

Whereas baleen whales tend to feed more or less independently or co-operatively singly or in dispersed groups (possibly maintained by long-distance acoustic communication), some odontocetes are thought to co-operate in large, concentrated groups, herding particularly shoaling pelagic fish. Whilst searching for food, many dolphin species move in tight schools that are distributed over a large area, possibly in acoustic or visual (by breaching) contact with one another, and using broad-band echolocation clicks to find fish shoals. Once found, they spread out; some individuals dive down to the school and herd it to the surface by swimming around and under the fish in an ever-tightening formation. In the case of at least dusky dolphins, the larger the group the more effective it is thought to be in herding fish, and feeding may continue for two or three hours (Wursig and Wursig 1980). Of course such behaviour will depend also upon the size of the fish shoal and its own behaviour. The fish shoal is often forced to the surface where individuals may be seen flying through the air to escape capture. As with the method employed by many baleen whales, the water surface serves as a wall, and hence probably helps to prevent their escape. The dolphins may also project loud sounds and trains of echo-clicks which could serve to further bunch the fish and even appears to stun some (Norris and Mohl 1981). Nevertheless, they probably capture individual prey items.

Herding and crisscrossing behaviour has been observed in spotted and spinner dolphins, common dolphins, dusky, white-beaked and bottle-nosed dolphins, and probably occurs also in other delphinids (see Norris and Dohl 1980b for a general review). Three main types of food herding that we have observed in white-beaked dolphins off the west coast of Scotland are illustrated in Figure 6.12. As with studies of other herding dolphin species, it is very difficult to be certain that the action is co-operative, or if it is organised by particular individuals. However, our observations of the synchrony of movement including dives and surface rushes, and the disbanding of groups after vigorous feeding followed by their re-grouping before a further feeding action suggest that they are co-operative. Certainly the results are very effective, and I have often witnessed very tight shoals of fish at the surface, with individual fish lying on the surface in an apparent state of shock immediately on completion of a frenzied feeding activity. Communication between individuals may occur by various whistles since vocal activity is often great at this time. It may also result from repeated breaching, elaborate somersaults and tail slapping, although these probably function pri-marily to corral or panic the fish.

Some species use sloping sandy shores to trap their prey. On the west coast of Africa, Mauritanian fishermen actually co-operate with bottle-

Figure 6.11 Method of fish capture by toothed whales. Fish shoals may be trapped against a wall formed by the water surface, and then picked off individually

Figure 6.12 Food-herding by white-beaked dolphins. Three typical methods of food herding used by white-beaked dolphins off the west coast of northern Britain in summer: (a) small groups of dolphins converge by porpoising on a single area, and this serves to bunch the fish shoals together; (b) a group steadily moves in U-shaped formation in the direction of a smaller number of individuals, apparently trapping the herded fish shoal in so doing; (c) the group 'surface-rushes' alongside one another in a wide band over a short distance, and other dolphins converge on them to trap the fish shoal. In the final stages of herding, the fish apparently panic and scatter in all directions, to be picked off by dolphins and northern gannets that have been attracted to the area

(a)

(b)

(c)

nosed and Atlantic hump-backed dolphins to capture mullet (Busnel 1973). The dolphins herd the fish into shallow water. Fishermen then place gill nets among the fish, allowing the dolphins to feed at the same time. The dolphins even respond to the slapping of the water with sticks, as a cue to food. Similar co-operative feeding has been reported for the harbour porpoise and California sea lion in Monterey Bay (Fink 1959).

Killer whales also commonly hunt co-operatively. When feeding in tidal rips upon salmon, they have been observed herding the fish, slapping the surface with their flippers or tail flukes and making squeals or ratchet-like whistling sounds. After long whistles and honks, they converge on their prey, trapping them between the shore and the rushing tide (for herding methods, see, for example, Condy et al. 1978; Lopez and Lopez 1985; Martinez and Klinghammer 1970; Norris and Prescott 1961). Other larger prey have also been seen herded by killer whales. These include elephant seals, California and southern sea lions, grey seals and walruses (Plate 12). In one instance off the west coast of Britain, a small group of killer whales were observed trying to corral a group of grey seals and their pups, and in another the male killer was seen capturing a grey seal and then, on killing it, leaving it to the other group members before returning to feed (Evans 1980). Such behaviour is relatively sophisticated and suggests a level of co-operation as developed as that exhibited amongst various primates. We shall return to this in the next chapter.

Some toothed whales hunt either singly or in small groups. This includes some of the squid feeders such as the sperm whale and beaked whales of the genus *Mesoplodon*, although bottlenose whales and pilot whales, which both feed primarily upon squid, often feed in large groups co-ordinated possibly by particular whistles made in different contexts. Actual food capture has not been observed in most of these species but the Russian cetologists, Bel'kovich and Yablokov (1963) and Berzin (1972) have suggested that sperm whales may stun their prey using sonar. In that species, the spermaceti organ may function as a reverberation chamber to produce the burst-pulse signals (Norris and Harvey 1972). Norris and Mohl (1981) have speculated that other odontocetes may use sonar to stun prey. They support this by field observations of immobilised fish amongst feeding dolphins (which, amongst other people, I have also witnessed at the end of frenzied feeding activity); and by experiments using similar sounds that have immobilised captive fish and squid. Recently this possibility was tested on guppies by Zagaeski (1983) from Boston University by discharging high energy sound pulses at them. The result was a transient loss in their orienting ability for about 15 minutes though only when their pulses were slightly above the maximum reported for bottle-nosed dolphins. Although the evidence is not yet conclusive, this promises to be an interesting area of study.

Coastal species such as the harbour porpoise, hump-backed dolphins and often the bottle-nosed dolphin usually hunt in small groups or even singly, although if there is a large amount of food they may form a loose aggregation. In these circumstances they still tend to feed semi-independently, and this may reflect the density of their prey and their schooling behaviour.

ENERGY BUDGETS

Animals need energy to move, grow and maintain various life processes. As noted above, this is essentially provided by food. However, food varies in quality depending upon the species or group whilst the energy required by an individual may vary depending upon the stage in its life cycle. We should, therefore, look at the balance between energy inputs and outputs that an individual should experience at any point in time. Such a budget or balance sheet is not simple to calculate and we are still relatively far from achieving an accurate one for any animal species.

To give some idea of the complexities contained in calculating a realistic energy budget, I shall briefly go through an idealised budget for cetaceans and those factors that need to be taken into account. Energy comes primarily in the form of food; some compounds may possibly also enter by absorption through the skin from sea water but if this occurs it is likely to make only a very small contribution (Gaskin 1982: 82–3). Some types of food have a higher energy content than others, depending upon the relative amounts of protein, fat (lipid), carbohydrate, water and other materials such as cellulose or chitin (Table 6.3). The calorific values (a measure of energy content) of plankton such as euphausiids, and many pelagic fish are around 4–10 kJoules (0.96–2.39 kcal) per g body weight. The corresponding values for squid are rather lower at about 3–3.5 kJoules (0.72–0.84 kcal) per g body weight. This implies that more energy per unit body weight could be obtained by feeding upon fish or plankton than upon squid. However, these are potential maximum energy values obtainable and they will depend also upon the digestibility of the food. Fish protein has high digestibility whereas chitin present in

Table 6.3: Energy contents of plankton, squid and fish

Animal Group	Family	No. of species	PER CENT WET WEIGHT			Calorific Value (kJ per g.)	Source
			Water	Protein	Lipid		
Plankton	Euphausiidae	1	76–80	10–11	2.4–6.3	4.2–4.5	1, 2
	Mysidae	1			4.2	3	
	Amphipodidae	1			3.8	3	
Cephalopoda	Loliginidae	5	74–184	16–19	0.3–1.3	2.9–4.7	4, 5
	Octopodidae	2	80–81	15–18	0.5–0.75	2.9–3.4	5
	Ommastrephidae	6	76–80	16–21	0.3–3.0	3.1–4.5	5
	Onychoteuthidae	3	79	18	0.7	1.4–4.0	4, 5
	Sepiidae	3–4	78–82	16–19	0.7–0.8	3.0–3.5	5
	Gonatidae	1				3.8	6
Fish	Myctophidae	?			8–14	5.6–8.0	2
	Nototheriidae	?			0.9–2.3	4.1	2
	Clupeidae	2	61–69	15–20	7.5–20	6.7–12.1	5, 7–8
	Salmonidae	2	67–78	17.5–22	0.5–14	7	
	Osmeridae	1	78.5	15	3.5	4.2	5
	Gadidae	4	73–84	14–20	0.1–5.0	4.1–7.1	7
	Ammodytidae	2	63.5	19.5 7–9	5.8–7.3	5.7–8	
	Scombridae		62	16	18.5	10.3	5

Reference sources: 1 Clarke (1980); 2 Clarke and Prince (1980); 3 Cummins and Wuycheck (1971); 4 Croxall and Prince (1982); 5 Montevecchi et al. (1984); 6 Clarke et al. (1985); 7 Murray and Burt (1969); 8 Harris (1984).

Note: Lipid levels (and consequently calorific values) may vary both between species within a family and within a species depending on their size and the time of year. Thus, pre-spawning young and post-spawning squid are likely to have higher calorific values compared with post-spawning young and pre-spawning old individuals; gravid female euphausiids have calorific contents of 5.45kJ per g compared with 3.84kJ per g for mature males. Amongst fish, calorific values of adults range from 3.3–4.6kJ per g wet weight for cod (*Gadua morhua*), 4.1kJ per g for whiting (*Merlangius merlangus*) through 5.1kJ per g for saithe (*Pollachius virens*), and 7.1kJ per g for rockling (*Ciliata* sp.) (all Gadidae), to 9.2kJ per g for herring (*Clupea harengus*) and 10.9kJ per g for sprat (*Sprattus sprattus*) (both Clupeidae). Furthermore, whereas the last value applies to mature sprat over 100mm length, calorific contents for sprat of 40–90mm length are 6.7kJ per g, and 5.6kJ per g for larval sprat. Likewise, larval sandeel (*Ammodytes* sp.) have calorific values of 5.8kJ per g compared with 6.5kJ per g when mature (over 60mm length). Capelin (*Mallotus villosus*) calorific contents average around 4.2kJ per g, but vary from c. 3.8kJ per g at the end of winter to 6.7kJ per g in late summer (see text).

Chemical composition as expressed above excludes per cent ash and residues such as chitin and carbohydrate, but together these generally amount to only 1–5 per cent.

euphausiids makes them relatively indigestible. Furthermore, some fish have higher calorific contents due to differences in the amount of fat they contain. Thus the calorific value of adult sprat is about two and a half times that of whiting or capelin (see footnote to Table 6.3). Even within a species its calorific value may vary greatly. The overall weight of a fish increases, approximately, as the cube of the length so that an adult fish might be twice its juvenile length but have an overall calorific content 20–30 times that of the juvenile stage (a 60mm sprat may contain c. 10 kJoules of energy but one of 140mm length c. 200–300 kJoules — Harris 1984: 120–1). Lipid levels may also vary between winter and summer, so that the same adult individual at the end of a summer feeding can have lipid levels of 15–16 per cent compared with 2.5 per cent at the end of the winter (Stoddard 1968).

The total energy consumed in a day by a cetacean will depend upon not only the calorific content of its prey but also the number and size of the individuals eaten. To determine this requires knowledge of the feeding rates of cetaceans. David Sergeant (1969) from Canada obtained theoretical estimates based on heart-body weight ratios, and found that feeding rates varied inversely with body weight within the range of 4–13 per cent of body weight. The smallest species such as the harbour porpoise should require about 13 per cent its body weight, whilst above about 600kg the food requirement remained more or less constant so that most large rorquals required 4–6 per cent their body weight. Although the relationship is probably broadly true, these calculations made a number of unrealistic assumptions and, since then, studies by Paul Brodie in Canada and Christina Lockyer in the UK have revised them downwards. It now appears that the large baleen whales may consume only around 1.5–2 per cent of their body weight daily on average through the year, though this is still essentially a theoretical estimate and has not been verified.

One of the problems with calculating energy budgets is to distinguish between estimates derived theoretically (which may represent optimum values) and those that actually occur in the wild, which may be some way below (or above) the expected values. The long-term energy requirements may vary so that food intake is higher than would be necessary for a balanced energy budget. Thus during the 120-day period of summer feeding, the Southern Ocean large baleen whales take about 4 per cent body weight daily. This represents an excess of immediate needs, and much of it is stored as fat in the form of a thick layer of blubber, and fat in the interstices of the tail muscle fibres (Lockyer et al. 1985). The lipid energy store in blubber and muscle is later used during winter months when food is scarce, and daily feeding rates decline to perhaps 0.4 per cent body weight (Lockyer 1981a). It should also be borne in mind that evolution has not necessarily achieved optimal results so we should not always equate theoretical maxima with what one may observe in the wild.

We have looked at the positive side of the energy equation; what of the negative side — the energy costs or output? As noted above, not all food is digested so there is some initial loss of energy here. Excretion of potentially toxic nitrogenous compounds takes place by the production of urine, which represents a further loss, as is the actual digestive process (termed SDA or specific dynamic action), which inevitably uses some energy by increased metabolism. Water vapour from the lungs provides another energy loss, but most heat loss appears to be through the body surface.

The metabolic rate (the rate at which chemical reactions within the body take place) in warm-blooded animals such as cetaceans is maintained at a stable and relatively high level. This is achieved by using energy mainly from respiration to maintain a steady body-core temperature (at 36–37°C). Since cetaceans live in an environment usually less than 25°C temperature, they require insulation to minimise heat loss. This is achieved primarily by the layer of blubber that they possess, but also by a specialised heat-exchange system (see below, and Chapter 1). Heat loss will also be affected by the ratio of the surface area to volume, such that smaller species will lose relatively more heat than larger ones and so have a relatively higher metabolic rate. A complication in estimating heat loss across the skin is that blubber thickness, particularly in the large baleen whales, varies with season. As described above, it reaches a maximum at the end of the summer feeding period and a minimum at the end of the winter. Thus Paul Brodie estimates heat loss for a large rorqual in the subtropics to be no more than 50 per cent that in polar waters during summer. It will also vary with sex, age and size, and the lipid content may vary (by as much as 50 per cent) from one part of the body to the other. Because of these variations (and the fact that lipid is also stored in the liver and bone), variations in blubber thickness alone should not be used in energetic calculations (Brodie 1975). Recently, Brodie and Paasche (1985) overcame some of these problems by using temperature probes, inserted in newly killed fin and sei whales. They found that live whales possessed low mid-core temperatures which decreased further towards the blubber. In terms of energy consumption, the temperature gradation results in a lower temperature at the muscle-blubber interface, a reduction of the temperature gradient across the blubber insulation with, ultimately, more economical heat regulation.

Energy is lost particularly through movement. This is very difficult to estimate and will depend upon the type of movement. It is likely to be much greater during vigorous breaching or lunging activities than when engaged in normal swimming. It will also be higher (possibly exponentially) with increased swimming speed. The energy to power the muscles for locomotion comes from respiration which obviously differs during a dive to before and after.

Although this is still a controversial subject, the basal or resting metabolic rate of cetaceans appears to be rather similar to that of terrestrial mammals. This may not mean that the energy per unit size of animal required for resting is comparable since cetaceans are thought to be negatively buoyant and so may need to move continually. The sight of large whales drifting apparently effortlessly on the surface tends to argue against this, but at least under most circumstances (when the sea is not flat calm) it may apply.

Other energy losses come from particular biological activities, notably growth and reproduction (particularly lactation by the female). Some growth occurs whilst the young animal is still a fetus so that by the time of birth it may be one quarter the length of the mother (see Table 8.4). This is a higher value than for most terrestrial mammals and necessi-

Table 6.4: Energy budgets of some cetaceans

Species	Sex	Age/status (yrs)	Body weight (kg × 10³)	Annual food intake (kg × 10³)	Annual energy intake (kcal × 10⁶)	Annual Energy Expenditure (kcal × 10⁶)				Temporary Energy Store (as fat)
						Mainten.	Growth	Pregn.	Lact.	
Mysticetes										
Blue whale	male	5/puberty	72.0	361	361	267	18	—	—	204
		14–15/young ad.	97.0	491	491	371	3	—	—	279
	female	5/puberty	87.0	434	434	324	24	—	—	250
		14–15/young ad.	114.0	578	578	438	5	—	—	317
		25+/mature yr 1	118.0	597	597	457	12	60.5	70	765
		yr 2	119.0	603	603	(calculated over full 2 year breeding cycle incl. 11 months pregnancy + 7 months lactation)				
Fin whale	male	6/puberty	43.5	180	180	171	9	—	—	76
		14–15 young ad.	51.5	261	261	205	2	—	—	87
	female	6/puberty	47.5	203	203	183	10	—	—	82
		14–15/young ad.	62.0	318	318	241	3	—	—	98
		25+/mature yr 1	64.5	326	326	250	7	39.5	56	272
		yr 2	65.3	331	331	(calculated over full 2 year breeding cycle incl. 11 months pregnancy + 7 months lactation)				
Odontocetes										
Sperm whale	male	9.5/puberty	9.4	99	78.8	56.1	3.63	—	—	—
		19/sex. mat.	18.0	203	162.1	113.3	3.63	—	—	—
		26/harem status	27.4	318	254.0	172.3	5.08	—	—	—
		45/mature	43.6	549	439.5	317.9	–	—	—	—
	female	9/puberty/ sex. maturity	6.35	69	55.5	42.3	1.99	—	—	—
		30+/mature	13.5	153	122.6	89.7	–	16.8	22.9	–
Harbour porpoise	male	4+/mature	0.051	0.78	0.982	0.902	?	—	—	0.15
	female	4+/mature	0.051	0.78	0.982	0.902	?	0.087	0.175	0.15

Reference sources: Blue, fin whales from Lockyer (1981a) but with modifications (see below) following Lockyer (in press); sperm whale from Lockyer (1981b) but with modification (see below) following Best et al. (1984); harbour porpoise from Yasui and Gaskin (in press).

Notes: The kiloJoule is the metric equivalent of the kilocalorie, but since the latter is still prevalent in the enegetics literature, I have retained its use here.

For those wishing to make the conversion, 1 kcal = 4.1868 kJ.

(1) For mysticetes, annual food intake has been calculated as 35g/kg body weight per day for 120 days of summer feeding + 3.5g/kg body weight per day for 245 days. Calorific value of food (plankton) consumed has been averaged at 1,000 kcal/kg.

For sperm whales, annual food intake has been calculated as 30g/kg body weight per day (to 40g/kg per day in fully mature males), throughout the year. Calorific value of food (squid) consumed averaged at 800 kcal/kg.

For harbour porpoise, annual food intake has been calculated as 35g/kg body weight per day for 291 days + 70g/kg body weight per day for 74 days of summer feeding. Calorific value of food (fish) consumed has been averaged at 1,260 kcal/kg.

(2) Resting metabolic rates have been taken as 7.3–8.7 kcal/kg body weight per day for blue and fin whales (varying with size); 5–8.5 kcal/kg per day for sperm whales (varying with size); and 29–30.5 kcal/kg per day for harbour porpoise. Basal metabolic rate (BMR) = 85% resting metabolic rate, and active metabolic rate = 10 × BMR.

(3) Costs of pregnancy and lactation for fin and blue whales have been modified, following Lockyer (in press), based on energy outputs of 2,940 kcal/kg for fetal growth to 1,750kg (fin whale) or to 2,630kg (blue whale) and an additional metabolic cost (heat of gestation) $Q_G = 4,400M^{1.2}$, where M = average fetal weight in kg. (this amounts to 34.3 x 10^6 kcal in the fin whale and 35.0 x 10^6 kcal in the blue whale. An additional gestational cost has been similarly calculated for the sperm whale over entire 15 months of pregnancy (virtually all in the last 9–10 months). The costs of lactation have also been modified following revised estimates of energy content of milk (Lockyer in press; Best et al. 1984) — 3,320 kcal per kg with 90 per cent gland efficiency in blue and fin whales, and 2,820 kcal per kg in the sperm whale. Milk production is estimated at 90kg/day in blue and 72kg/day in fin whales over a period of 7 months (210 days); and 20kg/day for one year in the sperm whale.

It will be noted that in blue and fin whales, the values for annual energy outputs exceed energy input. Since the input to energy storage as blubber is, if anything, a minimal value (see Lockyer in press), this suggests that the input of energy from feeding has probably been underestimated, possibly because food intake is higher than previously thought during migration or on the winter breeding grounds.

tates an extra demand on the mother's energy reserves. The main reason why the young is born at a relatively large size is probably its unfavourable surface-area to volume ratio in the much cooler aqueous environment that it enters.

Most baleen whales have reproductive cycles geared to their seasonal migrations between summer feeding and winter breeding, and this influences the energetic strategy adopted. For balaenopterids, the energetic cost of pregnancy increases exponentially in the second half of the gestation period. Christina Lockyer (1981a) has estimated for fin whales that in the latter six month period of pregnancy there is an increased food intake of between 50 and 60 per cent above normal intake, equivalent to 20–30 per cent over the entire 18 month period of gestation and lactation. The great majority of this increased food intake is laid down as reserve for the seven months' lactation.

The sperm whale, on the other hand, adopts a very different strategy. It does not have the same seasonal constraints on feeding and reproduction. Thus in the female sperm whale, food intake increases during the latter half of pregnancy by about 10 per cent, which in this case is equivalent to a 1 to 2 per cent increase spread over the entire 16 month period of gestation plus 2–3 years suckling.

The net costs of lactation for balaenopterid whales, but probably also for other species, are much higher than those of pregnancy (see Table 6.4). When the young are born they must grow fast to quickly overcome the unfavourable energy balance due to their small size. This is achieved through the provision of milk that is much richer in fat (30–37 per cent yielding between 15,500 kJoules or 3,700 kcal (white whale) and up to 18,000 kJoules or 4,300 kcal (large rorquals) per kg body weight) than in most terrestrial mammals (Gaskin 1982:97). The efficiency at which this is converted into growth and development (termed assimilation efficiency) is also very high (calculated to be 85–95 per cent for fin and blue whales). When converted to account for different calorific values of food taken in and tissues produced, this declines to net growth efficiencies of 30–40 per cent for fin and blue whales (still relatively high values).

As the calf gets older its growth rate slows down, particularly as weaning takes place. At this time it is probably more mobile as it seeks to find food for itself. At puberty, assimilation efficiencies remain at about 80 per cent although net growth is now between 5 and 7 per cent. Assimilation efficiencies remain high through adulthood at about 80 per cent when growth is virtually zero.

The result for both mother and young of high energy costs of lactation may be that baleen whales have to miss one or two years between breeding (Lockyer 1978). This is supported by observed cycles in body fat condition (Lockyer 1986) and by recent estimates of calving intervals (see Table 8.3). Even with small odontocetes an annual breeding cycle may be difficult, particularly for species such as the harbour porpoise that may have difficulty obtaining their overall energy requirements due to their unfavourable surface-area to volume ratio (Gaskin 1982: 101–3; but see Yasui and Gaskin in press). Tentative energy budgets have now been constructed for a few species (see Table 6.4). We shall consider later, in Chapter 8, how these may be extended to the population to give a better idea of what factors will determine their dynamics, and also relationships between species within the ecosystem as a whole.

7 Social organisation and behaviour

Whales and dolphins are essentially social animals even if some species only come together for limited periods of their life cycle. Living in groups has four possible advantages: (1) it helps with food finding (as shown in the previous chapter); (2) it helps with defence against predators; (3) it helps to bring individuals together for reproduction; and (4) it may spread the costs and increase the efficiency of calf rearing. In this chapter we shall explore some of the ways that cetaceans are organised socially and look at their social behaviour. These will be considered against a background of the above needs — survival through maximising food-finding and successful avoidance of predation, and reproduction.

Methods of study, particularly in the past, have depended heavily upon observations of animals in captivity. Although these have certainly contributed to our knowledge the results always need to be interpreted with caution because of the very unnatural conditions in which at least some species live. This is likely to be species dependent, according to their social organisation and home range use, and ideally captive studies of a species should be related to results obtained in the wild. Recently there has been a burgeoning of studies in the wild, allowing not only information from a wider range of species (to include large whales that are not normally kept in captivity) but also observations in a wider range of contexts that are more or less natural. However, they too have limitations. One cannot always be sure that the animals are not responding to the observer (or his actions, such as the application of numbered tags or radio transmitters). Indeed, cetaceans often react to the presence of a human diver. Furthermore, the view one obtains is a very limited and somewhat biased one. A great majority of our observations are made at or just above the sea surface. Although individuals may be followed indirectly by radiotelemetry or acoustic means, and even observed directly by subaqua diving or underwater capsules, these usually add little more than brief glimpses to the lives of these mysterious creatures.

GROUP SIZE AND SOCIAL STRUCTURE

Group sizes vary both between species, and within species depending upon the activity (for example feeding, courtship, migration) they are engaged upon. A study of such variations may give us some insight as to the relative importance of the above four factors. Before we do so, however, it is important to realise that to recognise a group and estimate its size are not necessarily easy tasks. Some baleen whale species could be dispersed over a very large area but form an integral unit in regular acoustic contact with one another. Our ability to recognise whether or not this is so is necessarily limited. Even when animals are within sight of one another, it is not easy to be sure whether they form a group or are independent. This is the case, for example, for the harbour porpoise and some pelagic dolphins. Finally, because most of our observations are made from above the surface, there is a possibility of overlooking members of the group underwater and so underestimating its size.

Mysticetes or Baleen Whales

Bearing in mind the above uncertainties, the dispersion of baleen whales tends to differ from that of many odontocetes. Whereas odontocetes often occur in schools, baleen whales do not group so tightly. As noted above, individual or pairs of whales may be in acoustic contact with many others over a large area. Thus, if one defines a social group as individuals in communication with one another, then probably most species occur at least in some situations in groups numbering tens or even hundreds of individuals. It is difficult to determine the actual distances that individuals are in contact with each other, but aggregations may be observed particularly during feeding, and also for some species (for example right and gray whales) on calving grounds, or during migration (for example gray and humpback whales). Bowhead whales may aggregate in groups of up to several hundred to feed, and tens to socialise. Southern right whales in one of their main calving areas, Peninsula Valdés in Argentina, form mother-calf pairs and several dozen of these may be seen along a few kilometres of coastline. Similar aggregations during feeding or breeding are also observed at least in right, humpback, fin and Bryde's whales. It should also be remembered that all the larger baleen whales now exist at much smaller population sizes than they did historically, due to over-hunting by man. In the past, therefore, these aggregations may have numbered many more than they do now. This may apply, for example, to the blue whale and right whales.

In most circumstances, when engaged in normal travel, baleen whales do not group closely together. Most sightings are of single or two animals, and usually do not exceed four or five individuals, although whales may group together under certain circumstances. Bowheads, for example, have been observed skim feeding in echelon formation and comprising 2–10 individuals (Wursig et al. 1984b), and gray whales migrate in pulses of 5 to 50 animals, though these are often subdivided into mother-calf pairs (Jones et al. 1984). These group sizes are typical for all baleen whales (see Table 7.1). The absence of close grouping, or schooling, of baleen whales very probably reflects the need to feed more or less individually. The large daily food intake required by their large size probably could not sustain a greater number in a restricted area. This may be more important than the need to group together for protection against their main predators, sharks and killer whales. However, some species (right, bowhead or gray whales) may temporarily cluster together

Table 7.1: Typical group sizes and social structure of mysticetes

Species	Typical group size	Group composition	Source
Blue whale	1, 2(5)	Not known	1–3
Fin whale	1, 2–10(30)	Not known	1–5
Sei whale	1, 2–5(30)	Female-calf; mature male(s), female(s) (females predominate at high latitudes; males at lower latitudes during breeding season); immatures of both sexes (females predominating) + females with calves (at lower latitudes)	1–3, 6
Bryde's whale	1, 2–5(30)	Not known	2–3
Minke whale	1, 2–3(40)	Not known	2–5, 7
Humpback whale	1, 2–3(20)	female-calf; male, female-calf; several males, female with/ without calf; mature males, mature females	8–14
Gray whale	1, 2–18(50)	Female-calf; all male; mixed	1, 15–18
Bowhead whale	1, 2–10(50)	Female-calf, all male; mixed	19–21
Northern/Southern right whale	1, 2–12(100)	Female-calf, all male; mixed	1, 22–24
Pygmy right whale	1, 2–8	Not known	25–26

Reference sources: 1 Nemoto 1964; 2 Gaskin 1982; 3 Leatherwood et al. 1983; 4 Evans 1980; 5 Evans et al. 1986; 6 Budylenko 1977; 7 Dorsey 1983; 8 Darling 1983; 9 Darling et al. 1983; 10 Baker and Herman 1984; 11 Mobley and Herman 1985; 12 Tyack 1981; 13 Tyack and Whitehead 1983; 14 Winn and Winn 1985; 15 Darling 1977a,b; 16 Rice and Wolman 1971; 17 Jones et al. 1984; 18 Wursig et al. 1986; 19 Everitt and Krogman 1979; 20 Nerini et al. 1984; 21 Wursig et al. 1984a,b, 1986; 22 Clark 1983; 23 Payne in press; 24 Omura et al. 1969; 25 Baker 1985; 26 Ross et al. 1975

Notes: Group sizes are particularly difficult to determine in baleen whales which form more dispersed groupings, although possibly still in acoustic contact. Most sightings of baleen whales tend to be of single or two individuals; larger groups may occur in association with activities such as feeding, migration, mating or birth, and probably represent aggregations of individuals/family groups. Composition of groups is rarely known, primarily because of the difficulties in sexing individuals (particularly in balaenopterids).

to form a defensive circle when threatened by a potential predator, just as do some African plains ungulates (such as wildebeest). In those circumstances, the whales form a circle with flailing tails (rather than heads as in wildebeest) pointed outwards. The large odontocete, the sperm whale, has also been observed adopting a defensive circle (the so-called 'marguerite' formation). Otherwise, these large whales probably rely upon their individual power derived from their large size, and their ability to swim fast to escape. Of course some whales do not escape by this means but these are often young or sick animals.

Baleen whales do not appear to be organised into structurally complex groups. Although we cannot be certain of the precise nature of social groups because dispersed individuals may form discrete units maintained by vocal contact, it seems likely that close bonds only exist for mother and calf. When two animals have been seen close together, in very many cases they have been a mother and calf. Any other social unit is almost certainly a fluid one. Individually recognisable southern right whales may occur in the same group one day and then alone or in different groups the next day (Payne in press). Gray whales and humpbacks behave similarly (Jones and Swartz 1984; Mobley and Herman 1985; Swartz 1986). When aggregations form at feeding grounds, there is some limited co-operation between individuals (see Chapter 6), but in many cases it is possible that the animals have assembled simply because of a mutual attraction to a food concentration. Without a better understanding of the role of vocal communication between individuals, we cannot say very much more. On the breeding grounds, however, there is more substantial evidence that whales communicate information which may serve in obtaining a potential mate. Humpback whales are well known for their complex 'songs' which are made largely or wholly on the breeding grounds. In these circumstances a lone whale sings and is either approached by other lone individuals which appear to displace it, or moves towards a mother and calf which it then escorts (Tyack 1981). These mothers are sometimes sexually receptive and this may be the main way that humpbacks obtain a mate. In the case of the southern right whale, vocalisations may also play a part since individuals will respond by swimming towards the sounds of another southern right whale played back from an underwater loudspeaker (Clark and Clark 1980).

For a long time the mating system of the baleen whales was thought to be monogamous and groups of two individuals automatically assumed to be male and female pairs. As with most mammals, and perhaps also birds, the idea of monogamy being the rule is now probably suspect, and it seems more likely that no long-term bond exists. Mating, in all baleen whale species that have been studied closely, appears to be promiscuous involving several partners (see Table 7.3). However, one should be reminded that observations of mating behaviour do not necessarily lead to conceptions, and without genetic evidence to test for paternity (a singularly difficult thing to obtain from large whales, though not impossible), we can do little more than guess.

Odontocetes or Toothed Whales

Odontocetes tend to group together into schools, which may often be quite large (Table 7.2), although their stability in the long term is probably only seen in a few species. Smallest group sizes occur in some of the specialised taxa, such as the beaked whales and river dolphins. Neither are very well known. Amongst beaked whales, those few sightings that exist of members of the genera *Mesoplodon*, *Ziphius*, *Tasmacetus* and *Berardius* suggest these whales live mainly singly or in small groups of two to five animals. Occasionally larger groups have been recorded, and there have been mass strandings of otherwise little known species, for example of 25 Gray's beaked whales at the Chatham Islands, New Zealand. Cuvier's whale is one of the better known beaked whales and has been seen in groups of up to 25 animals but usually occurs in tight schools of 3–10 individuals. The bottlenose whales of the genus

Table 7.2: Typical group sizes and social structure of odontocetes

Species	Typical group sizes	Group composition	Source
Sperm whale	1, 2–50+	Maternity/nursery group: females-calves, immatures; temporary harem group: females-calves, immatures, older male; males usually solitary or in bachelor groups (immature groups of larger group size), and occurring to higher latitudes	1–5
Pygmy sperm whale	1, 2–6(10)	Not known	6
Dwarf sperm whale	1, 2–10	Females-calves; adults of both sexes with calves; immatures	6
Narwhal	(1–2)3–20(1,000+)	Females-calves; adults of both sexes with/ without calves; adult males; immatures	7–9
White whale	(1–4)5–20(1,000+)	Females-calves with immatures; adults of both sexes with/without calves; adult males	10–11
Irrawaddy dolphin	(1)2–10	Not known	12
Baird's beaked whale	(1)2–20(30)	Females-calves; adults of both sexes with/ without calves; adult males	13
Northern bottlenose whale	1, 2–10(35)	Females-calves; adults of both sexes with/ without calves; adult males	14–16
Cuvier's beaked whale	1, 3–10(25)	Not known	17–18
Mesoplodon beaked whale	1, 2–10	Not known	17–19
Melon-headed whale	150–1,500	Not known	17–19
Pygmy killer whale	10–50(300)	Not known	17–19
False killer whale	10–50(300)	Herds of mixed age and both sexes	17–21
Killer whale	1, 2–40(100+)	Females-calves and immatures with/ without adult male; immature males; adult males (sometimes alone)	15–18, 23–26

163

Table 7.2 (continued)

SOCIAL ORGANISATION AND BEHAVIOUR

Species	Typical group sizes	Group composition	Source
Long-finned pilot whale	1, (2)10–50(1,000+)	Females-calves and immatures with adult males; adults of both sexes; adult males (sometimes alone)	15–18, 27–29
Short-finned pilot whale	1, (2)5–50(500)	Females-calves and immatures with adult males; adults of both sexes; mainly adult males	17–19, 28, 30
Rough-toothed dolphin	1, 2–50(500)	Not known	17–19, 27–28
Tucuxi	(1)2–5(25)	Not known (but apparently tight knit)	17, 28, 31
Indo-Pacific/Atlantic hump-backed dolphin	1–2, 3–10(20)	herds of mixed age and both sexes	32
White-beaked dolphin	1, 2–20(1,000+)	Herds of mixed age and both sexes	15–16, 18, 27
Atlantic white-sided dolphin	(1)10–100(1,000+)	Herds of mixed age and both sexes; possibly some age segregation	15–18, 27
Dusky dolphin	1, (2)6–15(500)	Herds of mixed age and both sexes	28, 33–34
Pacific white-sided dolphin	(1)10–100(1,000+)	Herds of mixed age and both sexes	17, 19, 35
Hourglass dolphin	(3)6–15(40)	Not known	17, 36
Fraser's dolphin	40–800 (based on few sightings)	Not known	17, 37–39
Common dolphin	(1)10–500(1,000+)	Herds of mixed age and both sexes	15–19, 27–28, 40
Bottle-nosed dolphin	1, 2–25(1,000) (inshore groups smaller)	Adult males and females with calves; adult females-calves and immatures of both sexes; immature males	15–19, 27–28, 41–49
Risso's dolphin	1, (2)5–25(300) (inshore groups smaller)	Females-calves and immatures with adult male; lone adult males; possibly groups of immature and/or adult males	15–17, 50–51

164

Species	Group size	Composition	References
Spotted dolphin	(1)5–500(1,000+) (inshore groups smaller)	Herds of mixed age and both sexes	17–19, 52
Striped dolphin	(1)5–300(3,000)	Females-calves; adults of both sexes; immatures of both sexes	16–19, 27–28, 53
Spinner dolphin	(1)6–250(1,000+)	Adult males and females with calves; adult females-calves and immatures of both sexes; immature males	18, 19, 52, 54
Clymene dolphin	(1)5–200(500)	Not known	18, 51
Southern right whale dolphin	(1)5–100(1,000+)	Not known	34, 55–56
Northern right whale dolphin	(1)5–200(2,000+)	Not known	17–18, 57
Hector's dolphin	1,2–8(300)	Not known	17, 34, 56, 58
Black dolphin	(1)6–14(40)	Not known	17, 36, 55
Commerson's dolphin	1,2–12(100+)	Not known	17, 36, 55, 60–61
Harbour porpoise	1,2–10(250+)	Females-calves; adults of both sexes with/without calves; immatures; adult males	15–18, 27–28, 51, 62–64
Burmeister's porpoise	1,2–8 (but few records)	Not known	17, 59, 65–66
Vaquita	1,2–5(40)	Not known	55, 67
Dall's porpoise	1,2–20(3,000+)	Herds of mixed age and both sexes	17, 19, 68–70
Finless porpoise	1,2–12(50)	Females-calves; adults of both sexes with/without calves; immatures; adult males	17, 71–73
Indus/Ganges susus	1,2–10	Females-calves; otherwise group composition not known	17, 28, 74–76
Boto	1,2–15(20) (but generally solitary)	Not known	17, 28, 31, 77
Baiji	1,2–4(12)	Not known	17, 28, 72–73, 78
Franciscana	1,2–5	Not known	17, 79–81

Table 7.2 (continued)

Reference sources: 1 Best 1979; 2 Berzin 1972; 3 Ohsumi 1971; 4 Gordon pers. comm.; 5 Whitehead and Gordon 1986; 6 Ross 1984; 7 Silverman and Dunbar 1980; 8 Best and Fisher 1974; 9 Mansfield et al. 1975; 10 Brodie 1971; 11 Sergeant 1973; 12 Lloze 1973; 13 Kasuya 1986; 14 Benjaminsen and Christensen 1979; 15 Evans 1980; 16 Evans et al. 1986; 17 Leatherwood et al. 1983; 18 Kasuya 1986; 14 Benjaminsen and Christensen 1979; 15 Evans 1980; 16 Evans et al. 1986; 17 Leatherwood et al. 1983; 18 Leatherwood et al. 1976; 19 Leatherwood et al. 1982; 20 Mead 1979; 21 Purves and Pilleri 1978; 22 Balcomb et al. 1979, 1980; 23 Bigg 1982; 24 Condy et al. 1978; 25 Erickson 1978; 26 Martinez and Klinghammer 1970; 27 Tomilin 1967; 28 Yablokov et al. 1972; 29 Sergeant 1962; 30 Kasuya and Marsh 1984; 31 Layne 1958; 32 Saayman and Tayler 1973, 1979; 33 Wursig and Wursig 1980; 34 Baker 1972, 1983; 35 Leatherwood et al. 1984a; 36 Brownell 1974; 37 Berzin 1978; 38 Miyazaki and Wada 1978b; 39 Tobayama et al. 1973; 40 W.E. Evans 1971, 1974; 41 Wells et al. 1980; 42 Shane et al. 1986; 43 M. Caldwell and D. Caldwell 1972a; 44 Wursig and Wursig 1977; 45 Wursig 1978; 46 Saayman and Tayler 1979; 47 Gruber 1981; 48 Hansen 1983; 49 Hussenot 1980; 50 Leatherwood et al. 1980; 51 P.G.H. Evans unpubl.; 52 Perrin et al. 1982, 1985; 53 Miyazaki and Nishiwaki 1978; 54 Norris and Dohl 1980a,b; 55 Watson 1981; 56 Gaskin 1968, 1972; 57 Leatherwood and Walker 1979; 58 Baker 1978; 59 Aguayo 1975; 60 Mermoz 1980; 61 Brownell and Praderi 1985; 62 Watson 1976; 63 Gaskin et al. 1975; 64 Kinze 1985; 65 Brownell and Pilleri 1978; 22 Balcomb et al. 1979, 1980; 23 Bigg 1982; 24 Condy et al. 1978; 25 Erickson 1978; 26 Martinez and 70 Kasuya 1978; 71 Kasuya and Kureha 1979; 72 Pilleri et al. 1980; 73 Zhou et al. 1980; 74 S. Jones 1982; 75 Aminul Haque et al. 1977; 76 Kasuya and Aminul Haque 1972; 77 Best and da Silva 1984; 78 Zhou et al. 1977, 1982; 79 Pilleri 1971; 80 Praderi 1979; 81 Brownell and Praderi 1976.

Notes: Minimum and maximum group sizes are given in parentheses. Many species are commonly recorded alone as well as in groups, and this is indicated accordingly. The social structure of no species is properly known and it is likely that some of the above designations of different types of grouping will be revised in the future. In particular, those species recorded as possessing mixed age/sex composition may on further study show sub-group segregation in the manner indicated for some of the better known species.

Hyperoodon may also form larger groups of 15–20 individuals but typically occur singly, in twos, or groups of four to ten. Terje Benjaminsen and Ivar Christensen (1979), who have made a particular study of the northern bottlenose whale, suggest (on the basis of Norwegian catches) that groups may segregate by sex and age during migration. These results derive from limited sample sizes and so need further verification. It has also been suggested that large dominant males may establish and maintain relatively stable groups of females and young but the evidence is scanty. The river dolphins also appear to live mainly singly, in twos or small groups. The boto usually is solitary but may aggregate in groups of 12 to 15 during the dry season in northern South America. The baiji of the Yangtze River also may form groups of ten or 12 but two to six is more usual, and this is the usual group size for the franciscana of temperate South America. The two susus of Indo-Pakistan are generally found alone or in twos, rarely numbering more than ten individuals, and, if they do so, they occur in loose groups. Although poorly known, it does not appear that any species of river dolphin has more than a very simple social structure.

The sperm whale has been studied in some detail (see Berzin 1972, Best 1979, Ohsumi 1971) although most of the information in the past has come indirectly, from whale catches, and it is only recently that detailed observations have been made at sea. This species forms a variety of different school types which may vary with season and location (see Figure 7.1). In high latitudes, usually only lone adult males or bachelor schools are seen (although recently there have been records of small groups of females with young off the coast of Scotland). In warmer waters, five school types have been observed: a nursery school comprising adult females, calves and juveniles of both sexes (but with three-quarters of the school being female); a harem school which is similar but temporarily joined by one adult male during the breeding season; a juvenile school which includes individuals of both sexes; a bachelor school comprising only young adult males; and a bull school of sexually active males. We have referred to these groups as schools because they appear to have some stability. Indeed nursery schools have contained tagged females recorded within the same group ten years later. However, it is not known whether adult males return to the same harem each season. Observations in the Indian Ocean (by Jonathan Gordon, Hal Whitehead and colleagues) and off the Galapagos (by Hal Whitehead and colleagues) indicate that females and immature males belong to schools which may comprise around 20 individuals. However, school members are generally seen associating together in subgroups of 2–10 individuals. The composition of these subgroups can be very labile, changing from hour to hour. The larger school, on the other hand, does seem to have a more stable membership; seven individuals from one school off Sri Lanka were resighted associating together in the same area one year later (J. Gordon pers. comm.).

The size of the school also varies with type and location, from one to over 100 animals. Groups in the open sea have been reported as numbering 3–7 individuals, but averaging 20 animals along the coast. However, it is likely that this is determined by the feeding situation, and off Sri Lanka the larger groups apparently occur offshore. A harem school typically contains one male and about 14 females (but may vary

Figure 7.1 Latitudinal distribution of sperm whale schools of different social structure (derived from Best 1979, Gaskin 1982, Ohsumi 1971). Note that lone males and bachelor male herds tend to move into higher latitudes than females with calves. Males probably only join herds of females with young for short periods, for the purposes of mating

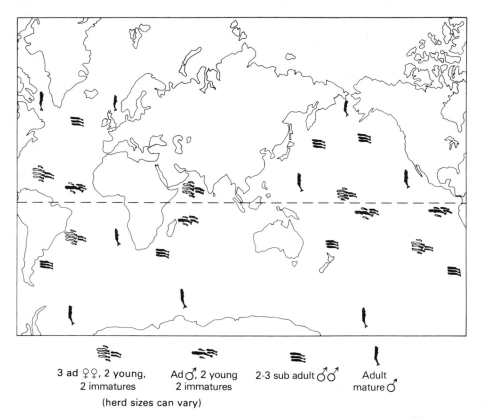

3 ad ♀♀, 2 young, Ad ♂, 2 young 2-3 sub adult ♂♂ Adult
2 immatures 2 immatures mature ♂
(herd sizes can vary)

from 10 to 40). Older males are usually solitary or occur in small groups except during the breeding season when they may compete to gain control of a harem. We are also still uncertain whether most successful mating is accomplished by those older bulls that are present only during the breeding season, or by younger males that are present in the school throughout the year. The mating system of the sperm whale is generally described as polygynous. However, the earlier remarks concerning our uncertainty of genetic paternity apply also to this species, and we cannot yet be certain that males are not actually promiscuous. Indeed recent field observations suggest that males form only temporary harems. Many further questions remain unanswered. Is group membership more stable among females than males? If males have a greater tendency to leave their natal groups, is this the consequence of ejection by temporary harem masters? Do adult males return to their natal groups or does this represent a permanent dispersal, perhaps to prevent inbreeding?

Both the pygmy and dwarf sperm whale seem to occur in smaller groups of less than ten animals. The social structure of the former is not known, but the dwarf sperm whale appears to occur in at least three different kinds of groups. These comprise females with calves; adults of both sexes without calves; and immatures.

Both white whale and narwhal may occur in very large groups. In the case of the white whale, they occur more or less throughout the year though they are closely aggregated on the breeding grounds but spread out during feeding. Within the group there is obvious segregation by age and sex. Two main types have been recognised: nursery groups of females with their calves (up to the age of two years); and groups of adult males. During mating there is temporary movement of males into the female groups. Unlike sperm whales, however, these sub-groups are commonly aggregated into groups that may number hundreds to several thousand individuals. The group structure of the narwhal is similar, numbering several hundreds or thousands of animals and comprising groups of females with calves, and tusked males often of similar large body size. Narwhals in broad Arctic fiords tend to be less tightly aggregated than white whales, which favour smaller estuaries. Both species are thought to be polygynous though as yet on little evidence.

The killer whale shows strong social cohesion of groups. Long-term studies in Vancouver and Washington State by Ken Balcomb, Mike Bigg and co-workers suggest that members of the group (commonly referred to as a pod) remain together for life, and pods are stable from one generation to the next (Balcomb et al. 1980; Bigg et al. 1976; Ford and Fisher 1983). The size of these pods typically varies from four to 40 individuals, although groups of 100 or more have occasionally been observed, possibly the result of temporary coalition of several pods. Usually larger groups split up into two or more smaller ones as the population grows. These comprise one adult male (easily recognisable by its much larger size and very tall dorsal fin), three or four adult females and several subadults of both sexes. Lone individuals or small groups also occur. As with some other mammalian carnivores, these groups may be at a disadvantage. The Vancouver studies suggest that the larger pods prey upon abundant shoals of Pacific salmon, the smaller pods being relegated to feeding on other less nutritious prey. Group sizes vary between regions and whilst commonly numbering 30–40 animals off the coast of Norway, they rarely exceed ten individuals around the British coasts (Evans 1980, in preparation).

Both pygmy and false killer whales are pelagic species and commonly form groups of up to 50 or 100 individuals. The former species is still poorly known but false killers appear to have a tight social structure comprising individuals of both sexes and all ages. The melon-headed whale is also poorly known but groups appear to be large, between 100 and 1,500 individuals.

Pilot whales are also very gregarious, forming groups that may number several hundreds or thousands, although typically 50 or less. These groups were once thought to be segregated by age and sex but more recent information presents conflicting results. Nevertheless, pilot whales are thought to be polygynous, with a large adult male holding a harem of females and young of both sex (Kasuya and Marsh 1984). Again, better evidence is needed. It may be that two or three males have access to females in a group since I have observed on a few occasions, groups of females and young with more than one apparently adult male (recognised by the large melon and conspicuous long dorsal fin) present.

The smaller dolphins can be divided into two types: inshore species such as the bottle-nosed and hump-backed dolphins, and porpoises such as the harbour and finless porpoise, which live mainly in small groups rarely above ten individuals; and pelagic dolphins such as those of the genera *Stenella*, *Delphinus* and *Lagenorhynchus*, which may form groups numbering several hundred or thousands. The latter groups probably represent only temporary aggregations associated with feeding or migration, and groups typically number between five and 100 individuals. The shape of the group may also change according to context. When travelling, pelagic dolphins often occur either as a tight group or in a line abreast (as do other pelagic odontocetes such as pilot whales) or echelon. At the start of feeding, these may spread out to form a number of small tight sub-groups and lone individuals which may then co-operate in some manner (though not necessarily) when pursuing food (see Figure 6.12). In my experience the broader lines or echelons tend to occur when the travelling group is larger, although Steve Leatherwood and William Walker (1979) have observed herds of 40 or more right whale dolphins in concentrated groups. When feeding concentrations occur even the inshore dolphins will aggregate in larger numbers. In the case of harbour porpoise we have observed loose groups numbering up to 100 feeding actively in localised regions in southwest Ireland and Shetland. At this time they appeared to be feeding upon dense shoals of sprats or sandeels. Similar (though smaller) aggregations have been seen in bottle-nosed and hump-backed dolphins.

Our knowledge of group sizes and social structure of dolphins derives from a number of field studies. The most detailed ones have been made by Bernd and Melany Wursig on bottle-nosed and dusky dolphins in Argentina; by Ken Norris and Thomas Dohl on the spinner dolphin in Hawaii; by Graham Saayman and Colin Tayler on the hump-backed dolphin in South Africa; and by Randall Wells, Blair Irvine and colleagues on the bottle-nosed dolphin in Florida. Studies have also been carried out on the harbour porpoise in Canada by David Gaskin and co-workers. Other studies have started up more recently. We, for example, have been working on white-beaked and Risso's dolphins in North Scotland. In some of the above studies, animals have been tagged or radio-tracked, but usually reliance has been placed on recognising individuals by unique markings.

Many of these studies suggest that the social structure of both inshore and pelagic delphinids is generally rather fluid. Individuals that are present in one group in the morning may be within another group by the afternoon, or the next day, and this may be tens of kilometres distant. There does, however, appear to be a core group of individuals which remain in association with one another over extended periods. They may not stay together throughout that period, individuals moving away for periods of several weeks or more before returning to the same group (see

Figure 7.2 Bottle-nosed dolphin school dynamics (from Wells et al. 1983b). Tagged dolphin interactions during three weeks in May–June 1976. Each horizontal line represents a tagged dolphin. Sightings of the individual are indicated by its identification number and its age-sex class designation. Boxes enclose groups. Letters following dates indicate more than one sighting of members of a group during a given day. M=adult male, F=adult female, C=calf, m=subadult male, f=subadult female, and a number followed by '?', within a box, indicates the number of unidentified dolphins in the group: M? indicates an unidentified adult male. Note that some individuals associate together for a period of time, others come and go, and some leave but return some days/weeks later.

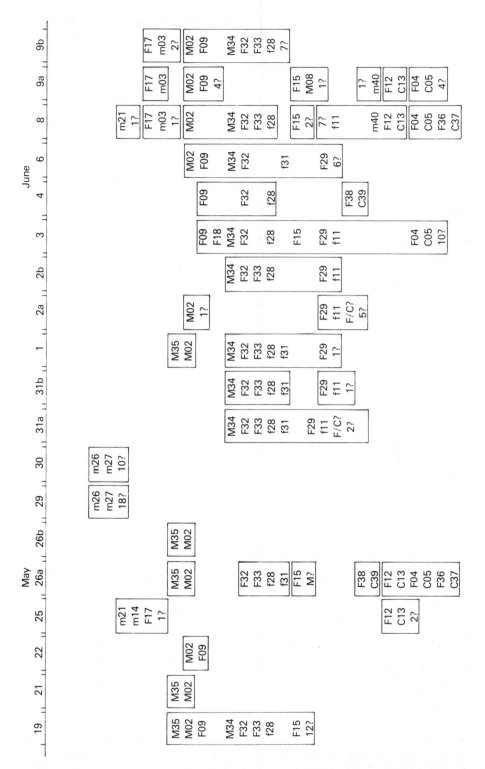

Figure 7.2). We know very little about the relatedness of individuals within these more stable sub-groups except that mothers and calves may remain together for many years. On the other hand, these same females may have long-term affiliations with other adults that are possibly unrelated. Segregation by sex and age is not uncommon. All-male groups of harbour porpoise have been observed in the Bay of Fundy. In Florida, bottle-nosed dolphins occur in groups of the following composition (in decreasing order of frequency): females with calves; subadult males; adult females; and less commonly, subadult females; and adult males. Breeding groups rarely contain adult males and the latter rarely mix with subadult males. A similar social structure has been suggested for the striped dolphin off Japan by Miyazaki and Nishiwaki (1978), but dusky dolphins on the other hand often occur in groups of both sexes with young included (Wursig and Wursig 1980), and this seems to be the case for white-beaked dolphins in Scotland (Evans in prep.). Studies on bottle-nosed dolphins in captivity suggest that there may be some dominance hierarchy system, with dominance displayed in the forms of jaw claps, biting, ramming or tailslaps against subordinates (Bateson 1974; Brown and Norris 1956; D. Caldwell and Caldwell 1972a; Caldwell et al. 1965; Norris 1967; Saayman et al. 1973). In the wild, dominance may be expressed by positioning of individuals (in some cases, mothers and small calves occupying the centre of groups) or by the formation of small sub-groups, often segregated by sex, forming part of a larger socially interacting (often resident) unit (Leatherwood 1977; Norris and Dohl 1980b). Individual females and their calves have been recorded associating together for 3–6 years, and even up to 8 years, although group composition is clearly dynamic and changes frequently for at least a portion of the group (Shane 1980; Shane et al. 1986; Wells et al. 1980; Wursig 1978; Wursig and Wursig 1977, 1979).

Discussion of variation in group sizes among cetaceans has centred upon the role that the quantity and distribution of food supplies might play. However, we should not forget that groups may develop for other reasons, notably in defence from predators and to increase opportunities for animals to meet for mating purposes. The latter could be achieved by large mixed groups being maintained through the year, by synchronised migrations of different age and sex classes, or by some mixture of the two where segregated groups show some stability but with a certain amount of fluidity imposed upon this. A number of cetacean species have now been shown to fall into one of these groupings. The advantages of grouping to avoid predation may relate more to increased surveillance for potential predators than to actual physical defence. Ken Norris and Thomas Dohl (1980b) go so far as to suggest that protection from predation is probably the reason for the formation of cetacean schools. I think this is unwarranted. The variations we see in group size and structure appear to be at least food related. We know that both killer whales and sharks can prey upon many different cetacean species from small dolphins to the large baleen whales — direct observations and scarred animals testify to this. However, we have no evidence that variations in predation pressure between species accord with the group size variations we witness, whereas food concentration and dispersion clearly do. Interactions between cetaceans and predators appear to be scarce (though opportunities to record it are also scarce). However, man has probably imposed a much greater predation pressure by his efficient exploitation of the great whales. In those circumstances, large groups are likely to have been at a definite disadvantage since man is capable of the slaughter of entire herds. The argument is clearly fraught with problems. Too little is known of the role of either predation or food dispersion (whether it is clumped, or distributed evenly or at random), and maybe the question can never be answered because of the difficulty of determining whether the absence of a selection pressure (for example predation) is the cause or the consequence of an observed group size.

The results of the field studies described above suggest loose associations (except for a mother-calf bond) and a possibly promiscuous mating system for most delphinids. The Risso's dolphin, however, appears to live in groups of more stable composition. Our studies in Scotland indicate that groups comprise one adult male, typically 4–6 females and young probably of both sexes. Although animals are viewed at close quarters, they are not captured and the sex of each individual cannot always be determined with certainty. This applies particularly to young animals. Nevertheless, the indication is of a polygynous mating system. Recognisable individuals (both adult males and females) have been observed within the same group over an extended period of several weeks and from one year to the next. The same area is apparently occupied by the group seasonally over at least three years.

Suggested mating systems for various cetaceans are summarised in Table 7.3. If these are verified, there are a number of conclusions that may be drawn. We have seen that baleen whales tend not to form large tight groups in the way that some small odontocetes do, and I have suggested that this results from their large energy demands which could not sustain larger numbers of individuals on the localised plankton swarms they feed upon. These concentrations may be relatively stable during a summer season, and so could usefully be defended, although they might not support more than a few individuals. However, the formation of even temporary harems seems unlikely because most mating occurs when there is little feeding, and therefore few opportunities for a male to maintain a group of females in a polygynous mating system. Instead, it seems more likely for these species to be either monogamous or promiscuous. Monogamy tends to occur where the long-term association of the male parent with the female and young is likely to increase the chance of his offspring surviving. For this to operate, food should be a relatively scarce resource which can be provided to the young by the male. In the case of baleen whales, where for several months the food is provided by the mother alone (in the form of milk), this is not likely to occur. Furthermore, the food resource needs to be sufficient to sustain both male and female (and their young) throughout the year unless site fidelity is so strong that both adults return to exactly the same area from one year to the next. If these sites are not very discrete so enabling pairs to readily come into contact with one another, then a promiscuous mating system is more likely to occur. The loose aggregations at times of mating of many baleen whale species, as exemplified by humpback and right whales, further argue in favour of promiscuity being the norm, and it seems extremely unlikely that any baleen whale has a monogamous mating system (see Brownell and Ralls, 1986, for a recent review of mating systems of baleen whales).

Table 7.3: Putative mating systems of cetaceans

Polygynous mating system with adult male associating with group of females for protracted period (the length of which is variable):

Sperm whale (Berzin 1972, Best 1979, Ohsumi 1971, Whitehead and Gordon 1986, Gordon pers. comm.)
Long-finned pilot whale (Sergeant 1962)
Short-finned pilot whale (Kasuya and Marsh 1984)
Killer whale (Balcomb *et al.* 1979, 1980; Bigg 1979, 1982)
Risso's dolphin (Evans *et al.* 1986, unpubl.)
Possibly northern bottlenose whale (Benjaminsen and Christensen 1979)

Promiscuous mating system where adult males compete for complete mating access to females:

Humpback whale (Darling 1983; Tyack 1981; Tyack and Whitehead 1983; Winn and Winn 1985)
Pygmy right whale (Baker 1985; Ross *et al.* 1975; Brownell and Ralls 1986)
Possibly blue, fin, sei, minke and Bryde's whales (Brownell and Ralls 1986), narwhal (Silverman and Dunbar 1980) and white whale (Pippard and Malcolm 1978; Sergeant 1973)

Promiscuous mating system where adult males compete for some mating access to females (and sperm competition may be most important):

Southern right whale (Kraus 1986, Payne in press)
Bowhead whale (Everitt and Krogman 1979)
Gray whale (Jones and Swartz 1984; Swartz 1986; Norris *et al.* 1983)
Spinner dolphin (Norris and Dohl 1980a,b)
Dusky dolphin (Wursig and Wursig 1980)
Bottle-nosed dolphin (Wursig 1978; Wursig and Wursig 1977, 1979; Wells *et al.* 1980; Shane *et al.* 1986; Saayman and Tayler 1973; Tayler and Saayman 1976)
Indo-Pacific hump-backed dolphin (Saayman and Tayler 1973, 1979)
Possibly most other delphinids and more social phocoenids

Notes: The reference sources given above provide descriptions of the social organisation of that particular species; they do not necessarily interpret these as a particular mating system. The grouping given above follows Brownell and Ralls (1986) for baleen whales, and for odontocetes they are as interpreted by the present author.
River dolphins are so poorly known that there is no information on their social organisation or mating system. If some species prove to be territorial, as has been suggested, for example, for the susus, there is a possibility that a monogamous mating system (linked to site fidelity) may have evolved, as could possibly occur for some of the more solitary phocoenids. However, temporary aggregations reported in some species may provide opportunities for a promiscuous mating system to prevail.

Odontocetes are mostly either fish-feeders or squid-feeders, or have mixed diets. If they range over a broad expanse of sea searching for clumped food concentrations, they may aggregate in large groups. The food source, particularly if it is schooling fish, can sustain a large number of animals in close proximity to one another. Inshore species seem to search for their food in smaller groups. Possibly the food source is not concentrated enough to support larger numbers. Fish schools appear to be more ephemeral in their geographical location than are plankton swarms which commonly occur along frontal systems. They are, therefore, less easy to defend and males would have difficulty supporting a discrete group of females in a localised area on such a resource. We might thus expect primarily fish-feeders to have a promiscuous mating system unless they are resident in a localised area supported by a regular food supply. Our knowledge of the ecology of squid is very poor but they do not appear to be social. As to their fidelity to particular sites, we can only conjecture. However, since those species that feed mainly upon squid appear to have polygynous mating systems, presumably males holding harems of females can sustain them on a regular source of food. This need not necessarily be the evolutionary route to that mating system. It may be, for example, that the slow growth to sexual maturity or long period needed for the maturation of skills for the capture of squid require the group to have a stable membership over an extended period. Either of these could lead to the opportunity for a single male to have mating access to a group of females. Furthermore, the protracted period of gestation and lactation in these species means that even if the normal sex ratio of sexually mature adults was 1:1, fewer females would be available to mate than males. Thus barely 35 per cent of female sperm whales come into oestrus each season so that there may be an annual surplus of males. This would inevitably lead to competition for females and may be a further route to polygyny. Males would try to monopolise access to females since they are a scarce resource; the fitter males might then have the opportunity to monopolise several females. Before leaving this discussion, I should point out its speculative nature and emphasise the fact that we are still far from certain of the mating system of almost any cetacean species.

The social organisation of cetaceans has often been compared to terrestrial mammals, usually either ungulates (particularly bovids such as the African buffalo — Wells *et al.* 1980b: 308–10) or primates (such as the chimpanzee or baboon — Saayman and Tayler 1979; Tayler and Saayman 1972; Wells *et al.* 1980b). There are some similarities to all these and also differences, some of which appear more fundamental than others. However, I would caution such comparisons between taxa that have widely different evolutionary histories. More would be gained by comparing social structure and group size of a particular species that may live in a variety of habitats. The bottle-nosed dolphin would obviously be a good subject and a study of pelagic groups would be most interesting.

HOME RANGE SIZE AND HABITAT USE

In the previous chapter we saw something of the energetic demands upon a whale or dolphin and how it meets these demands by the way it forages for food. If all its food requirements could be met within a restricted area, we might expect it to have a small home range; if not, it will need to range over a larger area. We also saw that there is a danger of the animal exhausting its food supplies unless these are allowed time to recover before being exploited again. Cetaceans move around to find food (and probably secondarily to escape predation and find mates) and the area over which they range must serve those needs either in the short term or over the long term. Short-term home ranges may differ from those over a twelve month period. Thus, baleen whales may spend the summer months in a small area but then migrate at the end of the season once the food resource has become scarce. The annual migration may involve a round trip of many thousands of kilometres (over 20,000 in the case of the gray whale — Jones and Swartz 1984).

Our knowledge of the size of short-term (seasonal) home ranges is very limited for most baleen whales. During calving they are probably quite small when animals congregate on localised breeding grounds. Individual whales may be recognised by the pattern of callosities on the bonnet or forehead (right whales — see R. Payne *et al.* 1983), markings on the flipper and underside of the tail flukes (humpback whale — see Katona *et al.* 1979; Kraus and Katona 1977), or by scars, pigmentation patterns and nicks in the dorsal fin (minke whale — see Dorsey 1983). By these means it has been shown that humpback whales spend protracted periods on the Silver and Navidad Banks in the Caribbean; likewise, southern right whale individuals spend their winter within the protected bays of Peninsula Valdés in Patagonia. On the feeding grounds both species appear to range over larger areas although short periods may be spent in very localised regions. The same individuals may visit exactly the same area each year, both when feeding and when breeding. This site fidelity is also exhibited by other rorquals. The minke whale, for example, has been recorded returning to the very same feeding areas in subsequent summers. Eleanor Dorsey (1983), observing in the inshore waters of Washington State, has also shown that recognisable individuals occupied exclusive adjacent home ranges over a summer season. Three such ranges were found in an area of about 600 sq km, each one shared by up to at least seven minke whales. Those individuals appeared to feed and travel independently of one another. Occasionally two or three individuals surfaced simultaneously parallel to one another and it is possible that this represents at least limited co-operation as seen occasionally in feeding aggregations of humpbacks. We cannot say if the exclusive home ranges of these minke whales represent territories; no overt acts of aggression were observed that might indicate that the areas were defended.

The use that a baleen whale makes of its home range is still poorly known for most species, but protracted observations of humpbacks, fin and minke whales, gray, bowhead and right whales suggest that particular areas may be visited repeatedly for feeding. Tidal rips or, in the case of the bowhead, thin ice edges are quartered by one or more whales for periods up to a few hours.

As with other aspects of natural history, our knowledge of home range size and habitat use is extremely limited for both the pelagic beaked whales and the river dolphins. It is known that individuals of certain beaked whale species may range over some distance. However, these may primarily represent seasonal migrations and home ranges within a season could be much smaller. Northern bottlenose whales, for example, have favoured feeding areas in the Greenland and Norwegian Seas where they traditionally concentrate. The association with subsurface sea mounts of Baird's beaked whales, reported from California, could lead to beaked whales having relatively restricted home ranges and, in turn, to population isolation which might explain the large number of *Mesoplodon* species that exist in the world's deep oceans.

The home range of river dolphins appears to be determined greatly by water flow and the rise and fall of water levels controlled by seasonal

1. Dusky dolphin breaching off New Zealand (photo: S. Leatherwood)

2. Southern right whale breaching, Peninsula Valdés, Argentina (photo: A. Taber)

3. Southern right whale and calf, Peninsula Valdés, Argentina (photo: A. Taber)

4. Minke whale lunge-feeding, eastern Pacific (photo: R. Pitman)

5. Fin whale surfacing showing open blowhole, Iceland (photo: A. Martin)

6. Humpback whale breaching off Iceland (photo: T. Waters)

7. Sperm whale with open jaw, off Sri Lanka (photo: T. Arnbom)

8. Herd of long-finned pilot whales in lateral formation, off western Ireland (photo: P.G.H. Evans)

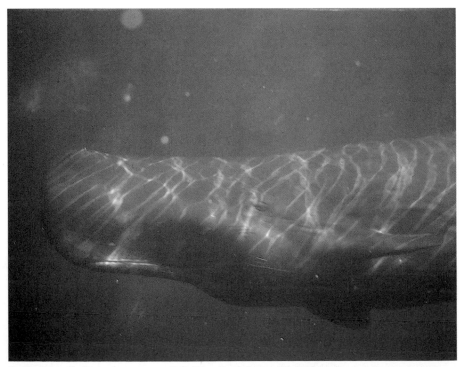

9. Sperm whale underwater, off Sri Lanka (photo: T. Arnbom)

10. Mixed herd of long-finned pilot whales and bottle-nosed dolphins, off western Ireland (P.G.H. Evans)

11. Killer whale breaching, Puget Sound (photo: K. Balcomb)

12. Killer whale attacking sea lion from shore, Patagonia (photo: A. Taber)

13. Bowhead whale killed by eskimos in aboriginal whale fishery, Barrow, Alaska (photo: H. Braham)

14. Sperm whale after harpooning,
Denmark Strait south of Greenland
(photo: A. Martin)

15. Pilot whale 'grind' in the Faroe
islands (photo: A. Martin)

16. Herd of narwhals, Baffin Bay (photo: A. Martin)

17. Common dolphin breaching, west of Ushant, Brittany (photo: P.G.H. Evans)

18. White-beaked dolphin breaching, Minches, western Scotland (photo: P.G.H. Evans)

19. Gray whale spyhopping, San Ignacio lagoon (photo: S. Leatherwood)

20. Long-snouted spinner dolphins bow-riding in Red Sea (photo: A. van den Berg)

rains. The susus, for example, are usually confined to the main channels of the river in the dry season, but when the rains come, they disperse into tributaries and swollen creeks. The same applies to other species such as the boto and baiji, and the latter, preferring deep channels, will enter lakes during spring floods. When hunting, the boto apparently orient themselves upstream or into a current, where, like other river dolphins, they forage individually. Unlike the previous species, the franciscana does not usually enter freshwater but lives in shallow water 40m (20 fathoms) or less. There has been a suggestion that the susus at least are territorial, but this needs further verification.

Only recently have sperm whales been studied at sea in any detail, mainly by Jonathan Gordon, Hal Whitehead and their co-workers. Observations have been made primarily in tropical areas, off the coasts of Sri Lanka and around the Galapagos Islands. Off Sri Lanka one school of identified individuals was tracked over c. 140km during a 10 day period and it moved first north and then south along a 50km section of the continental shelf edge (Gordon pers. comm.). Interestingly, the same whales were found in exactly the same location when they were resighted a year later, suggesting a surprising degree of long-term site fidelity for such an oceanic animal. Sperm whale calves observed off Sri Lanka were found to associate closely with several other school members in addition to their mothers. They were often found alone at the surface with such adults who may have been performing a 'babysitting' role. Field observations (from Sri Lanka) suggest that calves may suckle from more than one female, and further support for communal suckling (particularly from older females) comes from the finding of traces of milk in young up to 13 years old (Best *et al.* 1984:65–6). Observations on short-finned pilot whales suggesting a similar system of communal suckling have been made recently by Toshio Kasuya and Helene Marsh (1984:285–7).

Killer whale pods also have large home ranges that may extend for 320–480km, as in Puget Sound, Washington State where they have been studied since 1976 by Ken Balcomb, Mike Bigg, James Boran, Sara Heimlich and Richard Osborne (Balcomb *et al.* 1979, 1980; Bigg 1979, 1982; Bigg *et al.* 1976). During a single day they would regularly travel 120–160km whilst foraging for food. The distribution of these pods has been correlated closely with the occurrence of salmon, an important prey, and particular habitats appear to be favoured. These include tidal rips, kelp beds, underwater sea mounts and shoreline cliffs (indeed, similar habitats to those that many cetacean species favour and where we might expect food to be concentrated — see Chapter 6). No particular diurnal pattern of behaviour has been found, activity being most closely associated with the tidal cycle. Over half of the time (53 per cent) spent by the pod was divided almost equally between travelling and feeding/foraging. Twenty per cent of the time was spent in playful foraging (where animals would engage in various acrobatics), 13 per cent in more obvious play, 12 per cent in rest or sleep, and 2 per cent in intermingling (Boran *et al.* 1981; Osborne 1981). This gives us some idea of the time necessary to obtain food and helps with the calculation of energy budgets as detailed in the previous chapter.

Home range size and habitat use by the smaller odontocetes, the dolphins and porpoises, are best illustrated by one or two examples, taken from some of the most detailed field studies carried out to date. The dusky dolphin studied by Bernd and Melany Wursig (1980) at Golfo San José, southern Argentina, ranges over an area of approximately 1,500 sq km. Night-time is spent in small schools of 6–15 animals no more than a kilometre offshore. During this period they appear to be at rest, with only slow movements. In the morning they then move into deeper water (of 2–29m but mainly 2–6m depth), 2–10km from shore. At this time they appear to be searching for food and groups swim in a line abreast with each animal 10m from the next. In this way they can cover an area of sea up to 150m wide. Feeding then starts and may involve the co-operative herding of large schools of fish by aggregations of up to 300 dolphins. By mid-afternoon feeding may be concentrated in one area and during this time and the subsequent period individuals start to interact socially in play and sexual activity. In the evening the large school splits up into smaller groups once more which then return inshore for the night. When dusky dolphins were approached by killer whales they moved into water less than 1m deep; on the other hand, killer whales have not infrequently been observed picking off marine mammals from the immediate vicinity of the coast (see Plate 12; also Lopez and Lopez 1985).

Although generally pelagic, spinner dolphins in Hawaii tend to remain close to the coast. Here they may range up to 50km from day to day, although they seldom range further than 100km (Norris and Dohl 1980a). Unlike the dusky dolphin, the daytime is spent resting and socialising in relatively shallow protected bays, perhaps because it is calmer here or perhaps to escape killer whale and shark predation. Late in the day, Hawaiian spinners move offshore where they feed during the night at depths of 100m or more on organisms in the deep scattering layer (the sound-reflecting layer caused by stratified, dense concentrations of plankton and fish).

The home range of a group of bottle-nosed dolphins studied in Sarasota Bay, Florida was approximately 85 sq km (Wells *et al.* 1980). Within this group, individuals had smaller home ranges which varied according to the age or sex of the individual. Females with calves have the largest home ranges (c. 40 sq km) followed by subadult males, whilst they were smallest in adult males, adult females (without calves) and subadult females, in decreasing order (between 15–20 sq km). Segregation by age and sex occurred in this manner and such sub-groups often had home ranges centred on different parts of the bay. Within Sarasota Bay, sub-groups of bottle-nosed dolphins have preferred core areas where they spend most of their time and membership of these sub-groups is relatively stable for periods of up to four months (although they may change group affiliations as noted earlier). Typically, a sub-group would be found in one part of the home range for several days, milling over shallow seagrass beds or deeper channels whilst apparently feeding; this pattern would then shift to another part of the home range where it would be repeated. Home range size varies between different regions just as do group size and group composition. In southern Argentina, individual bottle-nosed dolphins might move 300km and then return to the original location (Wursig and Wursig 1979). When inshore, individuals usually fed alone but when feeding in deeper water offshore, they would do so in groups. Other studies have been carried out on free-ranging bottle-nosed dolphins, in Texas (Gruber 1981; Shane 1980), southern California (Hansen 1983), and in the Molène archipelago, Brittany (France) (Hussenot 1980). Though differing in detail, their results support those presented above, indicating relatively permanent social units that are closely tied to definable home ranges. Within these populations, the age and sex of an individual affects its social associations and movements, with some associations (particularly those of mothers and young) extending into the long term (see Shane *et al*. 1986 for a review).

Harbour porpoises have been followed in New Brunswick, Canada through radio-tagging and the use of natural marks (Gaskin *et al*. 1975; Watson 1976; Yasui 1980; Yurick 1977). Individuals (and sometimes small groups) of either sex, and female and calf pairs (sometimes accompanied by a yearling) are the most common groupings seen. These typically followed a similar pattern of movement from day to day, hugging the edges of basins and shallow trenches. Distances moved by a radio-tagged adult male over a four-day period amounted to at least 40km though not exceeding 20km within a day. This species appears to be closer to its energetic limit than the killer whale detailed above. Within a 24 hour period, 76 per cent of the time was spent apparently foraging or feeding, 21 per cent in normal travel and 3 per cent in rest (Watson 1976).

SOCIAL BEHAVIOUR — AGGRESSION, PLAY, AND PARENTAL CARE

The consequences of sociality, even if it is only for short periods, are that individuals interact and communicate with one another. We shall first look briefly at three forms of social behaviour which are essentially non-sexual: aggression, play and parental care. The first two may involve individuals of either sex and different age groups; the latter concerns the more restricted case of a mother-calf bond.

Aggression

The common response to a potential predator (shark, killer whale or playback of killer whale sound) appears to be for the cetacean to flee, often silently, having first formed a tight group (if it already exists in a school). However, sometimes aggression will be shown and the predator is pursued or attacked. Thus a humpback whale has been observed warding off an attacking group of killer whales by turning on its back and slashing out with its powerful tail. Southern right whales have also defended themselves against killer whales by slashing repeatedly with flukes and pectoral fins. Dolphins (for example bottle-nosed and hump-backed dolphins) have also been seen chasing off shark predators and even killing them (Saayman and Tayler 1979; Wells *et al*. 1980). Aggression, therefore, serves a useful purpose in predator defence. It may also be important in a social context. Aggression has rarely been observed among baleen whales although it may have escaped notice, and in certain species (such as the humpback), tail-slapping, tail-swishing and even breaching probably serve partly as a threat signal (Baker and Herman 1984). In feeding areas, groups of humpbacks may sometimes push and shove one another for access to a food concentration, whilst on the breeding grounds, escorts accompanying mother-calf pairs may display intense aggression towards other approaching humpbacks (Baker *et al.* 1981; Darling 1983; Tyack 1981; Tyack and Whitehead 1983). Southern right whale females may be surrounded by 2–6 (sometimes up to 14) competing males and in this situation pushing and head butting frequently occurs, leading to scars and gouges on the skin (Cummings 1985; Kraus 1986; Payne and Dorsey 1983). Group mating has been reported in bowhead whales (Everitt and Krogman 1979), with as many as six whales involved, but aggressive behaviour has not yet been observed. Gray whales have also been observed in mating groups of up to 18 animals, remaining together for up to two hours although changing composition as individual whales leave or join (Jones and Swartz 1984; Swartz 1986).

Dolphins and toothed whales commonly rake one another with their teeth and scarring is a widespread phenomenon. Studies in captivity have suggested the development of hierarchies where dominant animals will show aggression towards subordinates (particularly young males). In the wild it has often been the younger individuals, usually of the male sex, which have had the most extensive scarring (identifiable as made by others within the species by the pattern of tooth marks). Bull sperm whales may fight established males to take over a harem of females and to do this they use their prominent teeth in a raking action as well as butting with their huge barrel-shaped heads (possibly one reason for its greater development in the male) (see Best 1979). The teeth of sperm whales start to erupt in the lower jaw at 4–5 years of age in males (slightly later in females). The complete set of lower teeth may not show until 30–40 years old, whilst the upper teeth start to erupt at 20 years old or may not appear until much later in life, if at all. The late appearance of the teeth may, therefore, relate more to their use in aggressive encounters than to feeding.

The fact that only the male narwhal normally has a tusk may serve a similar function, since studies in Alaska by Helen Silverman suggest that when competing for females, males engage in aggressive behaviour, scarring one another during jousting contests (Silverman and Dunbar 1980). Scars attributed to tusk action have been found on the heads of adult males which are also more likely to have broken tusks. It is interesting that in those species thought to have polygynous mating systems, there is some sexual dimorphism that might be used either in direct combat for females (for example tusk, large head or melon) or as a character inferring sexual status (for example, a tall dorsal fin). As seems to be the case for some polygynous terrestrial mammals, perhaps sexual selection has favoured the evolution of these characters independent of other selection pressures. For a general review of aggressive behaviour, the reader should consult Norris (1967), and for a review of aggression in relation to mating behaviour, read Brownell and Ralls (1986).

Play

Play behaviour is commonly seen in both baleen and toothed whales. It is generally found in young animals where its function is considered to be the learning of various important actions and these may continue to be practised through later life. The right whale calf spends its early life close to its mother circling and moving back and forth but always within her vicinity (Taber and Thomas 1982). During this period it will also learn to breach and does so repeatedly, exceptionally up to 80 times in an hour. Other play involves rolling upside down, possibly a prelude to courtship when adults often roll upside down to bring themselves belly to belly with their sexual partner. The calf will also practise slapping the water with its flipper which later serves a defensive function against killer whales; or it may use the flipper to stroke or hug its mother much as is done in later life during courtship and other social interaction. In these ways the young animal learns to master the behaviour actions that will be a vital part of adult life. As the calf grows older it is more likely to play with other yearling or sub-adult right whales (Thomas 1986).

For social dolphins, play may commonly be seen between individuals both young and adult, as well as between mother and young. Often one can see young animals repeatedly practising aerial leaps and spins, and fin- and head-slaps. They will ride the surf or the bows of a vessel, and such scenes will probably be the commonest view for many people. During bow-riding, animals will constantly pass back and forth with frequent boisterous leaps. More than once in these circumstances I have been showered by a white-beaked dolphin in what appeared to be a very purposeful sideways splash beside the boat. Others have had similar experiences with other species such as bottle-nosed dolphins, and larger whales such as the right whale have been observed riding the surf or splashing beside a boat. These apparent playful actions practised out of context may at other times serve important functions of communication, food-herding and predator defence. Social and sexual behaviour is also practised with much tactile contact by young animals, stroking one another with the penis or flippers, swimming belly to belly or touching flippers in a manner similar to holding hands. These actions are carried out throughout life, and they probably function not only in courtship but to maintain familiarity between group members (the penis may serve as a tactile as well as a sexual organ). They are also sometimes directed to animals of other species such as man, and there are many accounts of lone dolphins befriending humans and often playing with them (see, for example, Alpers 1960; Doak 1982; Dobbs 1977; Saayman and Tayler 1971; Webb 1978). Play is also very well known among captive animals in dolphinaria and helps to enliven public shows.

Parental Care

The bond between the mother and calf is a special facet of behaviour which follows a similar pattern across all cetacean species. At birth the mother will assist its calf, usually born tail first, to the surface to gain its first breath (Figure 7.3). During this time the mother may be attended by others (usually nonpregnant females), sometimes referred to as 'aunts', and these have been observed assisting the mother in taking the young to the surface (M. Caldwell and Caldwell 1966; Norris and Dohl 1980b). There are even some accounts of these aunts helping the mother herself if she is in difficulty. These assisting actions take the form of the individual being supported from underneath by one or more others, which then swim to the surface (Figure 7.4). An attending female has been seen to actually bite through the umbilical cord of a captive dusky dolphin during birth of her young, but usually the mother does this herself. Most of these observations have been made on captive animals and it is not

Figure 7.3 Birth and parental care in dolphins. Young are born tail first and are quickly assisted to the surface for their first breath by the mother and, sometimes, by other females. During swimming, the young may press its flipper against the mother's side and thus be assisted in its locomotion

clear the extent to which they occur in the wild.

Aunts show great interest in the calf after birth and typically closely follow the mother-calf pair. They probably afford some protection by increased surveillance, and may 'baby-sit' the calf while the mother is feeding. This would be particularly useful for those species such as the sperm whale that need to dive beyond the depths of the young for food. It is also helpful for other species such as the pelagic dolphins that may need to swim beyond the speed of their young to pursue prey. Humpback whales, on the other hand, appear to isolate themselves prior to birth and this period may last for days or possibly weeks during which time a strong bond forms between the pair (Darling *et al.* 1983; Glockner and Venus 1983; Herman and Antinoja 1977). As we shall see in the next section, this behaviour is then exploited by males that temporarily escort the pair for purposes of courtship and mating. However, in most cetacean species, if mother-calf pairs come together (with or without aunts) to form nursery groups, they are segregated from males and these play no part in parental care. Where there is male contact it may involve high-speed rushes by males towards the mother-calf pair, interpreted by Ken Norris and Thomas Dohl (1980b) as being to bring the pair back into the centre of the larger group. Until we know more about the spacing relations and social structure of these groups, this point must remain equivocal.

Throughout the early period of life the calf keeps very close to its mother, positioning itself above the midline forward of the dorsal fin of the mother. The calf's flipper may actually be pressed against her side and this allows it to move with her without a great expenditure of energy. Otherwise the calf is precocious and many of the senses and actions necessary for survival are well developed very early in life. The calf, as in all cetaceans, is dependent upon its mother for food which it obtains from the fat-rich milk. The female sperm whale, for example, provides its calf daily with about 20kg of milk, containing about one-third fat (Lockyer 1981b). Suckling in this species continues for at least two years and the

Figure 7.4 Epimeletic (caring) behaviour in dolphin mother-calf pair. Young in distress (or even when stillborn) may be carried on the snout of the mother. Such supportive behaviour may sometimes even be applied to other cetacean species, and there are similar reports of dolphins assisting humans

young whale may even suckle after weaning for several more years (Best *et al.* 1984). In the case of the gray whale, the calf spends over 90 per cent of the first few weeks of its life within close proximity of its mother, and may maintain contact even as a yearling after a six month migration to feeding grounds (Taber and Thomas 1982; Thomas 1986).

In the bottle-nosed dolphin, almost immediately after birth, the mother may whistle nearly continuously for several days presumably to provide a strong acoustic imprinting stimulus. Studies by Melba and David Caldwell (1979) have shown that this early whistle is relatively uniform but then acquires a 'signature' characteristic which may serve for individual recognition, though this has yet to be verified (see Figure 7.9).

As the calf grows older, the bond with the mother weakens. More time is spent away from her and interactions with other young increase. Aggressive behaviour may also increase and this could serve partly as a spacing function. If any hierarchical system develops it is usually related to age (older animals being dominant to younger ones) or in nursery groups may be centred upon older females. Finally the bond is broken (though it may last two or three years), and in the case of odontocetes, the young may form groups of similar aged individuals either of the same sex, usually male (such as the sperm whale, killer whale, bottle-nosed dolphin and harbour porpoise) or of mixed sex (such as the spinner and dusky dolphin). Studies of infant and calf behaviour have concentrated upon the bottle-nosed dolphin in captivity, and for details of this and other aspects of social behaviour, the reader should consult D. Caldwell and Caldwell (1972a); M. Caldwell and Caldwell (1966, 1972); Defran and Pryor (1980); Leatherwood (1977); McBride and Webb (1948); Tavolga (1966); Tavolga and Essapian (1957).

SEXUAL BEHAVIOUR — COURTSHIP AND MATING

For successful sexual reproduction, potential mates must locate each other and then perform various actions that will ensure that mating is between members of the same species. Just as we humans may also show some choice in the mate we take, we can expect other species to do likewise even if there is no conscious intent involved.

Except for those species restricted to rivers or the coast, whales and dolphins occupy a wide expanse of relatively uniform sea. Movements, particularly of the more pelagic species, may range over great distances. Those species which live essentially alone or in small groups (often mother-calf pairs) might have the most difficulty meeting others of the opposite sex. However, most of these are baleen whale species which undergo definite seasonal migrations. They have favoured breeding and feeding areas, and, so far as we can tell, for many species individuals are faithful to those sites from year to year. Seasonality and site fidelity are probably the main ways that these whales can readily find a mate, and there is generally strong synchrony in the timing of mating and birth, although sexual activity may occur at different times of the year. During the southern winter (between July and November), southern right whales gather to calve in shallow sheltered bays such as at Peninsula Valdés in Argentina (Clark 1983, Payne in press). Mothers and their

Figure 7.5 Courtship behaviour: the nuclear female-calf pair, and satellite male humpback whale (derived from Tyack and Whitehead 1983). A cow and calf are joined by an adult male, which stops its singing and escorts them for a period of time. The cow, calf and primary escort group then attract secondary escorts which may or may not displace the male. Unsuccessful escorts and the displaced male leave the cow and calf, and recommence singing

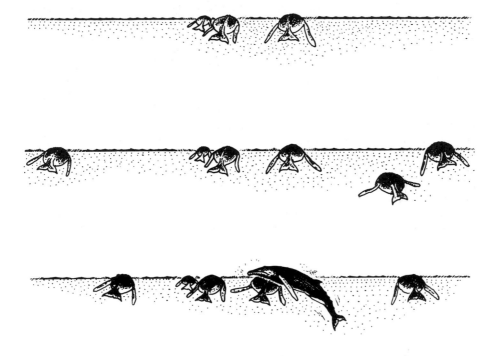

young occupy the areas closest to shore whilst other groups of up to ten adults and subadults engage in active social and sexual behaviour at the entrance to the bays. However, it is thought that matings at this time do not lead to conception and instead occur primarily in deeper waters on the feeding grounds just prior to or during migration. Female right whales may be surrounded by up to six males and triads commonly occur where one male may support the female from below whilst the other mates with her. So far we have no idea whether these individuals are related to one another but the degree of coming and going in the area would suggest that they are not. A similar fluid system exists for the humpback (Tyack and Whitehead 1983; see Figure 4.5 and p. 193). Since gestation is approximately 12 to 13 months for most baleen whales, effective mating probably takes place in the late summer to late autumn just prior to or during migration to the breeding grounds.

In the gray whale, sexual behaviour has been observed throughout the year but this may involve primarily males (Darling 1977b, 1983), and conceptions are concentrated over a short three-week period centred around the beginning of December (Jones and Swartz 1984; Norris *et al.* 1983; Swartz 1986). At this time the whales are at or near the end of their southward migration, which in the Northeast Pacific takes them close to the North American coast. Sexual behaviour may involve five or more individuals rolling and milling around, usually in the shelter of the lagoons of Baja California, where the calves will be born 13 months later. As with the right whale, mothers and calves tend to occupy the shallow portions deep inside the lagoons whilst males and subadults concentrate in the areas around the lagoon mouths (Norris et al. 1983). As many as 7 or 8 mating groups have been observed in an area about 100m in diameter, with males leaving or joining, and females repeatedly copulating with more than one male during the same mating bout (Jones and Swartz 1984; Norris et al. 1983; Swartz 1986).

So far as we can tell, for most baleen whales, those matings leading to conception occur primarily just before or during return to the breeding grounds. Courtship often involves groups of animals, usually identified as a female and a number of males (gray whale — Norris et al 1983, Rice 1983; bowhead — Everitt and Krogman 1979; southern right whale — Kraus 1986), although with rorquals this has only been determined for the humpback (Glockner 1983). Females of southern right, bowhead and gray whales apparently commonly copulate with more than one male, and interactions between males are not highly aggressive. This has been interpreted as reflecting sperm competition (sperm-producing males attempting to displace or dilute the sperm of others within the female), and has been related to the large testes and long penises that those three species (particularly the right whale) possess (Brownell and Ralls 1986). Larger testes are required to produce the large numbers of sperm needed under those conditions, and the longer penises presumably help to deliver the sperm closer to the ova. On the other hand, the mating systems of humpback whales (and maybe other balaenopterid whales and the pygmy right whale) appear not to be selected in this way. Humpback males compete primarily by monopolising females, preventing other males from copulating with them (Figure 7.5); females commonly copulate with only one male, male-male interactions are often highly aggressive, and males have relatively small testes and shorter penises.

Toothed whales differ from baleen whales in showing less striking seasonality in mating and birth. This applies particularly to those species living in the tropics or subtropics although there is still usually a seasonal peak in births. Sociality among toothed whales helps to ensure that the sexes meet, and it may be that the readiness of females to mate is relayed by various cues. Such cues include changes in the shape and colour of the genital area in several dolphin species, possible discharge of hormones in the feces or urine, and certain behavioural actions. Ken Norris and Thomas Dohl (1980b) have observed a well-defined defecation period during the morning hours when clouds of fecal material were produced underwater through which most school members swam. Clearly if activities such as these are synchronised they would provide a good way for males to receive sexually based chemical cues. As with baleen whales, courtship leading to mating involves belly contact either in an upright position or with the female lying motionless belly upwards just beneath the surface (Figure 7.6). In the latter position the female swims beneath the male, but usually the pair swims with the male gliding beneath the female. Such behaviour may be practised by animals of any age (and sometimes of the same sex), and at different times of year. It does not always lead to mating and when it does may not necessarily result in conception. Courtship may take various forms including chases, simul-

Figure 7.6 *Mating behaviour: (a) humpback whale; (b) sperm whale. Mating may be preceded by the male gliding beneath the female and then upturning for belly to belly contact. Sometimes the positions may be reversed, whilst belly contact in a vertical position has also been observed*

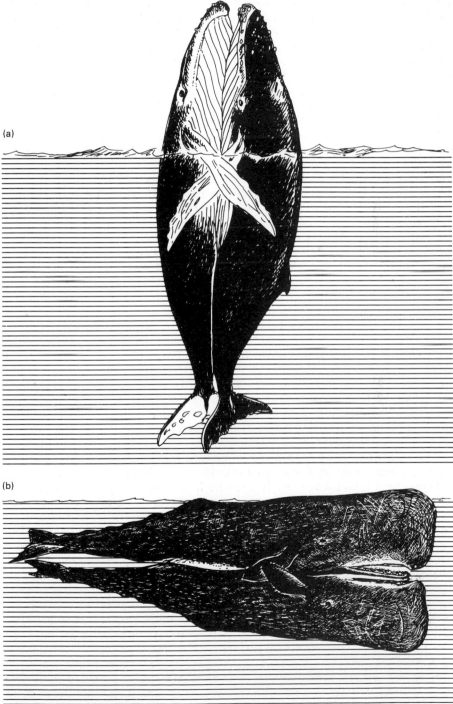

(a)

(b)

taneous surfacing, breaching and flipper contact. Such visual and tactile methods of courtship are conspicuous; the use of sound is less easily witnessed but evidence is accumulating to suggest that such signals may be quite important in conveying information relating to the identity and sex of the sender, and emotional content. Harbour porpoises and bottle-nosed dolphins, for example, both produce pulsed yelps during courtship. We shall consider these aspects of communication further in the next section.

COMMUNICATION, CO-OPERATION AND INTELLIGENCE

With cetaceans, one question more than any other hangs on the lips of the enquiring public — Are dolphins really as intelligent as man? This question in practice involves more than a comparison of levels of intelligence, but also includes comparisons of a variety of human attributes. In fact the question that is really in people's minds appears to be 'How similar are dolphins to man?' Entire books have been written on the subject, arguing often hotly opposing positions. There is room here to do no more than briefly review the subject and the reader should consult the following references for further details: Fichtelius and Sjolander (1972); Frost (1978); Gaskin (1982:141–152); Herman (1980a); McIntyre (1974); Wursig (1983).

Consideration of these questions requires more than just a strict comparison of language, learning skills, planned or innovative behaviour. It requires consideration of the different evolutionary courses that dolphin and man have taken and the environments in which they live. Man has evolved in a terrestrial environment where generalisation has been selected for. His bipedal habit with dexterous limbs aided by an opposable thumb have helped him to develop tools to perform tasks. These developments have taken place alongside the evolution of a large brain with a convoluted cortex, needed to process information of a variety of kinds and for learning. Particular developments of the voice box (larynx) have allowed man to transfer information between individuals through language. In language and the large brain lie the origins of culture.

Dolphins (and other cetaceans) have evolved in an aquatic environment. Anatomical and physiological adaptations have led to specialisations such as the streamlining of the body and loss of separate flexible digits. The aqueous medium is much better than air for transmitting sound, but not much better for the transmission of taste or smell (except over short distances). Except at the surface, the sea is a shadowy place where vision can scarcely operate. Where it does so, it seems to rely upon contrasting black and white patterns of pigmentation. Sound is, therefore, likely to be one of the more important senses for cetaceans, although anatomical constraints on movement of the jaws and tongue as well as the construction of the larynx might possibly limit the scope for complex language.

Now that we see something of the respective backgrounds of man and dolphin, let us look at those features of cetaceans that have been most closely compared with man. We will start with communication since this may be seen as the essence of the relationship in the minds of many people.

Communication

Few people can fail to be moved by the eerie and plaintive songs of the humpback whale brought to our ears mainly from the studies of Roger and Katy Payne and an LP record that has become a bestseller. The great variety of moans, snores and groans are repeated according to identifiable patterns forming an ordered sequence of themes comprising motifs and phrases just as do the songs of birds (Payne and McVay 1971; also Figure 7.7). These sounds are usually in the frequency range 40Hz to 5kHz and can be detected by hydrophones over 30km away (Winn and Winn 1978). They may last from 6 to 35 minutes before being repeated. Such song sessions can continue through the day and night with only brief one minute pauses for breath. Howard and Lois Winn (1978) recorded one whale in the Caribbean singing non-stop for at least 22 hours. The basic unit of the song is the syllable sounding as 'cries', 'yups', 'chirps', etc. Each syllable is equivalent to a note in our music and about 20 such syllables have been recognised. Syllables are grouped into small repeating sequences called phrases and groups of similar phrases are called themes. There are six basic themes. The motifs and phrases may be repeated any number of times though the individual phrases can vary considerably in length.

Although the song of an individual has its own signature, within one season all whales within a particular region sing broadly the same song. However, whales from the North Atlantic sing a different song to those in the North Pacific which in turn differ from those in the South Pacific (Winn et al. 1981). On the other hand, individuals from separate breeding grounds in Baja California and Hawaii were found singing the same song despite a 4,800-km distance between them (Payne and Guinee 1983). Two years later both populations had made identical modifications to their song. Further studies of recognisable individuals by James Darling of Santa Cruz proved that the whales from the different breeding areas had been in contact on feeding grounds off south-east Alaska (Darling and Jurasz 1983).

The songs of the humpback whale are continually changing over time (K. Payne et al. 1983; Guinee et al. 1983). All individuals within a population change their songs in the same way. The changes are both progressive and rapid, each component perhaps changing every two months, although many elements of the song are changing at any one time. During a season a song may change components adding extra parts and varying the pitch. One part of the song may undergo rapid changes for several months and then remain unchanged whilst other parts are modified. An entire song is changed after about eight years. In this way humpback whale songs fall somewhere between those of certain songbirds that increase their repertoires throughout life by mimicry and humans who create new songs from nothing.

Why these songs should continually change is unclear. It has been shown that overall changes do not simply reflect changing membership in a singing population. Recognisable individuals have been shown to change their songs along with the rest of the population — a clear case of cultural evolution. Although we do not know why the songs change

189

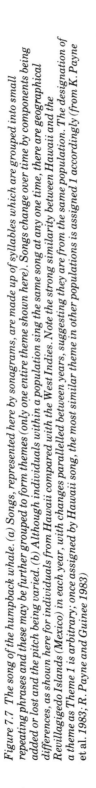
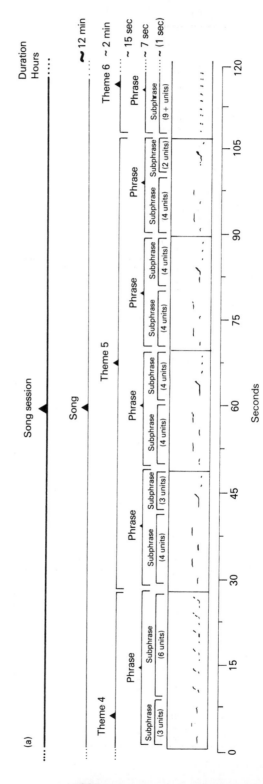

Figure 7.7 The song of the humpback whale. (a) Songs, represented here by sonagrams, are made up of syllables which are grouped into small repeating phrases and these may be further grouped to form themes (only one entire theme shown here). Songs change over time by components being added or lost and the pitch being varied. (b) Although individuals within a population sing the same song at any one time, there are geographical differences, as shown here for individuals from Hawaii compared with the West Indies. Note the strong similarity between Hawaii and the Revillagigedo Islands (Mexico) in each year, with changes parallelled between years, suggesting they are from the same population. The designation of a theme as Theme 1 is arbitrary; once assigned by Hawaii song, the most similar theme in other populations is assigned 1 accordingly (from K. Payne et al. 1983; R. Payne and Guinee 1983)

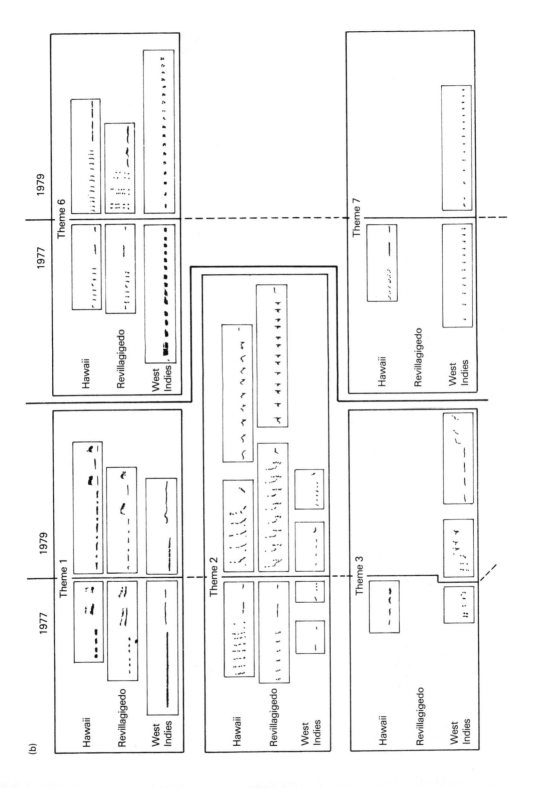

Figure 7.7 (continued)

(c)

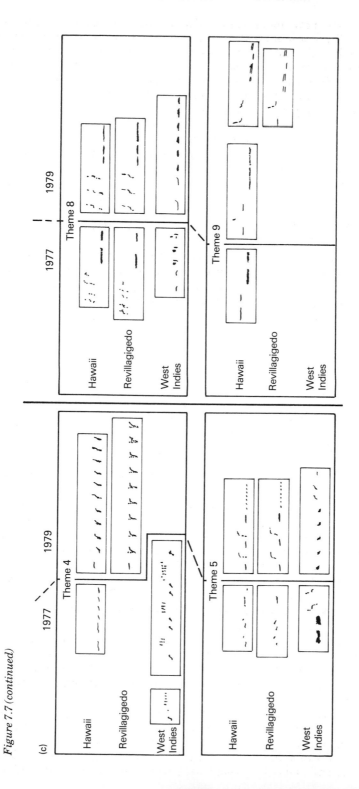

continually, we now have some idea of the function of singing in humpbacks. Singing is almost entirely confined to the breeding grounds (it may occasionally take place also on migration). Peter Tyack (1981), working with the Paynes, has used a combination of directional arrays of underwater hydrophones, simultaneous observation, and either sexing by underwater observation (see Glockner 1983), or by skin sampling of the singers for sexing of chromatin (see Winn *et al.* 1973). By these means he has been able to identify that the singers are invariably males. On arrival in winter at the breeding grounds, they start singing, mainly in shallow coastal areas of 20–40m depth with smooth bottom contours possibly for ease of sound propagation.

A singing whale is almost always alone. It moves back and forth in a particular area but it may change these areas or song-posts from day to day. Sometimes another lone male will approach, the two swim together for a short while and the original singer moves silently but rapidly away. The new arrival that has displaced it then starts singing in the other's place (Figure 7.5). A singer would also approach a mother and calf pair. If accepted he stops singing and swims with them for a few hours or even a day. In this manner the male acts as her 'principal' escort, and there may be gentle touching of flippers, rolling or protracted dives involving the two adults. During this latter period (which may last ten or 15 minutes) it is possible that mating takes place, the calf remaining on the surface to be joined later by the two. If the trio swims into the vicinity of another singing male, he will approach and pursue them at speed. As soon as the female is reached, he also stops singing and will then jostle for position close to her. Aggressive behaviour may then ensue with each whale thrusting at the other with its tail flukes, ramming one another, lunging or blowing bubbles underwater. They also produce vocal sounds including song segments out of context, low grunts and high trumpet calls. These sounds may be heard up to 9km away and will attract a stream of other singing males which converge on the trio. These have been referred to as secondary escorts surrounding the cow, which appears to be the nuclear animal (Tyack and Whitehead 1983). Beside her is the calf and the principal escort whose position is constantly challenged by them. These groups may number 15 animals and eventually the principal escort is displaced by another. He rarely retains his position for more than seven or eight hours, so that fidelity to a single mate seems unlikely. Eventually the animals in the group lose interest, returning to well-spaced positions where they start singing again, and the trio of cow, calf and principal escort swims on.

From playback experiments using different types of sound, Peter Tyack has suggested that one function of humpback song is as a spacing mechanism for courting males advertising their sexual availability to females. We have still much to learn about the function of this elaborate display, but it does suggest that these whales may have lekking grounds (like various gamebirds) where males compete with one another for access to females.

Recently, studies have been carried out on other whale species to record the variety of sounds they produce and the contexts in which they are made. The aim has been to see if different sounds serve particular communicatory functions — do they form some sort of language? In captivity and the wild, the vocal and behavioural reactions of white whales to playbacks of a variety of their sounds have been studied by David Morgan (1979). He found that both syntax and content appeared to be important in communication, and that novel sounds tended to result in the animal either approaching the sound or becoming silent. Certain specific sounds (e.g. the harmonic long, loud whistle, the squeal, the jaw clap, etc.) and certain combinations of sounds had a specific meaning if they were played back in the proper context. In the wild, off the coast of Newfoundland, Algis Taruski (1979) has studied the different types of whistles made by long-finned pilot whales, and related these to various behavioural and environmental contexts. He found seven contour categories of whistle, mostly related to individual signature-type signalling, but two appeared to have emotional content (see Figure 7.9).

Christopher and Jane Clark (1980) from Rockefeller University have used a combination of observation and hydrophone arrays linked to a portable mini-computer to examine the vocal repertoire of southern right whales on their calving grounds at Peninsula Valdés, Argentina. They have also found that particular calls are made in different contexts. When many males are gathered together, aggressive growlings take place and it appears that they are competing for a nearby female. When one of two competing males leaves, more high-pitched melodic sounds are produced instead and these may rise in pitch with apparent increased excitement. By playback experiments they were able to show that right whales responded to contact calls by approaching the loudspeaker but ignored calls of humpback whales. Contact calls are clearly important for many baleen whales that live dispersed, singly or in small groups. Particularly at night (perhaps because it is quieter then), the fin whale produces low frequency 20Hz calls of almost pure tone, sounding like blips, which theoretically could be picked up by other whales 80km or more away (maybe 800km if made in a deepwater channel) (Payne and McVay 1971). That whales actually do respond to calls over long distances is indicated by an observation made by Patterson and Hamilton (1964) off Bermuda, where a directional hydrophone array detected a fin whale emitting individual pulsed signals for a period of three hours as it travelled in a particular direction. Then another individual, 5km away, started to call and the first whale then radically changed its direction to move towards it. However, although fin whales sometimes utter 20Hz single pulse shouts 40–80 decibels strength, probably for longer distance communication, it is thought unlikely that they function much beyond about 25km (Watkins 1981).

Amongst the toothed whales, the sperm whale may also be able to communicate over long distances, since it often occurs at great depths (in the SOFAR channel) where it has been recorded making loud sounds. It produces clicks, which are sometimes in a distinctive pattern rather like a morse code, except that all clicks are of the same length. Clicks are emitted more or less continuously when whales are diving, and this may serve some echolocatory function. During feeding, individuals within a group have been tracked diving in a radiating manner to feed on the sea bottom some distance from one another before returning to within 10m of each other. Clicks are emitted as they rise to the surface and this may serve to co-ordinate feeding and keep the group together. William Watkins and William Schevill (1977) considered that these clicks or 'codas' had a personal signature, but Jonathan Gordon and colleagues in the Indian Ocean have found that the pattern of clicks made by an individual often changes markedly, with embellishments added or deleted. It also seems that one whale will answer another with exactly the same coda, and the same coda may be heard on many occasions from a number of different individuals. Similar results have been found recently by Watkins in the Caribbean and also the Mediterranean, so that populations may have distinct codas. Because the interval between sound pulses that comprise a single click varies with the size of the head and hence the size of the animal, Jonathan Gordon (in prep.) has suggested that males may be assessing one another on this basis, much as toads are thought to do on the depth of their croaks, or red deer on the amount of roaring, or reed warblers on the size of their song repertoire. By such methods a male can determine something of the prowess (its age and/or its condition) of a rival without having a potentially damaging contest with it. Another species recently thought to show individual variation in vocalisations is the narwhal with discrete pulsed calls (Ford and Fisher 1978).

An important function of the sounds made by many baleen and toothed whales seems to be one of identification — the location of the whale, its sex, status, emotional or activity state, possibly even its individual identity. Further information may relate to the identity of the group or population. Recent studies by John Ford and Dean Fisher (1983) in the coastal waters of British Columbia indicate that the latter may be important for killer whales. As we have seen earlier, killer whales live in extended matriarchal family groups which are very stable. They produce a variety of clicks, whistles and pulsed calls. The two former appear to be used during social interaction as contact calls. However, most of the sounds heard when the animals are spread out and foraging are repetitious and stereotyped pulsed calls which may be organised into discrete categories. Twelve such distinct calls have been recognised and all of these may be heard within a 30-minute period whatever the behaviour of the pod at the time. However, the small transient pods are significantly more silent than the large resident ones. This may reflect their different diet (concentrating on marine mammals rather than Pacific salmon) or it may be that they wish to avoid detection by the resident pods. These calls apparently are shared by most members of the pod and are highly stable for periods of ten years or more. Although pods have group-specific dialects there are some similarities between particular pods suggesting that they form a 'clan' with a common ancestor. In Vancouver three such clans have been recognised, one containing eight pods and the others only two or three. The clan with eight pods shows the richest repertoire and is thought to be of greater age. The suggestion is that new pods have formed by budding off from the ancestral group, taking with them some of its vocal characteristics. Interestingly, a pod may share a number of the stereotyped calls but have lost one or two, and maybe formed a new call. Although dialects are common amongst songbirds, they generally exist on a geographical basis in contrast to the situation in killer whales where they appear to be group-specific even within a localised area (Figure 7.8).

The existence of dialects requires vocal learning. Such dialects are rare in mammals, occurring notably in cetaceans and primates. Even within primates it is only man that shares with cetaceans the ability to use cultural means to transmit dialects by imitation. It is also only man and killer whales that have dialects among neighbouring groups that are known to react with and hence affect one another.

Further comparisons between the vocabulary of man and dolphins have concentrated upon one species, the bottle-nosed dolphin, in captivity. A very large amount of work has been done in this area, and for details the reader is referred to D. Caldwell and Caldwell (1972b), M. Caldwell and Caldwell (1979) and Herman (1980b).

One of the early and more famous experiments to show that dolphins communicated information to one another was carried out by Jarvis Bastian (1967) from California. In 1965, he placed a pair of bottle-nosed dolphins in adjacent tanks isolated visually from one another but in sound contact. The female was then taught to push a set of paddles for which it received a reward. The male was provided with an identical set

Figure 7.8 Song dialects in the killer whale (from Ford and Fisher 1983). Killer whale pods in the coastal waters of British Columbia (see map below) retain distinct calls common to members of the pod, despite those pods having overlapping distributions. Pods A1, A4 and A5 are closely related and share calls; pod B overlaps with them but has only three calls (Nos 5, 7 and 8) in common; pod J has no calls in common with the other pods. Call variants are indicated by roman numbers I, II, III

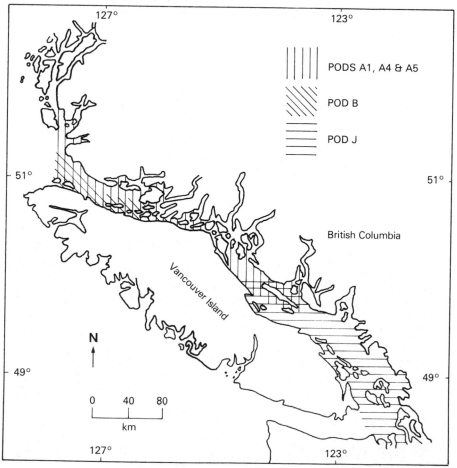

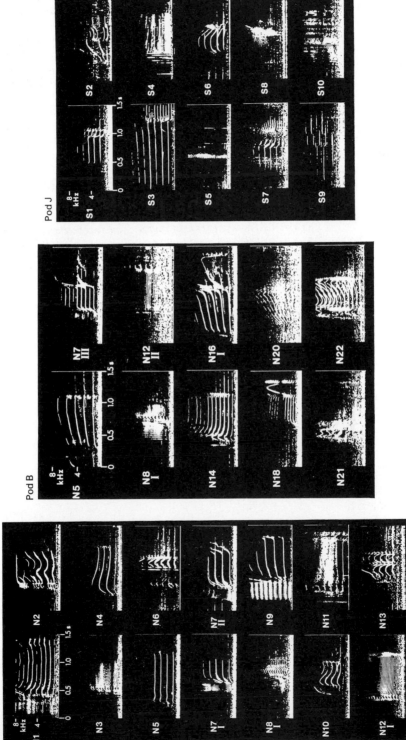

but given no training, yet he learned to push one of the paddles. Because many sounds were heard emitted by the two animals during the tests, it was assumed that the female had passed on the necessary information to the male. Of course that information may have been passed inadvertently and the male trained himself independently.

The vocal repertoire of dolphins is clearly very varied (see Herman and Tavolga 1980 for a review, also covering mysticetes). It contains whistles and squeaks, squawks and groans, rattles and clicks and many other sounds. They can be divided into pulsed sounds such as clicks and burst pulses (chirps, chuckles and click-trains), and unpulsed sounds like whistles and squeaks.

The latter are not produced by certain odontocetes, such as sperm whales and river dolphins, harbour porpoise and Heaviside's dolphin. When used they seem to relate to increased excitement. They are made

Figure 7.9 'Language' in Delphinids: the contexts in which different calls are made by (a) pilot whales (derived from Taruski 1979, with additional data from P.O. Thompson); and (b) bottle-nosed dolphins (based on Dreher and Evans 1964; Evans and Prescott 1962; M. Caldwell and Caldwell 1979, with additional data derived from Herman and Tavolga 1980). Typical calls are represented schematically against the common context in which they are made. Some calls which may serve as personal signatures (see(c))

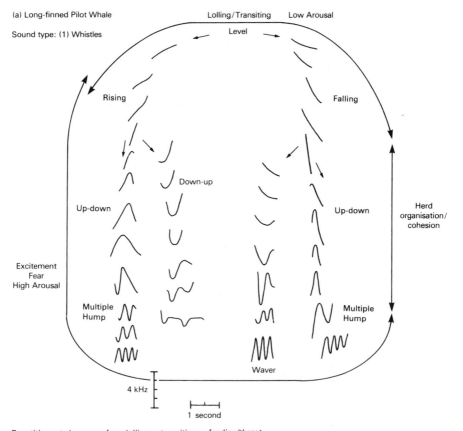

(b) Bottle-nosed Dolphin (and possibly other small social delphinids)

Sound type: (1) Whistles

Low arousal	High arousal	EMOTIONAL STATE
Lolling/transiting	Feeding/threat (excitement/fear)	BEHAVIOURAL CONTEXT
(many variations of these)		TYPICAL SCHEMATIC SONAGRAM TRACES (showing frequency changes)
Repetition rate increased from lolling → transiting → feeding/threat		

(2) Tonal Pulses

navigation/ hunting	play-chase agonistic encounters	courtship/ mating	threat	alarm/ fright/ distress	BEHAVIOURAL CONTEXT
clicks	squawk	yelp	buzz	squeaks, cracks, pops	DESCRIPTION OF SIGNAL
Animals usually silent during periods of rest and on predator approach (before actual threat)					

(c) Signature whistles of Bottle-nosed dolphin

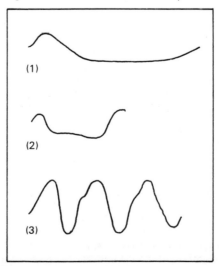

during feeding, by animals introduced to a new tank, when stranded or in a state of distress or alarm, or by the mother to its newly born calf.

Many pulsed click-sounds are used for echolocation and navigation but some also have a social function. Pulsed yelps can be given in courtship, pulsed squeaks during distress, buzzing click-trains during aggressive confrontation. Since high frequency clicks travel only short distances it is thought that they are suitable for communication only within small groups in close contact with one another. Unpulsed whistles, on the other hand, carry better over long distance and so might be most useful in large groups or aggregations. This might explain their presence in species like the spinner dolphin and bottle-nosed dolphin which at least at times may form large groups and their absence in relatively non-social species. Some whistles seem to serve as a signature. These may be used for communication of individual position and group cohesion during normal travel or foraging. A captured male spotted dolphin whistled almost continuously probably in alarm or distress. When these sounds were played back to members of its school they fled; when played to another school they showed curiosity (Fish and Lingle 1977; Herman and Tavolga 1980: 173–4). Perhaps each group has its own vocabulary of calls, developed by mimicry. Some contexts in which particular sounds are made are illustrated in Figure 7.9.

Captive studies have emphasised the capacity for vocal mimicry in dolphins. They learn to imitate signals extremely rapidly and are very accurate at it. Studies of vocal mimicry have been carried out in Hawaii by Douglas Richards, James Wolz and Louis Herman (1984). They trained a captive bottle-nosed dolphin to mimic computer generated model sounds by modifying its whistle. New model sounds, not heard previously, could be mimicked immediately often very faithfully and with high reliability in repeated tests. In further trials, the dolphin was able to relate the sound to a particular object (for example ball or hoop) presented at the same time, and then use them to give the appropriate whistle. In this way the dolphin had given unique vocal labels to those objects, an ability that compares with those of some birds and, less directly, with great apes.

Experiments in the United States by John Lilly and others, and in Holland by Wilhelm Dudoc van Heel, have succeeded in getting cetaceans to respond to human vocalisations. In Holland, a killer whale has been trained to recover objects using human sound cues and has even repeated a human sound spontaneously. In the United States, dolphins have been trained to perform tasks using a whistle language similar to that used to train sheep dogs, and to respond to human words. A few years ago, Lilly even constructed an elaborate computer system to relay translated messages between human and dolphin (referred to as JANUS or Joint Analog Numeric Understanding System). However, the experimental results of those studies have yet to be published and, to my knowledge, Lilly's work is no longer in progress.

Louis Herman and his colleagues have also studied the question of language in great detail, and established a two-way communication. Herman's studies have shown that dolphins are capable of understanding simple auditory or gestural language elements even when they are combined into two-word or three-word sentences. He has tested this by training dolphins to perform actions such as to fetch a ball or go through a hoop using gestures or word signals such as the words 'fetch' or 'ball'. The words are first taught separately and then when combined the dolphin responds appropriately. For two dolphins, one trained on acoustic and the other on gestural instructions, performance was equivalent with about 80 per cent correct responses during a week's worth of some 600–700 two-word instructions. Once the dolphin has learnt to fetch a ball it may be asked to take it to the hoop by saying 'ball-fetch-hoop', or the converse may be asked by using the words in the order 'hoop-fetch-ball'. In this way the order of the words conveys the meaning, and Herman has found that dolphins can respond appropriately, though performance is less good, averaging abour 50 per cent correct response with this three-word language (Herman 1980b).

Later studies have greatly expanded these descriptions of the cognitive abilities of dolphins. They have shown that a language-trained dolphin can store in its memory and then report to others that an arbitrary object is present or absent in its environment (Herman and Forestell 1985).Their studies further show that dolphins can understand and respond appropriately to sentences of unique meaning from 2–5 words length, and following syntactical rules (Herman et al. 1984). One subject was tutored in an acoustic language whose words were computer-generated sounds, presented through an underwater speaker. Another was tutored in a visually-based language whose words were gestures of a trainer's arms and hands. The results showed that the words of the languages had come to represent symbolically the objects and events referred to in the sentences. Arbitrary rules of syntax could be understood, as could the function of words early in the sentence on the basis of succeeding words. The ability of the dolphins to use both sound and vision in these tasks emphasised their ability to use both modes for sentence comprehension. In this respect they show greater flexibility than the apes who are apparently largely restricted to the visual modality at least for the production of language.

These studies are very exciting. They show that, like man, dolphins have a well-developed auditory memory, strong abilities for imitation (both vocally and in motor tasks) and learning through observation, a capacity for forming, generalising and learning rules and to symbolise. The speed at which dolphins were able to comprehend at least a simple language bodes well for future acquisition of a more complex vocabulary imposed upon them. The ability to form and act upon abstract concepts has now been demonstrated in a number of studies. This has extended to the concept of 'newness', as shown, for example, by the ability of a captive rough-toothed dolphin to be trained to accept a fish reward for every new behaviour it introduced, and then rapidly to invent behaviours (Pryor et al. 1969).

We should, however, be somewhat cautious in extrapolating from such studies when considering dolphin intellect. As Louis Herman has been quick to emphasise, some of these cognitive abilities may not be used in the wild. This depends very much upon the demands placed upon a dolphin in its natural environment and, as we have seen, these differ greatly from those placed on man. Communication in dolphins as in some other cetaceans is clearly complex and elaborate. However, all attempts to demonstrate the existence of a natural language in dolphins have been unsuccessful. Furthermore, whilst dolphins may be able to represent their world through arbitrary auditory signals, they appear to be unable to do so in solely visual terms. Indeed visual memory for form and brightness was found to be very limited although it could be improved if visual information is represented by an auditory code. Notwithstanding these essential differences there is remarkable similarity in the cognitive characteristics of dolphins and non-human advanced primates like the chimpanzee. Information seems to be processed in much the same way with similar capacities and limitations. This may explain the similarities in brain development between the two groups.

Intelligence and Brain Size

Many people have cited the large brains of dolphins as evidence for their comparable intelligence with advanced primates (Gihr and Pilleri 1979; Jansen and Jansen 1969; Kruger 1966; Lilly 1967, 1978; Morgane 1974, 1978; Pilleri and Busnel 1968; Tower 1954). The weight of the brain as a percentage of the body weight varies between 0.25 and 1.5 in a number of odontocetes, compared with 1.9 per cent in man. Furthermore, the neo-cortex of the brain, the part with which we create, innovate and reason, covers 98 per cent of the dolphin's cortex, higher even than man. However, it is also much thinner, and comparisons of brain size, convolutions of the cortex, zonal differentiation and neurone density show great variation in some of these features between cetacean species, mostly without obvious pattern. For recent reviews of the cetacean brain, the reader should consult Ridgway (1986) and Morgane et al. (1986a,b).

Using the above findings, Jerison (1973, 1978, 1980) has suggested that they indicate that some cetacean species possess unusual mental processes although this may serve different purposes to those in humans. Jerison considers that the encephalisation quotient, EQ (the ratio of the brain volume to body surface area) is a better measure for comparing the development of mental processes between species. These show an increase both evolutionarily (from c. 1.0 for Eocene cetacean skulls to 2.0 for Miocene toothed whale fossils) and between living taxa, from 1.5 in a river dolphin to 5.6 in the bottle-nosed dolphin, with phocoenids having intermediate values. The EQ of humans is c. 7.4, that of the chimpanzee is c. 2.5, but almost all other mammals are substantially lower than 2.0. Much of this development may relate to the processing of acoustic information which probably reaches a peak with the social dolphins, like the bottle-nosed dolphin, where communication, co-operation and competition among peers is thought to be particularly important (Gaskin 1982:141–2; Herman 1980b; Wood and Evans 1980). Louis Herman (1980b) suggests that these developments of the brain and the resulting cognitive skills have derived from the demands of social living, aided by an extended maturation period for the young and a high level of parental care. In those ways, the evolutionarily divergent dolphins and primates may face similar selection pressures.

Altruistic or Selfless Behaviour

Do Cetaceans Show Altruistic Behaviour? Before leaving the question of dolphin intelligence, we should briefly look at one other feature that many people consider places cetaceans close to man. This is altruistic or selfless behaviour. It may take the form of so-called epimelitic or care-giving behaviour: for example adult common dolphins (thought to be females) coming to the aid of a mother and its calf (M. Caldwell and Caldwell 1966); or a group of sperm whales taking up a so-called 'marguerite' formation like the radial spokes of a wheel around an injured adult (Nishiwaki 1962), although a similar formation has been observed during mating (Best *et al.* 1984). Alternatively, it may take the form of co-operation such as collective food-herding described for many social dolphins, or a male right whale supporting a female while another male mates with her.

Sometimes these 'helping' activities appear misdirected: they have been used on already dead individuals or towards animals of another species, notably man (as described first by Aristotle and subsequently by many others). The former would be interpreted as not very intelligent behaviour and the latter has been viewed as dolphins trying to establish a bond with man.

Although there is always the danger that such behaviours are interpreted in human terms (for example food-herding may sometimes simply reflect separate individual responses to a food concentration), sufficient careful observations have now been assembled to provide reasonably strong evidence that such truly altruistic behaviour exists in cetaceans.

Conditions for Its Existence: (a) Kin Selection. Altruism should not necessarily be considered a behaviour that requires high intellect or intelligence. It is seen in bees, birds and many other groups, and in many cases can be explained in genetic terms. If individuals that help one another are related, the advantages will lie in the genes that they share. This is termed kin selection. The conditions for its existence have been found, for example, in certain social hymenoptera, in the Belding's ground squirrel and the Florida scrub jay; it is also of course at the basis of parental care. In cetaceans, however, all the evidence that we have accumulated would suggest that those conditions (i.e. relatedness among helping individuals) are unlikely to apply at least for most species. Cetacean schools appear to be too fluid for stable social groups of related individuals to exist, except perhaps for the killer whale and maybe one or two other species. Where verified, helping seems almost always to involve members of the same sex, often centred around the mother and her calf. With sexual segregation occurring in many species this may be inevitable, but although it may not explain its maintenance, it could explain how it arose (if those females were related).

Perhaps the strongest argument against altruism being maintained by kin selection is its occurrence across species, genera and other taxa (see, for example, Brown and Norris 1956; Leatherwood and Walker 1979; Norris and Dohl 1980b; Norris and Prescott 1961; Saayman and Tayler 1979). However, we should be a little careful in interpreting all those observations as indicating altruistic behaviour. Certainly mixed species groups travelling or feeding together may simply reflect either mutual attraction to a food source or one species using another as a cue to the presence of food or to help in navigation (Evans 1982).

Conditions for Its Existence: (b) Reciprocal Altruism. Altruistic behaviour could also be maintained by what is termed reciprocity (though it would have to arise in the first place some other way). If a group of individuals lived together for a protracted period and could recognise one another, one individual might perform an altruistic act on the basis that there is some chance of the recipient reciprocating at a later date. The cost to the helper of an altruistic act must, however, be small compared to benefits to the recipient. Human beings are thought commonly to perform altruistic acts for these reasons. They are conscious of their actions (though not always), though such self awareness is not necessary for the existence of an altruistic act.

Amongst other animals, there are precious few good examples of reciprocal altruism, and they seem to require groups with stable long-term membership. One of the best known examples is found in the olive baboon, where an unrelated male may help another male to steal a female by engaging her consort in a fight whilst he sneaks in and mates with her. This behaviour sounds a little like the triad right whale groups where a male assists another to mate with a female, though here we have no information whether they are related. Furthermore, there is no evidence that right whales form stable groups though they may not need to if individuals could recognise one another by their excellent long-term memory of signature calls. The studies on right whales (or other species) do not yet suggest this degree of individual recognition but of course we are still far from understanding the full content of vocalisations by any species. For the time being, we cannot really say whether cetaceans might help each other for the above reasons. The evidence is not very strong, and it might be better to look elsewhere for an explanation.

Conditions for Its Existence: (c) Cultural Evolution. So far we have considered the evolution of helping through natural selection, primarily in genetic terms. Although this could easily be how the act of helping arose initially, it is possible that the trait has become generalised to non-relatives, maintained by cultural means (i.e. transmitted from one generation to the next through teaching or tradition). In this way cetaceans could further resemble man. We should not take the comparison too closely because, as explained throughout this chapter, there are important differences. However, this area of study promises some exciting development.

Connor and Norris (1982) have written a useful review on the subject of altruistic behaviour which I had overlooked at the time of writing. My conclusions appear to be very similar to theirs except that I consider that altruism in cetaceans initially spread through kin selection not reciprocity. Both agree that it has become generalised, rather than directed at particular individuals; otherwise it could not be maintained, since individuals are often almost certainly unrelated, and opportunities for reciprocation are low, given the fluidity of social groups.

Those who have had the privilege to interact with a whale or dolphin, be it in captivity or the wild, almost invariably are moved by the experience. I certainly have been. Though this may tell us more about our own personality than the nature of dolphins, it is interesting to consider why this relationship may exist in a way that does not seem to be present in the wild for any other species. I suggest that it is due to two characteristics of cetaceans. First is the fact that they are top predators in the sea, and so face predation from only a few species — some sharks, killer whales, and in recent times, man. Although they certainly show fear in the presence of sharks and killer whales, and sometimes also towards human divers, they may not yet be able to recognise as predators humans that kill them from above the water aboard a variety of platforms. After a time, if whaling vessels bear certain unique characteristics, then one might expect cetaceans to learn to associate these with danger and to take avoidance action. However, motor-driven whaling ships may be difficult to distinguish from other motorised vessels that are harmless, and in the great majority.

The second factor that may play a role is that the nature of a cetacean's food supply favours individuals to be inquisitive — to explore any new objects that come their way as they search for a very patchily distributed food source. Superimpose upon these two features the importance of social interaction, play and the learning of skills, and one can perhaps see a few of the reasons why some cetaceans, particularly the social dolphins, may readily interact with man. This should not lessen our respect for these creatures nor allow us to exploit them in the disgraceful way that we have done throughout our history.

8 Life history

In the last chapter we looked at whales and dolphins essentially as individuals. We shall now look at some of the features they possess at the population level. These can be considered under three broad headings: reproduction, mortality and competition. The first two are essentially biological parameters of the species whilst the third relates to interactions within and between species which may affect those life history parameters.

REPRODUCTION

All species of whale and dolphin, without exception, typically produce a single young: they differ from most other mammals which have litters of young. Female cetaceans do actually have paired mammary glands but twin fetuses have only very rarely been recorded (0.6 per cent in humpback to 2.3 per cent in sei whales — Gambell 1968, Kimura 1957, Ohsumi 1977a). Almost invariably one or both of these apparently die. The season of births is relatively restricted, at least in baleen whales and those species breeding at high latitudes. In the tropics and subtropics there is some indication that breeding seasons are more protracted although even these show a peak in births (see Tables 8.1 and 8.2). Seasonality of breeding is no doubt related to climatic seasonality which influences the availability of food. As we have seen in earlier chapters, the summer months in temperate and Arctic regions experience an explosion of food production. This results from longer days and calmer weather, higher temperatures and greater sunlight combining to produce concentrations of planktonic plants — algae, diatoms and the like. Upon these feed large quantities of zooplankton (euphausiids, amphipods, copepods and mysids), which in turn are fed upon by baleen whales, fish and squid, and the two latter are then taken by toothed whales and dolphins. However, whereas the small odontocetes (for example the common dolphin and harbour porpoise) appear to give birth during this period of food abundance, the larger baleen whales (such as the gray whale and humpback whale) feed during this time but then migrate long distances to give birth in warm waters during the winter (Figures 8.1 and 8.2). An exception is the Bryde's whale which makes only local seasonal movements in the tropics to warm temperate region.

Seasonal Migrations

Many people have considered why the baleen whales should undergo these long migrations: the general conclusion has been that they need warm waters for the growth and development of their relatively small young but cannot find enough food to·sustain them throughout the year. Because of this they move to feed in rich areas at high latitudes which enables them to build up an energy store in their body. However, I suggest there is no reason why these species should not remain in high latitudes. Indeed, one baleen species, the bowhead whale does so, and others such as the fin and minke whale may make only relatively short latitudinal movements. If the young of baleen whale species were to have difficulty with the temperatures of high latitude seas, then one should expect odontocetes to do so, particularly the smaller species such as the harbour porpoise with their less favourable volume-surface area ratio (requiring relatively more energy to prevent heat loss; see pp. 155 and 158). Yet the harbour porpoise may be found breeding in subarctic waters. Instead I would suggest that these long migrations are a reflection of the evolutionary history of mysticetes. The areas of high plankton productivity have not always been where they are at present. It is conceivable that the early baleen whales evolved alongside zones of productivity in low latitudes. Then as a result of the retreat of the Tethys Sea, opening of various dispersal routes, and fluctuations in ocean temperature, they may have dispersed polewards following plankton concentrations but returned annually to the original regions they occupied. Thus nowadays the movements between low and high latitudes are maintained primarily by tradition, much as some European songbirds migrate annually to the African continent. I should emphasise that this explanation is speculative and we do not really know where precisely the early mysticetes evolved nor the routes they took in their evolutionary history. It is an alternative view to the more established ones presented above, and postulates that there are no strong selection pressures favouring breeding in equatorial waters.

Breeding Areas

Tradition probably plays an important role in the maintenance of particular breeding areas — both calving and mating grounds (usually but not necessarily in the same areas). The shallow sheltered bays inshore of Peninsula Valdés, southern Argentina and in the Gulf of California are mating/calving grounds for southern right whale and gray whale respectively. They are used annually with at least some individuals faithfully returning year after year. For most species, however, we have little idea where they breed let alone whether individuals are faithful to those sites over a period of time. We might expect such fidelity to breeding area since, where known, they appear to have been used for many years. The requirements for breeding are not known precisely, but seem to involve a calm sea area. Some have suggested that inshore waters are used because of the protection they afford from predators. However, if this is the case, then it is not very effective, as witnessed by observations of attacks by sharks and killer whales, in the latter case sometimes even driving their prey ashore. Nevertheless safety from predation is likely to be one force operating in the choice of a breeding

Table 8.1: Breeding seasons of mysticetes

Species	Location	Peak months of conception	Peak months of birth	Source
Blue whale	Antarctic; South Africa	June/July	May	1–5
Pygmy blue whale	Antarctic	Feb–Apr	?Mar/Apr	1–4, 6
Fin whale	Antarctic; South Africa	June/July	May	1–5, 7
	North Atlantic	Dec/Jan	Nov/Dec	
	North Pacific	Dec/Jan	Nov/Dec	
Sei whale	Antarctic; South Africa	July	June	1–5, 8–10
	North Atlantic	Nov–Feb	Nov/Dec	
	North Pacific	Oct–Nov	Nov/Dec	
Bryde's whale	South Africa (inshore)	Year round	Year round	1–5, 10–13
	(offshore)	March	Feb/March	
	North Pacific (inshore, Japan)	Dec, but protracted	?Nov, but protracted	
	(offshore)	Protracted	Protracted	
	South Pacific	Protracted	Protracted	
Minke whale	Antarctic; South Africa; Brazil	Aug–Sept	May/June	1–5, 14–15
	North Atlantic	Feb	Dec	
	North Pacific	Feb/Mar	Dec/Jan	
	Huanghai Sea	July–Sept	May–July	
Humpback whale	Antarctic; Australia	July/Aug	July/Aug	1–5, 16–20
	Northwest Pacific	Feb	Jan	
	Caribbean	Feb	Jan/Feb	
Gray whale	Northeast Pacific	Nov/Dec	Jan–Feb	1, 21–23
Bowhead	Arctic	Mar/May	Apr/May	1, 24
Pygmy right whale	Southern hemisphere	?protracted	?protracted	1, 25–26
Southern right whale	South America; South Africa	Aug/Oct	May/Aug	1, 27–29
Northern right whale	Northern hemisphere	?Jan-Mar (but possibly also Aug-Sept)	?Nov-Jan	1, 30–31

Reference sources: For general references which include more detailed sources, see: 1 Lockyer 1984; 2 Harrison 1969. Other sources: 3 Lockyer 1981a; 4 Brown and Lockyer 1984; 5 Mackintosh 1965; 6 Ichihara 1966; 7 Lockyer in press; 8 Gambell 1968; 9 Masaki 1976; 10 Rice 1977; 11 Best 1977; 12 Ohsumi 1977a, 1980; 13 Omura 1966; 14 Best 1982; 15 Peilie 1982; 16 Chittleborough 1965; 17 Dawbin 1966a; 18 Nishiwaki 1959; 19 Herman and Antinoja 1977; 20 Winn and Winn 1985; 21 Swartz 1986; 22 Rice and Wolman 1971; 23 Rice 1983; 24 Nerini et al. 1984; 25 Ross et al. 1975; 26 Baker 1985; 27 Taber and Thomas 1982; 28 Payne in press; 29 Best 1981; 30 Kraus 1986; 31 Klumov 1962.

Note: See footnotes in Table 8.2.

Table 8.2: Breeding seasons of odontocetes

Species	Location	Peak months of conception	Peak months of birth	Sources
Sperm whale	Northern hemisphere	Mar-May	Apr-June	2, 7–9
	Southern hemisphere	Aug-?Jan	Oct-Dec(?Feb)	2, 10–11
White whale	Arctic	Apr-May	(Apr)July/Aug(Sept)	3, 12–14
Narwhal	Arctic	Apr	July-Aug	3, 15–17
Baird's beaked whale	Northwest Pacific	Oct-Nov	Mar-Apr	4, 18
Northern bottlenose whale	North Atlantic	Apr-May	Apr-May	4, 19
Melon-headed whale	Southern hemisphere	?July-Aug	?July-Aug	20–21
False killer whale	Northern/southern hemispheres	Protracted	Protracted	20, 22
Killer whale	Northern hemisphere	(Sept)Oct-Dec(Jan)	?Oct-Jan	20, 23–25
Long-finned pilot whale	North Atlantic	Apr-May/July-Nov	July-Oct/Nov-Mar	26–28

(different peaks may represent separate populations, though breeding probably protracted)

Table 8.2 (continued)

Species	Location	Peak months of conception	Peak months of birth	Sources
Short-finned pilot whale	North Pacific	(Jan)Apr-May(Sept)	(Apr)July-Aug(Oct)	29
Tucuxi	South America (but breeding seasons probably vary with peak births during periods of low water)	Dec-Feb	Oct-Nov	30
Indo-Pacific humpbacked dolphin	South Africa	?	Dec-Feb (but protracted)	31
White-beaked dolphin	North Atlantic	July-Oct	May-Aug	27–28, 32–33
Atlantic white-sided dolphin	North Atlantic	June-Aug	May-July	27–28, 32–33
Dusky dolphin	New Zealand / Argentina	?July-Sept / ?Jan-Mar	June-Aug / Dec-Feb	34 / 35
Pacific white-sided dolphin	North Pacific	?Sept-Nov	July-Sept	20, 36–38
Common dolphin	North Pacific / North Atlantic/Black Sea	?Apr-June/Oct-Dec / ?July-Oct	Mar-Apr/Sept-Oct / June-Sept	20, 38–40 / 27–28, 32, 40–42
Bottle-nosed dolphin	Northern hemisphere (possibly two seasonal breeding peaks: spring and autumn)	?Mar-May(June-July)Aug-Sept	Mar-May(June-July)Aug-Sept	1, 27–28 / 32, 40–43
Risso's dolphin	North Atlantic	?	Apr-Sept	27–28, 32
Spotted dolphin	Tropical Pacific (breeding season protracted but with two seasonal (spring and autumn) peaks in northern stock and only a spring peak in southern stock)	?Mar-June/Sept-Nov	Mar-June/Sept-Nov	20, 44–5

Striped dolphin	North Pacific	Dec-Feb/June-Aug	Jan-Mar/July-Sept	46
	North Atlantic	Aug-Dec	Sept-Jan	27–28, 40, 47
Spinner dolphin	North Pacific eastern form:	?Apr-July	Mar-June	45
	whitebelly form:	?Mar-May/Aug-Oct	Feb-Apr/July-Sept	45
Commerson's dolphin	Tierra del Fuego	?Nov-Feb	?Sept-Mar (with possible peak around Nov-Feb)	48
Harbour porpoise	North Atlantic	(Apr)June-Aug(Oct)	(Mar)May-July(Sept)	5, 27–28, 32, 49–53
Vaquita	Gulf of California	?	Apr (but based on little data)	54
Dall's porpoise	Northwest Pacific	(Aug)Sept(Oct)	Aug-Sept	5, 55–56
	Northeast Pacific (coastal)	all year round	all year round	5, 56
Finless porpoise	Inland Sea of Japan	?(Apr)May-June(July)	(March)Apr-May(June)	5, 57
	Yangtze River, China	?Mar-May	Feb-Apr	58–60
Ganges/Indus susus	Indo-Pakistan	?May(-Sept)	Apr(-July) (but protracted, with possible second peak in Oct-Nov)	6, 20, 61
Boto	Central Amazon	?July-Sept	May-July	6, 30
	Upper Amazon	?Sept-Nov	July-Sept	6, 20, 62
	(but breeding seasons probably vary with peak births during periods of high water)			
Baiji	Yangtze River, China	?Apr-June/(Aug-Sept)	Feb-Apr/(June-July)	6, 58–59
Franciscana	South America	?(Dec)Jan-Feb(Mar)	(Oct)Nov-Dec(Jan) (but possibly protracted)	6, 63–64

Table 8.2 (continued)

Reference sources: For general references with more detailed sources, see: 1 Harrison 1969; 2 Best *et al.* 1984; 3 Braham 1984; 4 Mead 1984; 5 Gaskin *et al.* 1984; 6 Brownell 1984. Other sources: 7 Clarke 1956; 8 Berzin 1972; 9 Ohsumi 1965; 10 Best 1974; 11 Gambell 1972; 12 Brodie 1971; 13 Sergeant 1973; 14 Seaman and Burns 1981; 15 Best and Fisher 1974; 16 Mansfield *et al.* 1975; 17 Hay 1980; 18 Kasuya 1977, 1986; 19 Benjaminsen and Christensen 1979; 20 Leatherwood *et al.* 1983; 21 Bryden *et al.* 1981; 22 Purves and Pilleri 1978; 23 Jonsgard and Lyshoel 1970; 24 Christensen 1984; 25 Bigg 1982b; 26 Sergeant 1962; 27 Evans 1980; 28 Evans *et al.* 1986; 29 Kasuya and Marsh 1984; 30 Best and da Silva 1984; 31 Saayman and Tayler 1979; 32 Fraser 1974; 33 Sergeant *et al.* 1980; 34 Baker 1972, 1983; 35 Wursig and Wursig 1980; 36 Leatherwood and Walker 1982; 37 Leatherwood *et al.* 1984a; 38 Ridgway and Green 1967; 39 W.E. Evans 1975; 40 Harrison 1972; 41 Collet 1981; 42 Tomilin 1967; 43 Mitchell 1975a; 44 Perrin *et al.* 1976; 45 Barlow 1984; 46 Miyazaki 1977, 1984; 47 Duguy *et al.* 1978; 48 Lockyer *et al.* in press; 49 Fisher and Harrison 1970; 50 Møhl-Hansen 1954; 51 Van Utrecht 1978; 52 Smith and Gaskin 1974; 53 Gaskin and Blair 1977; 54 Brownell 1983; 55 Kasuya 1978; 56 Morejohn 1979; 57 Kasuya and Kureha 1979; 58 Chen *et al.* 1984; 59 Zhou *et al.* 1980; 60 Pilleri *et al.* 1980; 61 Kasuya 1972; 62 Harrison and Brownell 1971; 63 Harrison *et al.* 1981; 64 Kasuya and Brownell 1979.

Notes: The above reference source lists are not exhaustive and the reader should consult the general references for further sources. However, the data contained in the table have taken account of those references secondarily cited. A question mark denotes uncertainty in the periods given, and usually is the result of back calculation of mating seasons derived from estimated gestation periods. Data presented refer to those better known locations. It should be noted that breeding seasons may vary between localities (and between years) so that it is not necessarily wise to extrapolate.

A number of species have been excluded from the above table because too few data are available for them.

Figure 8.1 Migration patterns of rorqual whales: (a) blue whale; (b) humpback whale. Both undergo extensive latitudinal migrations, although the former tends to migrate offshore and does not have discrete breeding areas whereas the latter tends to have coastal migrations and more clearly defined breeding grounds. As a consequence of this, the migration patterns of humpback are much better known than those of the blue whale (derived from Gambell 1979 for the blue whale; Chittleborough 1965, Dawbin 1966a, Mackintosh 1965, Martin et al. 1984b, Winn and Winn 1985 for the humpback). Note that humpback population in the Red Sea may be resident

(a) Blue Whale

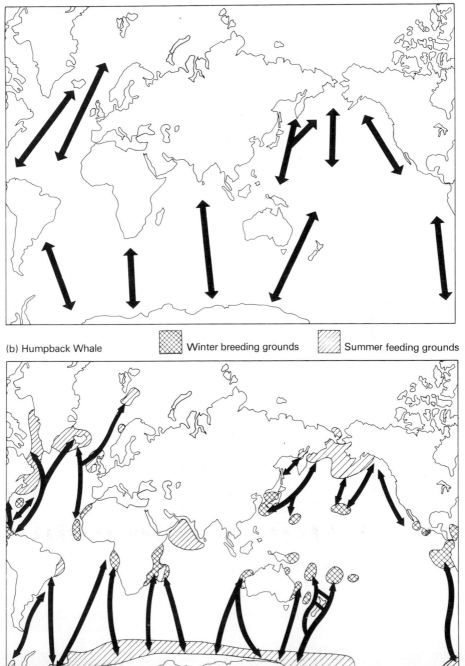

(b) Humpback Whale   Winter breeding grounds   Summer feeding grounds

area if mothers and their calves remain in a single region for any length of time. For most cetacean species, breeding areas in the Northeast Atlantic are almost certainly some distance offshore. The coincidence of offshore movements by most species just prior to the start of the breeding season supports this (Evans *et al.* 1986). So these species at least do not respond to their potential predators by calving close to the shore. On the other hand, the Atlantic coasts of northwest Europe are often exposed to strong tidal currents and the full force of winds across the Atlantic. There are few areas which could be considered very sheltered where calm water persists. Where these do occur, for example in the deeply indented coastline of the Shetland Isles with its sheltered geos, and of parts of western Ireland, these form breeding or nursery areas for both harbour porpoise and bottle-nosed dolphin.

Baleen Whale Reproduction

Although, for the large baleen whales, annual migrations help to achieve some synchrony for mating, only a proportion of females will conceive in any one year. This results from the protracted periods of gestation and lactation that all those species have. Pregnancy results from ovulation and conception during autumn migration or in winter on the breeding grounds. It is not known for certain whether females are spontaneous ovulators coming into oestrus only once a year or whether they are polyoestrus (with several oestrus cycles). There is some evidence that the inshore form of Bryde's whale is polyoestrus (Best 1977), and Chittleborough (1965) obtained evidence of polyoestry in humpbacks if conception failed to occur.

Gestation periods are approximately one year, presumably linked closely to the annual migrations, with mating taking place usually sometime after arrival on the breeding grounds, and calving in the same area ten to twelve months later (see Table 8.3). The gray whale probably conceives either towards the end of the southwards migration or soon after arrival on the breeding grounds since its gestation period is 13 to 14 months. Mating has been observed in this and other species at various other times of the year, but it is probable that these sexual encounters rarely if ever lead to conception.

The timing of mating and births probably results in the sequence patterns of migration that are seen for different sexes and age classes of certain whale species, such as humpback and gray whales. In the California gray whale, for example, the southwards migration is led by females in the late stages of pregnancy, apparently travelling singly and at a greater speed than the rest. Next come the recently impregnated females who have weaned their calves the previous summer. Then come immature females and adult males, and finally the immature males. These travel usually in groups of two but groups of up to eleven may occur. They tend to travel more slowly, particularly towards the end of the migration. The return migration is led by the newly pregnant females, followed by adult males and non-breeding females, then immatures of both sexes, and finally the females with their newborn

Figure 8.2 Migration patterns of the gray whale (derived from M.L. Jones et al. 1984). With coastal breeding grounds and migration routes, the movements of this species are probably the best known of any whale species

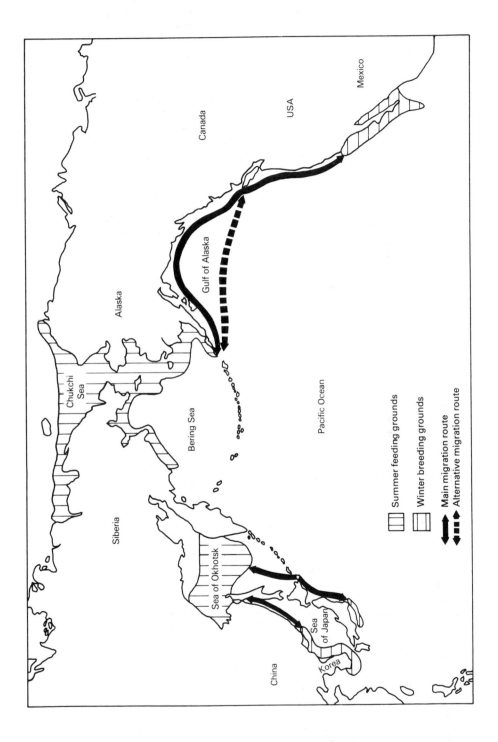

Table 8.3: Gestation and lactation periods, and calving intervals for mysticetes

Species	Location	Gestation period (months)	Lactation period (months)	Calving interval (years)	Source
Blue whale	Antarctic/South Africa	11	7	2–3	1–4
Pygmy blue whale	Antarctic	<12?	?	?	5
Fin whale	Antarctic/South Africa	11	7	2–3	1–4
	Northern hemisphere	11–12	?		
Sei whale	Antarctic/South Africa	11–11.5	6	2–3	1–4, 6–8
	North Atlantic	>10.75	?6		
	North Pacific	>10.5(west) 12–13(east)	7(west) 9(east)		
Bryde's whale	South Africa/North Pacific	12	?6	2	1–4, 9
Minke whale	Antarctic/Brazil/South Africa	10	4	1–2+	1–4, 10–14
	North Atlantic	10	<6		
	North Pacific	10	6		
Humpback whale	Antarctic; Australia	11.5	10.5–11	(1)2+	1–4, 15–17
	Northwest Pacific	10–11	1011(12)		
	Northeast Pacific	12			
Gray whale	North Pacific	13.9	7	2	18–21
Bowhead whale	Arctic	c.12–13	5–6	2+	22
Pygmy right whale	Southern hemisphere	c.12	?5–6	?	23

Northern/ southern right whales	Northern/southern hemispheres	10	?12	3(2–4)	2, 24–26

Reference sources: For more general references with detailed sources, see: 1 Harrison 1969; 2 Lockyer 1984; 3 Lockyer 1981a; 4 Slijper 1979. Other sources: 5 Ichihara 1966; 6 Gambell 1968; 7 Masaki 1976; 8 Rice 1977; 9 Best 1982; 10 Best 1982; 11 Jonsgard 1951; 12 Larsen and Kapel 1983; 13 Mitchell and Kozicki 1975; 14 Williamson 1975; 15 Chittleborough 1965; 16 Winn and Winn 1985; 17 Nishiwaki 1959; 18 Rice and Wolman 1971; 19 Rice 1983; 20 Yablokov and Bogoslovskaya 1984; 21 Blokhin 1984; 22 Nerini *et al.* 1984; 23 Ross *et al.* 1975; 24 Kraus 1986; 25 Klumov 1962; 26 Payne in press.

Notes: Data indicated '?' or 'c.' are either unknown or of limited reliability, mainly through sparsity of data. Age of weaning may not correspond with mother's lactation period if communal suckling occurs.

calves. Presumably the newly pregnant females move north as soon as they can to make the maximum use of time in Arctic seas, building up food reserves to nourish their developing fetus. They then move south as quickly as possible to give birth to their calves (see Jones *et al.* 1984; Swartz 1986 for reviews of gray whale migration behaviour; also Figure 8.2).

In nearly all other baleen whale species, newly pregnant females are the first to migrate to feeding grounds but, unlike gray whales, they are usually the last to leave, possibly due to a need for extra energy stores in those species, for their shorter gestation periods. Juvenile blue, fin and sei whales tend not to penetrate such high latitudes as adults whilst lactating female minke whales are almost absent from higher latitudes of the Antarctic (Best 1982; Lockyer 1981a; Lockyer and Brown 1981).

The fetus in mysticete whales grows faster than in any other mammal,

Figure 8.3 Fetal growth in weight of various rorquals and sperm whale (from Lockyer 1981a, b). Note the accelerated growth of the fetus, particularly in rorquals, during the latter half of pregnancy. Growth rate constants (a) = 0.52 (blue), 0.47 (fin), 0.35 (sei) and 0.25 (sperm whales)

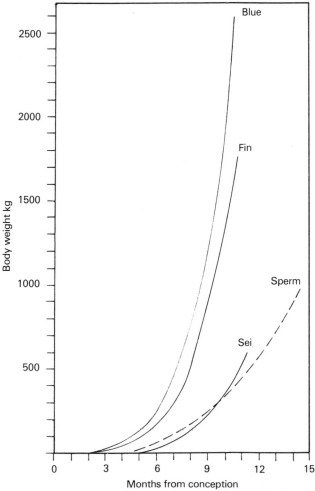

and particularly in the latter stages of gestation (see Laws 1959, Mikhalev 1980 for growth patterns using body length; Frazer and Huggett 1973, 1974, and Lockyer 1981a for growth in weight; see also Figure 8.3). This accelerated growth generally coincides with arrival on the feeding grounds. When the young are born they are therefore relatively large, and rapid growth continues for several months, nourished by their mother's milk with its high fat content. Lactation lasts between four and ten (possibly twelve) months depending on the species (see Table 8.3) and in that time the suckled young may increase its weight by five to eight times (Figure 8.4). Ovulation is usually suppressed over this period (although there are some post-partum ovulations in the fin and sei whales), so it is not possible for a female to conceive again until at least towards the end of lactation (Lockyer 1984). This imposes a minimum reproductive cycle of two years for all but the minke whale, and recent studies suggest that three years or more is

Figure 8.4 Growth rates of mysticetes: (a) blue whale; (b) fin whale; (c) sei whale; (d) humpback whale; (e) minke whale (from Brown and Lockyer 1984). Average curves of body length at different ages ↓ = Age at sexual maturity

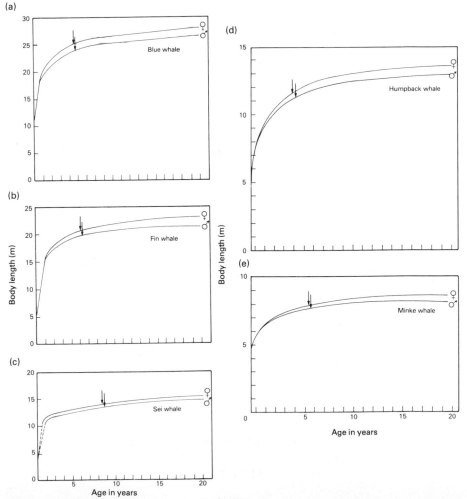

likely to be more typical for most species (Table 8.3). Variation in calving interval probably exists between individuals as well as between species, both being affected by the high energetic costs of lactation (lasting half a year or more in many species and thought to be much greater than those of gestation). These costs may be greater upon recently mature females than on older ones, since they are still actively growing. During a two-year cycle, Christina Lockyer estimates that the net costs of reproduction (gestation and lactation) forms about 19 per cent of total energy costs in fully mature female fin whales but 26 per cent in recently mature ones (Lockyer 1981a). This may mean that in years of low food availability, many younger fin whales rest for one year after weaning their first calf. A generalised breeding cycle for a fully mature fin whale is given in Figure 8.5.

Sexual maturity is estimated in female whales by the presence of evidence for at least one ovulation with or without pregnancy — either a corpus luteum or a corpus albicans. The corpus luteum is the mass of tissue which is left after ovulation when a mature follicle ruptures from the ovary; it persists only when fertilisation occurs leading to pregnancy, otherwise regressing to form a scar-like corpus albicans. It is much more difficult to estimate sexual maturity in males. The increased weight of the testis tends to be used as the criterion for sexual maturity for practical reasons, but, ideally, measurements of the diameter of the testis tubule, and histological evidence (spermatogenesis and the presence of sperm) should also be collected (see Perrin and Donovan 1984:1–24 for a review).

Age determination is also a problem, and for a long time the number of ridges on baleen plates was used as an index of age (Ruud 1945; Ruud *et al.* 1950), though wear on the tip and lack of growth after maturity made it of limited use. However, in 1955 a method of age determination was developed by the British zoologist Peter Purves by counting the light and dark layers in the ear-plug of whales, after sectioning (Purves 1955; Figure 8.6). It was thought that two pairs of layers (made up of one pale and one dark) were laid down each year and a consistent relationship with body length supported this (Ichihara 1959; Laws and Purves 1956; Nishiwaki 1957; Purves and Mountford 1959). However, there were increasing doubts during the 1960s when several zoologists thought that although two pairs of layers might be deposited annually in the early years of life, it was more like one pair later on. This crisis was overcome when Roe was able to show that, in fin whales at least, one pale and one dark lamina did indeed form an annual growth layer (Roe 1967).

In young animals minor laminations may be laid down giving rise to spurious bands. Whether these alternating bands are produced through some internal rhythm or are determined by the seasonal variation in food intake is still not clear. However, the method has now been applied to other species, with some supporting evidence (see, for example, for sei —

Figure 8.5 Generalised breeding cycle of the fin whale (from Lockyer and Brown 1981). During pregnancy the female may spend c. 5 months feeding, in preparation for the energy costs of lactation. In the second year, after weaning, the female may rest and feed over a 4-month period before the next conception. Some individuals may need to rest for a longer period, and hence miss a year before reproducing, whilst others possibly reproduce annually (as is thought to occur in many minke whales)

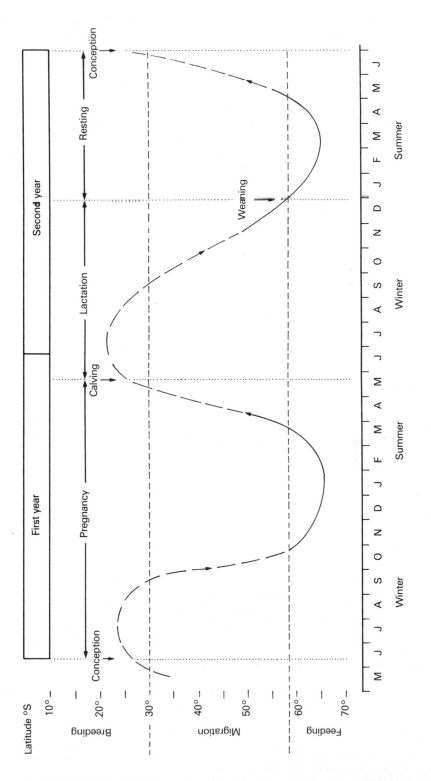

Figure 8.6 Method to determine age of baleen whales by ear-plug layers. A fin whale ear plug cut to expose growth layers in the core, appearing as alternating light and dark bands. Each pair constitutes a growth layer and in most species (the possible exception being the humpback) is apparently deposited annually

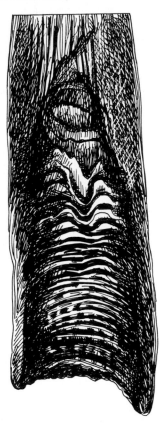

Lockyer 1974, Masaki 1976; Bryde's — Best 1977, Ohsumi 1980; minke – Best 1982, Kato 1983, Masaki 1979, Ohsumi *et al.* 1970; gray whale — Rice and Wolman 1971). There are still difficulties in interpretation of some of the layers (although in sei and minke whales, which have very dark layers, bleaching the plugs with hydrogen peroxide has helped increase their readability — Lockyer 1974). This applies particularly to young animals and smaller species such as the Bryde's and minke whales which have thin growth layers (because of the size of their ear plugs). These uncertainties have been important in the use of such criteria in assessing the influence of human exploitation and decisions relating to the regulation of whaling (see Chapter 9).

Present estimated ages of sexual maturity are given for baleen whales in Table 8.4. As will be discussed later in this chapter, there is some good evidence that these have changed for a number of species during this century. For all species they presently lie somewhere between four and ten years with no obvious pattern related to size or ecology. Females generally grow slightly larger than males, and it is thought that this may be because of extra energy demands to take care of their young which requires storage of much fat.

Table 8.4: Size and growth parameters for mysticetes

Species	Location	Length at birth (m)	Length at sex. maturity (m) ♂	♀	Age at sex. maturity (yrs)	Adult length (m) ♂	♀	Source
Blue whale	Antarctic; South Africa	7.0	22.6	24.0	5	c.25.0	c.26.5	1-3
Pygmy blue whale	Antarctic	c.6.3	c.18.9	19.2	c.5-6	c.23.5		4
Fin whale	Antarctic; South Africa	6.4	19.0	20.0	10→6/7	c.20.5	c.22.0	1-3, 5
	North Atlantic	?	16.8-17.6	17.7-19.1	11→8	c.18.5	c.20.0	1-2, 6
	North Pacific	6.4	17.4-17.7	18.3-18.6	8-11/12→4/6	c.18.5	c.20.0	1-2, 7
Sei whale	Antarctic; South Africa	4.5	13.6	14.0	11→8	c.14.5	c.15.0	1-3, 5
	North Atlantic	?	12.9	13.3	8	c.14.0	c.14.5	1-2, 8
	North Pacific	4.4	12.8(west) 12.9(east)	13.3(west) 13.4(east)	10→6 10	c.13.7	c.15.0	1-2, 9-10
Bryde's whale	South Africa (inshore)	3.96	12.0	12.5	c.10	c.13.1	c.13.7	1, 11
	(offshore)	3.96	13.0	?12.5	8-11	c.13.7	c.14.4	1, 11
	North Pacific (coastal Japan)	3.95	11.9	12.0	9	c.12.9	c.13.3	1, 12
	(pelagic) South Pacific	>3.95 <4.15	11.9 11.6-12.4	12.0 12.2-12.8	10/8 10	c.12.9 c.13.7	c.13.3 c.14.4	1, 13 1, 14
Minke whale	Antarctic; South Africa; Brazil	2.8	7.2	8.0	14→6/7	c.8.5	c.9.0	1-3, 15-19
	North Atlantic	2.6	6.9	7.3-7.45	7.3	c.8.0	c.8.5	1-2, 20-21
	North Pacific	2.8	6.9	7.3	?	c.8.0	c.8.5	1-2, 22
	Huanghai Sea	2.5-2.7	?	6.6-7.0	?	?	c.8.0	23

Table 8.4 (continued)

Species	Location	Length at birth (m)	Length at sex. maturity (m) ♂	♀	Age at sex. maturity (yrs)	Adult length (m) ♂	♀	Source
Humpback whale	Antarctic; Australia	4.3	11.5	12.0	?4–5	c.13.2	c.14.8	1–3, 24
	Northwest Pacific	4.1	11.6	12.0	?5	c.13.5	c.15.0	1–2, 25
	(ages at sex. maturity may be twice these values, based on 1 growth layer/year)							
Gray whale	North Pacific	4.6	11.1–11.4	11.7–11.8	8 (male) 8–12 (female)	c.13.2	c. 13.3	1, 26–28
Bowhead	Arctic	4.5	11.6	12.2–14.0	4	c.14.0?	c.14.6?	1, 29
Pygmy right whale	Southern hemisphere	c.1.6–2.2	?	?	?	c. 5.5–6.4		1, 30
	(all estimates for this species uncertain due to small sample size)							
Southern right whale	Southern hemisphere	5.5	13.0–16.0		?	c. 15.0– 18.5		1, 31
	South Africa; South America	6.1	?	?	?	?	?	1, 32
Northern right whale	Northern hemisphere	?4.4–4.8	?	?	?	?	?	1, 33–35

Reference sources: Much of the above table is derived from: 1 Lockyer 1984. Other sources are: 2 Lockyer 1981a; 3 Brown and Lockyer 1984; 4 Ichihara 1966; 5 Lockyer 1979; 6 Lockyer 1981c; 7 Ohsumi 1986a; 8 Lockyer and Martin 1983; 9 Masaki 1976, 1978; 10 Rice 1977; 11 Best 1977; 12 Omura 1962; 13 Ohsumi 1977a; 14 Ohsumi 1980; 15 Masaki 1979; 16 Kato 1983; 17 Ohsumi 1986b; 18 Best 1982; 19 Williamson 1975; 20 Jonsgard 1951; 21 Mitchell and Kozicki 1975; 22 Omura and Sakiura 1956; 23 Peilie 1982; 24 Chittleborough 1965; 25 Nishiwaki 1959; 26 Rice and Wolman 1971; 27 Yablokov and Bogoslovskaya 1984; 28 Blokhin 1984; 29 Nerini *et al.* 1984; 30 Ross *et al.* 1975; 31 Whitehead and Payne 1981; 32 Best 1981; 33 Klumov 1962; 34 Slijper 1979; 35 Kraus 1986.

Notes: Data indicated '?' or 'c.' are either unknown or of limited reliability, either through sparsity of data, or because they are based on extrapolations from other species, e.g. pygmy blue whale. Growth is probably best expressed in terms of body weight. However, since such data are not so readily available (at least for so many cetacean species), size is expressed here in terms of body length. Where possible, adult lengths are derived from asymptotic growth curves.

Age at sexual maturity is based on growth layers in the ear plug, interpreted as one layer (one dark and one light lamina) being laid down *per annum* (but see text for discussion of possible variation and difficulties in readability); data for humpback whales are based here on two growth layers *per annum* although it is possible that, as interpreted for other mysticetes, one layer is laid down *per annum*.

Arrows indicate changes in estimated age at sexual maturity over time, presumed due to smaller population sizes and hence reduced competition, after human exploitation.

Toothed Whale Reproduction

The toothed whales also have definite peak periods of breeding (conceptions) although these are often less seasonally pronounced (Table 8.2). In the sperm whale, it appears to occur between April and June in the northern hemisphere and between October and December in the southern hemisphere, although in the latter case it may be slightly earlier in the Southeast Pacific than these figures from South Africa indicate. Both mating and births occur in subtropical or tropical waters and there do not appear to be discrete breeding areas. Since the breeding cycle is six months out of phase between northern and southern hemispheres, it is considered that, like the baleen whales which are also out of phase, sperm whales from the two hemispheres rarely if ever interbreed.

The gestation period of the sperm whale is much longer than any of the baleen whales, probably in the region of 15–16 months (though it may possibly extend to 19 months — Best *et al.* 1984). Growth of the fetus increases three to four months after conception, accelerating rapidly about four months later, though not at the same rate as blue and fin whale fetuses. The young are therefore born mainly around August in the northern hemisphere and February to March in the southern hemisphere. Males and females are born at about the same size, but after two to three years males start to grow faster and because they continue growing longer they may reach a size one and a half times the length and three times the weight of the females (Figure 8.7).

The lactation period appears to be rather variable (Table 8.5). There is some evidence (on the basis of lactose in the stomach — see page 237) that some males may continue to suckle up to 13 years of age and females to 7½ years of age (perhaps due to differences in social group membership), although lactation periods are generally given as two years. It apparently lasts longer in older mothers, and there is a possibility that communal suckling occurs if juveniles do suckle intermittently at an older age. Alternatively, those young may represent past offspring that have resumed nursing when a subsequent calf born to their mother died before being weaned.

Age determination of odontocetes is carried out by sectioning teeth and counting the growth layers in the dentine (in some species alternatively the cementum) (Perrin and Myrick 1980; Sergeant 1959; also Figure 8.8). They are usually represented as one narrow translucent and one broader opaque lamination considered to form an annual growth layer. The readability of these layers varies greatly between species and may result in different counts between observers on the same material. For the smaller odontocetes (when relatively young), checks have been made by injecting tetracycline which is then deposited in growing dentine and detected under UV light (Best 1976; Gurevich *et al.* 1980; Nielsen 1972). If the animal is then recaptured a known number of years later this can be related directly to the additional number of growth layers. When this has been done, it has usually substantiated the suggestion that two laminations are laid down annually (viz. the earplugs of baleen whales).

The results of determining the age of sperm whales indicate that females become sexually mature at seven to twelve years (depending on geographical location) and males rather later, puberty commencing at 9–11 years, but sexual maturity generally being reached only at 18–19

Table 8.5: Gestation and lactation periods, and calving intervals for odontocetes

Species	Location	Gestation period (months)	Lactation period (months)	Calving interval (years)	Source
Sperm whale	South Africa	15–16 (possibly to 18.9)	19–42 (increasing with age)	5.2(west coast) 6.0–6.5 to 5.2(east) (after exploitation)	1
	North Atlantic/North Pacific	16–17	?	?	1, 7–8
Pygmy sperm whale	South Africa	c.11	?	?	9
White whale	Arctic	14.5	20–24	3	2, 10–12
Narwhal	Arctic	14–15	20	3?	2, 13–15
Baird's beaked whale	North Pacific	17 (possibly down to 10)	?	c.3?	3, 16–17
Northern bottlenose whale	North Atlantic	12	12+	2(3)	3, 18–19
False killer whale	North Atlantic	15.5 (possibly down to 11)	?	?	4, 20–21
	North Pacific	?	18	?	
Killer whale	North Atlantic	(11)12	?	3–3.5/8.3	4, 21–24
	North Pacific	12–16	>12	?	4, 24–25
	Antarctic	?	?	7.3	4, 24
Long-finned pilot whale	North Atlantic	15.2–16.2	22	3.3+	4, 26
Short-finned pilot whale	North Pacific	15–16	24+ (possibly to several years in older females)	3–10 (increasing with age)	4, 27–28
Tucuxi	South America	10–10.3	?	?	4, 29

Species	Region				References
White-beaked dolphin	North Atlantic	10?	?	?	21
Atlantic white-sided dolphin	North Atlantic	10–12	18	2–3?	4, 30
Dusky dolphin	New Zealand	11	18	?	31–32
Pacific white-sided dolphin	North Pacific	10	?	?	4, 21, 33–34
Common dolphin	North Atlantic/Black Sea	10–11	19	1.3–2.3	4, 21, 34–36
	North Pacific	11.5	19	2.6	4, 34
Bottle-nosed dolphin	All regions	12(13)	19	2–3 (possibly down to 1.3)	4, 21, 34, 37–38
	South Africa	11.5–12	?	?	4, 9
Spotted dolphin	Eastern tropical Pacific	11.5 (possibly 9–10)	13/17/26	2.5/2.7/3.4 (varies between localities and years)	4, 21, 39–40
	Japan	11.2	26/27	3.5/3.9 (varies between years)	4, 41–42
Striped dolphin	Eastern tropical Pacific	12?	14	3.3	4, 21, 40
	Japan	12	8/12/13/17/20	4.2 to 1.4 (varies between years, due to exploitation)	4, 42–43
	Japan	13.2	6.6	3.17	44
Spinner dolphin	Eastern tropical Pacific	9.5–10.7	15/18/19	2.9/3.0/3.3 (varies between localities/stocks)	4, 40, 45–46
Commerson's dolphin	Tierra del Fuego	c.11	?	?	47
Harbour porpoise	North Atlantic	(8–)11	8	1–2	5, 48–51

227

Table 8.5 (continued)

Species	Location	Gestation period (months)	Lactation period (months)	Calving interval (years)	Source
Dall's porpoise	Japan	(7–9)11.4	6–42(average 24.8)	c.3	5, 52
	Bering Sea/ North Pacific	11	c.24	c.3	5, 52
Finless porpoise	Inland Sea of Japan	11	6–15(average <12)	c.2?	5, 53
Boto	South America	>10?	?	?	6, 29, 54
	(uncertain, based on very few specimens)				
Baiji	Yangtze River, China	c.10?	?	?	6, 31, 55–56
Franciscana	South America	10.5	8–9	c.2?	6, 54, 57
Indus susu	Indus river, Pakistan	10–11	?	2	58

Reference sources: For more general references with detailed sources, see: 1 Best 1984; 2 Braham 1984; 3 Mead 1984; 4 Perrin and Reilly 1984; 5 Gaskin et al. 1984; 6 Brownell 1984. Other sources: 7 Clarke 1956; 8 Ohsumi 1965; 9 Ross 1984; 10 Brodie 1971; 11 Sergeant 1973; 12 Seaman and Burns 1981; 13 Best and Fisher 1974; 14 Mansfield et al. 1975; 15 Hay 1980; 16 Omura et al. 1955; 17 Kasuya 1977; 18 Benjaminsen 1972; 19 Benjaminsen and Christensen 1979; 20 Purves and Pilleri 1978; 21 Harrison 1969; 22 Christensen 1984; 23 Jonsgard and Lyshoel 1970; 24 IWC 1982, 32:617–31; 25 Nishiwaka and Handa 1958; 26 Sergeant 1962; 27 Kasuya and Marsh 1984; 28 Marsh and Kasuya 1984; 29 Best and da Silva 1984; 30 Sergeant et al. 1980; 31 Leatherwood et al. 1983; 32 Baker 1983; 33 Leatherwood and Walker 1982; 34 Harrison et al. 1972; 35 Tomilin 1967; 36 Collet 1981; 37 Ridgway and Benirschke 1977; 38 Tavolga and Essapian 1957; 39 Perrin et al. 1976; 40 Perrin and Oliver 1982; 41 Kasuya et al. 1974; 42 Kasuya 1976; 43 Kasuya 1972; 44 Miyazaki 1984; 45 Perrin et al. 1977; 46 Perrin and Henderson 1977; 47 Lockyer et al. in press; 48 Møhl-Hansen 1954; 49 Fisher and Harrison 1970; 50 Van Utrecht 1978; 51 Silijper 1979; 52 Kasuya 1978; 53 Kasuya and Kureha 1979; 54 Harrison and Brownell 1971; 55 Chen et al. 1984; 56 Zhou et al. 1980, 1982; 57 Harrison et al. 1981; 58 Khan and Niazi unpubl.

Notes: Data indicated '?' or 'c.' are either unknown or of limited reliability, mainly through sparsity of data. Age of weaning does not necessarily correspond with mother's lactation period since communal suckling might occur (theoretically possible, though yet to be proved) or young may suckle intermittently from their mother, particularly when she has had another infant. In the sperm whale, for example, males are thought to suckle to 13 years age, and females to 7.5 years age (Best 1984); a similar situation may occur with the young of older short-finned pilot whales (Kasuya and Marsh 1984).

Species for which there are insufficient reproductive data are excluded from the above table. Note also that variations in estimated gestation/lactation periods may be due to different methods of calculation as well as to varying localities and times of sampling. Exploitation appears in some cases to result in reduced calving intervals and/or lactation periods. Estimates of calving intervals are only approximate and are likely to vary between individuals, populations, localities and times (probably due to varying food availability and density-dependent effects).

Figure 8.7 Growth rates of odontocetes: (a) sperm whale; (b) long-finned pilot whale; (c) white whale; (d) northern bottlenose whale; (e) killer whale; (f) striped dolphin; (g) Dall's and harbour porpoises (from Lockyer 1981b; Sergeant 1962; Braham 1984; Benjaminsen and Christensen 1979; Christensen 1984; Miyazaki 1984; Gaskin et al. 1984). Average curves of body length at different agec. For all species, they assume that two dentinal growth layers are laid down per year, although in some cases, for example white whale, it is possible that one later is laid down each year, whilst there may also be variability with age (↓ = age at sexual maturity)

(a)

Sperm whale

(b)

Long-finned Pilot whale

229

Figure 8.7 (continued)

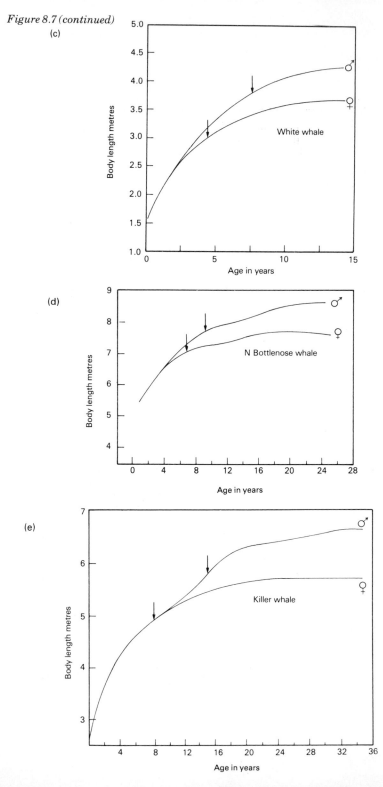

(f)

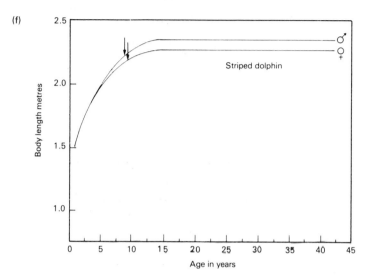

Striped dolphin

(g)

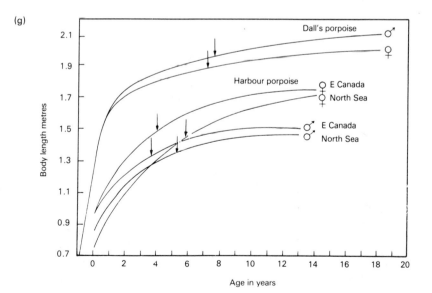

Figure 8.8 Method to determine age of toothed whales by dentine tooth layers. Here, a sperm whale tooth has been bisected with one half etched in 10 per cent formic acid and then rubbed with a pencil to show the growth layers. An annual growth layer appears as an alternating ridge and a trough

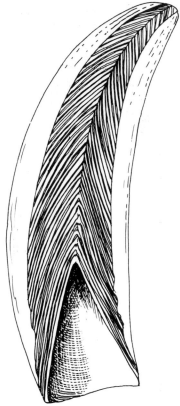

years of age (Best *et al.* 1984; Table 8.6). This may relate to male competition which requires that they continue to grow physically if they are to acquire a harem of females. The longer distance migrations that males make (possibly to avoid competition with females and their calves) may also contribute to the sexual dimorphism observed. For the male, social maturity (corresponding to the acquisition of a harem of females) is achieved at an age of about 26 years. With the protracted gestation and lactation periods, the interval between calving is also long, somewhere between five and seven years. There is some indication that the interval declined slightly between the 1960s and 1970s in response to exploitation (see p. 248). As implied by the variation with age in lactation periods, it also appears that older females calve at less frequent intervals than younger ones, probably reflecting female senescence (a similar pattern has been found in short-finned pilot whales — Marsh and Kasuya 1984; see also Marsh and Kasuya 1986 for a general review).

The larger whale species have been discussed in some detail mainly because of the great amount of information available derived from whale catches. Data for other odontocetes, where available, are summarised in Tables 8.5 and 8.6. Breeding seasons vary both between and within species depending upon the latitude. At high latitudes, although sexual

Table 8.6: Size and growth parameters for odontocetes

Species	Location	Length at birth (cm)	Length at sex. maturity (cm) ♂	Length at sex. maturity (cm) ♀	Age at sex. maturity (yrs) ♂	Age at sex. maturity (yrs) ♀	Adult length (cm) ♂	Adult length (cm) ♀	Source
Sperm whale	Southern hemisphere	400	1190	880	18–19	7–12	1580	1100	1, 7–9
Pygmy sperm whale	South Africa; Florida	120	270–300	260–280	?	?	307(mean)	303(mean) (270–340)	10–12
Dwarf sperm whale	South Africa; United States	c.100		210–220	?	?		210–270	10–11
White whale	Arctic	150–160	c.360	c.300	8–9	4–7	c.420	c.360	2, 13–15
Narwhal	Arctic	150–170	390	340	11–13	5–8	c.410 (max. 470)	c.350 (max. 400)	2, 16–17
Baird's beaked whale	North Pacific	450	1,000	1,050	8–10	8–10	1,190 (max.)	1,280 (max.)	3, 18–19
Northern bottlenose whale	North Atlantic	360	750	690	7–11	11	850	750	3, 20–22
Cuvier's beaked whale	Northern hemisphere	270	550	580	?	?	700 (max.)	754 (max.)	3, 17
False killer whale	Northern hemisphere South Africa	193 160	396–457	366–427	8–14	8–14	541	452	4, 23 4, 11

Table 8.6 (continued)

Species	Location	Length at birth (cm)	Length at sex. maturity (cm) ♂	Length at sex. maturity (cm) ♀	Age at sex. maturity (yrs) ♂	Age at sex. maturity (yrs) ♀	Adult length (cm) ♂	Adult length (cm) ♀	Source
Killer whale	North Atlantic	208–220	c.579	457–488	15–16	8–10	945(mean)	566(mean)	4, 24–26
	North Pacific	246/276							4, 26–27
	all regions	210–250							4, 28
	Antarctic							645(mean)	4
Long-finned pilot whale	North Atlantic	177	490	365	10–12	6–7	c.550	c.460	4, 29
Short-finned pilot whale	North Pacific	139.5	400	320	16	9 (7–12)	c.470	c.340–350	4, 30
Tucuxi	South America riverine	c.75	>140	128.5–138.5	?	?	146(mean)	145(mean)	4, 31
	coastal	?	?	?	?	?	177(mean)	176(mean)	4, 32
Atlantic white-sided dolphin	North Atlantic	110	230–240	201–222	?4–6	?5–8	250(mean)	224(mean)	4, 10, 33
Pacific white-sided dolphin	North Pacific	80–95	170–180	?	?	?	190(mean)	192(mean)	4, 34–36
Common dolphin	North Pacific	79	?	?	7–12	?	?	?	4, 37
	Tropical Pacific	81	200	?	6–7	?	208(mean)	196(mean)	4, 37–39
	North Atlantic	?	200	190	5–7+	6–7	243	211	4, 40
	Black Sea	80–90	170–180	150–170	3	2/4	178(mean)	170(mean)	4, 29, 41–42
Bottle-nosed dolphin	Northern hemisphere	98–130	245–260	220–235	c.11	c.12	270	250/259	4, 34, 43–44
	South Africa	84–112	210–240	210–230	9–11	?	239	241	4, 11
Spotted dolphin	Northwest Pacific	89	194	181	12	9	207	194	4, 45
	Tropical Pacific (offshore)	c.82.5	c.195	182	11	8	200(coastal) (offshore form c.20cm larger)	190(coastal)	4, 46–47

Striped dolphin	Northwest Pacific	100	219	216	9	9	238	225	4, 48
	Tropical Pacific	?	195–200	?	?	?	205	200	4, 49
Spinner dolphin	Tropical Pacific								
	Eastern stock*	77	160–170	164	6–9	5(4–5)	180	171	4, 47, 50
	Whitebelly stock	76	165–170	167	6–8	6(4–6)	180	175	4, 50
	Gulf of Mexico	?	c.190	c.188	?	7–10	201	201	4, 51
Commerson's dolphin	Tierra del Fuego	c.75 (due to rapid early growth spurt)	c.130–135	c.130–135	5–6	5–8 c.130–135			52
Harbour porpoise	North Sea	67–80	c.135	c.145	5	6	c.145	c.170	5, 53–54
	East Canada	78	c.134	c.144	3–4	3–4	c.150	c.175	5, 55–56
Dall's porpoise	Japan	100	c.196	c.186	7–8	7	c.207	c.197	5, 57
Boto	South America	79	>198?	>183?	?	?	c.190–230 (modal adult lengths)	c.180–220	6, 31
Franciscana	South America	76	131	140	2–3	2–3	131(mean)	140(mean)	6, 58

Reference sources: For more detailed sources, see the following general references: 1 Best et al. 1984; 2 Braham 1984; 3 Mead 1984; 4 Perrin and Reilly 1984; 5 Gaskin et al. 1984; 6 Brownell 1984. Other sources: 7 Best 1968; 8 Gambell 1972; 9 Lockyer 1981b; 10 Leatherwood et al. 1983; 11 Ross 1984; 12 Odell et al. 1984; 13 Brodie 1971; 14 Best and Fisher 1974; 15 Seaman and Burns 1981; 16 Hay 1980; 17 Ohsumi in Braham 1984; 18 Kasuya 1977; 19 Omura et al. 1955; 20 Benjaminsen 1972; 21 Christensen 1973; 22 Benjaminsen and Christensen 1979; 23 Purves and Pilleri 1978; 24 Jonsgard and Lyshoel 1970; 25 Christensen 1984; 26 Nishiwaki and Handa 1958; 27 Bigg 1982; 28 Tomilin 1967; 29 Sergeant 1962; 30 Kasuya and Marsh 1984; 31 Best and da Silva 1984; 32 Van Utrecht 1981; 33 Sergeant et al. 1980; 34 Harrison et al. 1972; 35 Fitch and Brownell 1968; 36 Ridgway and Green 1967; 37 Hui 1977; 38 Gurevich and Stewart 1978; 39 Evans 1975; 40 Collet 1981; 41 Sleptsov 1941; 42 Sokolov 1962; 43 Sergeant et al. 1973; 44 Harrison 1969; 45 Kasuya 1976; 46 Perrin et al. 1976, 1982; 47 Perrin et al. 1977; 48 Miyazaki 1977, 1984; 49 Gurevich and Stewart 1979; 50 Perrin and Henderson 1984; 51 Mead et al. 1980; 52 Lockyer et al. in press; 53 Møhl-Hansen 1954; 54 Van Utrecht 1978; 55 Smith and Gaskin 1974; 56 Gaskin and Blair 1977; 57 Kasuya 1978; 58 Kasuya and Brownell 1979.

Notes: Data indicated '?' or 'c.' are either unknown or of limited reliability through sparsity of data. Growth is best expressed in terms of body weight. However, since such data are not so readily available (at least for many odontocetes), size is expressed here in terms of body length. Where possible, adult lengths are derived from asymptotic growth curves or as averages of lengths of physically mature individuals. Otherwise, they are expressed as mean values of adults (some of whom will not be physically mature).

Table 8.6 (continued)

Age at sexual maturity is based on growth layers in the dentine (in some species, the cementum) of sectioned teeth, with one growth layer group (termed GLG), made up of one narrow translucent (by transmitted light) and one broader opaque lamination, interpreted as laid down *per annum* in all species (see Perrin and Myrick 1980 for details). Exceptions are white whales (2 GLGs/year — Brodie 1971; IWC 1982:114, after examination of a captive specimen of known age) and narwhal (3 GLGs/year until age 3 in males or 4.5 GLGs/year until age 2 in females, and 1 GLG/year thereafter — Hay 1980). It is also possible that 2 GLGs are laid down in the first year of life in other odontocetes (as suggested for sperm whale — Best *et al.* 1984, and spotted dolphin — Perrin *et al.* 1976).

Values for length and age at sexual maturity represent averages (rounded to the nearest year), calculated by a variety of methods (see above general references for details). The age of sexual maturity is not necessarily equivalent to the age at which an animal actually breeds if it is excluded socially. This is thought to occur, for example, in some putatively polygynous species; males reach social maturity at about 17 years in the short-finned pilot whale (Kasuya and Marsh 1984) and about 25 years in the sperm whale (Best 1979; Lockyer 1981b), although it is likely (as Best *et al.* (1984) have suggested for sperm whales) that some younger males breed successfully.

In a number of cases, more recent knowledge and larger sample sizes have resulted in revised estimates of various parameters. These have been incorporated in the above review to give 'best' estimates wherever possible. However, all sources of references examined are given (secondary sources to be found in the general references), whether or not those published values are included here.

Only species for which there is sufficient information on growth and development are included in this table.

* = population severely reduced by human exploitation, possibly resulting in changes to various biological paremeters (see Perrin and Henderson 1984)

activity may occur in most months (perhaps to maintain social bonds), births are more strongly seasonal, between spring and autumn for the smaller species but often in winter for larger odontocetes (such as the killer whale and long-finned pilot whale). In lower latitudes births are less seasonal.

Gestation periods for most odontocetes are between ten and twelve months, although this is extended to 15 or 16 months in certain species, usually those for which squid are important prey. I suggest that this may result from the longer time needed for fetal growth arising from a lower energy content of squid (see Table 6.3). As with mammals in general, it appears that the gestation period is reasonably inflexible whereas lactation periods may vary greatly within a species. On the other hand, it is much more difficult to estimate the lactation period and some of the variation observed may relate to this. Three methods are used. The first and most common method takes the gestation period of a species and multiplies this by the proportion of the sample lactating divided by the proportion that is pregnant (including some which may be both pregnant and lactating). This is based on the assumption that the length of time spent in lactation will be directly proportional to the proportion of mature lactating females sampled. There are various potential biases related mainly to sampling (but also to the possibility of overlooking animals in early pregnancy). If, for example, there is some segregation of animals of particular status this could give a misleading overall estimate.

The second method estimates the age at weaning by calculating the age of the assumed oldest suckling calf in a sample containing a lactating female. This method has various biases associated with variation in growth rate of different calves and the fact that the calf that is suckling for the longest time may continue to do so for an unknown length of time. Furthermore, the average age of weaning will not necessarily tell one the lactation period, because it takes no account of the higher chance of some lactating females having lost their calves as the lactation period progresses.

The final method, developed recently by Peter Best on sperm whales, determines the presence of lactose (a constituent of milk) in the stomach of a calf by a direct chemical test (see Best *et al.* 1984). It also estimates the age at weaning and may be affected by bias if there is differential mortality between calves that continue suckling for a long time compared with those that are weaned earlier. It is also possible that calves may continue suckling only intermittently after the main shift to solid food, just as human babies will do, and this may involve mothers that are now suckling another, younger, calf of their own.

We have seen in some detail the potential problems for estimating lactation periods. The results shown in Table 8.5 suggest that, for the majority of odontocete species, length of lactation is between 18 and 20 months, although some solid food will be taken on average from six months of age. The maximum length of suckling is at least two years (possibly much longer — see Kasuya and Marsh 1984).

The consequence of these lengths of gestation and lactation is that the interval between calving in the majority of smaller odontocetes has to be at least two years. It appears that females may come into oestrus whilst lactating so that in some species (such as common dolphin) a mother may give birth again between one and two years later. It is also likely that there is a resting period which has been estimated at 4–5 months (range 2–15) so that most females probably do not calve more frequently than every two or three years. These values will be correspondingly longer for species like the pilot whales and killer whale with protracted gestation and lactation periods (see Table 8.5), although Kasuya and Marsh (1984:286) have shown that female short-finned pilot whales may simultaneously lactate and become pregnant.

Different species become sexually mature at very different ages, ranging from only three years in the common dolphin to 16 years in the killer whale. The larger species tend to reach sexual maturity later, and differences between the sexes are greatest in those species thought to be polygynous. In those cases, males are substantially larger than females and take much longer to reach sexual maturity. This may be the result of the increased time they need in competition with other males to take over a group of females, particularly if that group has a stable membership with a male 'harem-master' at least in residence for more than just a short period.

There is some evidence that, for those dolphin populations which are heavily exploited, the various reproductive parameters have changed over recent years. In the striped dolphin, which is hunted extensively off Japan, the pregnancy rate has increased and the lactation period decreased, as would be expected if there are fewer animals in the population to compete for food (Kasuya 1985a). Spinner dolphins in the eastern tropical Pacific reach sexual maturity faster (five instead of six years) in the most heavily exploited population, but, perhaps rather surprisingly, have a longer length of lactation (Perrin and Reilly 1984). Clearly the relationship between exploitation and different reproductive parameters is complicated and not yet fully understood.

Further details on various aspects of reproduction in whales and dolphins have been assembled in an excellent recent volume *Reproduction in Whales, Dolphins and Porpoises*, edited by Perrin *et al.* (1984), arising out of a special conference on the subject in California, 1981, organised by the International Whaling Commission.

MORTALITY

Natural (i.e. not man-induced) death may occur from a variety of causes, but only three are considered important. These are predation, parasitism and disease. Unnatural causes of death such as poisoning will be considered in a later chapter, whilst starvation is usually so closely linked with parasitism and disease that evidence for it as a direct cause of mortality is virtually absent. However, studies in Florida of a number of singly stranded pygmy sperm whales revealed lesions in the myocardium of the heart (indicative of thiamine deficiency) and suggest that inadequate nutrition may cause mortality (Bossart *et al.* 1983).

Predation

We have seen that cetaceans have few predators — notably sharks, killer and false killer whales (probably pygmy killers, and possibly pilot whales), and man. The importance of sharks and killer whales is difficult to determine. Actual observations not surprisingly are scarce (see Gaskin 1982:–3; Hancock 1965; Lopez and Lopez 1985; Martinez and Klinghammer 1970; Norris and Dohl 1980b; Rice 1968; Whitehead and Glass 1985), although the regular presence of scars on a wide variety of species (particularly inshore species) testifies to attacks by sharks being not uncommon, estimates ranging between 3 and 18 per cent of animals examined (McCann 1974; Norris and Dohl 1980a,b; Wood *et al.* 1970). Furthermore, 33 per cent of individually recognised humpbacks off Newfoundland and Labrador had scars attributable to the teeth of killer whales (Katona *et al.* 1980). One has to be careful to identify the source of scarring, because it is not necessarily clear, and many scars may arise by fighting between members of the same species. Parallel scar lines are most likely made by the teeth of members of the same species whereas circular scars (particularly around the head) represent attachment by the suckers on the tentacles of squid. Round or oval lacerations with radiating groove patterns, once thought to be lamprey wounds, are now known to be made by the teeth of the tropical shark (*Isistius brasiliensis*) which temporarily attaches to cetaceans by its suction-like lips (Jones 1971). Avoidance behaviour by cetaceans when killer whales approach (Arnbom *et al.* 1987; Saayman and Tayler 1979; Tayler and Saayman 1972; Wursig and Wursig 1979, 1980), or their sounds are played back underwater (Cummings and Thompson 1971b; Fish and Vania 1971) lend further support that these potential predators probably have some influence, whilst aspects of the ecology of many species (group size, calving grounds, etc.) show at least a secondary role of predation (Norris and Dohl 1980b). We naturally have more exact information of predation by man and most changes in biological parameters appear to be directly or indirectly caused by man. Direct human predation will form the subject of the next chapter.

Parasitism and Disease

There is no shortage of evidence for cetaceans having plenty of parasites (see Delyamure 1968; also Dailey and Brownell 1972). This does not necessarily mean that these will lead to cetacean death, however. Most animals, including man, will be a home for a diverse assemblage of parasites, bacteria and viruses, but only rarely will these actually show strong detrimental effects, unless the death of the host results in or is caused by production or dissemination of the next life cycle. Otherwise it would be disadvantageous for a parasite to cause the death of its host, since such an act would remove its home or source of nourishment and so could lead to its own death.

Some baleen whale species have conspicuous infestations of barnacles and amphipod crustaceans (called whale lice although they are not insects) attached to their skin (particularly around the head region, on the flippers and tail flukes but also, in the case of whale lice, in folds of skin) (Figure 8.9). Epizootic barnacles and whale lice (mainly of the genus *Cyamus* and related forms) occur mainly on the humpback, gray and right whales, though some of these also occur on sperm whales. For a review of cyamid crustaceans, the reader should consult Leung (1967).

Unlike whale lice, barnacles are not particularly species-specific. However, they do not appear to be able to settle on the swifter moving

Figure 8.9 Parasites and commensals of cetaceans. Organisms such as (a) acorn barnacles of the genus Coronula, *and (b) stalked barnacles (cirripeds) of the genus* Conchoderma *are essentially commensal upon whales; (c) pseudo-stalked barnacles of the genus* Xenobalanus *burrow deeper, but nevertheless probably cause little harm; (d) the lernaeid parasitic copepod,* Penella, *burrows into the blubber with its abdomen protruding and hanging down from the skin, both this and (e) the amphipod whale louse of the genus* Cyamus *actually feed on the whale's skin, although neither is likely to cause more than minor irritation*

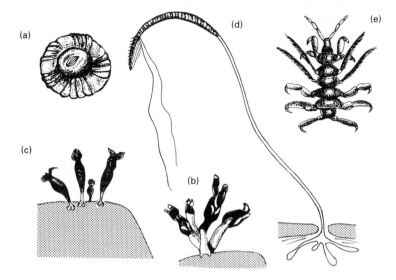

rorquals and only rarely occur on dolphins. On the other hand, the skin, blubber and baleen plates of rorquals and other mysticetes are frequently infested with copepods (varying from small *Balaenophila* to the very large *Penella*), and ciliate protozoa.

Three different kinds of barnacles occur on the surface of whales: acorn barnacles such as those of the genera *Coronula* and *Cryptolepas*; stalked or ship barnacles such as those of the genus *Conchoderma*; and pseudo-stalked barnacles such as those of the genera *Xenobalanus* and *Tubicinella*. Although *Conchoderma* will occur on dolphins when it can settle on teeth where they are exposed by a crooked, healed fracture of the jaw, only the pseudo-stalked barnacles (particularly *Tubicinella*) burrow into the skin to any extent and hence occur regularly on the faster-moving dolphins. However, all three kinds derive only nourishment and do not seem to cause any infection or inflammation. In this way they should more accurately be regarded as commensals rather than parasites. Many baleen whales also have a thin yellow-green film of diatoms (for example *Cocconeis ceticola* on the blue whale) over their skin which is acquired during their summer stay in polar waters, and has helped to identify some of the migration patterns of those species (Nemoto 1956; Nemoto *et al.* 1980; Omura 1950a).

The cornified growths around which whale lice gather develop before birth so they cannot be seen as a response to parasitic infection. Instead they appear to represent an overgrowth of the epidermis which is then grazed by these crustaceans. In general, none of these external parasites is thought to have a strongly detrimental effect. The same may not be true, however, for certain internal parasites.

Very many different species of nematodes and tapeworms live in the stomach and intestine of both mysticetes and odontocetes, and the same species may occur in different cetaceans (see Delyamure 1968 for a review). Nematodes of the genus *Crassicauda* infest the kidneys and urino-genital system, and various species may inhabit the bronchi of the lungs. Some tapeworms reach a length of 15m and nematodes may occur in such abundance that as much as 50kg of them has been recorded from the stomach of a sperm whale. Parasitic flukes (almost exclusively in the adult phase) occur in the liver, gall bladder, brain, lung and intestine. Heavy infestations of many of these parasites almost certainly have important detrimental effects. William Perrin and Joseph Powers (1980) have estimated the mortality induced by *Crassicauda* infections in spotted dolphins to be at least 1–3 per cent per year (or between 11 and 14 per cent of natural mortality). This suggests that parasitism may be an important mortality factor facing small cetaceans. It supports the results of another study by Joseph Geraci and colleagues (1978) which indicated reproductive failure in Atlantic white-sided dolphins through invasion of mammary glands by a closely related nematode. Recently, Richard Lambertson (1986) found 82 out of 87 fin whales (94 per cent) to be infected by *Crassicauda*, and considered that severe infections could be lethal by congestion of the kidney and consequent renal failure. Moderate infections could also cause extensive injury to the vascular system. Mortality due to this nematode was estimated at 4–5 per cent per year (or over half of the estimated total natural mortality).

Our knowledge of the role of disease in cetaceans is still extremely limited. Post-mortem examination by Richard Stroud and colleagues, of stranded cetaceans (and seals) along the Oregon and Washington coasts, indicated bacterial infections and parasitism to be important causes of death, each respectively thought to account for over one-quarter of the dead marine mammals found (Stroud 1979). For a review of marine mammal diseases, see Howard (1983).

Strandings and their Causes

The cause of strandings has continued to perplex biologists. Many animals that are found on our coasts probably died first at sea, and their bodies then drifted ashore. It is extremely difficult to determine how freshly dead a beached cetacean is since it may remain intact for some time before there is a visible deterioration in condition. Post-mortem analyses may be done on a mixture of animals that have stranded live or dead. Heavy parasitic fluke infections of the brain have been found in some strandings (see, for example, Ridgway and Dailey 1972). A recent study of the pathology of 43 stranded small cetaceans in Califorinia by William Walker (1981) and colleagues revealed brain lesions caused by the trematode worm *Nasitrema* sp. in 91 per cent of these. Their effects on the air sinuses, inner ear and brain were considered to be the major cause of stranding (see Cowan *et al.* 1986 for further details). Heavy nematode infections of the ear (and the acoustic sinuses) have also been found in stranded specimens of a variety of cetacean species (as noted above; see also Dailey and Perrin 1973). They are thought to affect either their sense of balance or their sonar abilities. Otherwise, many strandings are of animals damaged by boat propellers, drowned in nets, or new or recently born young that presumably were ailing or had lost their mothers.

Most public attention has been given to mass strandings and one suggestion has even been that these represent a method of population regulation mediated by increased stress amongst herds at high population density (Sergeant 1982). For this to apply, one would need to invoke group selection, and the conditions for this are probably too restrictive to apply to cetaceans in this way. Some species are more inclined to mass strand than others. They include pilot whales, sperm whale, pygmy sperm whale, false killer and melon-headed whales, and to a lesser extent the killer whale and Atlantic white-sided dolphin. All but the last species form groups with some apparent social cohesion. All but the last two are essentially pelagic, rarely coming into inshore waters. These factors may be important in understanding why such strandings occur. If normally pelagic animals come close to the coast, perhaps because they are collectively following food prey or because they are following one or more animals that direct the movement of the herd, then they could easily become lost. Their navigation (by sonar or other senses) could be confused by shallow sandbanks, magnetic anomalies or unfamiliar topographic features (see, for example, Klinowska 1986). Alternatively, the 'herd leader(s)' might be diseased or sick in some way, or senile.

Once close to the coast, however, it is difficult to understand why cetaceans should come ashore. Even when towed back to sea, they often strand again. Perhaps acoustic signals deflected off shallow sloping land (or sandbanks) are rather distressing for them, and they leave the sea conceivably to escape their constant rebounding. Or they may be weakened by illness or starvation and find it difficult to keep rising to the surface for breath. Shallow water or dry land would provide a respite where, faced with the risk of drowning, an animal could at least continue to breathe. Weakness of a stranding individual or 'standing by' behaviour of its comrades may thus be one explanation for repeated strandings, with social contact maintained acoustically within a group, given its likely strong social cohesion. We are obviously still far from knowing why whales strand alive, and in any case it is very likely that more than one factor is involved. Whatever causes live strandings (see Geraci and St Aubin 1979 for a review on the subject), some useful methods to save stranded animals have been assembled by Frank Robson in a book entitled *Strandings: ways to save whales* (1984).

Population Dynamics: Sex Ratios, Reproductive and Mortality Rates

We have seen the major causes of mortality: let us next examine how these affect the populations of different cetacean species. Mortality starts at conception although rarely has information been available before birth to calculate it. A recent study of fetuses derived from the whaling industry, by Jon Seger and Robert Trivers (1983) from Princeton University, has produced some very interesting results. They found a significant excess of males in various baleen species (most marked in the humpback and blue whales). Female fetuses were slightly larger than male ones for all five species examined (as they are throughout life) and they appear to grow slightly faster in all species except the minke whale. They also have some interesting evidence that there is a greater preponderance of males early on but that this then declines. Humpback and blue whales with the highest excess of male fetuses also show the highest rates of differential mortality before birth.

Within a species, there are also differences between large and small mothers. In humpback, blue and minke whales, larger females are more likely to produce sons than are smaller females whereas larger fin and sei whales are more likely to produce daughters. Why should this be? The answer is not clear but a possible explanation provided by Seger and Trivers is that it relates to sex ratio theory which predicts that parents will try to equalise their 'investment' (expenditure of energy) in the production of male and female offspring (Fisher 1930; Trivers 1972). More male fetuses are conceived than female ones but these use less energy by growing more slowly, and they suffer a higher mortality so reducing the number of males during the gestation period. This should apply only if mothers that lose a fetus then have a higher chance of reproducing successfully next time.

With species that may conceive in successive years (presumably bearing little reproductive cost), this reproductive compensation is less likely to be effective. We may, therefore, not expect it to operate in sei, fin and minke whales, with maximum pregnancy rates ranging between 0.6 and 0.85. In those cases, larger females, arriving in polar seas after smaller ones, have less opportunity to compensate for lost fetuses. Thus large females equalise their investment in the sexes at an effective sex ratio at conception nearer 1:1 than smaller females who equalise their investment by producing relatively more sons. On the other hand, in humpback and blue whales, with pregnancy rates around 0.5, such reproductive compensation may not apply. Larger females arrive in polar seas before smaller ones and it is they that would equalise investment in the sexes by having more sons.

These relationships are clearly rather complex and we are far from understanding precisely how they work. If the results obtained generally hold, then they are most interesting, although providing a theoretical explanation for them requires further work. Other studies would suggest that individuals of most rorqual species more usually reproduce at intervals greater than one year (see Lockyer 1984), so that arguments that involve reproductive compensation may be less strong. Furthermore, the effects of exploitation, particularly upon blue and humpback whales, may alter the age structure and reduce intraspecific competition which would have further consequences on the reproductive strategies of different sized females.

At birth the sex ratio of the above baleen species (and other cetaceans) appears to adjust to approximately 1:1. Although in most animals juvenile mortality is substantially higher than for adults, in whales there is less evidence for this. Both juvenile and adult rates of mortality in the sperm whale have been given as about 6 per cent per annum and similar rates for adults and juveniles have been found in sei whales (Allen 1980:10). However, estimates for those species are based on very little direct evidence, and higher mortality rates for juveniles are more usual among mammals. Gray whales show a much higher juvenile mortality rate (11 per cent per annum) compared with adults (5.5 per cent) (Reilly 1984b), and the same may be true of short-finned pilot whales (Kasuya and Marsh 1984).

Natural adult mortality rates seem to decline in various baleen whales as the size of a species increases. Thus, among three rorqual species, it is highest in the minke whale (9–10 per cent per annum), less so in sei whales (7.5 per cent) and lowest in the fin whale (4 per cent) (Ohsumi 1979).

In some species, mortality rates may be higher in males than females (Ralls et al. 1980). For example, in some dolphins of the genus *Stenella*, adult mortality is between 4 and 7 per cent higher in males than in females (Kasuya 1976), and about 4 per cent higher (averaged over all age classes) in male short-finned pilot whales (Kasuya and Marsh 1984). On the other hand, it is slightly higher in female gray whales than in males (Reilly 1984b). In the case of the short-finned pilot whale, there is some evidence that mortality rate increases after a certain age which differs between the sexes (28 years in the male and 46 years in the female — Kasuya and Marsh 1984). Although this could relate to the polygynous habit of this species, with males possibly competing for groups of females, the sperm whale, which has a similar breeding system, shows no evidence of differential mortality between the sexes, with an estimated mortality rate of 6 per cent (Ohsumi 1979). Indeed in most species examined, the mortality rate does not seem to differ between the sexes and the sex ratio of the population has been found to be approximately 1:1 (though this will not necessarily be reflected in groups sampled, because of segregation by age and sex).

The limited information we have suggests that mortality rates are low and that cetaceans are usually long-lived. Among odontocetes, smaller species have shorter life spans. The harbour porpoise, for example, is thought to live for about 15 years (Gaskin and Blair 1977; Van Utrecht 1978); the bottle-nosed dolphin for 25 years (Sergeant et al. 1973); white whale for 25–30 years (Brodie 1971; Sergeant 1973); northern bottle-nose whale up to 37 years (Christensen 1973); the spotted dolphin for 40–50 years (Perrin et al. 1976); the narwhal for 50 years (Hay 1980); killer whale for 50+ years in the male; and 80+ years in the female (Balcomb pers. comm.); short-finned pilot whale up to 63 years (Marsh and Kasuya 1984); sperm whale for 65–70 years (Lockyer unpubl.), and the Baird's beaked whale possibly up to 70 years (Kasuya 1977). Baleen whales are also long-lived. Humpback whales live to at least 30 years (Chittleborough 1959), minke whales for 40–50 years, sei whales to 65 years, and fin whales for 85–90 years (Lockyer unpubl.). All these values are maximum rather than average life spans.

COMPETITION AND THE RESPONSE TO EXPLOITATION

It is a generally held principle that animal species cannot coexist if their requirements completely overlap (Gause 1934). If two species occupying the same area share precisely the same diet, they are thought to come directly into competition with one another. During the course of evolution, it appears that many closely related species have diverged slightly to reduce competition with one another, and the web of animals that make up an ecosystem, be it forest or coral reef or whatever, are thought to have assorted themselves to avoid excess competition. In practice, it is very difficult to identify whether competition exists between two species. One would expect any serious competition to have been minimised already by natural selection.

The presence in a region of closely related species such as the white-beaked and white-sided dolphins in the North Atlantic or five species of rorquals in the Southern Ocean might be taken as a potential for strong competition. In the case of the former, they appear to concentrate in different habitats, white-sided dolphins being rather more pelagic, and their diets consequently differ slightly, but there is still much overlap. In the case of the Southern Ocean whales, they each have slightly different favoured prey and this might help reduce competition. Of course, if suitable food is presently superabundant then there may be no cause for competition, and perhaps the great concentrations of krill in the Antarctic are more than sufficient for every animal's needs. However, it is clear that this has not been the case when one looks at the consequences of over-hunting of the great whales.

In the early years of this century the vast whale resources inhabiting the Southern Ocean were discovered by European whalers. First they concentrated upon the largest and, therefore, most economically productive species, the blue whale. In 60 years, numbers were reduced from some 200,000 to a mere 6,000. As numbers dwindled, the whalers moved to other smaller species, the fin whale then sei whale and finally minke (see Figure 9.3). Humpbacks and right whales had already been over-exploited. In the Antarctic, krill (*Euphausia superba*) are pivotal organisms in the complex food web (see Figure 8.10). In this region, all rorquals tend to feed mainly on krill, and the Japanese cetologist, Takahisa Nemoto (1959, 1962), has shown that there is considerable overlap in food preference, feeding area and timing of feeding for all the Antarctic baleen whales. Richard Laws (1977a, b) and Neil Mackintosh (1973) have calculated that the overall reduction of baleen whale stocks from about 43 million tonnes in the 1900s to about 6.6 million tonnes today has made available a 'surplus' of about 153 million tonnes of krill. It has been further estimated that the total whale density in the Antarctic summer feeding area has declined from a biomass of 2.6g/sq m to 0.4g/sq m, a truly massive reduction. These changes to the food web of the Southern Ocean have had important effects on a variety of biological parameters and, as we shall see below, provide some of the best evidence for the existence of competition.

The reduced abundance of the large blue, fin and humpback whales has had an effect upon the smaller sei and minke whales as well as upon the larger whales themselves (Gambell 1973, 1976a,b; Kawamura 1978; Laws 1977b; Lockyer 1979, 1984). About double the proportion (50–55 per cent) of mature non-lactating female blue whales are now pregnant compared with the rate before the 1930s (Figure 8.11). This implies that the interval between successive births is approximately half. Similar changes have taken place in fin and sei whales, and at present a very high proportion of minke whale females appear to be pregnant. Furthermore, declines in the mean age of sexual maturity have been observed in various species — from 10 to 6 years in fin, 11.4 to 7 years in sei and 14 to 6 years in minke whales (Figure 8.11). There have been some doubts expressed in these figures in recent years due partly to the difficulties of determining age from ear plugs and the effects that variability in estimations will have on the mathematical calculations.

Figure 8.10 Food web in the Southern Ocean (from UNEP (1978)). Figures in boxes denote annual production at each trophic level, and those alongside lines annual consumption, in millions of tons (one ton = 1.016 tonnes)

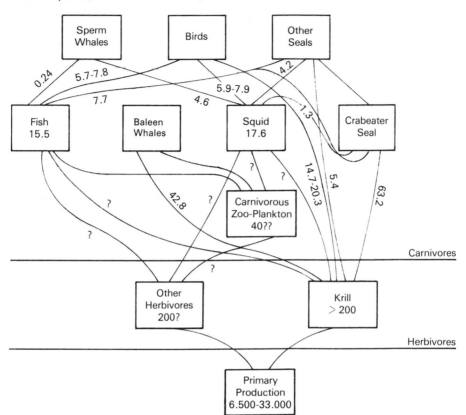

There is also a need in population modelling to use age at first birth rather than age at sexual maturity, and this cannot be estimated reliably by adding on the gestation period to the age at maturity since ovulation cannot be equated with conception, and even less with live birth (DeMaster 1981, 1984; Lockyer 1984).

Estimates of changes in pregnancy rates are confused by pooling of data between regions and dates, the variability of which can introduce biases or mask trends (Masaki 1978; Mizroch and York 1984). In particular, the age at sexual maturity may be determined from the transition phase in ear plug growth layers between widely spaced ones (which may or may not be irregular) whilst juvenile and the more compact and regular layers of the adults. This has been described for fin and sei whales (Kato 1983; Lockyer 1972, 1974; Masaki 1979). Cooke and de la Mare (1983) considered that the observed declines in age of sexual maturity may be an artifact of the variability in reading this phase, as well as to truncation biases of the observed curves (see also Cooke 1985, Kato 1983). However, even if these marked trends are revised somewhat in future, there is direct evidence that declines in age at maturity have occurred in a number of fin whale stocks, for example in the Antarctic

Figure 8.11 Changes in reproductive parameters of the great whales in response to exploitation (from Brown and Lockyer 1984). The apparent decline in mean first age at sexual maturity (left side) in fin, sei and minke whales over time, and the apparent increase in percentage of pregnant females in the exploitable population (right side) in fin, sei and blue whales. Those graphs on the left side apply to the Antarctic between 0° and 60° W, whereas those on the right side apply to all areas in the Antarctic

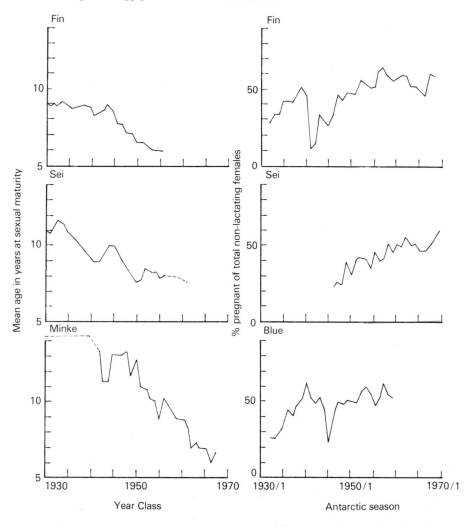

and North Pacific (Ohsumi 1986a,b), and good evidence for a similar decline in Antarctic minke whales (Lockyer 1984).

Despite apparent declines in the age at which the various baleen whale species become sexually mature, the size at which they have reached sexual maturity has remained constant, for fin and sei whales at about 90 per cent maximum length. This suggests that those whales must be growing faster. Christina Lockyer (1978, 1981c) has explored the feasibility of these increased growth rates on an energetic basis. Her results indicate that an extra 20–25 per cent food annually could cover the energetic costs that a fin whale would have to make to reach sexual maturity four years earlier. Minke whales would require a similar food increase of 27 per cent to attain sexual maturity eight years earlier. Of course all these calculations are fraught with difficulties and uncertainties. Individuals within a species show much variation in a number of these parameters, for example. Nevertheless they lie within the bounds of possibility given the amount of krill thought to be released by the reduction of the great whales mentioned above.

Changes in pregnancy rates, individual growth rate and attainment of sexual maturity appear to correlate with the history and pattern of exploitation, being greatest in those areas with the longest histories of exploitation (Lockyer 1984). Although some other parameters are more relevant, such as the age at first parturition rather than age at sexual maturity, these findings represent fairly strong evidence that the reduction in density of various whale species has released food to the remaining individuals of that and related species.

One possible consequence of changes in growth rates and age of sexual maturity has been noted in a previous chapter. This is the process known as paedomorphosis (see page 87), and it may explain how the recently recognised subspecies, the pygmy blue whale, and species such as drawf and pygmy sperm whales, pygmy right whales and pygmy killer whales have evolved.

Useful reviews of the effects of exploitation of whales (and seals) and the importance of species interactions in the Southern Ocean may be found in Beddington and May (1977, 1982), Gambell (1973) and Laws (1977a,b, 1985). Similar density dependent effects (notably a decline in age of sexual maturity) were previously described for the Antarctic crabeater seal, another species that feeds particularly upon krill, although recent studies show that both counts are unreliable and suggest the results may be a consequence of individuals that mature earlier dying sooner (Bengtson and Laws 1984). Otherwise there are only a few good examples amongst mammals, notably the African elephant and humans. However, other cetacean species have shown comparable responses to exploitation. These include the sperm whale (with a decline in calving interval from 6 to 5.2 years between 1962 to 1965, 1967, and 1973 to 1975 — Best *et al.* 1984), spinner dolphins in the eastern tropical Pacific (Perrin and Henderson 1984), and striped dolphins in the western North Pacific (Kasuya 1985a). As noted earlier in this chapter, the responses of different biological parameters do not necessarily vary as one might expect, and we have much to learn yet of the interplay between the many different factors involved.

9 Whales and man – history of whaling

The First Whalers

The earliest evidence of whales in the history of man goes back into the mists of time — 5,000–6,000 (perhaps up to 8,000) years ago in Alaska (Donovan 1982: 36; Laughlin and Harper 1982); and 4,000 years ago in Norway (Clarke 1947). Whale carvings in Norse stone age settlements, the bones of whales in kitchen middens of Alaskan Eskimos, Canadian Inuits and other Arctic peoples all hint at the use that early man made of these animals. It is probable that at first these sometimes large packages of meat and oil were used only when served up to Stone Age peoples as stranded animals upon their beaches. However, the great abundance of whales in Arctic regions through the summer must have attracted the early hunters to find ways to capture them. With open boats and hand-crafted spears they will have pursued their quarry. Only those species that were slow-moving and came close to their shores were available to hunt — species such as the bowhead and North Atlantic right whale, which now are probably closer to extinction than any other of the great whales. It is possible that by the time that modern whaling had come upon the scene, populations of these species were already mere remnants of their former size. The gray whale, whose bones have been found upon the coasts of the North Atlantic, may have been one of the early casualties. Just as the Steller's sea cow was hunted to extinction in the Bering Sea, so the gray whale is now extinct in the Atlantic.

Dolphins in Ancient Culture

Not every society was exploiting cetaceans for food. In the Mediterranean, the Ancient Greeks had obviously incorporated dolphins into their culture. Drawings appear on frescoes in the Minoan temple of Knossos, 3,200 years old, and whale and dolphin motifs are found on Greek vases, coins and even buildings. Dolphins also were the subject of various Greek myths and legends. The most famous is that of Arion, the lyric poet and musician, who on returning to Corinth from Italy with riches he had won at music competitions, was set upon by the crew of the boat that he travelled in. He asked one last favour, that of the chance to play a tune, and on being granted this, his music attracted a school of dolphins. As

249

they approached the boat, Arion leapt overboard and was carried by one of them on its back to safety ashore. This legend recurs with slight variations many times in Greek mythology.

One of the earliest students of cetaceans was the Greek philosopher, Aristotle (384–322BC). He must have actually dissected animals since his descriptions of their anatomy and physiology are so detailed. Others following him, such as the Roman authors Pliny and Galen, repeated much of his descriptions except that they caused further confusion by fanciful embellishment and reference to cetaceans as fishes. Indeed this myth was perpetuated up until the eighteenth century, when in 1758, the Swedish biologist Linnaeus recognised whales and dolphins as mammals. Some biologists and anatomists, including Aristotle, and Ray and Tyson in the seventeenth century, had actually recognised the mammalian characters of cetaceans, though they still listed them as fishes. During the sixteenth and seventeenth centuries, various books on Natural History had continued to assemble imaginary information, such as the unicorn depicted in Konrad Gesner's *Historia Animalium* in 1551. This horse with cloven hooves, a lion's tail and a horn in the middle of its forehead was even incorporated into the royal coat of arms of England by King James I. This may reflect the arrival of similar narwhal tusks from remote arctic regions to southern Europe, where they were often used for their supposed medicinal properties.

Early Whaling Methods

Early whaling may have concentrated upon deliberately trying to drive whales ashore. This method has been used on tightly knit schools of long-finned pilot whales to good effect for centuries in the Faroe Islands. At various times in our history, it has also been adopted in the islands of Shetland and Orkney, Newfoundland and Cape Cod for long-finned pilot whales, along the coasts of Greenland for narwhal and white whale, and quite independently, along the coasts of Japan, the Solomon Islands and various other Pacific islands for various schooling dolphins mainly of the genus *Stenella*. Some of these continue to this day, and rely upon species that may occur in large but fairly cohesive social groups, which as in mass strandings may follow each other ashore during the drive.

The Eskimos of Greenland and Alaska used a light skin canoe or kayak with a paddle, an ice scraper, a harpoon and its line to which a seal-skin float was attached, the receptacle for the line, a bird-spear with its throwing board, and two lances. Once harpooned, the movement of the prey would be restricted by the float and if necessary additionally by a wooden hoop serving as a sea anchor. When the animal had grown tired of trying to escape, it would be lanced and pulled ashore. By this means small whales such as narwhal and white whale, and even sometimes the giant bowhead were taken. Broadly similar methods using large dug-out canoes, an enormous harpoon, a line made of whale sinew, and a large number of seal-skin floats were adopted by the Indians of Vancouver and Washington on the Pacific coast of North America. They hunted mainly the gray whale and smaller killer whale, but also sperm whales, right whales, and humpbacks amongst others. In the Bering Sea, the natives of the Aleutian Islands, Kamchatka and the Kurile Islands apparently used poisoned lances to kill their prey, abandoning the gray or bowhead whale until its body came ashore a few days later.

European Whaling

In Europe, whaling was first recorded with the Norse Vikings of Scandinavia between AD800 and 1000, although rock carvings to be found in northern Norway suggest that Stone Age man also hunted whales by canoe around 2200BC (Clarke 1947, Slijper 1979). In the twelfth century, the Basques were hunting right whales quite extensively in the Bay of Biscay and possibly also in the North Sea (Aguilar 1981, de Smet 1981). As noted above, these early fisheries concentrated upon the right whales partly because they were slow-moving and so could be pursued first from promontories and then by canoe or some other form of open boat. They were also easier to recover since they float after death, due to their high oil content. At the same time they were profitable both for baleen and for oil (in addition to their use as a source of meat). For these reasons they were termed the 'right' whales, and were probably quite quickly over-hunted.

Whaling gradually spread northwards up the European coast and across to the whale rich coasts of Novaya Zemlya, Spitsbergen and Jan Mayen, where bowheads as well as northern right whales were valuable prey. Basque boats were even recorded in the western Atlantic towards the end of the sixteenth century. However, most whaling was concentrated in the European Arctic and by the 1600s, the Dutch and British, followed by the Germans and then French had started whaling in these Arctic waters. Whaling was certainly no longer a subsistence activity, and the whaling from the coasts of France, Spain and Portugal ceased as whales became scarce and greater profits could be found elsewhere. Whalebone for umbrellas, whips, crinolines and other items of clothing, and whale oil for lamps became particularly important products. The sailing ships that travelled to these waters were 30m or more in length, weighing between 250 and 400 tonnes, typically with a crew of 30–50 men. Although it was expensive to equip such a vessel (c. £1,200), it was more than repaid by the profits, particularly derived from the valuable whalebone, which could amount to c. £4,000 per whale.

Whaling in the New World

During the seventeenth century, commercial whaling was also developing from the coast of New England in eastern North America, and northwards as the rich whaling grounds of the Davis Strait and Baffin Bay were discovered. Northern right whales, bowheads and humpbacks probably formed the main prey. Throughout this period, the whales in all these Arctic regions were struck with hand harpoons from rowing boats, tied to inflated seal-skin or wood floats, and then towed ashore to land or ice floes. When whales became scarcer along the coast and in the bays, they were flensed and processed in the sea alongside the boat, the blubber being cut up into small pieces rather than placed immediately into large boilers as on shore.

In 1720, the European whalers joined the Americans on the hunting grounds off the icy coasts of Greenland and Canada (see Lubbock 1937; Scoresby 1820, reprinted 1969). The bowhead and northern right whale continued to be hunted intensively, particularly by the British who of all nations must take responsibility for the whales' demise in these regions. During the seventeenth and first half of the eighteenth century, the

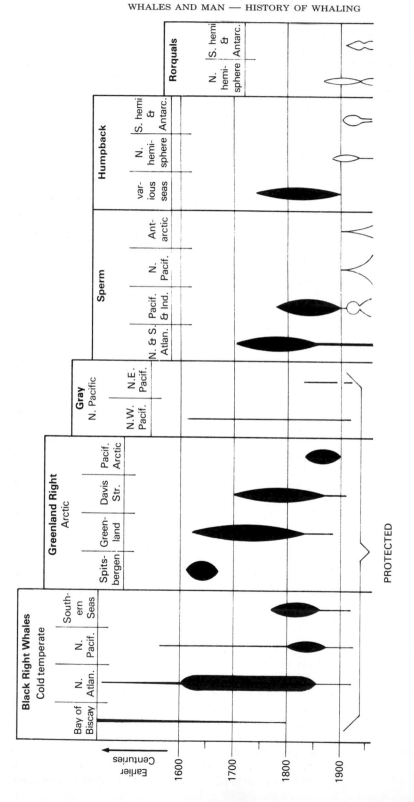

Figure 9.1 History of whaling (from Mackintosh 1965). Species of whales hunted in past centuries, to show the phases of old whaling (black) which was mainly with open boats and hand harpoons; modern whaling is indicated in outline. The width of the bars is not proportional to the numbers caught and is intended only to indicate the development and decline of local phases of whaling

Dutch fleets also wrought havoc on these Arctic whales, but by the end of the eighteenth century had been completely superseded by the British, eager to collect the spoils that their own rise as a power enabled. By 1820, whaling around Spitsbergen had practically ceased, with activities now concentrated in the Davis Strait and Baffin Bay. As both bowhead and northern right whale declined, the whalers turned their attentions increasingly to humpbacks and other large whales. Over-hunting caused the decline of whaling for bowheads and right whales in the North Atlantic by the late 1700s, and soon after the start of exploitation, similar declines occurred during the mid-1800s in the North Pacific. British Arctic whaling eventually ceased in 1912.

The Spread of Whaling in the Seventeenth and Eighteenth Centuries

Elsewhere during the seventeenth and eighteenth centuries whaling was generally only practised on a local and rather modest scale, probably based upon methods used by visiting European and American whalers. Such areas included the west and east coasts of North America and, later in the nineteenth century, the Pacific islands such as Tonga. In Japan, coastal whaling had been performed using small rowing boats, harpoons, lines and lances, much in the way Europeans did at the time. This method may have been used from very early times since Japan, like Norway, has probably always been very dependent upon the sea for food, but there are few records of any kind before 1700. Around 1600, another method of hunting developed, involving a large fleet of boats and heavy nets towards which the whales were herded before being lanced and finally towed to the shore. Right whales and humpbacks were the main species of large whale taken in this way.

As the capability of vessels developed to travel further afield, so whalers started to pursue other species, particularly the sperm whale of the deep seas. In the eighteenth and nineteenth centuries, the whalers of the New England coast of the United States (particularly Nantucket and Cape Cod), and of Britain, moved southwards in the Atlantic to the Azores, the bays of Brazil and Argentina, the Falkland Islands and South Africa (where the Dutch also operated from shore stations). They also moved around Cape Horn westwards into the Pacific, and around the Cape of Good Hope eastwards into the Indian Ocean. In the first half of the nineteenth century, major whaling bases started up in Hawaii and elsewhere — in South Africa, Mozambique and the Seychelles.

Yankee Whaling for Sperm Whales, and other Nineteenth Century Whaling

Throughout the world (excepting Japan and Indonesia), sperm whales are considered unpalatable and so for centuries were relatively protected despite being slow-swimming and easily caught. Their populations also tend to be concentrated in warm waters away from the major centres of whaling activity. However, during the eighteenth century there was an increasing demand for lamp oil and candles, and the oil from sperm whales was ideally suited to these purposes. This was the time of Moby Dick, the white sperm whale that Herman Melville immortalised in his book of the same name. Sperm whaling flourished particularly from 1820 to about 1850 but then declined rapidly during the next decade, mainly

Figure 9.2 Map of main whaling areas in the world: (a) up to 1970; (b) from 1970 to 1985. Whaling did not necessarily occur in the areas shown throughout the period concerned. By 1986, whaling had been reduced to activities under the heading of subsistence whaling off Alaska, Greenland and the Soviet Arctic, St Vincent and Indonesia, and scientific whaling around Iceland and Korea; commercial whaling by Japan, the Soviet Union and Norway continues either in local waters or in the Antarctic, but the first two nations undertake to stop in 1987–8. North Pacific factory ship whaling ceased from the 1979 season

(a) Whaling up to 1970

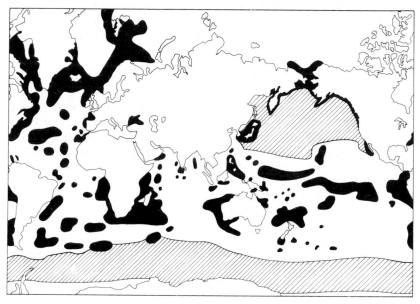

(b) Whaling between 1970 & 1985

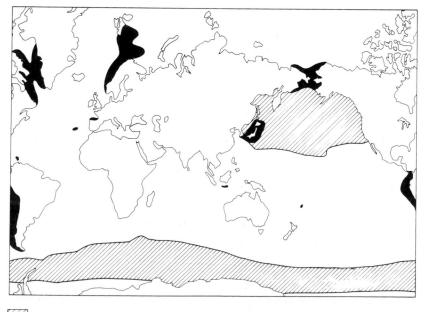

Factory ship whaling

for economic reasons (petroleum replacing sperm oil to light lamps) rather than due to substantial declines in numbers. Other species continued to be hunted. Although the populations of right whales and bowheads of the North Atlantic were now severely depleted, those in the North Pacific had escaped the attentions of large scale whalers. But not for long. During the first half of the nineteenth century, whaling for right whales started up in the higher latitudes of the Pacific, off New Zealand, Australia (particularly Tasmania) and the Kerguelen Islands, and in the cooler waters of the North Pacific, operating out of San Francisco. From 1840 onwards, bowheads were hunted in the Bering, Chukchi and Beaufort Seas. However, populations of both species in these regions had declined markedly by the end of that century.

Origins of Modern Whaling

The pursuit of right whales, bowheads, gray and sperm whales was made possible by their slow speed of swimming, rarely more than five knots (9km/hr). The humpback whale also is relatively slow-swimming, but had the disadvantage of sinking readily after death. Sailing boats like the Yankee square riggers that ranged the open seas for sperm whales were easily capable of capturing their prey, but they were not able to pursue the faster moving rorquals. But in the second half of the nineteenth century, two innovations had significant impact upon those whale species that had until then escaped man's greedy hands. In 1868, a Norwegian, Svend Foyn, following earlier experiments by the American whaler Thomas Welcome Roys, developed an explosive grenade harpoon, a cannon from which it could be fired, and a method for mounting it on the bow of a vessel. At about the same time, sailing ships were replaced by steam-driven vessels. Together these allowed the fast-moving rorquals to be pursued, killed by the head of the harpoon (the grenade) as it exploded in the back or side of the whale. Since the harpoon was attached to a line from the ship, this then secured the whale and prevented its sinking. These developments heralded the start of modern whaling.

This next phase of whaling spread rapidly from the Northeast Atlantic (Norway, Spitsbergen, north Scotland and western Ireland) to areas throughout the world. By the end of the nineteenth century, whalers had reached the waters off Newfoundland, the west coast of Africa, and into the Pacific. Then, in 1904, the whalers started to exploit the richest area of all — the Antarctic feeding grounds of the great whales, the blue, fin and sei whales. Very quickly, operations moved to the Southern Ocean and it soon became the whaling centre of the world with South Georgia and the South Shetlands forming the major bases. Norway was essentially the main whaling nation, with UK subsidiaries a runner up, until after World War II when replaced by Japan, who had arrived on the scene in 1934.

Antarctic Whaling

For the first 20 years, Antarctic whaling was land-based but in 1925 the first modern factory ship started operations. Whaling could now take place away from coastal floating factories or shore stations. The ship had a slipway and winches on the stern deck which allowed the whale to be hauled on board for processing. One of the first modern factory ships was the British-owned 'Southern Empress', with a massive cubic capacity of hull (below the upper deck) of 12,596 tonnes. A rapid expansion of the whaling industry occurred, helped on by the great increase in demand for whale oil. The discovery that liquid animal fats could be converted to solid fats by the process of hydrogenation gave rise to a thriving industry for the manufacture of soap and margarine, and the whale oil was also used for the production of nitro-glycerine.

The humpback catches had been the first to decline in the Antarctic. They had formed 95 per cent of the total whale catch in the 1910–11 season, but comprised only 2 per cent of the total seven years later. The largest and most valuable of the rorquals, the blue whale, then dominated the catches and continued to do so through the 1930s, with 29,000 taken in 1930–1 from South Georgia, before declining to very few by the middle 1950s (they were eventually totally protected in the Antarctic in 1965, and throughout the world two years later). As these populations declined, the industry moved to ever smaller species, the fin whale, then sei and finally minke whale (Figure 9.3). The story of Arctic whaling was being mirrored in the Southern Ocean, in this case with populations of successive target species declining to commercial extinction.

Whale Products

Outside the Antarctic, small numbers of sperm whales continued to be hunted following the decline of the industry in 1860. Annual world catches averaged around 5,000 until 1948, then in the early 1960s they expanded rapidly due to a fivefold increase in the price of sperm oil, caused by the United States government buying to stock strategic materials for their space rocket programme. In recent years, until further quotas were imposed, about 20,000 have been taken each year, mainly in the North Pacific and the southern hemisphere.

Until recently, the most important product of modern commercial whaling was oil, from baleen whales to produce margarines and other foodstuffs and from sperm whales first for lamp oil and then for specialised lubricants. However, from about 1950, meal for animal foodstuffs and chemical products became increasingly important, although baleen whale meat became even more highly valued for human consumption by the Japanese during post-war famine conditions there. The Soviet Union, the other major whaling nation in recent years, on the other hand, used very little whale meat, concentrating instead upon sperm whales for their oil. By the late 1970s, whale catches in the Antarctic were yielding 29 per cent meat, 20 per cent oil and 7 per cent meal and solubles (Allen 1980). The whaling industry was dominated until the 1930s by Norway and Britain, with Holland and the United States also taking substantial numbers. Since World War II, however, these nations have all abandoned deep-sea whaling which is now practised only by Japan and the Soviet Union.

Attempts to Regulate Whaling

The gluttony of the whaling industry not only caused marked reductions in the populations of the great whales, but it also swamped the market temporarily with whale oil. In the early 1930s, whaling companies agreed voluntarily to limit production with quotas on catches and the amount of oil produced (at around 2.5 million barrels per year).

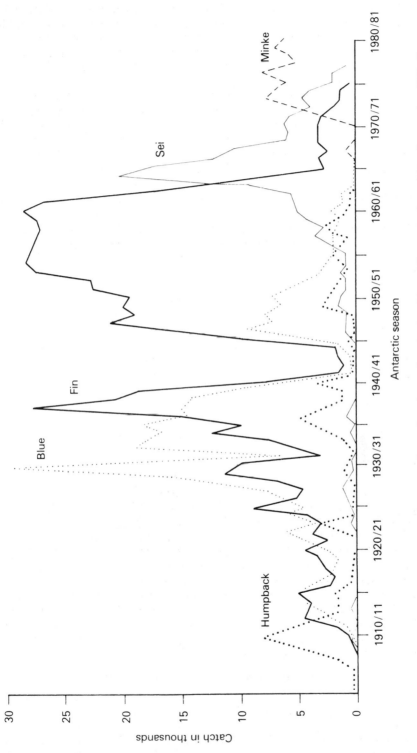

Figure 9.3 Catches of the great whales since 1900 in the southern hemisphere (updated from Allen 1980, derived from International Whaling Statistics, Oslo). Note the successive importance of each whale species in the fishery

However, the entry in 1934 of Japan into the fray, followed by Germany, ruined this intention. By the 1937–8 season, catches were as large as ever with 46,000 whales taken in the Antarctic region.

In 1931, the League of Nations drew up an International Convention for the Regulation of Whaling but this did not come into effect until 1935, mainly because Britain was slow to ratify it. However, the convention was not ratified by either Japan or Germany, who like the nations before them put short-term self interest first. Some regulation did come into effect, though mainly to maximise oil production. This was the concept of the Blue Whale Unit (BWU) where it was considered that one blue whale produced the same amount of oil as two fin, or two and a half humpbacks or six sei whales. It achieved its purpose but was disastrous on conservation grounds. It meant that whalers would concentrate upon the largest individuals since these yielded the greatest amounts of oil, whilst depleted stocks continued to be reduced because of lack of individual species recognition. The industry imposed minimum lengths for the taking of blue and fin whales and set particular opening dates for the whaling season. In 1937, another agreement called the International Agreement for the Regulation of Whaling was signed in London by Norway, UK and Germany, but not by Japan. This adopted the above agreements extending them to humpback and sperm whales. It also introduced a number of other useful measures: the prohibition of catching females accompanied by calves; the closing of waters north of 40°S (except the North Pacific) to pelagic whaling; the formation of a sanctuary in the Pacific sector of the Antarctic; and the protection of right whales and the gray whale. The following year, the humpback was given protection south of 40°S latitude, having been reduced to very small numbers.

After a short respite during World War II, whaling resumed with Norway and Britain, followed by the Soviet Union, Japan, South Africa and Holland all entering the fray. In 1950–1, the 20 factory ships operating in Antarctica caught 32,566 whales on a quota of 16,000 BWU, set in 1944.

In December 1946, another attempt was made to regulate whaling activities internationally with the signing of an International Convention for the Regulation of Whaling by representatives of 14 governments. This established the International Whaling Commission (IWC) which incorporated the 1937/8 agreements into its regulations, thus giving full protection everywhere to right whales and the gray whale, and to humpbacks in the Antarctic, regulating the timing of the catching season and minimum sizes of individuals, and protecting certain areas in the Antarctic. A quota of 16,000 BWU was also set for the Antarctic, as established two years previously. Unfortunately, different species should have received different levels of protection, and these regulations did little to stop the further decline of some species whilst maintaining the industry on the more abundant ones. Furthermore, the extent to which member nations observed these regulations was questioned. Blue whale catches crashed once again in the 1950s, followed by fin whales in the early 1960s and sei whales in the late 1960s. In the following decade, the factories finally turned their attention to the smallest of all rorquals, the minke whale.

At the first meeting of the IWC in 1949, it regrettably removed the total ban on humpbacks and allowed a quota of 1,250. Not only was this quota almost certainly too high, but it was also totally ignored with catches ranging from around 1,500 to 2,100. A scientific sub-committee had recommended the earlier quota and in future years attempted to regulate the hunting of humpbacks by limiting the season to only three days. This met with strong opposition from some of the whaling nations and it was not until 1956 that it came into effect. Attempts to reduce the quotas generally were unsuccessful as was a move to introduce national quotas. Catches continued to increase, reaching a peak of 16,433 BWU in 1960–1. From 1962 onwards, Antarctic catches declined sharply as the stocks collapsed and in the following year a committee of three scientists (later increased to four) which had been set up in 1961, made a number of recommendations for the management of the remaining whale stocks. They recommended a variety of restrictions including a complete ban on whaling of blue and humpback whales. The response by the IWC for the 1963–4 season was some reduction in whale quotas, plus a ban on humpback whaling in the Antarctic and for blue whales in most of the Antarctic.

During the early 1960s, Britain and then Holland pulled out of the Antarctic, followed towards the end of the 1960s by Norway. This left only Japan and the Soviet Union, each with three factories, in the Antarctic. In 1972–3, after continued recommendations by their scientific committee, the IWC at last abandoned the Blue Whale Unit in the Antarctic (it was never used in the North Pacific). Although that species had been totally protected from 1967, the system of Blue Whale Units was still being used for other species. Now for the first time in the Antarctic (though adopted four years earlier for the North Pacific), separate quotas were set for fin, sei, minke and sperm whales.

Management of Whale Stocks

In 1975, another important modification was made. This was termed the New Management Procedure and it divided whale stocks into three categories: (1) Protection Stocks which were more than 10 per cent below the level giving the maximum sustainable yield (MSY), calculated on the basis of principles first used in the study of fish populations; (2) Sustained Management Stocks where stocks were between 10 per cent below and 20 per cent above the level giving the MSY; and (3) Initial Management Stocks whose abundance exceeded 20 per cent above the MSY level. No catching was allowed in the Protection Stocks; quotas were set for Sustained Management Stocks to keep them near the MSY level; and for Initial Management Stocks to bring them gradually towards MSY levels. These new management procedures were based upon the concept of density-dependent population regulation, supported by the apparent changes in various biological parameters in response to exploitation, as described in the previous chapter. In essence, the notion is that whale populations, like those of many other animals, annually produce a surplus of individuals which can be harvested by man on a sustainable basis indefinitely without causing its decline (Figure 9.4). The maximum population that may be harvested to achieve this result is referred to as the maximum sustainable yield. There are a great many problems with this management policy which have been voiced increasingly by scientists during the 1970s and 1980s. We shall consider these briefly in turn.

Methods of Stock Assessment

Firstly any management policy depends upon some estimate of population sizes, their survival and productivity. Such stock assessments are based primarily upon mathematical analyses of catch and effort statistics together with relevant biological information. They use a combination of the following six methods (reviewed by Gambell 1976a,b; Allen 1980).

(1) DeLury method — the numbers caught in successive years are added together and this accumulated catch is plotted against the catch per unit effort for each of those years. A line is then fitted to these points and extrapolated to zero to give an estimate of the stock size in the first year of the series (Figure 9.4). Because both recruitment (i.e. addition to the population by reproduction) and natural mortality will also be occurring, compensations for these need to be used in this model (DeLury 1947, Chapman 1970), whilst a modified version of this method, taking account of density dependent recruitment was developed by Chapman (1974).

Figure 9.4 Rationale behind harvesting of whales: (a) recruitment curve; (b) maximum sustainable yield (MSY) curve (from Gambell 1976, derived from Jones 1973). (a) As the fin whale population declines through harvesting, the proportion recruited into the breeding population increases (possibly because of relaxed competition for food); (b) from the recruitment relationship, a sustainable yield curve is derived, indicating an intermediate population size (in this case, 50 per cent of the original population) which theoretically could be maintained indefinitely

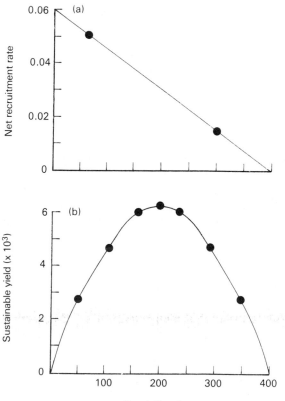

(2) Mortality coefficient methods — total mortality estimates are derived from logarithmic regression of the catches of each fully recruited year class (i.e. the number of animals of a particular age that have entered the breeding population) in two successive years. This requires both catch and effort statistics and data on age composition. Estimates are generally calculated by month, by sex, and by area with an average pooled estimate derived from these (Chapman *et al*. 1964). Since such estimates may vary greatly, the results may be averaged over a number of seasons to provide a smoothed catchability coefficient (Doi *et al*. 1970). Mortality estimates can also be determined using only a single year's catch and the age compositions of the fully recruited year classes. Such methods provide an estimate of total mortality. The natural mortality rate can be calculated from the age compositions obtained at the start of whaling, or alternatively from the difference in abundance of successive year classes of older whales that were fully recruited before heavy exploitation occurred (so long as they have a similar catching history). Mortality due to hunting is calculated as the total mortality less the natural mortality and the total population catch may thus be obtained from the known catch and the estimated fishing mortality.

(3) Least squares method — this uses age composition data to estimate directly the recruitment into the exploited phase of the fishery. The catches of a year class are compared in one season when it is partially recruited to catches the following season when it is fully recruited. This provides an estimate of the proportion of new recruits in a year class fully recruited for the first time, and by working back in time, the proportion of new recruits in all the catches can be estimated. Population size may then be estimated using this calculated recruitment by computing the value which minimises the sum of the squares of the differences between the actual catches and those expected from the population (Allen 1966, 1968).

(4) Recruitment curve method — The Japanese cetologists, Doi, Ohsumi and Nemoto, have developed mathematical models which try to mirror the population history of a species given certain levels of exploitation. From a variety of possible reproductive curves, they estimate what recruitment is likely to be each year. Using an assumed population size (unexploited population stock) as a starting basis, deducting annual catches and adding on estimated annual recruitment they are able to estimate the expected population given that level of exploitation (Doi *et al*. 1967, 1970; Ohsumi 1972, 1973; Ohsumi *et al*. 1971).

Models using variable biological parameters have more recently been used in attempts to refine the population equations and make them more realistic. Allen (1976) introduced a model that took account of the fact that juvenile mortality rate and hence recruitment into the population is likely to be density dependent. A further refinement was then applied to sei whales where observed changes in pregnancy rates and female age at maturity were incorporated into the model (IWC 1978). Much attention has been given recently to refining these mathematical models and the reader is advised to consult the latest reports of the IWC to keep up to date with developments.

261

Sperm whales have a rather different social structure (i.e. harem) to baleen whales, with males and females having different life history characteristics (growth, age at maturity, etc.), probabilities of reproduction and rates of harvesting. This has meant that the models applied to baleen whales were not suitable for this species, and in particular, the effects of the ratio of mature males to mature females have had to be taken into account. Allen and Kirkwood (1977) developed a model for sperm whales (termed the La Jolla model), using the age structure of the population and incorporating generalised growth and size distribution functions for each of the two sexes. This has recently been refined for male sperm whales in two alternative length-specific models for a more realistic simulation of the observed growth curves (Beddington and Cooke 1981; Cooke *et al.* 1983; Shirakihara and Tanaka 1983; Shirakihara *et al.* 1983; Tanaka 1983).

(5) Whale marking — The mark-recapture method is well known and frequently used by zoologists to estimate population size. This method has been used for whales by firing 23cm-long (diameter 1.5cm) numbered stainless steel darts (referred to as Discovery tags after the first experiments carried out by the Discovery Committee) from a 12-bore shotgun into the whale (minimum length 11m). These tags appear to do little damage (owing to the very thick blubber layer) and are recovered after the animals have been killed by whalers (Brown 1978). The proportion of recovered marks to the total effective hits gives a factor to relate the associated catch to the total population. Since some whale marks are not reported on recovery, it is necessary to apply some correction factor to the calculation, or to compare the proportions recovered from different marking experiments within one season and use the ratio of these recoveries to obtain a measure of total mortality during the time between the experiments (Doi *et al.* 1970).

Recently, mark-resighting methods have been used where animals are either tagged on the dorsal fin (applied primarily to small odontocetes); or with a streamer fired into the blubber (apparently not much more successful, due to being lost or overlooked); or recognised by an assumed unique set of markings (most successful on gray, right and humpback whales). The ratio of marked to unmarked individuals on first sampling may then be related to the ratio on second sampling to derive an estimate of the total population size. This method, known as the Petersen method or Lincoln Index, has some important assumptions that unfortunately are often violated. Most important are the fact that there should be no addition or loss to the population (by births, mortality or migration) between the sampling periods and individuals should have an equal chance of recapture/resighting. If multiple recaptures/resightings are made, these constraints can be minimised, and a triple-catch method has been developed by Bailey (1951), and more recently, a sophisticated method taking into account stochastic variation has been developed by Jolly (1965). Tagging has been used particularly on the large whale species (though increasingly on smaller species), but has various drawbacks — they are difficult to apply, may become detached and can cause tissue damage in some cases (Evans *et al.*

1972; Brown 1978; White *et al.* 1981). Natural markings are obviously preferable though often more difficult to re-sight and one rarely has an independent check of their uniqueness. However, they are being used increasingly, and species recognised in this way include humpback (Katona *et al.* 1979, 1980), gray (Darling 1983), southern right (R. Payne *et al.* 1983), northern right (Kraus and Prescott 1983), sperm (Gordon 1983) and killer whales (Balcomb *et al.* 1980, Bigg 1982) — most successful; bottle-nosed (Wells *et al.* 1980, Wursig and Wursig 1979), dusky (Wursig and Wursig 1980), hump-backed (Saayman and Tayler 1979), white-beaked and Risso's dolphins (Evans 1981, in prep.) — moderately successful; and blue (Sears 1983), fin (Edds 1981, Mattila et al. 1983, Sadove 1982), minke (Dorsey 1983, Edds 1981) and pilot whales (Evans unpubl.) — less successful.

(6) Sightings estimates — Sightings obtained from boat transects can be used to derive an estimate of the density of whales of a particular species within a known area on one or both sides of the ship's track. The numbers per unit area can then be extrapolated to the total area of the region concerned to calculate an estimate of the total population (see, for example, Doi 1970, 1974; Doi *et al.* 1967, 1983; Hammond 1986a, b; Ohsumi *et al.* 1971). This method has been used particularly for those species which cannot be assessed on the above methods because they are currently under protection, but also on minke whales with annual cruises in different Antarctic areas in collaboration with Japan and USSR, using their vessels on loan. Corrections have been applied to take account of the sightability of different species, some species spending less time at the surface than others, and some showing positive or negative reactions to the vessel. Attention has also been paid to the probability of sighting under different sea conditions, the visual angle of observation and the actual area that is properly observed (Braham 1984; Hiby 1982a,b; Hiby *et al.* 1984; Reilly 1984a). Recently, surveys using boats towing an array of directional hydrophones have shown promise as a more efficient method of recording whale species since they detect whales underwater without need to sight them and often from great distances (Thomas *et al.* 1986a, b; Winn *et al.* 1975). However, they obviously do not detect individuals that are moving silently.

Some of the factors that need to be taken into account have been mentioned above under each method. Although each of these methods provides a separate estimate, a number of them are not independent of each other. Thus, one criticism has been that taking an average of a variety of estimates is not necessarily much better than taking one or two estimates. If the values used for recruitment or original population size or whatever are incorrect, this will affect a number of the estimates. Furthermore, in statistical terms it is not possible to put confidence limits on any of the above methods with the exception of sightings estimates. This favours the use of the latter method but it too has serious drawbacks. The most important of these perhaps is that the boat transects and the animals being censused should for statistical reasons both be distributed at random. Neither of these is the case, particularly the latter. Most of our evidence points to whales and dolphins having decidedly clumped distributions. One way to overcome this is to have a stratified sampling scheme where areas known to be of different density are subdivided and then within these are sampled randomly (see Burnham *et al.* 1980; Eberhardt 1978; Gaskin 1982:282–7; and Hammond 1986a, b, for reviews of line transect techniques). Current estimates of whale population sizes are based primarily on sightings (for example Antarctic minke whales, North Atlantic humpbacks) and on length/frequency analyses of catches.

Another criticism of the methods using catch-per-unit-effort analysis has been made by John Beddington (1979) on mathematical grounds. This is that they tend to overestimate abundance after the initial phase of exploitation, because catches are not likely to decline in a linear manner over time in relation to a decline in the population, since searching or handling efficiency may alter in response to decreased abundance.

Maximum Sustainable Yield

As noted earlier, the whole philosophy of whale management is based upon the concept of a maximum sustainable yield (MSY). A simplified form of the relationship between the population size of a whale and the net rate of recruitment (i.e. after subtraction of deaths) is given in Figure 9.4. This is derived from an analysis of fin whale populations in the Antarctic by R. Jones (1973). We have seen in the previous chapter how larger numbers of animals are produced as the population decreases. In this figure it is represented as a linear relationship but in fact it is likely to be curvilinear as indicated by the hatched line. When each population size is multiplied by its net recruitment rate, the resulting curve represents the excess of recruits over natural deaths (Figure 9.4). This is, therefore, the excess which theoretically could be harvested indefinitely without changing the overall population size, in other words the maximum sustainable yield. Usually the MSY is somewhere above 50 per cent of the original population size in the mathematical models that have been developed. Although sexes may be combined for the calculations, the values may differ between the sexes, particularly if some members of one sex are not available to breed, as happens for example in the polygynous sperm whale where only some males are able to acquire females and those may mate with an entire harem of females. Thus in the case of the sperm whale, the females are considered separately. Another modification is that since the population being exploited is rarely in equilibrium, it is better alternatively to consider the replacement yield (RY) which takes catch figures that will leave the population at the end of the year the same as it was at the beginning (Gulland and Boerema 1973). Finally, the above harvesting regimes are based on numbers of animals, but in some cases (for example the sperm whale where much growth continues during the time of its life that it is being exploited) MSY by weight would be a better long-term strategy.

John Beddington and Robert May (1977) have pointed out some dangers of using MSY when the values are uncertain and could vary substantially. The problem is that a small error in the estimate could have a big effect and if a population was being exploited only a small amount above its MSY, this could lead to an accelerated decline. The New Management Procedure tries to take some account of this by allowing a safety margin upon its recommended quotas. Other difficulties are that the effects of exploitation may extend beyond these relatively simple population models. There could be social effects; the killing of certain large individuals may have a bigger impact than if animals were taken at random. There could also be effects upon other species. Such multi-species interactions seem very likely on the basis of the findings summarised in the last chapter (see May *et al.* 1979 for a useful review). And the definition of a stock is not based upon genetic information so that it is not equivalent to a biological population. This point is recognised (hence the term stock rather than population), and the imposition of separate quotas by various divisions of sea area (New Management Procedure) is an attempt to bring the two closer to one another. However, there is still a disturbing lack of information on the extent of gene flow between stocks, and marking or radio-tagging experiments do not necessarily answer these problems. An animal may move great distances but still return to mate with one of a few individuals occupying a particular region where they are hunted. The widespread use of biochemical methods such as electrophoresis could help to answer some of those questions (see Evans 1987b for a review). Preliminary studies in this direction have been carried out by Shiro Wada in Japan, A. Arnason in Iceland, Deborah Duffield in the United States and Kees Lankester in Holland. For the present, given the large number of uncertainties in the methods for obtaining estimates of population sizes and reproductive parameters, it is no wonder that scientists have expressed growing concern at its use in managing whale populations.

Economic Considerations

We have looked in some detail at the difficulties of using the information available to harvest whales on a long-term basis. This is further compounded by the fact that the whaling industry operates with interests centred upon economic returns. The economist Colin Clark (1975, 1981) has stressed two points that make a whaling industry difficult to manage on an ecological basis. The first is that there is no sole owner of the resource. Although the IWC tries to function in this way, it will always have to contend with the fact that there is essentially open access to whales and individual ships or even nations can cheat for their self-gain. Secondly, whalers are not concerned with maximising a sustainable biological yield but in maximising their short-term profits after subtraction of present costs (in economists' jargon, the Present Value of net economic return), and discounting the future. If the economic discount rate is greater or similar to the intrinsic growth rate of the whale population (probably between 2 and 5 per cent per annum), as appears to be the case, the Present Value criterion will tend to lead to stocks being depleted below MSY level. With high discount rates there is, just as in an open access situation, no motive to heed what happens in the future. The picture may be complicated by various other factors such as changes in harvesting costs, prices, etc. over time. There may also be a tendency to have an initial rapid phase of heavy exploitation which possibly could depress the stock below that value which maximises Present Value, followed by a slower phase in which the stock levels recover to or are maintained around the Present Value level. This could lead to the population declining to seriously low levels before the industry is forced to respond. These issues may help to explain why the history of man's exploitation of the sea, whether it be fish or whale, is a succession of chapters of disaster.

For further details on the history of whaling, the reader is referred to the first chapter of Slijper's (1962, reprinted 1979) classic treatise on whales, the excellent *History of Modern Whaling* by J.N. Tonnesen and A.O. Johnsen (1982), J.T. Jenkins' (1921) *A History of the Whale Fisheries*, B. Lubbock's (1937) *The Arctic Whalers* and John Bockstoce's (1986) *Whales, Ice and Men*. Scammon's (1874) treatise on American whaling, and Scoresby's (1820, reprinted 1969) *Account of the Northern Whale-fishery* are also highly recommended reading. Problems related to modern whaling and its management are reviewed in Neil Mackintosh's (1965) *The Stocks of Whales* and Radway Allen's (1980) *Conservation and Management of Whales*, whilst the concept of MSY and its limitations are discussed in papers by Allen, Clark, Gulland, Holt and Price in FAO's (1981) *Mammals in the Seas*, Vol. 3, and in a general review by May *et al.* (1979).

10 Whales and man – the present day

COMMERCIAL WHALING FROM 1970–1985

Since around 1970, whales have become increasingly politicised animals. Concern for their plight was being voiced by an ever larger number of biologists; and conservation organisations such as Friends of the Earth and Greenpeace started to campaign energetically on their behalf. In 1972, the United Nations Conference on the Human Environment met in Stockholm and called for a ten year moratorium on whaling (though admittedly not on the basis of scientific evidence available to them). This was subsequently adopted by the UN General Assembly and by the General Assembly of IUCN, but it was rejected by the member states of the IWC with six nations voting against, four in favour and four abstaining. At that time, the scientific committee considered a ban on whaling unnecessary.

In the same year the United States passed a Marine Mammal Protection Act which prohibited the taking or import of marine mammals and their products except by certain Indian, Aleut and Eskimo populations for subsistence or native handicrafts and clothing. However, some permits were issued to allow the taking of certain species for scientific research and public display. A waiver was also incorporated to allow incidental mortality of dolphins in the United States tropical purse-seine tuna fishery. A Marine Mammal Commission was set up as a result to administer these regulations and promote research on marine mammals. Although a welcome move in the right direction, the United States continued to have problems on their doorstep — the hunting of endangered bowhead whales by the Eskimos of Alaska; the horrific number of incidental takes of spotted and spinner dolphins in the Eastern Pacific tuna fishery; and the ever-increasing capture of small cetaceans for zoos and dolphinaria, and their associated mortality.

In 1973, the Convention on International Trade in Endangered Species of Wild Fauna and Flora (CITES) was signed in Washington and came into force from 1975. By 1978, 46 countries had become party to the Convention. As its name implies, its concern was to regulate international trade in animals and plants (and their products) whether alive or dead, so as to protect them from potential extinction. Differing levels of

267

protection were given according to their status. Thus, among cetaceans, full protection was given to the gray whale, two right whale species, humpback, blue whale, some stocks of fin and sei whale, and the Ganges susu.

With the introduction in 1975 of the New Management Procedures by the International Whaling Commission, a major advance had been made in the regulation of whaling. However, many quotas that were set presented an unhappy compromise between biological advice from the scientific committee and the economic wishes of representatives of the major whaling nations. Furthermore, outside criticism pointed to the many uncertainties in the details on which the quotas were based.

Alternatives to Whale Products

There were two other cries as the public turned its attention to the issues. Sadly these had largely been overlooked by the scientists. First, the purpose of whaling was called into question. Clearly from the point of view of the individual whalers there were commercial profits involved. But on a national basis, this was no longer so clearcut. Modern pelagic whaling is carried out by two nations, Japan and the Soviet Union, with catches shared approximately equally between them. However, whereas the Soviet Union concentrates upon sperm whales for oil, being little interested in whale meat for domestic consumption, Japan has had an increasing interest in baleen whales for meat. Since about 1950, meal, largely for animal foodstuffs, and other chemical products, termed solubles, have been produced in increasing quantities. Oil comes both from sperm whales where it is used as a lubricant in the cosmetic, textile and leather industries, and in the making of pencils, crayons and candles; and from baleen whales where it is used in margarines, soap and various foodstuffs. Meat from sperm whales is used only for animal feed whilst from baleen whales it is used for human consumption. Other products include spermaceti and ambergris, both from sperm whales, which are used also in the cosmetic industry. In recent years many suitable alternatives have been found for some of these products. Notable among these is the oil extracted from the seeds of the jojoba shrub (*Simmondsia chinensis*), a plant of arid regions of the United States and elsewhere in the world. This oil has been found to be an excellent lubricant and is able to replace sperm whale oil for most of the above purposes. However, it is rather a slow-growing plant and the development of high-yielding economic strains will take a while.

In the Western world, whale oil has largely been replaced by vegetable and fish oils, whilst meat for animal feed has been replaced by fishmeals. In Japan, whale meat is still considered an important part of the human diet, although an estimate in 1972 indicated that it made up less than 1 per cent of the total protein consumption (Allen 1980), and will have declined further since then. Nevertheless, culturally it has some significance for the Japanese people, hence their reluctance to give it up.

Humanitarian Considerations in Whaling

The second cry was definitely one from the heart. Many humans began to question the moral case for whaling. The issues of intelligence and the evolutionary position that whales occupy in the sea were put forward as arguments against killing whales (see Frost 1978). I have discussed these issues (i.e. cetacean intelligence and comparisons with man) at some length in the last chapter but my own view is that even if whales were found not to be very intelligent and comparable beings to man, the moral decision over whether to kill them should be the same as that applied to deer or grouse or fish.

A more relevant moral question is surely the way the animal is killed. The current method for killing large whales is a harpoon about 1.5m long, weighing 55kg. The head of the harpoon has four barbs (claws) to which is screwed an explosive grenade. On firing from a cannon mounted on the deck of the whale catcher, the harpoon penetrates the back, the claws open when a strain comes on the whale line and resistance acts on the trailing edge of the claws; then by a delayed action fuse, the grenade explodes. The claws help secure the animal which if the harpoon was placed correctly then dies instantaneously. However, studies in the 1970s suggest that times before death were sometimes much longer than this, amounting to on average 3.72 minutes for minke whales, 4.0 minutes for sei whales and 6.12 minutes for fin whales (Ohsumi 1977b). As the species becomes larger, so the killing time increases, and some sperm whales may take up to 15 minutes before dying (Best 1975). Often more than one harpoon would have to be fired into the animal. Smaller species such as the minke whale are captured by the 'cold grenade' technique. A 50mm non-explosive harpoon is fired into the animal which is then winched in and, if still alive, it is electrocuted. This prevents damage to the meat but is almost certainly even less humane. Whatever effect shock may have in numbing the pain, as has been claimed by some, these lengths of time before dying are surely inhumane.

Various attempts have been made to find more humane alternatives. These include the use of electrical harpoons, harpoons with a charge of compressed carbon dioxide, and even a phial of prussic acid. None of these seems to have been very satisfactory nor reduced the death times, although new explosive harpoons now have been developed and introduced by Norway and Japan for minke whaling. Improvements include modifications to the grenade base and the use of penthrite or black powder in the grenade. Killing times have been reduced to 2.5 minutes in Japan, using penthrite grenades, although around 15–20 per cent have failed to detonate even on hitting the whale, and some of the meat has been rendered unusable (IWC 1984).

Whaling Regulations, 1975–1985

Pressure from both scientists and the public continued during the late 1970s. In 1976, the Food and Agriculture Organization held a Scientific Consultation on Marine Mammals in Bergen, Norway, with conservation and management important elements of the meeting (see FAO 1978–82). In 1977, at the 29th Annual Meeting of the IWC in Canberra, Australia, it was agreed to maintain the New Management Procedures adopted two years previously. Quotas were generally reduced, particularly for sperm whale catches in the North Pacific, but the latter were amended and raised once more at a meeting later that year. The IWC decided to take control of medium-sized whales such as bottlenose (which received total protection in the North Atlantic), other beaked whales, pilot and killer whales. This was an important move since, previously, whaling activities for these species were scarcely regulated. More recently, the scientific committee of the IWC recommended that other small cetaceans, in particular the narwhal and white whale, be included in the IWC purview, but this was rejected by the members. In 1978, at the annual IWC meeting in London, a further reduction of about 5 per cent was imposed upon the quotas, with some variation between stocks. By 1979–80, more than three-quarters of the permitted catch comprised minke whales, with 14 per cent made up by sperm whales. Only minke whales were to be hunted pelagically. Sperm whales were to be taken only from shore stations in the North Atlantic (Iceland and Spain), North Pacific (Japan and Korea) and from South America (Brazil, Chile and Peru).

At this same 1979 meeting (also held in London), a 10 million square kilometre sanctuary was set up at the recommendation of the Seychelles in the Indian Ocean (north of the Equator and west of 100°E, including the Arabian and Red Seas). This served to protect one important breeding ground for the sperm whale. Besides the two pelagic whaling nations, Japan and the Soviet Union, coastal whaling was still being carried out by the following countries: Brazil, Chile, Denmark (in Greenland and the Faroes), Iceland, Norway, Peru, Portugal (Azores), Spain, United States (Alaska), the Republic of Korea and Japan. In 1979, Australia had dropped out of whaling, following South Africa (1976), the United States (1972), Canada (1972) and New Zealand (1964), although like the UK, Holland and others, all but Canada have remained within the IWC. At the time, some nations were not members of the IWC and so were not governed by their regulations. These included Chile, Peru, Spain and Portugal (Republic of Korea joining in 1978). However, all but Portugal are now members of IWC, joining in 1979.

In the past, some ships have operated independently under flags of convenience. These 'pirate' vessels almost certainly did not observe the regulations the IWC imposed, not that all member states of IWC did so either. There have been accusations that quotas are sometimes exceeded, and restrictions on size, sex and species not always observed. Although an International Observer scheme has been in operation since 1972, there has been concern expressed by IUCN and others that this is not always truly independent and infringement of regulations continues.

After repeated calls at annual IWC meetings for a moratorium on commercial whaling, eventually in 1982 a three-quarters majority adopted the recommendation, to come into effect in 1986. Three countries (Soviet Union, Japan and Norway) lodged objections. Until the ban was to come into effect, the IWC imposed severe quotas. For the 1985 season in the North Atlantic, annual catches of 281 fin, 100 sei and 1,117 minke whales were permitted. In the North Pacific, 357 Bryde's and 320 minke whales could be taken. In the southern hemisphere, 164 Bryde's and 4,224 minke whales were permitted. No sperm whales could be caught. These quotas were set to allow the whaling nations some leeway before a complete phasing out of commercial whaling, at least for the time being, from the winter of 1985/6.

This might seem to be the end of whaling and conservationists could breathe a sigh of relief. However, it is not. Unfortunately, the IWC has no statutory control. Although it has come a long way since its formation in 1946 as a club of whalers (and ex-whalers), with its attempts to be self-regulatory, any restrictions imposed are essentially voluntary (and consequently in some cases have not been observed). If a nation does not agree to them, it can object (within 90 days) and then set its own quotas. Japan, Norway and the Soviet Union have done this, although the Soviet Union and Japan have undertaken to end Antarctic whaling in 1987. Japan will end coastal minke and Bryde's whaling in 1987, and coastal sperm whaling the following year. Alternatively, there is nothing (but public pressure) to stop a nation pulling out of the IWC which would mean it need not pay any attention to the IWC's management policies nor to international scientific opinion.

At present, one problem seems to be that the opinion of scientists within Norway and Iceland over population sizes of whales such as the minke is at variance with that of others in the scientific committee. Iceland, on the other hand, has exploited another loophole in the regulatory procedure, that of issuing permits to catch whales (even if otherwise protected) for 'scientific' purposes. In this way they would continue to hunt not only minke whales but also fin and sei whales (80 each of the two former and 40 of the latter between 1986–9). The aim they say would be to obtain more scientific information for better management of these whales, although it has also been put forward as a way of raising funds for research. The Republic of Korea also continues whaling for 'scientific' purposes. On the other hand, Denmark (Faroes) has ended its research take, and Norway has not made any proposals under this heading.

In many ways Japan has a pivotal role to play in the future of commercial whaling. It has the biggest domestic whaling industry and consumes nearly all the whale meat produced by other countries (such as Iceland for example). Much of the interests of this commercial whaling industry are controlled by Japan. These interests have played a political role in the IWC decisions, and have forced some of the smaller countries such as Jamaica (who had taken a conservationist line following encouragement from environmentalists) to withhold their objections and even to leave IWC, for fear of trade pressures. If Japan withdrew its demand for whale products, whaling on its present commercial basis would probably collapse. Even this, however, would not necessarily mean that no whales would be hunted, and it brings us to the final issue that requires attention in man's unhappy exploitative relationship with whales, that of subsistence whaling.

SUBSISTENCE WHALING

The proposed ban on whaling applies to what is termed 'commercial' whaling to distinguish it from 'subsistence' or 'aboriginal' whaling. Such whaling refers to the catching from small vessels (or from the beach) of whales specifically to satisfy material and cultural needs in local communities (FAO 1978). Let us examine the different whaling activities around the world that are attributed to this definition.

Alaskan Bowhead Hunt

The most controversial must be the whaling by native Inupiat Eskimos for bowhead whales in Alaska. For a useful overview of the problem, I recommend the reader consults a paper by Edward Mitchell and Randall Reeves (1980), whilst the IWC special publication on subsistence whaling discusses at length both Alaskan and Greenland whaling (Donovan 1982).

Once hunted by Inupiat with ivory or stone-tipped harpoons and seal-skin floats, and later by American and European whalers (to the 1930s), bowheads continue to be taken by the Inupiats. This species is almost certainly the most seriously endangered of all the large whales. Its total world population is estimated at about 4,000, with most in the Bering Sea. The traditional hunting methods of the Eskimos are still used to a large extent, including nineteenth-century bomblances and umiaks (canoes), although modern inventions have also been introduced. They may use fibreglass speed boats equipped with outboard engines, motorised sleds and even bulldozers to pull up the carcass before transport of the meat away in a pick-up truck or snowmobile for later storage in a deep freeze. The numbers of bowheads caught have increased markedly from an average of 9 per annum between 1912 and 1967 to around 27 in the past decade (Chapman 1977). Whilst this increase has taken place, the numbers struck and lost have also greatly increased, so that the figures above almost certainly underestimate the actual numbers harvested. Despite repeated calls to cease whaling this species, the hunt has continued with compromise quotas being set by the IWC. Several times the United States has been unable to take a conservation stance at IWC meetings because of political pressures from its far-flung state, Alaska.

The argument that has been put forward, which applies to much subsistence whaling, is that it is not only materially necessary but is also of cultural necessity. The United States government in this case has rejected the claim that the whale products are necessary for the material survival of the Inupiat community, but has conceded to the cultural argument. Whilst sympathising with the desire to retain some elements of their traditional culture, I see the very fact that the community has moved from a traditional culture as the main cause of the problem. In the days when the family would starve if it wiped out a local population of whales or seals or seabirds, there was sufficient self-regulation to prevent the exploitation of that resource. Now, the Inupiat (and the Canadian and Greenland Inuits, Faroese and others) are no longer so ecologically restrained. They now live at least partly by a cash economy with imports and supermarkets, and a welfare state. Twelve years ago I remember walking into a supermarket in the remote settlement of Upernavik, northwest Greenland (where subsistence whaling continues) and seeing the shelves lined with radios and stereos, and the freezers filled with frozen chicken and duck, imported from Denmark. This transitional period to a cash economy is clearly a difficult one for the Eskimo, and one would obviously wish those communities to have the opportunity to share the economic development of the Western world. However, the Eskimos clearly need to show further self restraint if they are not to hasten the demise of species such as the bowhead.

One possible solution for the Alaskan Eskimos has been the proposal to substitute bowhead whaling with a small catch of the much more numerous gray whale in the hopes that these would satisfy both nutritional and cultural needs. Unfortunately, gray whales are not really a suitable substitute in that region because they arrive later (when ice conditions are less favourable), are more dangerous and difficult to hunt (tending to sink when killed), and their products are not so suitable for the Inupiat because the skin is encrusted with barnacles and the blubber is difficult to chew (Marquette and Braham 1982).

Elsewhere in the Arctic, the native people of Eastern Siberia also hunted bowheads but since the 1930s they have switched to gray whales, caught by a large Soviet catcher boat on their behalf. About 200 are taken each year. Although this whaling may be partly for local consumption by the native people, much is used to feed Arctic foxes for fur farming, and it is hardly operated in an 'aboriginal' manner. In its favour, however, it is probably more efficient and humane than when it was an aboriginal activity.

Subsistence Whaling elsewhere in the World

In some parts of the world subsistence whaling can indeed be said to operate in a fairly traditional manner. In Tonga, South Pacific and St Vincent, West Indies, whaling has dated back to the nineteenth century, when European and American whalers visited their shores and showed them the method of 'Yankee' whaling which involved open rowing boats and hand harpoons. These methods are still used in St Vincent, with less than a handful of humpbacks killed in any year, but other smaller cetaceans (such as short-finned pilot whales, spinner and striped dolphins) being taken also. Whaling in Tonga ceased in 1978. At least such whaling kept (by necessity) to relatively traditional methods, though now with motor boats. The same applies to two villages on the islands of Lembata and Solon in Indonesia, which probably more than any other can claim to be a subsistence activity. They have hunted for centuries by wooden sailing boats and long bamboo poles tipped with a metal blade (Soegiarto and Polunin 1982). The hunt dominates their culture and supplies them with most of their protein and oil. One island concentrates upon sperm whales (the only place besides Japan to consume their meat) and the other on Bryde's and minke whales (occasionally also taking small fin and blue whales). About 50 animals in total are taken each year.

In the North Atlantic, two island groups, the Azores and Madeira, belonging to Portugal, have been whaling for sperm whales (along with nations like Spain and Iceland) since the Yankee whalers visited them in the nineteenth century (Clarke 1956). Though styled on this former basis, with open boats and hand harpoons, they have moved with the times and use motor boats for towing out the rowing boats. They also caused greater damage by hunting mothers and their calves. The oil (and the teeth) were also exported until international trade was curtailed by CITES and other regulations. Both have within the last year or so ceased whaling, and indeed Madeira has now declared its coastal waters a marine mammal sanctuary.

Further north, whaling has been carried out for centuries, perhaps a millenium, in the Faroe Islands, halfway between Scotland and Iceland (see Joensen 1976). Their quarry has been the long-finned pilot whale which would sometimes visit their coasts in large herds in summer. Once a herd is sighted the Faroese put to sea in small boats and encircling the herd, drive it into one of a number of favoured bays. From here, with much banging and slapping the water with oars, the pilot whales (or 'grindhval' as they are called) are driven into shallow waters and onto the shore. A whaling lance is used to kill them or the spinal cord is severed at the neck with a knife (called a gaff). The justification of this annual slaughter (each drive is termed a 'grind') is its role in the Faroese culture and the fact that the whale meat is consumed locally. Some communities at least are very efficient and well organised, and the kill is performed humanely. The arguments against the hunt are that it is cruel, improperly controlled, and the meat is often wasted. Furthermore, the annual catch has increased markedly in the 1970s and 1980s, although this may reflect a recent increase in the pilot whale populations of the Northeast Atlantic (from sightings surveys — Evans *et al.* 1986), as part of a 110-year cycle (Hoydal 1985). My own personal observations in the Faroes do, nevertheless, suggest that in certain locations the kill may be relatively slow and without adequate control.

In Arctic waters, where bowheads and right whales were once hunted until almost extinct, the native people of West Greenland and eastern Canada have for centuries hunted white whale and narwhal (Kapel 1977a). In Greenland the otherwise protected humpback was also taken until recently (Kapel 1979), and off Newfoundland, a drive fishery for pilot whales (capturing nearly 10,000 in 1956) as food for mink operated between 1947 and 1972 (Mercer 1975). Although white whale and pilot whale have been hunted by these native peoples mainly for subsistence, in some areas narwhal are also taken for the international ivory trade. Over 1,000 of white whale and narwhal may be taken annually by each of these two countries. For those species, open boats or kayaks are used with hand-held harpoons, although the boats are often motor-powered and the harpoons supplemented with shoulder guns. The larger species in West Greenland are hunted by modern Norwegian-style methods — fast motorised catcher boats and harpoons fired from a fixed cannon on the bow of the deck. The meat is frozen and exported to Denmark. Humpbacks are theoretically to be protected from 1986, but a couple of hundred minke whales continue to be taken as a subsistence activity (Kapel 1977b, 1978). By those same arguments Norway is attempting to continue taking minke whales, in the Arctic waters west of Norway and around Spitsbergen and Jan Mayen. They too use large high-powered vessels and explosive harpoons, and export most of their frozen meat to Japan.

A Case Example of Subsistence Whaling — the Inuit Hunters of Greenland

The Inuit hunters of Greenland provide a good example of the various issues involved, and the following account derives mainly from Hertz and Kapel (1986).

Between one-quarter and one-fifth of the Greenland population is totally dependent on hunting (particularly seals but also cetaceans and seabirds) for subsistence, and hunting makes a considerable contribution to the nutritional requirements of the remainder (Kapel and Petersen 1982). Hunting of marine mammals is the dominant occupation in the northwestern, northern and eastern parts of Greenland, with the capture of white whale, narwhal and minke whale (and other smaller cetaceans) being concentrated in the summer and autumn periods when there is open water. During this period, hunting is carried out from small motor boats or dinghies with an outboard motor. In Thule district, narwhal are still harpooned from kayak. Minke whale hunting is carried out either as a collective hunt by a number of small boats or from fishing vessels with harpoon guns. In autumn, migrating white whales are captured in large nets placed along the coast at selected localities. The hunting cycle and choice of prey is dictated by the annual cycle and yearly variations in prey availability. Although Inuits may travel some distance between hunting sites within a district, they rarely move to other regions in pursuit of the prey. This need to utilise whatever prey animal is locally available has meant that, in West Greenland as a whole, an estimated 50–70 species are exploited (including 12 cetacean and six seal species). Alternative occupations such as agriculture are impossible in most regions, and fish resources are limited or presently unexploited.

On the other hand, the hunting communities are no longer isolated from the outside world and the hunting technology has changed considerably to what it was. Today, the hunters need rifles, ammunition, nets, lines, motors, oil, gasoline, etc. to maintain their hunting activity, and for this purpose a cash income is necessary. This might come from trading hunting products, or at least one member of the family having temporary jobs. The cash income is very low in the hunting districts, and an estimated one-third to half of the household income is used for hunting and fishing gear.

The main products from whale (and seal) are meat and other edible parts of the animal, mostly locally consumed by man and sled dogs. The requirements of a hunting family of five persons and ten dogs amount to an estimated 200–400kg per month (depending on the time of year). For larger animals, the catch is divided and shared usually according to traditional rules and moral codices. However, some of the catch is nowadays traded for cash income, particularly when there are short-term surpluses, and in the larger settlements where a major part of the population earns wages and cannot meet their nutritional needs by 'holiday-hunting'. Attempts to organise the export of seal and whale meat or blubber have now ceased (though seal skins are exported).

In hunting communities, the social life and cultural traditions are still closely connected with this activity, with women playing a significant role in cleaning and drying seal skin, and in flensing, and elderly persons providing advice before hunts. The commercial exploitation of marine mammals, such as the bowhead and humpback, by European and American whalers, has had an appreciable effect on hunting in Greenland. It is, therefore, understandable that Greenlanders should resent those countries now seeking to impose restrictions on peoples who for centuries have conducted subsistence harvesting with at least some ecological considerations embedded in their culture. Technological developments in catch methods should not necessarily be rejected if they result in improved living conditions and, for example, reduce loss rates. Although hunting communities have a long tradition of establishing regulatory rules, they clearly need to take account of the economic and cultural developments that are presently in part accounting for the conflict. Outside influences must work closely and sensitively with those people.

HUNTING OF SMALL CETACEANS

We have looked primarily at larger cetaceans, and this is where man's exploitation has been greatest. However, in a number of regions of the world, dolphins are also hunted (see Mitchell 1975a,b for useful reviews). Some of these are killed because of their perceived conflict with fishing activities. These will be reviewed in a later section. Other hunting has been directed at particular species for their meat. It is estimated that the annual take of dolphins, porpoises and small whales exceeds 100,000 (IWC 1982). In Southwest Greenland, approximately 1,000 harbour porpoise have been hunted annually in recent years (Kapel 1975). The same species used to be hunted in the Baltic Sea until the population was wiped out from virtually all of the region. Until 1977, the Norwegians hunted northern bottlenose whales in the Northeast Atlantic (Christensen 1975; Benjaminsen and Christensen 1979). The subsistence humpback whale fishery in St Vincent has included other smaller species such as pilot whales, killer and false killer whales (Caldwell and Caldwell 1975; Price 1985). Like other Caribbean Islands (and at least in the 1970s, the Seychelles), hunting on an opportunistic basis is carried out for most small cetacean species though numbers taken are probably small. A subsistence harpoon fishery for spotted dolphins (annual take 50–300) in St Helena operated until recently (Perrin 1985a).

Opportunistic hunting applies to whale catchers elsewhere, and in 1978 I remember the vessel operating from the Faroes catching not only fin whales but also small species such as killer whale and Atlantic white-sided dolphin. Norwegian whalers sometimes do likewise in north Scottish waters. Norwegians and Icelanders take long-finned pilot whales in the Northeast Atlantic, where both also capture killer whales, the latter partly for the aquarium industry. Between 1938 and 1967, 1,400 killers were taken by Norwegians in the Northeast Atlantic (Jonsgard and Lyshoel 1970). Small dolphin species are also sometimes taken, and recently a French boat with mounted harpoon was observed by a coastguard aeroplane, pursuing common dolphins in the English Channel.

Japanese and other Small Cetacean Fisheries

In the Pacific, small whale fisheries operate in Japanese waters using both traditional and Norwegian-type methods (Miyazaki 1983; Ohsumi 1975). Besides minke whales, small numbers of pilot whales, Baird's beaked, killer and melon-headed whales have been taken. In the 1950s, catches of several hundred Baird's beaked whales were recorded annually, but hunting is now limited to the coastal waters of the Boso Peninsula (Kasuya 1986). Fishermen elsewhere on the Pacific coast of Japan (notably the Izu Peninsula) have hunted dolphins, particularly striped and spotted dolphins, by driving them ashore and killing them with hand harpoons (Nishiwaki 1975). During the 1960s annual catches reached a peak of around 20,000 striped dolphins and in some years several thousand spotted dolphins are caught; since then numbers have declined, with 4,800 taken in 1981 (IWC 1983; Miyazaki 1983), and less since then. Dall's porpoise have also been harpooned annually for food, with a mean annual take of over 8,000 in recent years (Miyazaki 1983). More recently, a drive fishery on the Kii peninsula has seen an increase in catches mainly of striped dolphins (with 11,017 in 1980 from the village of Taiji alone) (Miyazaki 1980, 1983). Elsewhere, in the Pacific, spotted and striped dolphins have been caught in shore-drive fisheries in the Solomon Islands and Papua New Guinea (Dawbin 1966b). The killer whale formed the target of Soviet commercial catcher boats in the southern hemisphere during the 1979–80 whaling season, with 916 taken, along with the larger species also taken (but a moratorium was brought into effect in subsequent seasons).

Of other species, there is limited hunting for hump-backed dolphins in the Red Sea, Arabian Sea and Persian Gulf, of dusky dolphins on the South African coast, and bottle-nosed dolphins in Sri Lanka, West Africa, Venezuela and the West Indies, generally for human consumption (Mitchell 1975a; Northridge and Pilleri 1985). Along the coasts of southern Chile, fishermen catch particularly Commerson's and Peale's dolphins, but also Burmeister's porpoise for bait in the crab fishery and for meat (Sielfeld 1983; Torres et al. 1979). Concern has recently been expressed at observed declines in small cetaceans in this region, where over 4,000 were taken in 1978–9 (Torres et al. 1979). The Burmeister's porpoise is also taken in Peru, where as many as 2,000 are sold at markets annually (Brownell and Praderi 1982; Perrin 1985b). Finally, a possible threat to the boto in Brazil is the rapidly expanding market for dried organs (Perrin 1986). Possession by a man of the eyeball of a boto or a dried boto vagina by a woman is thought to ensure sexual irresistibility, and these are now widely available in street markets and even sold by mail order. However, Best and Da Silva (1986) suggest that these are taken from incidentally killed animals.

Black Sea Fishery

One of the largest dolphin fisheries to exist has been that in the Black and Azov Seas, where catches by the Soviets and others using guns and nets, reached a maximum of 250,000–300,000 animals per year between 1931 and 1941 (Smith 1982). At one stage mainly common dolphins were caught but, by the time of a complete closure of the fishery in the Soviet Union, Romania and Bulgaria in 1967, the catch was predominantly of harbour porpoise. Small numbers of bottle-nosed dolphins were also taken but these also had declined. The fishery was closed because of a major collapse in numbers caught (to a Soviet catch of 5,600–7,400 for 1964–6). However, the Turks continued the fishery and in 1973, almost 130,000 animals were reported killed (this may have represented an underestimate since there is thought to be a significant loss rate by shooting) (IWC 1983). After public pressure from other countries, Turkey eventually decided temporarily to cease hunting in 1983 (Perrin 1985b), but as I write, there are indications that the fishery may resume shortly on the basis of the putative threat the dolphins pose to fishing (Perrin 1986).

Live Capture Fisheries

Before leaving the subject of exploitation of cetaceans by man, one should not forget the ever increasing take of live animals for dolphinaria. These are mainly bottle-nosed dolphins (over 450 were estimated in 1975 throughout the world in holding tanks or on display — Ridgway and Benirschke 1977), but also include numbers of killer whales (notably from British Columbia, Canada; Washington State, USA; and Iceland), false killers, pilot whales, white whales, tucuxi, common, white-sided, spotted and Commerson's dolphins. Other species include Irrawaddy dolphin, Fraser's dolphin, northern right whale dolphin, Risso's dolphin, finless porpoise and boto. A census in 1983 reported 304 bottle-nosed dolphins in captivity in North America alone (Reeves and Leatherwood 1984), and 39 killer whales were listed by Hoyt (1984) in 20 locations around the world. A review of live-capture fisheries in the United States, Canada, Europe, South Africa, Australia and New Zealand, Japan, Indonesia and Hong Kong provided an estimate of more than 4,000 live captures of small cetaceans in recent decades, involving 32 species (mainly bottle-nosed dolphin, followed by Pacific white-sided dolphin and short-finned pilot whale) (Cornell 1984, IWC 1984). The mortality associated with this occupation (see Walker 1975) continues to cause concern, and there are very few dolphinaria in the world that can be said to have suitable conditions for the care of cetaceans in captivity. Indeed, some would say that it is not feasible to do so humanely.

CONFLICTS WITH FISHERIES

Some direct takes of cetaceans, particularly the smaller species, occur because of the perceived conflict between them and man in pursuit of a common source of food. This conflict takes the form of either direct competition for that food, usually a fish species, or, more commonly, interference with fishing gear which may also lead to incidental drowning (see next section). In those circumstances, fishermen may kill the animals to try to reduce the conflict.

It is generally rather difficult to separate the two forms of conflict since dolphins may damage gear in the process of taking fish from that gear. This occurs, for example, on Iki island, on the west coast of Japan, where, since the 1970s, large numbers of bottle-nosed dolphins, false killers and smaller numbers of other species have been driven ashore (Kasuya 1985b; Miyazaki 1983). This started because dolphins were actually taking fish off the hooks, and then scaring the fish away from the boats. For many years, the meat was disposed of in the sea, but now it is reduced to fertiliser. Between 1976 and 1982, 4,147 bottle-nosed dolphins and 953 false killers, as well as 525 Risso's and 466 Pacific white-sided dolphins, were taken, but in recent years they have either stayed away or been driven from the Iki fishing grounds (Kasuya 1985b).

In most areas of the world, coastal fishermen consider dolphins at least as some form of nuisance. This applies also to river dolphins and, for example, in the Amazon and Orinoco river systems of Brazil and Peru, commercial fishermen consider the boto a serious competitor to be shot whenever encountered, in contrast to subsistence fishermen who hold the dolphins in some respect (believing them to have superstitious qualities) and release them alive from their nets (Best and da Silva 1984, 1986; Perrin pers. comm.). In most cases, the retaliation by fishermen probably has little effect either on the populations or on their supposed damage. One exception may be the common dolphin in the Mediterranean where purse-seine and trawl fisheries in Spain, Italy, Yugoslavia, Turkey, Israel, Malta, Algeria and Morocco perceive dolphins as a threat.

Common dolphins have been directly caught in retaliation in southern Spain (and form incidental catches in southern Italy). Both direct and incidental catches are thought to have contributed to a recent decline in in this species in the western Mediterranean (Aguilar 1986).

In earlier decades, a bounty was issued by the Quebec Department of Fisheries for white whales in the St Lawrence River, on the basis that they had a serious effect on local fish stocks (Boulva 1981). More constructively, playbacks of recorded killer whale sounds have been used successfully in Bristol Bay, Alaska, to keep white whales from preying upon young Pacific salmon (Fish and Vania 1971; Mate and Greenlaw 1981). Killer whales themselves are frequently alleged to interfere with fishing activities, as for example in the Icelandic and Norwegian herring fisheries where culls have taken place in the past. False killers have also been indicted as causing extensive operational damage to gear in long-line fisheries for tuna and billfish in the Pacific and Indian Oceans (Mitchell 1975a).

We have looked briefly at some of the cases where cetaceans are thought to have a detrimental effect upon fisheries, but what of the converse, the possible negative effects of fisheries upon cetacean populations? In both cases our information on cetacean-fishery interactions is very poor, and research in this area is badly needed. Where the diet of cetaceans appears to coincide with the target of a commercial fishery, such as for tuna, anchovy, herring or capelin, then there is obviously potential competition. However, the relative importance of different food species to cetaceans in a particular area is still poorly known, and even when determined, the complex interactions between predator and prey populations require detailed study before conclusions can be drawn. The collapse of energy-rich herring stocks may have played some part in the virtual absence of cetaceans in the southern part of the North Sea (even though other factors such as pollution may be more important). The rise of the capelin fishery in eastern Canada and subsequent collapse of capelin stocks in the late 1970s is considered by Hal Whitehead and others to be having a negative effect on fin whales (Lynch and Whitehead 1984; Whitehead and Carscadden 1985). Capelin are major prey items for this species and the humpback, and it is thought that a food shortage might have allowed the latter to out-compete the former. In Shetland waters, the accelerated rise in the industrial fishery for sandeel, sprat and Norway pout could have a serious impact on the harbour porpoise and minke whale populations there, both of which are known to take these species.

Perhaps the most controversial area for potential cetacean-fishery interaction lies in the Southern Ocean. Here, we have seen how a depletion of the great whales has released a large quantity of krill annually produced which could be consumed by other organisms. This has been estimated at about 150 million tonnes of krill per year (Laws 1985). Since the total annual yield of the world's fisheries is estimated at 70 million tonnes, it is not surprising that many nations have looked excitedly at the possibility of exploiting this resource. However, as Table 10.1 indicates, this potential surplus may have been taken up by an increased abundance of seals (notably the crabeater seal) and seabirds (notably some of the penguin species). For these reasons any future krill fishery should proceed cautiously.

Table 10.1: Possible changes in patterns of consumption of krill by major groups of predators in the Southern Ocean

Predatory group	Annual consumption (tons $\times$ 10^6)	
	1900	1984
Whales	190*	40*
Seals	50	130*
Birds	50	130*
Fish	100	70
Cephalopods	80	100
Total	470	470

Reference sources: From Laws (1985), derived from Clarke (1983), Croxall (1984), Everson (1984), Laws (1977b, 1984).

Notes: The above values are in many cases (particularly for squid, birds and seals) based on uncertain determinations, and so should be viewed with caution. Nevertheless, the historical changes in whale numbers are reasonably well documented and there have been recent population increases in Antarctic fur and crabeater seals and in king penguins supporting those inferences.

* published estimates, adjusted in case of birds to allow for recent population increases. Other figures are tentative estimates based on indications from above sources and on back-projections of increases in seal and bird populations.

Useful reviews of cetacean-fishery interactions, centred mainly on the Southern Oceans, are those of Beddington and de la Mare (1985), Beddington and May (1982) and Laws (1985). Simon Northridge (1984) has also provided a very useful, detailed literature review of the subject.

Before leaving the topic of possible negative effects on cetaceans of fisheries, we should note that there are a few cases of co-operation between man and dolphins in pursuit of food. The most obvious one is that of the tuna purse-seine fishery, but because of the incidental kills this causes it will be considered in the next section. However, there are a few instances where neither party appears to be affected detrimentally. The best known example is that of the relationship between fishermen and Atlantic hump-backed dolphins along the Mauritanian coast (Busnel 1973). When mullet are schooling along the coast, the fishermen attract dolphins by beating the surface of the sea with sticks. The dolphins then help fishermen to herd fish into nets and, in so doing, gain a meal themselves by trapping them against the nets. In Burma, the Irrawaddy dolphin is said to help river fishermen by herding fish into their nets (Tin Thein 1977), and in the Amazonian basin boto may help fishermen herd fish into seine nets (Lamb 1954).

INCIDENTAL CATCHES IN FISHING NETS

As may be inferred from the preceding section, the rise in various fishing activities has also led to increased incidental capture in nets of many different species of cetaceans, particularly the smaller ones. Sometimes this incidental capture is deliberate. The best known example is the capture of several species of dolphins in the tuna purse-seine fishery in the eastern tropical Pacific (Allen 1985; Perrin *et al.* 1982). Deepwater spinner dolphins and pantropical spotted dolphins commonly associate with yellow-fin tuna. Tuna fishermen take advantage of this, using the dolphins to help locate shoals of tuna and then setting their purse-seine nets around the dolphin-tuna schools. In the past very many dolphins would become entangled in these nets and drown. During the 1960s and early 1970s between 200,000 and 500,000 dolphins, mainly spotted and spinner dolphins, but also common and Fraser's dolphins, were killed in such nets each year in the eastern tropical Pacific. Some of the populations have declined considerably, and the eastern Pacific stock of spinner dolphin is estimated to be reduced by 80 per cent (Smith 1983). To try to reduce this mortality, a special panel of fine mesh (called the Medina panel) has been added to the net. This part of the net is placed furthest from the fishing vessels and operated as the net is drawn tight. The tuna usually dive and are retained in the net whilst the dolphins are able to escape over the net rim, sometimes remaining immobile (probably due to stress) enabling them to be helped out of the net by hand from inflatables (Figure 10.1). This method seems to have reduced the mortality considerably, and the current incidental take is around 30,000–40,000 per year (though this may be partly due to reduced population sizes).

Small cetaceans are caught in gill-net, trawl, purse seine, set net and long-line fisheries throughout the world (Figure 10.2). However, probably most important are gill-nets, particularly those made of nylon monofilament which is not only much more durable but is more difficult for dolphins to detect by echolocation. Species worst affected are coastal ones such as the harbour and Burmeister's porpoises, vaquita and franciscana. The harbour porpoise suffered incidental catches exceeding 1,500 per year in the salmon drift net fishery off west Greenland in the early 1970s (Lear and Christensen 1975). Although changes to this fishery in the late 1970s should have reduced the catch, some of these have now been reversed, so we may expect further mortality. This species also suffers incidental mortality in various types of nets elsewhere, notably by trawls in Denmark, set nets or traps for cod or salmon in Scotland (Aberdeenshire), western Ireland, Iceland, Poland and Alaska; salmon and cod traps, herring weirs, salmon and mackerel gill-nets in the northeastern United States and eastern Canada (New England, New Brunswick, Nova Scotia and Newfoundland); herring gill-nets off Honshu, Japan; and nets set for sturgeon along the Kanin Peninsula, USSR (Gaskin 1984; also Evans 1980; Evans et al. 1986; Kinze 1985).

Between 10,000 and 20,000 Dall's porpoise may drown each year in Japanese gill-nets used offshore for salmon (Jones 1983); tucuxi are taken in fishermen's nets in the central Amazon region (Best and da Silva 1984, 1986) and Burmeister's porpoises in gill-nets off southern Chile and Peru (and probably elsewhere in South America) (Brownell and Praderi 1982); some finless porpoises are trapped wherever they occur along the coasts of China and Japan (Kasuya and Kureha 1979; Zhou et al. 1980); and in the Gulf of California, tens to hundreds of vaquita were taken annually in a commercial gill-net fishery for shark and totoaba (Brownell 1982, 1983). The vaquita may have been seriously reduced in numbers since the late 1940s, and is now considered vulnerable to extinction. Although the totoaba fishery closed in 1975 after collapse of the stocks, other fisheries and poaching still catch some

Figure 10.1 Areas where substantial incidental catches of cetaceans occur in fishing gear

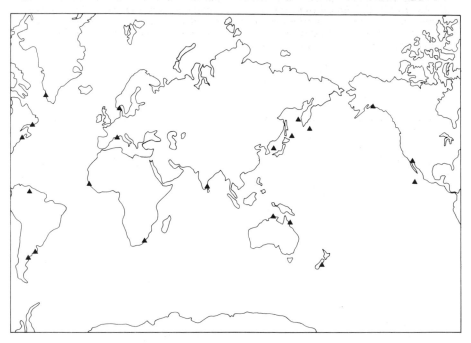

▲   incidental catch in fishing nets

porpoises (Perrin 1986). Around Sri Lanka, gill-net fisheries are thought to take an estimated 42,000 small cetaceans (40 per cent of which may be spinner dolphins) *per annum* (Alling *et al.* 1984).

Gill-nets set for shark either for food or to protect swimmers operate in many parts of the world, particularly Australia, South Africa, and South America. These cause drownings of many coastal dolphins (for example the franciscana, Irrawaddy, hump-backed and bottle-nosed dolphins) each year (Bannister 1977; Da Silva and Best 1984; Harwood *et al.* 1984; IWC 1982; Northridge 1984). Off the coasts of Argentina, Uruguay and Brazil, large numbers of franciscana have been killed each year since 1942. For one site in Uruguay, the estimated annual catch was 2,000 in the late 1960s and early 1970s although a move offshore in the shark fishery has led to a more recent reduction in mortality.

Dolphins and porpoises are not the only species affected by incidental catches. False killer whales (30–50 per year) are taken accidentally on the high seas in Japanese tuna long-line fisheries (Mitchell 1975b:914). Incidental catches of the Pacific tuna purse-seine fishery include melon-headed whale, pygmy killer whale, and short-finned pilot whale, although numbers are usually small (Allen 1985).

More importantly, however, have been entrapments of humpbacks and minke whales, and occasionally right and fin whales in traps, weirs or nets off New England and eastern Newfoundland (Perkins and Beamish 1979). This problem seems to have arisen mainly from the 1970s when humpbacks in particular started to feed closer inshore, possibly associ-

Figure 10.2 Incidental capture of dolphins in the purse-seine tuna fishery and method to reduce mortality. Dolphins accompany tuna shoals and are entrapped when a fishing boat encircles the fish with a purse-seine net. The bottom of the net is pulled in beneath the fish whilst a panel of finer mesh (Medina panel), sited on the far side of the net, is employed enabling dolphins to see it and escape over its rim, aided where necessary by divers

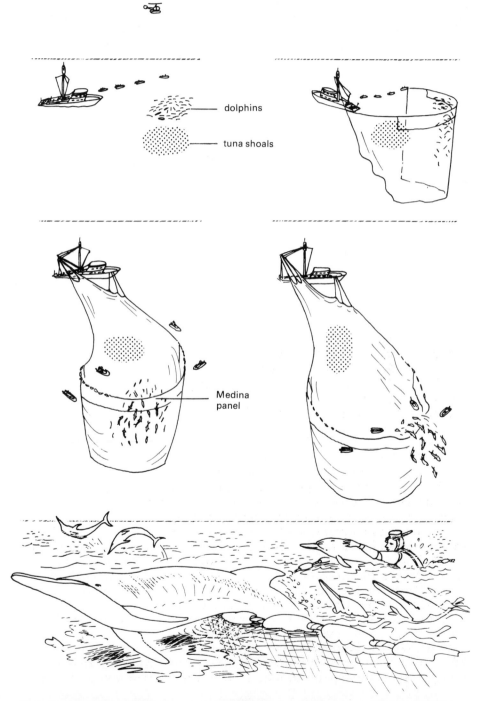

dolphins

tuna shoals

Medina panel

ated with the collapse in the capelin stocks and increased effort in the cod fishery. Between 1969 and 1978, at least seven humpbacks and ten minke whales are known to have died as a result, and by 1980 about 15 humpbacks were dying each year.

Studies by Jon Lien and colleagues in Newfoundland showed that the problem was serious to both whales and the fishing industry (Lien 1981). Damages to gear and lost fish in 1979 and 1980 were estimated to amount to 2–3 per cent of the total annual value of the Newfoundland fishery, whilst there were 58 entrapments in 1979 and 150 in 1980, with 70 per cent of the damage being caused by humpbacks. Efforts to reduce the problem have been partially successful. Some whales have been freed and released alive whilst modifications of the gear and the design of acoustic alarms set on the fishing gear to make them more easily detected have shown some success. In 1981, collisions with gear were greatly reduced, although this has been partly due to changes in the distribution of fishing activity and of baleen whales. Unfortunately in that year there was a substantial increase in pilot whale entrapments, due partly to their increased presence that year (Lien 1981).

The problem of incidental catches in fishing gear continues. In some cases it can be reduced by better education and help to the fishermen themselves, who may then be able to release the animals before they drown. Acoustic warning devices (either sonic or ultrasonic) that emit continuous pinging sounds (Perkins and Beamish 1979), or playback of killer whale sounds (Fish and Vania 1971) may help but are expensive to apply to large amounts of gear. The animals may also habituate to them or overlook them in their hot pursuit of concentrated prey.

HABITAT DESTRUCTION

If any cetacean species goes extinct in the next decade or two, it is more likely to be through changes to its habitat than to anything else. The species most affected are ones with restricted distributions, tied to rivers or coastal areas where their habitat requirements prevent them from escaping human activities. These are essentially the river dolphins and porpoises.

Most threatened of all cetacean species is the baiji of the Yangtze River (Changjiang) in China where collisions with vessels (and accidental entanglement in fishing gear) have reduced the population to perhaps as few as 200 animals (Chen et al. 1979; Perrin 1985b). It is now restricted to a few localities in the middle and lower reaches of the Yangtze where industrialisation is fast occurring. Although completely protected from exploitation, this will not save the species from deterioration of its habitat. Two proposals are presently underway for the construction of large semi-captive reserves to contain translocated animals, and a 135-km stretch of the Yangtze in Hubei province where fishing operations and boat traffic will be regulated (Perrin 1986).

The Indus susu is also on the brink of extinction with a population of somewhere between 450 and 600, restricted to the River Indus in the provinces of Sind and Punjab, Pakistan (Jones 1982; Kasuya and Nishiwaki 1975). The Ganges susu numbers perhaps several thousand in the Ganges, Brahmaputra and Meghna river systems of western India

(Jones 1982; Shrestha 1982). Modifications to the flow of these rivers by the construction of barrages for hydroelectric development have posed serious threats to these species. Although the Indus susu is in the most perilous state, it is receiving at least some protection in Sind Province. The Ganges susu, on the other hand, is still declining rapidly in the rivers of Nepal, where only about 40 are thought to remain, and further high dams are planned for this region in the near future (Perrin 1986, Shrestha 1982).

Habitat modification along the coasts of Brazil and Venezuela poses threats to the franciscana (Best and da Silva 1984; Perrin 1986), and in the upper reaches of the Gulf of California to the vaquita (Brownell 1982). Damming and other developments may also be having a detrimental effect on boto populations in South American river systems, particularly of the Amazon basin (Best and da Silva 1986; Perrin 1986).

The harbour porpoise and bottle-nosed dolphin, with their inshore distributions, also come into frequent contact with man's activities. The development of coastal resorts and sheltered bays in the Irish Sea, English Channel and southern North Sea may be partly responsible for their recent comparative absence in these regions (Evans 1980; Kayes 1985; Kroger 1986).

Larger cetaceans may also have critical requirements during parts of their life cycle. Humpbacks, right whales and gray whales use shallow coastal lagoons and bays for breeding. These are sometimes of restricted area and apparently used traditionally so that sudden damage to those habitats could be potentially serious. So far, there have fortunately been few such developments, although gray whale breeding lagoons in Mexico are in some peril (Perrin 1985b, pers. comm.). Feeding areas for coastal whale species are also vulnerable, and hydroelectric developments on the Manicouagan River, eastern Canada were thought to have seriously affected white whale populations in the outer St Lawrence estuary by closing important feeding grounds (Gaskin 1982:347; Pippard and Malcolm 1978). Offshore oil developments (oilrig and pipeline constructions, artificial islands, etc.) could pose threats to white whales, narwhals and bowheads in Arctic waters and other species in the North Sea, but so far there is no evidence of any direct effects (as opposed to oil or noise pollution). Indeed, hotwater outflow from oilrigs could actually be favourable feeding areas for some species.

HUMAN DISTURBANCE

Harassment of cetaceans by increased boat traffic is a problem only recently recognised as potentially serious. Information on possible effects is sparse and difficult to obtain. Some of it is obvious, such as the mortality from collisions with propellers that are often implicated in strandings of dolphins and whales. Concern has also been expressed recently over disturbance by whalewatchers to regular concentrations of whales — gray whales in the bays of southern California and Mexico; humpbacks in Glacier Bay, Alaska, and in Hawaii; and white whales in Bristol Bay, Alaska, and the St Lawrence estuary, Canada. In Baja California, low-flying aircraft and large numbers of speedboats were thought to be disturbing gray whale mothers and their calves (Reeves

1977). The shifting of whales between lagoons in the early 1970s has been correlated with shifting human activities. However, studies since 1975 by Richard Gard, Mary Lou Jones and Steven Swartz indicate no correlation between the two although the possibility exists that reproductive success is affected (Jones and Swartz 1984). A separate study of gray whales in Laguna San Ignacio by Marilyn Dahlheim and colleagues (1984) indicated that the whales produced sounds with maximum energy in the frequency range 20Hz-2kHz, outside the range of snapping shrimps which possibly produce most of the background biological sound, where most energy is between 2 and 5kHz. However, small vessels (powered by outboard motor) produced sounds mainly below 2kHz, in the same frequency range as the gray whale. Although this provides potential for acoustic interference, it was thought that it resulted primarily in the attraction and apparent curiosity displayed by gray whales towards small boats, particularly when idling or moving slowly (2–4 knots, or 4–7km/hour).

Some studies do indicate possible detrimental effects to whales. In Hawaii, Gregory Kaufman and Kevin Wood (1981) found, in 1980–1, that the presence of humpbacks varied inversely with the amount of daily boat traffic and with days on which military bombing practice took place. Low-flying aircraft, on the other hand, had no apparent effect. In Alaska, Scott Baker and Louis Herman have found clear and graded changes in the behaviour of humpbacks in response to vessel traffic even at distances of over 3km (Baker et al. 1982, 1983). These included longer dives, shorter periods at the surface, movements away from the path of vessels and temporary displacement of individuals from preferred feeding areas.

Among smaller cetaceans, negative responses to boat traffic have been found in the harbour porpoise in Washington State (by Chuck Flaherty), Denmark (by Carl Kinze) and northwest Scotland (by the author). I have also tested out different engine sounds upon white-beaked and Risso's dolphins in Northwest Scotland and found a marked negative response at high frequencies (above around 10kHz).

Many sea areas (for example the English Channel and southern North Sea) have seen a large increase in marine traffic which has been estimated to lead to a rise in ambient noise levels of about 10dB in such areas. However, these are predominantly in the frequency range 10–100Hz with very little above 1kHz (Ross 1976). Most dolphins and porpoises have hearing ranges of between 1 and 150kHz and so should not be affected by these, although mysticete whales with a hearing range of around 12Hz to 30kHz could obviously be affected. Speed boats (operating at 25 knots (46 km/hour) or more), on the other hand, generate much more sound in the 1–50kHz band range and so could certainly potentially affect dolphins and porpoises, although high frequency sounds are attenuated rapidly in shallow water. It has also been suggested that sidescan sonar (as used by many fishing fleets) and echo-sounders (that virtually every motorised vessel has) could disrupt the echolocation behaviour of small cetaceans. These transmit at 5–250kHz depending on the type of equipment and its usage. Thus they potentially could affect dolphins and porpoises, and some whales, although if the sounds are not very loud cetaceans may be able to ignore them.

Seismic exploration operates over frequencies mainly below 100Hz although certain types of equipment apparently emit frequencies of 1–1.5kHz (Haines 1974). The sounds these produce are transmitted very great distances, and I remember well putting a hydrophone into the sea and picking up seismic activity as a regular, almost deafening bang that could be heard 25km away from the vessel in question. No cetaceans were observed within 40km of this vessel despite frequent sightings beyond this (Evans 1981).

In a typical marine seismic survey, noise pulses with source levels 245–252dB re:1µPa at 1m are emitted every 10–15 seconds from an array of airguns towed by a ship (Barger and Hamblen 1980; Richardson et al. 1986). It seems possible that cetaceans, particularly baleen whales, could be affected, possibly by reducing the range over which animals can communicate since, up to several kilometres range, background noise increases by about 50db (i.e. to more than 150dB re:1µPa) at the frequencies used for communication (20–1,000Hz band). Received pulses are usually about one-quarter to three-quarters of a second duration, with most energy at 75–500Hz (Malme et al. 1983, 1984; Richardson et al. 1986).

A study in 1984 by Donald Ljungblad and others indicated strong avoidance reactions by bowhead whales in the Beaufort Sea to each of four seismic vessels (Ljungblad et al. 1985). However, similar studies by W.J. Richardson, C.R. Greene and others found only very mild reactions by bowheads (subjected to underwater noise levels of 107–158dB re:1µPa), although breathing rates generally increased (Richardson et al. 1985). Further studies were carried out using higher noise levels (248dB re:1µPa) and elicited avoidance for some at 7.5km distance, and all by about 2km distance (Richardson et al. 1986).

Chris Clark, Peter Tyack and others studied migrating gray whales off California subjected to seismic air-guns and arrays (Malme et al. 1983, 1984). They observed gray whales showing avoidance behaviour, moving into the surf zone and within the sound shadow of rocks. Responses consistently began when the sound source was at least 160dB re:1µPa, corresponding to ranges less than 5km for a full-scale array of airguns, and less than 1km for a single 1.6–1 airgun; they usually resulted in a deflection of movement of the whales.

These results suggest that whales tend to move away from full-scale seismic ships when seismic impulses are very strong (i.e. a ship within about 4–7.5km; received levels more than 160–170dB re:1µPa). There may also be responses at greater distances, although both gray and bowhead whales are more inclined to react to continuous noise from boats, offshore drilling, etc. when its broadband level is 120dB or less, rather than to the intermittent noise impulses that seismic vessels produce (Malme et al. 1983, 1984; Richardson et al. 1985, 1986).

POLLUTION

The last negative influence of human activities is that of pollution, by oil or other toxic chemicals. Increased industrialisation in many areas of the world poses a severe threat to cetacean populations, particularly the smaller species that occupy semi-enclosed waters (Figure 10.3).

Numerous studies have been published showing the presence of pesticides and heavy metals in the blubber, muscle, liver and brain of many cetacean species. As analytical methods improve and animals are sampled over wider regions, an ever increasing quantity of trace elements and chlorinated hydrocarbons have been found. There are no areas of the world, even the remote Arctic and Antarctic, that do not possess traces of hydrocarbon derived from industrial or agricultural activities. Petroleum tar balls may be encountered in every ocean almost anywhere in the world.

What are the most important trace elements and hydrocarbons in cetacean tissues? This is more difficult to answer than it might seem. The reason is that a number of trace elements, at least, occur naturally in the sea and in prey organisms. Their presence in whales and dolphins need not be harmful; indeed in some cases they are beneficial, being important in certain enzyme reactions (though above certain levels they can become toxic). Those that are known to be toxic include the insect pesticides DDT (and its derivative DDE) and dieldrin (and related endrin, aldrin, chlordane and heptachlor); polychlorinated biphenyls (PCBs), such as Arochlor, used in the plastics industry; and trace elements (called heavy metals) such as mercury, lead, cadmium, zinc, and copper (Moriarty 1975). Chlorinated hydrocarbons (DDT, dieldrin, PCBs etc.) have only recently been produced, primarily since 1940. They are virtually insoluble in water but soluble in lipids so that they can become concentrated in tissues like blubber where they will persist for long periods. If the animal uses up that fat store, the compound becomes 'activated' (i.e. metabolised) and it is in this state that it can cause damage. Otherwise the compound can persist in an inactive state for many years. When applied in solid form to agricultural land, compounds such as DDT are transported mainly by winds to the sea. PCBs probably enter the sea by direct discharge or via rivers. Heavy metals can enter by all these means, though probably mainly as particles in the air.

Once in the sea, the hydrocarbons remain inert until entering the food chain. Predator eats contaminated prey and is then in turn eaten so that the chemical becomes concentrated. Those organisms at the top of the food chain (for example marine mammals, seabirds and man) are thus most vulnerable to its toxic effects at high concentrations. DDT is a contact or stomach poison but can also affect the reproductive system; dieldrin and related compounds affect the nervous system; PCBs can cause liver damage or upset the enzyme systems in the liver, and also affect the reproductive system (Moriarty 1975).

When heavy metals enter the sea, they may form either inorganic or organic complexes (Bryan 1976). It is usually in the latter form that they are ingested by marine mammals. Mercury, cadmium, arsenic and copper have little or no affinity for lipids and so usually enter organs, notably the liver and kidneys, rather than blubber. In those organs, when they are not bound to proteins called metallothioneins, they can become mobilised in the bloodstream and become toxic. Lead, zinc, manganese and chromium may be found equally in lipids and organs. When mobilised from lipids into the bloodstream, many of these can be highly toxic. The brain is particularly sensitive to mercury contamination.

Geographic Distribution of Pollutants

Sampling of cetaceans has rarely been done on any systematic basis, mainly because of lack of resources. Few individuals of any species have been sampled, and since they were often already found dead, the levels of organochlorines or heavy metals may not reflect normal levels. Furthermore, analytical methods have rarely been compared between laboratories so values for a particular species, obtained in different regions, may not be strictly comparable. Despite these problems, however, a broad review of levels of these potentially toxic chemicals indicates that certain regions are particularly polluted. They generally fall within the temperate northern hemisphere and coincide with heavily industrialised regions or areas with intensive agriculture. Worst of all appear to be the Baltic (and Gulf of Bothnia) and the western Mediterranean Sea, but also bad are the southern North Sea, Bay of Fundy (New England, Nova Scotia, New Brunswick and Quebec), California and Gulf of Mexico, and coasts of Japan (Figure 10.3).

Pollutant Levels in Cetaceans

Reviews of contaminant levels in cetaceans are given world-wide by David Gaskin (1982); for the Pacific by O'Shea et al. (1980); the North Sea by NERC (1983); and Atlantic and Mediterranean coasts of France by Alzieu and Duguy (1979, 1981). They indicate levels to be highest for DDT, PCBs and mercury; and in those cetacean species that feed primarily on fish or squid and occupy coastal habitats for most or all of the year. These include high levels in the harbour porpoise of DDT and PCBs in the Bay of Fundy and southern California (Gaskin et al. 1971, 1982, 1983; O'Shea et al. 1980), PCBs on the French coast (Alzieu and Duguy 1981), and mercury in the North Sea (Koeman et al. 1973; NERC 1983); DDT and PCBs in bottle-nosed and common dolphins in southern California (O'Shea et al. 1980) and the western Mediterranean (Viale 1978), and in striped dolphins in France (Alzieu and Duguy 1978b); and heavy metals (mercury, iron and titanium) in fin whales, bottle-nosed and common dolphins, and Cuvier's beaked whale in the western Mediterranean (Viale 1978).

High levels of DDT (expressed here as total DDT in blubber) have also been found in common, Hector's and dusky dolphins in New Zealand waters (Baker 1978; Koeman et al. 1972); in Dall's porpoise in California and finless porpoise in Japan (O'Shea et al. 1980); DDT and PCBs in white whale in the Gulf of St Lawrence (Sergeant 1980) and killer whale in Puget Sound, Washington State (Peard et al. 1983); and in long-finned pilot whales, DDT and PCBs in eastern United States (Taruski et al. 1975), PCBs in France (Alzieu and Duguy 1978a) and DDT and mercury in the Faroes (Lehmann and Peterle 1971).

Levels are generally lower in sperm whales and in baleen whale species, typically ranging between 0.1 and 10 parts per million (ppm) wet weight (i.e. fresh, undried weight) for both DDT and PCBs (Aguilar 1983; Aguilar and Jover 1982; Alzieu and Duguy 1978a, 1981; Holden 1975; Saschenbrecker 1973; Sergeant 1980, 1981; Taruski et al. 1975; Wolman and Wilson 1970). These results are based on relatively few specimens and species, and sampling has included areas away from organochlorine pollution (for example Antarctic, Arctic). Higher levels have been

Figure 10.3 Major polluted regions of the world where cetaceans may be affected (derived from the Times Atlas of the Oceans *(1983)). Not surprisingly they coincide with those regions where high levels of organochlorine and heavy metal pollutants have been detected in cetaceans*

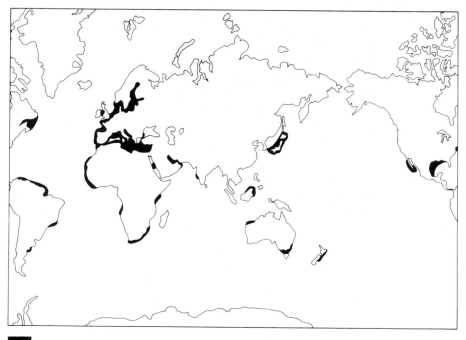

■ heavily polluted area

obtained along the French coast. Sperm whales generally have slightly higher levels than baleen whales, with maximum values of 53 ppm DDT and 39 ppm PCBs (Aguilar 1983; Alzieu and Duguy 1979).

Biological Effects on Cetaceans

It is very difficult to interpret high levels of these contaminants in terms of their potential harm. In the cases of DDT and PCBs, they are usually detected in the blubber where they probably cause little damage. On the other hand, high levels in odontocetes noted above refer typically to between 50–500 (max. 2,700) ppm DDT and 20–500 (max. 850) ppm PCBs (Gaskin 1982). Bottle-nosed dolphins in California had DDT levels ranging from 1,796 to 2,695 ppm and PCB levels of 420–450 ppm (O'Shea *et al.* 1980); an immature long-finned pilot whale had a PCB level of 840 ppm in the western Mediterranean (Alzieu and Duguy 1978a); and a striped dolphin in the same region had levels of 706 ppm DDT and 833 ppm PCBs (Alzieu and Duguy 1978b). Harbour porpoises in the Bay of Fundy had PCB levels up to 310 ppm (Gaskin *et al.* 1971, 1976); on the French coast, to 333 ppm (Alzieu and Duguy 1981); and off the west coast of Sweden, to 260ppm, with DDT levels to 289ppm in the Baltic and 560ppm in west Sweden (Otterlind 1976).

If these concentrations were mobilised from the blubber, as is likely during food shortage, or to the calf during lactation, they are likely to have serious effects (though this has yet to be tested adequately). Levels of mercury in the liver of animals from polluted regions are typically in the range 5–200 ppm wet weight (Gaskin 1982), although levels of greater than 604 ppm and 440 ppm have been found in common dolphins and Cuvier's whales in the western Mediterranean (Viale 1978).

Various studies suggest that levels of both DDT and PCBs are lower among females than males (except possibly in sperm whales — Aguilar 1983), and it is generally thought this is due to transfer of contaminants via the placenta or through lactation to the calf (see for example Alzieu and Duguy 1981; Gaskin 1982). This may further explain why David Gaskin and his co-workers have found a net decrease in residues with age in female harbour porpoises but an increase in males (Gaskin 1982:420; Gaskin *et al.* 1982). Similar results have been obtained in grey and ringed seals.

Our knowledge of the effects of these pollutants is still virtually zero. There is a strong need to carry out carefully controlled experiments on animals in captivity, as has been done recently on seals in Holland with some success. The Dutch workers (Peter Reijnders and his colleagues) have shown clear sublethal effects of DDT and PCBs on reproduction in harbour seals, and such studies should be repeated on a small cetacean such as the bottle-nosed dolphin, or possibly harbour porpoise if it can be bred reliably. It is also important that levels be monitored through the annual cycle of the animal, as David Gaskin (1982) has gallantly been trying to do, despite the logistical difficulties that one must face. This will help to determine the effects of drawing upon fat reserves, gestation and lactation, varying the diet, inshore-offshore movements, and so on. Long-distance movements obviously have important implications on whether an animal would actually accumulate large concentrations, and might be a further reason why baleen whales tend to have relatively lower levels. The role of natural trace element detoxification systems needs also to be studied. It could be that high levels of mercury, cadmium or zinc usually have little detrimental effect.

Oil Pollution

Oil pollution is a problem particularly facing certain seabird species, but it is also known sometimes to have a negative effect on seals. Its potential harm to cetaceans has scarcely been studied although David St Aubin, Joseph Geraci and colleagues (1985) have recently started experimental studies. Their preliminary results suggest that cetaceans, for example bottle-nosed dolphins, can visually detect thin films of crude oil and will avoid oil slicks even at night. Mysticete whales, feeding in oiled waters, risk fouling their baleen plates. This might apply particularly to right whales with their fine-fringed baleen plates. However, both migrating gray whales off California and rorquals off eastern United States have been reported swimming directly through oil slicks without showing any avoidance reaction (Gaskin 1982), though Leatherwood *et al.* (1983:29–30) do report avoidance of a natural oil seep by migrating gray whales in California. Oil slicks are likely to be more damaging in cooler waters where petroleum hydrocarbons are less likely to form less damaging tar balls. It is true that, unlike razorbills and guillemots, there is presently no evidence of oiled cetaceans being washed ashore. Nevertheless, with the large amount of oil polluting the seas, this subject area needs much more careful study.

We have made a brief survey of marine pollutants and their possible effects on cetaceans. However, we should not forget that the discharge of untreated sewage, pesticides or heavy metals in our coastal waters may first affect the food of cetaceans and so have important indirect effects that might otherwise go unnoticed. All these aspects point to the need for vigilance if we are to protect the whales and dolphins that come into contact with us.

11 Postscript

Prehistoric man, on putting to sea, almost certainly found an ocean abounding with whales and dolphins. In the 4,000 years that man has known these animals, he has thrown everything he can at them to cause their destruction. He has hunted population after population, and species after species of the great whales until bringing some to the verge of extinction. Some of the greatest overexploitation occurred during the present century. The most important period of whaling throughout its history (by a factor of ten) was as recent as 30–50 years ago, within the lifetime of many of us (Figure 11.1). The present biomass of large whales is estimated to be about 23 million tonnes, about one-third the value around 1900. And some species, such as blue, humpback and right whales, have had their populations reduced to a few per cent of their numbers before exploitation (Table 11.1). Certain species are showing a few signs of recovery after protection. The gray whale appears to be increasing in the Northeast Pacific, humpbacks increasing slightly in the Northwest Atlantic, and right whales in the Northwest Atlantic and off South Africa. The blue whale, on the other hand, despite 20 years of protection, shows no sign of recovery. It may take a couple of hundred years for the species to return to anything like its former numbers. Indeed, it may never happen. The world's oceans are a different place to what they were before whaling, and different species have filled parts of the vacant niche that the demise of the great whales had left (see Table 10.1 in previous chapter).

The relentless pursuit of whales first for essential food but later for additional products is a blot on man's history. Yet we can see how economics have encouraged it, particularly in the last two centuries. The history of whaling is the history of man. Until he learns how to manage his resources wisely without the overexploitation that has characterised both whaling and fishing industries, he will always be in conflict with his environment. The blame does not lie with the Japanese or the Russians, the two main whaling nations today; it lies with everyone. The more developed a nation has been, the more damage it has wrought. Britain and Holland may be more responsible than any others for the near extinction of the right whales, at least in the North Atlantic. But other countries have in turn made significant impacts. The United States

Figure 11.1 Estimated decline of the great whales during the present century (from Beddington and May 1982). Precipitous decline in the stocks of blue, fin, humpback and sei whales since 1910, with apparent recent increase of minke whales. The figures are for Area IV of the Southern Ocean (between 70° and 130° E)

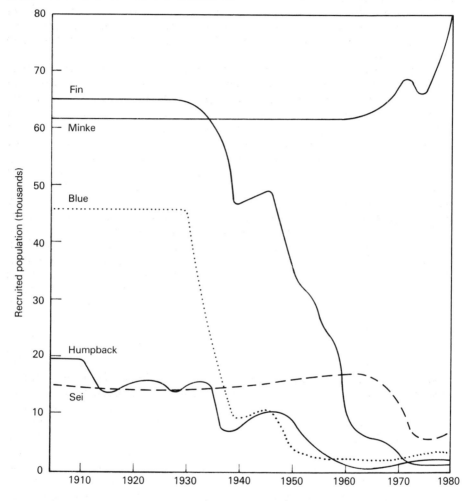

contributed to the decline of the great whales in the North Atlantic, but also dominated in the Pacific and Indian Oceans. With the advent of modern whaling about a century ago, Norway joined Britain to wreak havoc on the whales of the Southern Ocean. In recent years, the persistence of Norway and Iceland are presenting some of the biggest obstacles to protection of the remaining whales. The whale species closest to extinction is probably the bowhead. Were that to happen, the United States would be in the unhappy position of being finally responsible.

As I write this, the 38th meeting of the International Whaling Commission has just ended in Malmö, Sweden. The moratorium on commercial whaling that was voted in 1982 is now in effect, and will run at least to 1990. However, some of the major whaling nations may not abide by it. The Soviets and Japanese have promised to stop, but the

Norwegians continue. Norway presents its own population estimates to justify continued whaling of minke whales in the North Atlantic. On the grounds of 'scientific' whaling, Iceland and the Republic of Korea also intend to continue, with some compromise that such whales caught would be partly for local consumption. Much depends upon Japan and its trading for whale products, whilst the United States threaten an embargo on Norwegian fish exports, which amount to 70 times the value of their whale exports.

The justification of whaling on scientific grounds is a difficult one. It is certainly true that we need various biological parameters to monitor the population dynamics of any animal species. These include reproductive rates, estimates of survivorship and longevity, age of sexual and physical maturity, individual growth rates and, of course population estimates. In the past these have been derived from the whaling industry, but in recent years a number of vital parameters have been obtained without any harm to whales (Payne 1983; Perryman et al. 1984; Whitehead and Gordon 1986). Sightings surveys, the use of sidescan sonar and mark-resighting studies have together provided us with population estimates that are probably every bit as good as, if not better than, previous ones.

Some individuals of many whale species can be recognised individually by natural markings (Figure 11.2; and see p. 263 for references). This remains a problem for rorquals although techniques are being developed that will allow the identity of at least a minority of the population sampled. The individual recognition of animals is important for many studies, but some of the above biological information can be obtained without it. Sexing live whales has always been a problem because of the lack of secondary sexual characters, and it is rarely possible to see the genital organs of a whale as it swims (the penis is often tucked out of sight). Skin samples can be taken with a biopsy dart and analysed in the laboratory for sex chromatin bodies (Winn et al. 1973). However, this is laborious and not always practical. Recently, humpback whales have been sexed by swimming alongside and noting in ventral or lateral view the presence or absence of a hemispherical lobe behind the genital slit (Glockner 1983). This lobe is visible in females but absent in males. Similar studies need to be carried out on other species. These methods show promise for species like the right whales, gray whale and humpback, which are often slow-moving and more easily individually recognisable. But for the more elusive rorquals, we still have some way to go to finding suitable methods. That is not to say they do not exist. Often closer study has revealed some ingenious way to age, sex or individually recognise animals.

Age determination is in fact another problem. In toothed whales, it may be possible to extract a tooth whilst restraining a captured animal under anaesthetic. With baleen whales, the procurement of ear plugs is obviously not possible from living animals. Instead, one must rely upon following individuals of known age. This comes back to the need to mark whales individually, preferably soon after birth (another problem for rorquals that do not have discrete coastal breeding grounds) (Figure 11.3). If need be, they can be freeze-branded (Irvine and Wells 1972), or tagged either on the dorsal fin or with a plastic streamer, preferably with a unique marking (Evans et al. 1972; Irvine et al. 1982). The development of radio telemetry has helped study long-distance movements of a

Table 11.1: Past and present population estimates for the great whales

Whale species	Area	Pre-exploitation population	Present population	Per cent of pre-exploitation size	Year of full commercial protection
Sperm	S. hemi.	1,250,000	950,000	81	1985*
	N. hemi.	1,150,000	1,000,000		
Blue	S. hemi.	220,000	11,000	6	1967
	N. hemi	8,000	3,000		
Fin	S. hemi.	490,000	100,000	22	1986*
	N. hemi.	58,000	20,000		
Sei	S. hemi.	190,000	37,000	21	1986
	N. hemi.	66,000	17,000		
Bryde's	S. hemi.	30,000	30,000	100	1986*
	N. hemi.	60,000	60,000		
Minke	S.hemi.	350,000+	380,000	c.100	1986*
	N. hemi.	140,000	125,000		
Humpback	S. hemi.	100,000	3,000	9	1966*
	N. hemi.	15,000	7,000		
Gray	S. hemi.	–	–	<90	1935*
	N. hemi.	20,000+	18,000		
Bowhead	S. hemi.	–	–	15	1935*
	N. hemi.	30,000	4,400		
Right	S. hemi.	100,000	3,000	c.3	1935
	N. hemi.	?	1,000		

Reference source: International Whaling Commission (R. Gambell pers. comm.), based on recent published estimates or estimates provided to the IWC Scientific Committee.

Note: These estimates are in many cases very approximate, particularly those applied to pre-exploitation populations.

* = 'Subsistence' whaling permitted by IWC still takes bowheads (Alaska), gray whales (USSR and USA), minke and fin whales (Greenland). Similar whaling outside IWC regulations takes humpbacks (St Vincent), Bryde's, minke, fin and blue whales (occasionally off Indonesia).

Figure 11.2 Methods used to recognise cetaceans individually: (a) humpback tail flukes; (b) right whale head callosities; (c) dorsal fin variations. Species such as humpback and sperm whales often show their tail flukes when diving, enabling distinctive nicks along the trailing edge, or patterning of black, grey and white markings, to be recognised. Species such as right and gray whales have callosities distributed over their head, whose form and position can vary individually. Smaller species such as various small toothed whales and many dolphins may have individual scars over the head or back, and/or nicks in the dorsal fin, which in some cases allow individual recognition

number of whale and dolphin species (Evans 1974; Leatherwood and Evans 1979; Mate *et al.* 1983; Ray *et al.* 1978; Watkins *et al.* 1981). Transmitters have been made smaller, lighter and more streamlined so that they cause less hindrance; they are better waterproofed, and better attached (for small cetaceans, bolted through the dorsal fin if the animal has one, or mounted as a backpack on a harness; for large whales, implanted onto the back either by a long pole or by a dart, or as a suction tag fired from a crossbow). Gray whales tagged in this way with a 70g radio were tracked for 41 days at an average aerial range of 112km (Mate and Harvey 1984). Tracking such animals is expensive by boat or aeroplane, and the use of satellite radio telemetry on dolphins, gray whale and humpback whale have shown some promise (Jennings and Gandy 1980; Mate 1983, 1984).

Once sighted, the size of a whale or dolphin is obviously important for

Figure 11.3 Methods used to follow individuals: (a) 'Discovery' tag; (b) streamer tag; (c) numbered tag on dorsal fin; (d) freeze branding; (e) radio package. In addition to the use of natural markings, cetaceans may be marked for individual recognition using a variety of forms of tag (depending partly on species) or by freeze branding to kill those skin cells that produce pigment. Discovery tags work most successfully when fired deeper into the blubber so that rejection is less likely. However, they require the death of the animal to be re-sighted. Vinyl spaghetti streamers are more readily visible and may be colour-coded for limited individual recognition. Nylon button tags with numbers or letters give opportunities to mark more individuals uniquely. Cetaceans may actually be tracked by attachment of a radio, emitting signals at a particular sound frequency. The mode and site of attachment depends on the species but commonly the radio package is attached by bolts to the dorsal fin or blubber of the back. Recently, umbrella or barnacle tags have been used where several metal legs (holding a circular or rectangular plate) are embedded in the blubber and serve as anchors for the package. In the larger species, attachment is usually by firing from a special gun, although a 'remora' tag, which is fired from a crossbow and is held by a suction cup, has also recently been tested

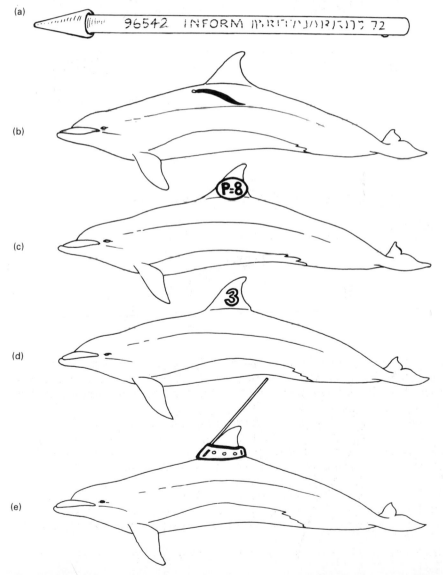

determining growth rates, particularly if it is individually recognisable. Various techniques have been developed using photogrammetry usually of the animal in lateral aspect near an object of known size (for example a floating sphere) (Whitehead and Payne 1981), but also from above by aerial stereo imagery (Cubbage and Rugh 1983). These have been mainly used on larger cetaceans, but could be used on dolphins particularly for comparison of calf to mother lengths.

In the last decade we have come a long way in the study of living whales and dolphins. The FAO Bergen meeting started a decade of scientific research on cetaceans which will hopefully continue if funds are obtained to put their Global Plan of Action into effect (Nielsen 1986). We have discovered a great deal about cetacean social organisation, and the exciting possibilities of the role of culture through acoustic mimicry in the evolution of the social behaviour of some of them. We still have a lot to learn – about mating systems, population substructuring in genetic terms, foraging behaviour and ecological parameters that determine their distribution, movements, breeding and feeding areas. We scarcely understand detailed aspects of their physiology, the mechanics of some of their senses and the precise roles they play in their lives. The more we learn the more we can marvel at the many remarkable adaptations that they have evolved for life in the sea.

Many people are now recognising cetaceans for their non-consumptive values, and whale-watching is becoming of some economic importance in areas such as Baja California (Mexico), Glacier Bay (Alaska), the Hawaiian Islands and Gulf of St Lawrence (Canada) (Barstow 1986). Sanctuaries have been set up or proposed in these and a number of other areas (Stellwagen Bank, off Cape Cod; Silver Bank, Dominican Republic; Madeiran Islands, off Northwest Africa).

On the negative side, however, the dangers of extinction through over-hunting still face a number of whales, and maybe always will. And we should not forget other modern pressures that man is imposing upon cetaceans, particularly the smaller species. It is perhaps remarkable that, despite man's attempts, no cetacean species has become extinct whilst man has been on this Earth (though the Atlantic population of the gray whale was apparently exterminated). This is testimony to the resilience of these slow-growing, slow-reproducing yet long-lived species. On the other hand, loss of habitat has probably caused more animal extinctions than any other human pressure. This, together with the combined effects of pollution, disturbance and conflicts with the fishing industry, probably represents the greatest threat to the future of many species. The river dolphins with their restricted habitat preferences, often close to man, are the most threatened. The baiji, and the Indus and Ganges susus among others may be extinct in a decade or two unless something drastic is done to save them. The coastal cetaceans, particularly the porpoises, are increasingly vulnerable and many are showing declines; the vaquita in the Gulf of California is considered by some to be the most endangered of all small cetaceans. We must act fast if our seas and coasts and rivers are to continue being graced by these fine creatures.

I have not done justice to the enormous amount of excellent work that is presently being carried out on all aspects of cetacean biology. However, I hope this brief synthesis will encourage the reader to take the subject further, following up studies through leads into the literature that I have provided. The next ten years promise to be a most exciting period in the development of our knowledge of whales and dolphins.

One of the most emotional moments of my life was six years ago, when in the company of long-finned pilot whales off the west coast of Ireland. I was moved not only by the power and grace of the whales themselves, but by the other humans with me and the feeling of elation that united all of us. I hope that everyone has the opportunity to share such experiences for a long time in the future.

Bibliography

Aguayo, L.A. (1975) 'Progress report on small cetacean research in Chile', *J. Fish. Res. Bd Can.*, *32*, 1123–43

Aguilar, A. (1981) 'The black right whale, *Eubalaena glacialis*, in the Cantabrian Sea', *Rep. Int. Whal. Commn*, *31*, 457–9

—— (1983) 'Organochlorine pollution in sperm whales, *Physeter macrocephalus*, from the temperate waters of the eastern North Atlantic', *Mar. Poll. Bull.*, *14*(9), 349–52

—— (1986) 'The common dolphin may be in trouble in the Mediterranean', *IUCN Cetacean Specialist Group Newsletter*, *2*, 5–6

Aguilar, A. and Jover, L. (1982) 'DDT and PCB residues in the fin whale, *Balaenoptera physalus*, of the North Atlantic', *Rep. Int. Whal. Commn*, *32*, 299–301

Aguilar, A., Grau, E., Sanpera, C., Jover, L. and Donovan, G. (1983) 'Report of the "Ballena 1" whale marking and sighting cruise in the waters off Western Spain', *Rep. Int. Whal. Commn*, *33*, 649–55

Aguilar, A., Sanpera, C., Grau, E., Jover, L. and Nadal, J. (1984) 'Resultados del crucero de investigacíon de cetáceos "Sur 82"', *Publ. Dept. Zool. Barcelona*, *10*, 93–100

Allen, K.R. (1966) 'Some methods for estimating exploited populations', *J. Fish Res. Bd Can.*, *23*, 553–74

—— (1968) 'Simplification of a method of computing recruitment rates', *J. Fish. Res. Bd Can.*, *25*, 2701–2

—— (1976) 'A more flexible model for baleen whale populations', *Rep. Int. Whal. Commn*, *26*, 247–63

—— (1980) *Conservation and Management of Whales*, University of Washington Press, Seattle, Wash.

—— (1981) 'The optimization of management strategy for marine mammals', *FAO Fish. Ser.* (5), [*Mammals in the Seas*] *3*, 77–91

Allen, K.R. and Kirkwood, G.P. (1977) 'Further development of sperm whale population models', *Rep. Int. Whal. Commn*, *27*, 106–12

Allen, P., Compton-Bishop, Q. and Gordon, J. (1980) 'Cambridge Azores Expedition Report', unpublished report, University of Cambridge, Cambridge

Allen, R.L. (1985) 'Dolphins and the purse-seine fishery for yellowfin tuna', in Beddington, J.R., Beverton, R.J.H. and Lavigne, D.M. (eds.), *Marine Mammals and Fisheries*, George Allen and Unwin, London, pp. 236–52

Alling, A., Gilligan, P.R., Gordon, J.C.D. and Papastavrou, V. (1984) 'WWF/IUCN Indian Ocean sperm whale project', unpublished report, Cambridge

Alpers, A. (1960) *Dolphins: The Myth and the Mammal*, Houghton Mifflin, Cambridge, Mass.

Aminul Haque, A.K.M., Nishiwaki, M., Kasuya, T. and Tobayama, T. (1977) 'Observations on the behaviour and other biological aspects of the Ganges susu, *Platanista gangetica*', *Sci. Rep. Whales Res. Inst., Tokyo*, *29*, 87–94

Arkowitz, R. and Rommel, S. (1985) 'Force and bending moment of the caudal muscles in the shortfin pilot whale', *Marine Mammal Science*, *1*(3), 203–9

Arnason, U. (1974) 'Comparative chromosome studies in Cetacea', *Hereditas*, *77*, 1–36

Alzieu, C. and Duguy, R. (1978a) 'Teneurs en composés organochlorines chez les cétacés et pinnipèdes frequentant les côtes françaises', *Cons. Int. l'Explor. Mer., Doc. C.M.* 1978/N:8
—— (1978b) 'Contamination du dauphin bleu et blanc de Mediterranée *Stenella coeruleoalba* par les composes organochlorines', XXVIe Congrès, Assemblée plenière, Antalya, 24 novembre–2 décembre 1978
—— (1979) 'Teneurs en composes organochlores chez les cétacés et pinnipedes frequentant les côtes françaises', *Oceanol. Acta*, 2(1), 107–20
—— (1981) 'Nouvelles données sur la contamination des cétacés par les organochlores', *Cons. Int. l'Explor. Mer., Doc. C.M.* 1981/N:8
Arnbom, T., Papastaurou, V., Weilgart, L. and Whitehead, H. (1987) 'Sperm whales react to an attack by killer whales', *J. Mammal.*, 68
Au, D. and Perryman, W. (1982) 'Movement and speed of dolphin schools responding to an approaching ship', *Fish. Bull., U.S.*, 80, 371–9
Au, D. and Weihs, D. (1980) 'At high speeds dolphins save energy by leaping', *Nature, Lond.*, 284, 548–50
Au, W.W.L., Floyd, R.W., Penner, R.H. and Murchison, A.E. (1974) 'Measurement of echolocation signals of the Atlantic bottlenose dolphin, *Tursiops truncatus* Montagu, in open waters', *J. Acoust. Soc. Am.*, 56, 1280–90
Au, W.W.L., Penner, R.H. and Kadane, J. (1982) 'Acoustic behavior of echolocating Atlantic bottlenose dolphins', *J. Acoust. Soc. Am.*, 71, 1269–75
Awbrey, F.T., Thomas, J.A., Evans, W.E. and Leatherwood, S. (1982) 'Ross Sea killer whale vocalizations: preliminary description and comparison with those of some Northern Hemisphere killer whales', *Rep. Int. Whal. Commn*, 32, 667–70
Bailey, N.J.T. (1951) 'On estimating the size of mobile populations from recapture data', *Biometrika*, 38, 293–306
Baker, A.N. (1972) 'New Zealand whales and dolphins', *Tuatara*, 20, 1–49.
—— (1977) 'Spectacled porpoise, *Phocoena dioptrica*, new to the subantarctic Pacific Ocean', *N.Z. J. mar. Freshwat. Res.*, 11, 401–6.
—— (1978) 'The status of Hector's dolphin *Cephalorhynchus hectori* (Van Beneden) in New Zealand waters', *Rep. Int. Whal. Commn*, 28, 331–4
—— (1981) 'The southern right whale dolphin, *Lissodelphis peronii* (Lacépède) in Australasian waters', *Natl. Museum of N.Z. Records*, 2(4), 17–34
—— (1983) *Whales and Dolphins of New Zealand and Australia*, Victoria University Press, Victoria
—— (1985) 'The pygmy right whale', in Harrison, R.J. and Ridgway, S.H. (eds.), *Handbook of Marine Mammals, Vol. 3*, Academic Press, London, pp. 345–54
Baker, C.S. and Herman, L.M. (1984) 'Aggressive behavior between humpback whales (*Megaptera novaeangliae*) on the Hawaiian wintering grounds', *Can. J. Zool.*, 62, 1922–37
Baker, C.S., Herman, L.M. and Stifel, W.S. (1981) 'Agonistic behavior in humpback whales: evidence for male-male competition'. *Abstract, Proc. of 4th Biennial Conf. on the Biology of Marine Mammals*, 14–18 Dec. 1981, San Francisco, Calif.
Baker, C.S., Herman, L.M., Bays, B.G. and Stifel, W.S. (1982) 'The impact of vessel traffic on the behavior of humpback whales in Southeast Alaska: 1981 season', Report to the National Marine Mammal Laboratory, Seattle, Wash.
Baker, C.S., Herman, L.M., Bays, B.G. and Bauer, G.B. (1983) 'The impact of vessel traffic on the behavior of humpback whales in Southeast Alaska: 1982 season', Report to the National Marine Mammal Laboratory, Seattle, Wash.
Balcomb, K., Boran, J. and Osborne, R. (1979) 'Killer whales, *Orcinus orca*, in Greater Puget Sound', *Abstract, Proc. of 3rd Biennial Conference on the Biology of Marine Mammals*, 7–11 Oct. 1979, Seattle, Wash.
Balcomb, K.C., Boran, J.R., Osborne, R.W. and Haenel, N.J. (1980) 'Observations of killer whales (*Orcinus orca*) in greater Puget Sound, state of Washington', U.S. Dep. Commer., NTIS PB80–224728
Bannister, J.L. (1977) 'Incidental catches of small cetacea off Australia', *Rep. Int. Whal. Commn*, 27, 506
Barger, J.E. and Hamblen, W.R. (1980) 'The air gun impulsive underwater transducer', *J. Acoust. Soc. Am.*, 68, 1038–45
Barlow, J. (1984) 'Reproductive seasonality in pelagic dolphins (*Stenella* spp.): implications for measuring rates', *Rep. Int. Whal. Commn (special issue 6)*, 191–8
Barnes, L.G. (1977) 'Outline of eastern North Pacific fossil cetacean assemblages', *Syst. Zool.*, 25(4) (for Dec 1976), 321–43
—— (1978) 'A review of *Lophocetus* and *Liolithax* and their relationships to the delphinoid Family Kentriodontidae (Cetacea: Odontoceti), *Nat. Hist. Mus. Los Ang. Co. Sci. Bull.*, 28, 1–35

—— (1984a) 'Whales, dolphins and porpoises: origin and evolution of the Cetacea', in Broadhead, T.W. (ed.), Mammals. Notes for a short course organized by P.D. Gingerich and C.E. Badgley, University of Tennessee Department of Geological Sciences, *Studies in Geology*, 8, 139–54

—— (1984b) 'Fossil odontocetes (Mammalia: Cetacea) from the Almejas Formation, Isla Cedros, Mexico', *PaleoBios*, Museum of Paleontology, University of California, *42*, 1–46

—— (1984c) 'Search for the first whale: retracing the ancestry of cetaceans', *Oceans*, *17*(2), 20–3

—— (1985) 'Evolution, taxonomy, and antitropical distributions of the porpoises (Phocoenidae, Mammalia)', *Marine Mammal Science*, *1*(2), 149–65

Barnes, L.G. and McLeod, S.A. (1984) 'The fossil record and phyletic relationships of gray whales', in Jones, M.L., Swartz, S.L. and Leatherwood, S. (eds.), *The Gray Whale Eschrichtius robustus*, Academic Press, New York, NY, pp. 3–32

Barnes, L.G. and Mitchell, E.D. (1978) 'Cetacea', in Maglio, V.J. and Cooke, H.B.S. (eds.), *Evolution of African Mammals*, Harvard University Press, Cambridge, Mass., pp. 582–602

Barnes, L.G., Domning, D. and Ray, C. (1985) 'Status of studies on fossil marine mammals', *Marine Mammal Science*, *1*(1), 15–53

Barstow, R. (1986) 'Non-consumptive utilization of whales', *Ambio*, *15*, 155–60

Bastian, J. (1967) 'The transmission of arbitrary environmental information between bottlenose dolphins', in Busnel, R-G. (ed.), *Animal Sonar Systems*, Vol. II, Laboratoire de Physiologie Acoustique, Jouy-en-Josas, France, pp. 803–73

Bateson, G. (1966) 'Problems in cetacean and other mammalian communication', in Norris, K.S. (ed.), *Whales, Dolphins, and Porpoises*, University of California Press, Berkeley, Calif., pp. 569–82

—— (1974) 'Observations of a cetacean community', in McIntyre, J. (ed.), *Mind in the Waters*, McClelland and Stewart, Toronto, pp. 146- 65

Bauer, G.B., Fuller, M., Perry, A., Dunn, J.R. and Zoeger, J. (1986) 'Magnetoreception and biomineralization of magnetite in cetaceans', in Kirschvink, J.L., Jones, D.S. and MacFadden, B.J. (eds.), *Magnetite biomineralization and magnetoreception in living organisms*, Plenum Press, NY, pp. 489–508

Beamish, P. and Mitchell, E. (1971) 'Ultrasonic sounds recorded in the presence of a blue whale (*Balaenoptera musculus*)', *Deep Sea Research*, *25*, 469–72

Beddington, J.R. (1979) 'On some problems of estimating population abundance from catch data', *Rep. Int. Whal. Commn*, *29*, 149–54

Beddington, J.R. and Cooke, J.G. (1981) 'Development of an assessment technique for male sperm whales based on the use of length data from the catches, with special reference to the North West Pacific', *Rep. Int. Whal. Commn*, *31*, 747–60

Beddington, J.R. and de la Mare, W. (1985) 'Marine mammal fishery interactions: modelling and the Southern Ocean', in Beddington, J.R., Beverton, R.J.H. and Lavigne, D.M. (eds.), *Marine Mammals and Fisheries*, George Allen and Unwin, London, pp. 143–64

Beddington, J.R. and May, R.M. (1977) 'Harvesting natural populations in a random fluctuating environment', *Science*, *197*, 463–5

—— (1982) 'The harvesting of interacting species in a natural ecosystem', *Sc. Amer.*, Nov 1982, 1–8

Bel'kovich, V.M. and Yablokov, A.V. (1963) 'The whale — an ultrasonic projector', *Yuchnyi Teknik*, 3, 76–7

Benjaminsen, T. (1972) 'On the biology of the bottlenose whale, *Hyperoodon ampullatus* (Forster)', *Norw. J. Zool.* 20(3), 233–41

Bengtson, J.L. and Laws, R.M. (1984) 'Trends in crabeater age at maturity: an insight into Antarctic marine interactions' in Siegfried, W.R., Candy, P.R. and Laws, R.M. (eds.), *Antarctic Nutrient Cycles and Food Chains*, Proc., 4th SCAR Symposium on Antarctic Biology, Springer Verlag, Berlin, pp. 669–75

Benjaminsen, T. and Christensen, I. (1979) 'The natural history of the bottlenose whale *Hyperoodon ampullatus*', in Winn, H.E. and Olla, B.L. (eds.), *Behavior of Marine Animals*, Vol. 3: *Cetaceans*, Plenum Press, New York, NY, pp. 143–64

Berzin, A.A. (1972) *The Sperm Whale*, Israel Program for Scientific Translation, Jerusalem

—— (1978) 'Whale distribution in tropical Eastern Pacific waters', *Rep. Int. Whal. Commn*, 28, 173–7

Berzin, A.A. and Vladimirov, V.L. (1981) 'Changes in the abundance of whalebone whales in the Pacific and the Antarctic since the cessation of their exploitation', *Rep. Int. Whal. Commn*, 31, 495–9

Best, P.B. (1967) 'Distribution and feeding habits of baleen whales off the Cape Province', *Division of Sea Fisheries Investigational Report South Africa*, 57, 1–44
—— (1971) 'Order Cetacea', in Meester, J. and Setzer, H.W. (eds.), *The Mammals of Africa: An Identification Manual*, part 7, Smithsonian Institution, Washington, DC, pp. 1–11
—— (1974) 'The biology of the sperm whale as it relates to stock management', in Schevill, W.E. (ed.), *The Whale Problem: A Status Report*, Harvard University Press, Cambridge, Mass.
—— (1975) 'Death-time for whales killed by explosive harpoons', *Rep. Int. Whal. Commn*, 25, 208–14
—— (1976) 'Tetracycline marking and the rate of growth layer formation in the teeth of a dolphin (*Lagenorhynchus obscurus*)', *S. Afr. J. Sci.*, 72, 216–18
—— (1977) 'Two allopatric forms of Bryde's whale off South Africa', *Rep. Int. Whal. Commn (special issue 1)*, 10–38
—— (1979) 'Social organization in sperm whales, *Physeter macrocephalus*', in Winn, H.E. and Olla, B.L. (eds.), *Behavior of Marine Animals, Vol. 3: Cetaceans*, Plenum Press, New York, NY, pp. 227–89
—— (1981) 'The status of right whales (*Eubalaena glacialis*) off South Africa, 1969–1979', *Investl Rep. Sea Fish. Inst. S. Afr.*, 123, 1–44
—— (1982) 'Seasonal abundance, feeding, reproduction, age and growth in minke whales off Durban (with incidental observations from the Antarctic)', *Rep. Int. Whal. Commn*, 32, 759–86
—— and Ross, G. (1984) 'Live-capture fishery for small cetaceans in South African waters', *Rep. Int. Whal. Commn*, 34, 615–18.
Best, P.B., Canham, P.A.S. and Macleod, N. (1984) 'Patterns of reproduction in sperm whales, *Physeter macrocephalus*', *Rep. Int. Whal. Commn* (special issue 6), 51–79
Best, R. and Fisher, H.D. (1974) 'Seasonal breeding of the narwhal (*Monodon monoceros* L.)', *Can. J. Zool.*, 52, 429–31
Best, R.C. and da Silva, V.M.F. (1984) 'Preliminary analysis of reproductive parameters of the boutu, *Inia geoffrensis*, and the tucuxi, *Sotalia fluviatilis*, in the Amazon river system', *Rep. Int. Whal. Commn* (special issue 6), 361–9
—— (1986) 'Yangtse perspective on Amazon dolphins', *Wildlife*, 4(10), 502–3
Bigg, M.A. (1979) 'Interaction between pods of killer whales off British Columbia and Washington', *Abstract, Proc. of 3rd Biennial Conference of the Biology of Marine Mammals*, 7–11 Oct. 1979, Seattle, Wash.
—— (1982) 'An assessment of killer whale (*Orcinus orca*) stocks off Vancouver Island, British Columbia', *Rep. Int. Whal. Commn*, 32, 655–66
Bigg, M.A., MacAskie, I.B. and Ellis, G. (1976) 'Abundance and movements of killer whales off eastern and southern Vancouver Island with comments on management', unpublished manuscript, Arctic Biological Station, Ste Anne de Bellevue, Quebec, Canada
Blokhin, S.A. (1984) 'Investigations of gray whales taken in the Chukchi coastal waters, U.S.S.R.', in Jones, M.L., Swartz, S.L. and Leatherwood, S. (eds.), *The Gray Whale Eschrichtius robustus*, Academic Press, New York, NY. pp. 487–509
Blokhin, S.A., Maminov, M.K. and Kosygin, G.M. (1985) 'On the Korean-Okhotsk population of gray whales', *Rep. Int. Whal. Commn*, 35, 375–6
Bockstoce, J. (1986) *Whales, Ice, and Men: the History of Whaling in the Western Arctic*, University of Washington Press, Seattle, Wash.
Bogoslovskaya, L.S., Votrogov, L.M. and Semenova, T.N. (1981) 'Feeding habits of the gray whales off the Chukotka peninsula', *Rep. Int. Whal. Commn*, 31, 507–10
Boran, J.R., Felleman, F.L., Heimlich, S.L. and Osborne, R.W. (1981) 'Habitat use of Puget Sound killer whales', *Abstract, Proc. of 4th Biennial Conference on the Biology of Marine Mammals*, 14–18 Dec. 1981, San Francisco, Calif.
Boschung, H.T. Jr, Caldwell, D.K., Caldwell, M.C., Gotshall, D.W. and Williams, J.D. (1983) *The Audubon Society Field Guide to North American Fishes, Whales and Dolphins*, Alfred A. Knopf, New York, NY
Bossart, G.D., Altman, N.H. and Odell, D.K. (1983) 'A cardiomyopathy complex in stranded pygmy sperm whales (*Kogia breviceps*)', *Abstract, Proc. of 5th Biennial Conference on the Biology of Marine Mammals*, 27 Nov–1 Dec. 1983, Boston, Mass.
Boulva, J. (1981) 'Catch statistics of beluga (*Delphinapterus leucas*) in northern Quebec: 1974 to 1976 final; 1977 to 1978 preliminary', *Rep. Int. Whal. Commn*, 31, 531–8
Braham, H.W. (1984) 'Review of reproduction in the white whale, *Delphinapterus leucas*, Narwhal, *Monodon monoceros*, and Irrawaddy Dolphin, *Orcaella brevirostris*, with comments on stock assessment', *Rep. Int. Whal. Commn* (special issue 6), 81–9
Bree, P.J.H. van (1977) 'On former and recent strandings of cetaceans on the coast of the

Netherlands', *Zeitschrift fur Saugetierkunde, 42,* 101–7

Brodie, P.F. (1971) 'A reconsideration of aspects of growth, reproduction, and behavior of the white whale (*Delphinapterus leucas*) with reference to the Cumberland Sound, Baffin Island, population', *J. Fish. Res. Bd Can., 28,* 13091-18

—— (1975) 'Cetacean energetics, an overview of intraspecific size variation', *Ecology, 56,* 152–61

Brodie, P.F. and Paasche, A. (1985) 'Thermoregulation and energetics of fin and sei whales based on postmortem, stratified temperature measurements', *Can. J. Zool., 63,* 2267–9

Brown, D.H. and Norris, K.S. (1956) 'Observations of captive and wild cetaceans', *J. Mammal., 37,* 311–26

Brown, R.G.B. (1980) 'Seabirds as marine animals', in Burger, J., Olla, B.L., and Winn, H.E. (eds.), *Behavior of Marine Animals, Vol. 4: Marine Birds*, Plenum Press, New York, NY, pp. 1–39

Brown, S.G. (1976) 'Modern whaling in Britain and the north-east Atlantic Ocean', *Mammal Rev., 6*(1), 25–36

—— (1977) 'Some results of sei whale marking in the Southern Hemisphere', *Rep. Int. Whal. Commn* (special issue 1), 39–43

—— (1978) 'Whale marking techniques', in Stonehouse, B. (ed.), *Animal Marking*, Macmillan, London, pp. 71–80

—— (1982) 'Southern right whale dolphins off the South West Africa coast', *The Marine Observer, 52,* 33–4

Brown, S.G. and Lockyer, C.H. (1984) 'Whales', in Laws, R.M. (ed.), *Antarctic Ecology, Vol. 2*, Academic Press, London, pp. 717–81

Brownell, R.L. Jr. (1974) 'Small odontocetes of the Antarctic', in *Antarctic Mammals*, Antarct. Map Folio Series, *Folio 18*, Amer. Geogr. Soc., New York, NY, pp. 13–19

—— (1982) 'Status of the cochito, *Phocoena sinus*, in the Gulf of California', *FAO Fish. Ser. (5), [Mammals in the Seas] 4,* 85–90

—— (1983) '*Phocoena sinus*', *Mammalian Species (198),* 1–3

—— (1984) 'Review of platanistid dolphins', *Rep. Int. Whal. Commn* (special issue 6), 149–58

Brownell, R.L. Jr and Chun, C. (1977) 'Probable existence of the Korean stock of the gray whale (*Eschrichtius robustus*)', *J. Mammal., 58*(2), 237–9

Brownell, R.L. Jr and Praderi, R. (1976) 'Present research and conservation problems with the franciscana, *Pontoporia blainvillei* in Uruguayan waters', paper presented at the ACMRR Scientific Consultation on the conservation and management of marine mammals and their environment, 31 Aug–9 Sept. 1976, Bergen, Norway. FAO ACMRR/MM/SC/19 (mimeo)

—— (1982) 'Status of Burmeister's porpoise, *Phocoena spinipinnis*, in southern South American waters', *FAO Fish. Ser. (5), [Mammals in the Seas] 4,* 91–6

—— (1985) 'Distribution of Commerson's dolphin, *Cephalorhynchus commersonii*, and the rediscovery of the type of *Lagenorhynchus floweri*', *Sci. Rep. Whales Res. Inst., Tokyo, 36,* 153–64

Brownell, R.L., Jr. and Ralls, K. (1986) 'Potential for sperm competition in baleen whales', *Rep. Int. Whal. Commn* (special issue 8), 97–112

Bryan, G.W. (1976) 'Heavy metal contamination in the sea', in Johnston, R. (ed.), *Marine Pollution*, Academic Press, London, pp. 185–302

Bryant, P.J., Nichols, G., Bryant, T.B. and Miller, K. (1981) 'Krill availability and the distribution of humpback whales in southeastern Alaska'. *J. Mammal., 62*(2), 427–30

Bryden, M.M., Harrison, R.J. and Lear, R.J. (1977) 'Some aspects of the biology of *Peponocephala electra*, on the east coast of Australia', *J. Mammal. 58,* 180–7

Budylenko, G.A. (1977) 'Distribution and composition of sei whale schools in the southern hemisphere', *Rep. Int. Whal. Commn* (special issue 1), 121–3

Burnham, K.P., Anderson, D.R. and Laake, J.L. (1980) 'Estimation of density from line transect sampling of biological populations', *Wildl. Monogr., 44,* 1–202

Busnel, R.-G. (1973) 'Symbiotic relationship between man and dolphins', *Ann. N.Y. Acad. Sci., 35,* 112–31

Busnel, R.-G. and Dziedzic, A. (1966) 'Acoustic signals of the pilot whale *Globicephala melaena*, and of the porpoises *Delphinus delphis* and *Phocoena phocoena*', in Norris, K.S. (ed.), *Whales, Dolphins and Porpoises*, University of California Press, Berkeley, Calif., pp. 607–46

Cadenat, J. (1959) 'Rapport sur les petits cétacés ouest-africains. Résultats des recherches sur ces animaux jusqu'au mois de mars 1959', *Bull. Inst. Fondam. Afr. Noire (A. Sci. Nat.), 21,* 1367–427

Caldwell, D.K. and Caldwell, M.C. (1972a) *The World of the Bottlenosed Dolphin*, Lippincott, New York. NY
—— (1972b) 'Senses and communication', in Ridgway, S.H. (ed.), *Mammals of the Sea; Biology and Medicine*, Charles C. Thomas, Springfield, Ill., pp. 466–502
—— (1975) 'Dolphin and small whale fisheries of the Caribbean and West Indies: occurrence, history, and catch statistics — with special reference to the Lesser Antillean island of St. Vincent', *J. Fish. Res. Bd Can.*, 32, 1105–10
—— (1983) *A Field Guide to Marine Mammals of the Southeastern United States and Caribbean Basin*, US Dept. of Commerce, NOAA, National Marine Fisheries Center, Miami, Fla.
Caldwell, M.C. and Caldwell, D.K. (1966) 'Epimeletic (care-giving) behaviour in Cetacea', in Norris, K.S. (ed.), *Whales, Dolphins, and Porpoises*, University of California Press, Berkeley & Los Angeles, Calif. pp. 755–89
—— (1967) 'Intraspecific transfer of information via pulsed sound in captive odontocete cetaceans', in Busnel, R.-G. (ed.), *Animal Sonar Systems: Biology and Bionics*, Laboratoire de Physiologie Acoustique, Jouy-en-Josas, France, pp. 879–936
—— (1970) 'Statistical evidence for individual signature whistles in the Pacific whitesided dolphin, *Lagenorhynchus obliquidens*', *Los Angeles County Mus. Nat. His. Foundation, Tech. Report No. 9*, pp. 1–18
—— (1972) 'Behavior of marine mammals', in Ridgway, S.H. (ed.), *Mammals of the Sea: Biology and Medicine*, Charles C. Thomas, Springfield, Ill., pp. 419–65
—— (1977) 'Social interactions and reproduction in the Atlantic bottlenosed dolphin', in Ridgway, S.H. and Benirschke, K.W. (eds.), *Breeding Dolphins: Present Status, Suggestions for the Future*. Marine Mammal Commission Report MMC-76/07, Washington, DC, pp. 133–42
—— (1979) 'The whistle of the Atlantic bottlenosed dolphin (*Tursiops truncatus*) — ontogeny', in Winn, H.E. and Olla, B.L. (eds.), *Behavior of Marine Animals, Vol. 3: Cetaceans*, Plenum Press, New York, NY, pp. 369–401
Caldwell, M.C., Caldwell, D.K. and Siebenaler, J.B. (1965) 'Observations on captive and wild Atlantic bottlenosed dolphins, *Tursiops truncatus*, in the Northeastern Gulf of Mexico', *Los Ang. Cty. Mus. Nat. Hist. Contrib. Sci.*, 91, 1–10
Casinos, A. (1981) 'On the distribution of *Globicephala melaena* (Traill, 1804) (Cetacea, Delphinidae) in the south-west Atlantic', *Sonderbruck aus Z. f. Saugetierkunde Bd.*, 46(4), 268–71
Casinos, A. and Vericad, J.-R. (1976) 'The cetaceans of the Spanish coasts: a survey', *Mammalia*, 40, 267–89
Cawthorn, M. (1978) 'Whale Research in New Zealand', *Rep. Int. Whal. Commn*, 28, 109–13
—— (1979) 'New Zealand progress report on cetacean research June 1977–May 1978', *Rep. Int. Whal. Commn*, 29, 123–5
Chapman, D.G. (1970) 'Re-analysis of Antarctic fin whale population data', *Rep. Int. Whal. Commn*, 20, 54–9
—— (1974) 'Estimation of population size and sustainable yield of sei whales in the Antarctic', *Rep. Int. Whal. Commn*, 24, 82–90
—— (1977) 'The Alaska bowhead whale controversy', *Marine Mammal Information, Dec 1977*, 1–2
Chapman, D.G., Allen, K.R. and Holt, S.J. (1964) 'Reports of the Committee of Three Scientists on the special scientific investigation of the Antarctic whale stocks', *Rep. Int. Whal. Commn*, 14, 32–106
Chen, P., Peilin, L., Renjun, L. and Kejie, L. (1979) *Distribution, Ecology, Behavior and Conservation of the Dolphins of the Middle Reaches of Changjiang (Yangtze River) (Wuhan-Yueyang)*, Institute of Hydrobiology, Academia Sinica, Wuhan (China)
Chen, P.-X., Liu, R.-J. and Lin, K.-J. (1984) 'Reproduction and the reproductive system in the beiji, *Lipotes vexillifer*', *Rep. Int. Whal. Commn* (special issue 6), 445–50
Chittleborough, R.G. (1959) 'Determination of age in the humpback whale, *Megaptera nodosa* (Bonnaterre)', *Aust. J. mar. Freshwat. Res.*, 10, 125–43
—— (1965) 'Dynamics of two populations of the humpback whale, *Megaptera novaeangliae* (Borowski)', *Aust. J. mar. Freshwat. Res.*, 16, 33–128
Christensen, I. (1973) 'Age determination, age distribution and growth of bottlenose whales, *Hyperoodon ampullatus* (Forster), in the Labrador Sea', *Norw. J. Zool.*, 21, 331–40
—— (1975) 'Preliminary report on the Norwegian fishery for small whales: expansion of Norwegian whaling to arctic and northwest Atlantic waters, and Norwegian investigations of the biology of small whales', *J. Fish. Res. Bd Can.*, 32, 1083–94
—— (1977) 'Observations of whales in the North Atlantic', *Rep. Int. Whal. Commn*, 27, 388–99

—— (1978) 'The killer whale (*Orcinus orca*) in the northeast Atlantic', *Fisker Hav.*, (*1*), 23–31.

—— (1980) 'Observations of large whales (minke not included) in the north Atlantic 1976–1978 and markings of fin, sperm, and humpback whales in 1978', *Rep. Int. Whal. Commn*, *30*, 205–8.

—— (1982) 'Killer whales in Norwegian coastal waters', *Rep. Int. Whal. Commn*, *32*, 633–42

—— (1984) 'Growth and reproduction of killer whales, *Orcinus orca*, in Norwegian coastal waters', *Rep. Int. Whal. Commn* (special issue 6), 253–8

Clark, C.W. (1975) *Mathematical Bioeconomics: The Optimal Management of Renewable Resources*, Wiley, New York, NY

—— (1981) 'Economic aspects of renewable resource exploitation as applied to marine mammals', *FAO Fish. Series* (5) [*Mammals in the Seas*] 3, 7–19

Clark, C.W. (1983) 'Acoustic communication and behavior of the southern right whale (*Eubalaena australis*)', in Payne, R. (ed.), *Communication and Behavior of Whales*, AAAS Selected Symposium 76, Westview Press, Col., pp. 163–98

Clark, C.W. and Clark, J.M. (1980) 'Sound playback experiments with southern right whales (*Eubalaena australis*)', *Science*, *207*, 663–5

Clark, C.W. and Johnson, J.H. (1984) 'The sounds of the bowhead whale, *Balaena mysticetus*, during the spring migrations of 1979 and 1980', *Can. J. Zool.*, *62*, 1436–41

Clark, J.G.D. (1947) 'Whales as an economic factor in prehistoric Europe', *Antiquity*, *21*, 84–104

Clarke, A. (1980) 'The biochemical composition of krill, *Euphausia superba*, Dana, from South Georgia', *J. Exp. Mar. Biol. and Ecol.*, *43*, 221–36

Clarke, A. and Prince, P.A. (1980) Chemical composition and calorific value of food fed to mollymauk chicks *Diomedea melanophris* and *D. chrysostoma* at Bird Island, South Georgia', *Ibis*, *122*, 488–94

Clarke, A., Clarke, M.R., Holmes, L.J. and Waters, T.D. (1985) 'Calorific values and elemental analysis of eleven species of oceanic squids (Mollusca: Cephalopoda)', *J. mar. biol. Ass. U.K.*, *65*, 983–6

Clarke, M.R. (1978) 'Buoyancy control as a function of the spermaceti organ in the sperm whale', *J. mar. biol. Ass. U.K.*, *58*, 27–71

—— (1979) 'The head of the sperm whale', *Sc. Am.*, *240*(1), 106–17

—— (1980) 'Cephalopoda in the diet of sperm whales of the southern hemisphere and their bearing on sperm whale biology', *Discovery Rep.*, *37*, 1–324

—— (1983) 'Cephalopod biomass — Estimation from predation', *Mem. Nat. Mus. Victoria*, *44*, 95–107

—— (1986) 'Cephalopods in the diet of odontocetes', in Bryden, M.M. and Harrison, R.J. (eds.), *Research on Dolphins*, Clarendon Press, Oxford, pp. 281–322

Clarke, R. (1956) 'Sperm whales of the Azores', *Discovery Rep.*, *28*, 237–98

Collet, A. (1981) 'Biologie du dauphin commun *Delphinus delphis* L. en Atlantique Nord-Est', Doctoral thesis, University of Poitiers

Condy, P.R. (1977) 'Whale observations in the pack ice off the Fimbul Ice Shelf, Antarctica', *S. Afr. J. Antarct. Res.*, *7*, 7–9

Condy, P.R., van Aarde, R.J. and Bester, M.N. (1978) 'The seasonal occurrence and behaviour of killer whales *Orcinus orca*, at Marion Island', *J. Zool., Lond.*, *184*, 449–64

Connor, R.C. and Norris, K.S. (1982) 'Are dolphins reciprocal altruists?', *Amer. Natur.*, *119*, 358–74

Cooke, J.G. (1985) 'Has the age at sexual maturity of southern hemisphere minke whales declined?', *Rep. Int. Whal. Commn*, *35*, 335–340

Cooke, J.G. and Beddington, J.R. (1981) 'Further development of an assessment technique for male sperm whales based on length data from the catches', *Rep. Int. Whal. Commn*, *32*, 239–42

Cooke, J.G. and de la Mare, W.K. (1983) 'The effects of variability in age data on the estimation of biological parameters of minke whales (*Balaenoptera acutorostrata*)', *Rep. Int. Whal. Commn*, *33*, 333–8

Cooke, J.G., de la Mare, W.K. and Beddington, J.R. (1983) 'An extension of the Sperm Whale Model for the simulation of the male population by length and age', *Rep. Int. Whal. Commn*, *33*, 731–3

Cornell, L.H. (1984) 'Census of captive marine mammals', *Am. Assoc. Zool. Parks Aquariums Ann. Proc.*, 246–52

Cowan, D.F., Walker, W.A. and Brownell, R.J. Jr (1986) 'Pathology of small cetaceans stranded along Southern California beaches', in Bryden, M.M. and Harrison, R.J. (eds.),

Research on Dolphins, Clarendon Press, Oxford, pp. 323–68

Croxall, J.P. (1984) 'Seabirds', in Laws, R.M. (ed.), *Antarctic Ecology, Vol. 2*, Academic Press, London, pp. 533–616

Croxall, J.P. and Prince, P.A. (1982) 'Calorific content of squid (Mollusca: Cephalopoda)', *Br. Antarct. Surv. Bull.*, 55, 27–31

Cubbage, J.C. and Rugh, D.J. (1983) 'Stereo imagery in size measurement of bowhead whales', *Abstract, Proc. of 5th Biennial Conference on the Biology of Marine Mammals*, 27 Nov–1 Dec. 1983, Boston, Mass.

Cummings, W.C. (1985) 'Right whales *Eubalaena glacialis (Muller, 1776) and Eubalaena australis* (Desmoulins, 1822)', in Ridgway, S.H. and Harrison, R.J. (eds.), *Handbook of Marine Mammals, Volume 3: The Sirenians and Baleen Whales*, Academic Press, Orlando, Fla, pp. 275–304

Cummings, W.C. and Thompson, P.O. (1971a) 'Underwater sounds from the blue whale, *Balaenoptera musculus*', *J. Acoust. Soc. Am.*, 50, 1193–8

—— (1971b) 'Gray whale, *Eschrichtius robustus*, avoid the underwater sounds of killer whales, *Orcinus orca*', *Fish. Bull., U.S.*, 69, 525–30

Cummings, W.C., Fish, J.F. and Thompson, P.O. (1972) 'Sound production and other behavior of southern right whales, *Eubalaena glacialis*', *Trans. San Diego Soc. Nat. Hist.*, 17, 1–13

Cummins, K.W. and Wuycheck, J.C. (1971) 'Caloric equivalents for investigations in ecological energetics', *Commun. Inst. Assoc. Theor. Appl. Limnol.*, No. 18

Dahlheim, M.E. and Awbrey, F. (1982) 'A classification and comparison of vocalizations of captive killer whales (*Orcinus orca*)', *J. Acoust. Soc. Am.*, 72, 661–70

Dahlheim, M.E., Fisher, H.D. and Schempp, J.D. (1984) 'Sound production by the gray whale and ambient noise levels in Laguna San Ignacio, Baja California Sur, Mexico', in Jones, M.L., Swartz, S.L. and Leatherwood, S. (eds.), *The Gray Whale Eschrichtius robustus*, Academic Press, New York, NY, pp. 511–41

Dahlheim, M.E., Leatherwood, S. and Perrin, W.F. (1982) 'Distribution of killer whales in the warm temperate and tropical eastern Pacific', *Rep. Int. Whal. Commn*, 32, 647–53

Dailey, M.D. and Brownell, R.L. Jr. (1972) 'A checklist of marine mammal parasites', in Ridgway, S.H. (ed.), *Mammals of the Sea. Biology and Medicine*, Charles C. Thomas, Ill., pp. 528–89

Dailey, M.D. and Perrin, W.F. (1973) 'Helminth parasites of porpoises of the genus *Stenella* in the eastern tropical Pacific, with descriptions of two new species: *Mastigonema stenellae* gen. et sp. n. (Nematoda: Spiruroidea) and *Zalophotrema pacificum* sp. n. (Trematoda: Digenea)', *Fish. Bull., U.S.*, 71, 455–71

Darling, J.D. (1977a) *Aspects of the behaviour and ecology of Vancouver island gray whales*, Eschrichtius glaucus Cope, MSc thesis, University of Victoria, Victoria, British Columbia

—— (1977b) 'The Vancouver Island gray whales' *Waters*, 2(1), 5–19

—— (1983) 'Migrations, abundance and behavior of Hawaiian humpback whales, *Megaptera novaeangliae* (Borowski)', PhD thesis, University of California, Santa Cruz, Calif.

Darling, J.D. and Jurasz, C.M. (1983) 'Migratory, destinations of North Pacific humpback whales (*Megaptera novaeangliae*), in Payne, R. (ed.), *Communication and Behavior of Whales*, AAAS Selected Symp. Ser., Westview Press, Boulder, Co., pp. 359–68

Darling, J.D. and McSweeney, D.J. (1985) 'Observations on the migrations of North Pacific humpback whales (*Megaptera novaeangliae*)', *Can. J. Zool.*, 63, 308–14.

Darling, J.D., Gibson, K.M. and Silber, G.K. (1983) 'Observations on the abundance and behavior of humpback whales (*Megaptera novaeangliae*) off west Maui, Hawaii, 1977–79', in Payne, R. (ed.), *Communication and Behavior of Whales*, AAAS Selected Symp. Ser., Westview Press, Boulder, Co., pp. 201–22

Da Silva, V.M.F. and Best, R.C. (1984) 'Freshwater dolphin fisheries interactions in the Amazon region (Brazil)', presentation at Sci. Comm. Meet. of the IWC SC/36/SM20, June 1984

Davies, J.L. (1963) 'The antitropical factor in cetacean speciation', *Evolution*, 17, 107–16

Davis, R., Finley, K. and Richardson, W.J. (1980) 'The present status and future management of arctic marine mammals in Canada', Science Advisory Board, *Report No. 3*, NWT, Can.

Dawbin, W.H. (1966a) 'The seasonal migratory cycle of humpback whales', in Norris, K.S. (ed.), *Whales, Dolphins and Porpoises*, University of California Press, Berkeley, Calif., pp. 145–70

—— (1966b) 'Porpoises and porpoise hunting in Malaita', *Aust. Nat. Hist.*, 15, 207–11

Dawson, W.W. (1980) 'The cetacean eye', in Herman, L. (ed.), *Cetacean Behavior*, Wiley Interscience, New York, NY, pp. 53–100

Defran, R. and Pryor, K. (1980) 'The behavior and training of cetaceans in captivity', in Herman, L.M. (ed.), *Cetacean Behavior*, Wiley Interscience, New York, NY, pp. 319–62

Delyamure, S.L. (1968) *Helminthofauna of Marine Mammals (Ecology and Phylogeny)*, Israel Program for Scientific Translations, Jerusalem (Acad. Sci. USSR, Moscow, 1955)

DeLury, D.B. (1947) 'On the estimation of biological populations', *Biometrics*, 3, 145–67

DeMaster, D.P. (1981) 'Estimating the average age of first birth in marine mammals', *Can. J. Fish. Aquat. Sci.*, 38, 237–9

—— (1984) 'Review of techniques used to estimate the average age at attainment of sexual maturity in marine mammals', *Rep. Int. Whal. Commn* (special issue 6), 175–9

Desportes, G. (1985) 'La Nutrition des Odontocetes en Atlantique Nord-Est', doctoral thesis, University of Poitiers, Poitiers

Diercks, K.J. (1972) *Biological Sonar Systems: A Bionics Survey*, Applied Research Laboratories, University of Texas, ARL-TR-72-34

Diercks, K.J., Trochta, R.T., Greenlaw, R.L. and Evans, W.E. (1971) 'Recording and analysis of dolphin echolocation signals', *J. Acoust. Soc. Am.*, 49, 1729–32

Di Natale, A. (1979a) 'Project Cetacea — II: sightings of sperm whales (Physeter catodon L.) in the central Mediterranean Sea', *CIESM, Réunion-intersession du Groupe de travail sur les Mammifères Marins*, Nov. 1979, Tunis

—— (1979b) 'Project Cetacea — IV: whalebone whales in the central Mediterranean Sea', *CIESM, Réunion-intersession du Groupe de travail sur les Mammifères Marins*, Nov. 1979, Tunis

Doak, W. (1982) *Dolphin dolphin*, Sheridan House Inc., New York, NY

Dobbs, H. (1977) *Follow a Wild Dolphin*, Souvenir Press, London

Dohl, T.P., Norris, K.S. and Kang, I. (1974) 'A porpoise hybrid: *Tursiops* x *Steno*', *J. Mammal. 55*, 217–21

Doi, T. (1970) 'Re-evaluation of population studies by sighting observation of whale', *Bull. Tokai Regional Fish. Res. Lab.*, 63, 1–10

—— (1974) 'Further development of whale sighting theory', in Schevill, W.E. (ed.), *The Whale Problem: A Status Report*, Harvard University Press, Cambridge, Mass., pp. 358–68

Doi, T., Ohsumi, S. and Nemoto, T. (1967) 'Population assessment of sei whales in the Antarctic', *Norsk Hvalfangst-Tidende*, 56, 25–41

Doi, T., Ohsumi, S., Nasu, K. and Shimadzu, Y. (1970) 'Advanced assessment of the fin whale stock in the Antarctic', *Rep. Int. Whal. Commn*, 20, 60–87

Doi, T., Kasamatsu, F. and Nakano, T. (1983) 'Further simulation studies on sighting by introducing both concentration of sighting effort by angle and aggregations of minke whales in the Antarctic', *Rep. Int. Whal. Commn*, 33, 403–12

Dolphin, W.F. and McSweeney, D.J. (1981) 'Aspects of the foraging strategies of humpback whales determined by hydro-acoustic scans', *Abstract, Proc. of 4th Biennial Conference on the Biology of Marine Mammals*, 14–18 Dec. 1981, San Francisco, Calif.

Donovan, G. (editor) (1982) 'Aboriginal/subsistence whaling (with special reference to the Alaska and Greenland Fisheries)', *Rep. Int. Whal. Commn* (special issue 4), 1–86

Donovan, G. (1984a) 'Blue whales off Peru, December 1982, with special reference to pygmy blue whales', *Rep. Int. Whal. Commn*, 34, 473–77

—— (1984b) 'Small cetaceans seen during the IWC/IDCR research cruise in the eastern tropical Pacific', *Rep. Int. Whal. Commn*, 34, 561–8

Dormer, K.J. (1979) 'Mechanisms of sound production and air recycling in delphinids: Cineradiographic evidence', *J. Acoust. Soc. Am.*, 65, 229–39

Dorsey, E.M. (1983) 'Exclusive adjoining ranges in individually identified minke whales (Balaenoptera acutorostrata) in Washington state', *Can. J. Zool.*, 61, 174–81

Dreher, J.J. and Evans, W.E. (1964) 'Cetacean communication', in Tavolga, W.N. (ed.), *Marine Bioacoustics*, Pergamon Press, Oxford, pp. 373–93

Duguy, R. (1977) 'Notes on the small cetaceans off the coasts of France', *Rep. Int. Whal. Commn*, 27, 500–1

—— (1983) 'Les cétacés des côtes de France', *Annales de la Societé des Sciences Naturelles de la Charente-Maritime (Suppl.)*, March 1983.

Duguy, R. and Robineau, D. (1982) *Guide des mammifères marins d'Europe*, Delachaux and Niestle, Neuchatel and Paris

Duguy, R., Casinos, A. and Di Natale, A. (1983) 'Distribution and frequency of marine mammals in the Mediterranean', *Rapp. P.-V. Réun. Ciesm.*, 28(5), 223–30

Duguy, R., Casinos, A. and Filella, S. (1978) 'Note sur la biologie de *Stenella coeruleoalba* dans le bassin occidental de la Méditerranée', *Congrès-Assemblée plénière, Comm. int. l'explor. scient. de la mer Med. XXVI*, Antalya, 24 Nov–2 Dec. 1978, 1–3

Duguy, R., Casinos, A., Di Natale, A., Filella, S., Ktarichakroun, F., Lloze, R., and Marchessaux, D. (1980) 'Repartition et frequencé des mammifères marins en Mediterranée', *Rapport de synthese du groupe de travail sur les Mammifères marins*, CIESM, XXVIIe Congrès, Cagliari, 1–9

Dustan, P., Smith, R.C. and Baker, K.S. (1981) 'Mesoscale patterns of oceanic chlorophyll and the distribution of marine mammals', *Marine Mammal Information*, June 1981, p. 4

Earle, S.A. (1979) 'Quantitative sampling of krill (*Euphausia pacifica*) relative to feeding strategies of humpback whales (*Megaptera novaeangliae*) in Glacier Bay, Alaska', *Abstract, Proc. of 3rd Biennial Conference on the Biology of Marine Mammals*, 7–11 Oct. 1979, Seattle, Wash.

Eberhardt, L.L. (1978) 'Transect methods for population studies', *J. Wildl. Mgmt.*, 42(2), 207–38

Edds, P.L. (1981) 'Dorsal fin variations in fin and minke whales in the St. Lawrence River', *Abstract, Proc. of 4th Biennial Conference on the Biology of Marine Mammals*, 14–18 Dec. 1981, San Francisco, Calif.

—— (1982) 'Vocalizations of the blue whale, *Balaenoptera musculus*, in the St. Lawrence River', *J. Mammal.*, 63, 345–7

Erickson, A.W. (1978) 'Population studies of killer whales (*Orcinus orca*) in the Pacific Northwest: A radio-marking and tracking study of killer whales', *Marine Mammal Commission Report*, Washington, DC, MMC-75/10

Essapian, F.S. (1955) 'Speed-induced skin folds in the Bottle-nosed porpoise *Tursiops truncatus*', *Breviora*, 43, 1–4

Evans, P.G.H. (1980) 'Cetaceans in British waters', *Mammal Review*, 10, 1–52

—— (ed.) (1981) *Report of NE Atlantic Scientific Cruise, 1980*, Occasional Publication, Mammal Society, London

—— (1982) 'Cetacean-seabird associations: a review', *Mammal Review*, 12, 187–206

—— (1987a) 'Ecology of cetaceans in Red Sea', in Marsden, C. and Head, S. (eds.) *Key Environments: Red Sea*, Pergamon Press, Oxford, pp. 305–14

—— (1987b) 'Electrophoretic variability of gene products', in Cooke, F.C. and Buckley, P.A. (eds.), *Avian Genetics*, Academic Press, New York, NY, pp.105–61

—— (in press) 'Seabirds foraging with marine mammals in temperate waters' in Burger, J. (ed.), *Seabirds and Other Marine Vertebrates: Commensalism, Competition and Predation*, Columbia University Press

Evans, P.G.H. and Nettleship, D.N. (1985) 'Conservation of Atlantic Alcidae', in Nettleship, D.N. and Birkhead, T.R. (eds.), *The Atlantic Alcidae*, Academic Press, New York, NY, pp. 427–88

Evans, P.G.H., Harding, S., Tyler, G. and Hall, S. (1986) 'Analysis of cetacean sightings in the British Isles, 1958–1985', unpublished Report to Nature Conservancy Council, Peterborough

Evans, W.E. (1967) 'Vocalizations among marine mammals', in Tavolga, W.N. (ed.), *Marine Bio-Acoustics, Vol. II*, Pergamon, New York, NY, pp. 159–86

—— (1971) 'Orientation behavior of delphinids: radio telemetric studies', *Ann. N.Y. Acad. Sci.*, 188, 142–60

—— (1973) 'Echolocation by marine delphinids and one species of freshwater dolphin', *J. Acoust. Soc. Am.*, 54, 191–9

—— (1974) 'Radio telemetric studies of two species of small odontocete cetaceans', in Schevill, W.E. (ed.), *The Whale Problem: A Status Report*, Harvard University Press, Cambridge, Mass., pp. 385–94

—— (1975) 'Distribution, differentiation of populations, and other aspects of the natural history of *Delphinus delphis* Linnaeus in the northeastern Pacific', PhD dissertation, Univ. of Calif., Los Angeles, Calif.

Evans, W.E. and Awbrey, F.T. (1986) 'Natural history aspects of marine mammal echolocation: feeding strategies and habitat' (unpubl. ms)

Evans, W.E. and Bastian, J. (1969) 'Marine mammal communication: social and ecological factors', in Andersen, H.T. (ed.), *The Biology of Marine Mammals*, Academic Press, New York, NY, pp. 425–76

Evans, W.E. and Maderson, P.F.A. (1973) 'Mechanisms of sound production in delphinid cetaceans: A review and some anatomical considerations', *Am. Zool.*, 13, 1205–13

Evans, W.E. and Prescott, J.H. (1962) 'Observations of the sound production capabilities of the bottlenose porpoise: a study of whistles and clicks', *Zoologica*, 47, 121–8

Evans, W.E., Hall, J.D., Irvine, A.B. and Leatherwood, J.S. (1972) 'Methods for tagging small cetaceans', *Fish. Bull., U.S.*, 70, 61–5

Everitt, R.D. and Krogman, B. (1979) 'Sexual behavior of bowhead whales observed off the north coast of Alaska', *Arctic, 32*, 277–80

Everitt, R.D., Fiscus, C.H. and DeLong, R.L. (1979) 'Marine mammals of northern Puget Sound and the Strait of Juan de Fuca. A report on investigations November 1, 1977 — October 31, 1978,' *NOAA Technical Memorandum ERL MESA-41*, Marine Ecosystems Analysis Program, Boulder, Co.

Everson, I. (1984) 'Zooplankton', in Laws, R.M. (ed.), *Antarctic Ecology*, Academic Press, London, pp. 463–90

FAO (Food and Agriculture Organisation) (1978–82) *Fish. Ser. (5), [Mammals in the Seas]* Vols. *1–4*, FAO, Rome

—— (1981) *Living Resources of the Seas*, FAO, Rome

Fay, F. (ed.) (1981) 'Marine mammals off the eastern Bering Sea shelf: an overview', in Hood, D.W. and Calder, J.A. (eds.), *The Eastern Bering Sea Shelf: Oceanography and Resources, Vol. 2*, University of Washington Press, Seattle, Wash., pp. 807–11

Fichtelius, K.-E. and Sjolander, S. (1972) *Smarter Than Man? Intelligence in Whales, Dolphins and Humans*, Ballantine Books, New York, NY

Fink, B.D. (1959) 'Observations of porpoise predation on a school of Pacific sardines', *Calif. Fish Game, 45*, 216–7

Finley, K.J. and Gibb, E.J. (1982) 'Summer diet of the narwhal (*Monodon monoceros*) in Pond Inlet, northern Baffin Island', *Can. J. Zool., 60*, 3353–93

Fish, J.F. and Lingle, G.E. (1977) 'Responses of spotted porpoises, *Stenella attenuata*, to playback of distress (?) sounds of one of their own kind', *Abstract, Proc. of 2nd Biennial Conference on the Biology of Marine Mammals*, Dec. 1977, San Diego, Calif.

Fish, J.F. and Vania, J.S. (1971) 'Killer whale, *Orcinus orca*, sounds repel white whales, *Delphinapterus leucas*', *Fish. Bull., U.S., 69*, 531–5

Fisher, H.D. and Harrison, R.J. (1970) 'Reproduction in the common porpoise (*Phocoena phocoena*) of the North Atlantic', *J. Zool. 161*, 471- 86

Fisher, R.A. (1930) *The Genetical Theory of Natural Selection*, Clarendon Press, Oxford

Fitch, J.E. and Brownell, R.L. Jr (1968) 'Fish otoliths in cetacean stomachs and their importance in interpreting feeding habits', *J. Fish. Res. Bd Can., 25*, 2561–75

—— (1971) 'Fish otoliths in cetacean stomachs and their importance in determining feeding habits', *Bull. Mar. Sci., 21*, 626–36

Ford, J.K.B. and Fisher, H.D. (1978) 'Underwater acoustic signals of the narwhal (*Monodon monoceros*), *Can. J. Zool. 56*, 552–60

—— (1983) 'Group-specific dialects of killer whales (*Orcinus orca*) in British Columbia', in Payne, R. (ed.), *Communication and Behavior of Whales*, AAA Selected Symposium 76, Westview Press, Boulder, Co., pp. 129–61

Fordyce, R.E. (1977) 'The development of the circum-Antarctic current ,and the evolution of the Mysticeti (Mammalia: Cetacea)', *Palaeogeography, Palaeoclimatology, Palaeoecology, 21*, 265–71

—— (1980) 'Whale evolution and Oligocene southern ocean environments', *Palaeogeography, Palaeoclimatology, Palaeoecology, 31*, 319–36

—— (1982) 'A review of Australian fossil Cetacea', *Memoirs of the National Museum*, Victoria, *43*, 43–58

—— (1983) 'Rhabdosteid dolphins (Mammalia: Cetacea) from the Middle Miocene, Lake Frome area, South Australia', *Alcheringa, 7*, 27–40

—— (1984) 'Evolution and zoogeography of cetaceans in Australia', in Archer, M. and Clayton, G. (eds.), *Vertebrate Zoogeography and Evolution in Australia*, Hesperion, Perth, pp. 929–48

Fordyce, R.E., Mattlin, R.H. and Dixon, J.M. (1984) 'Second record of spectacled porpoise from subantarctic Southwest Pacific', *Sci. Rep. Whales Res. Inst., Tokyo, 35*, 159–64

Fordyce, R.E., Mattlin, R.H. and Wilson, G.J. (1979) 'Stranding of a Cuvier's beaked whale, *Ziphius cavirostris* Cuvier 1823, at New Brighton, New Zealand', *Mauri Ora, 7*, 73–82

Fraker, M. (1980) 'Status and harvest of the Mackenzie stock of white whales (*Delphinapterus leucas*)', *Rep. Int. Whal. Commn, 30*, 451–8

Fraker, M.A. and Wursig, B. (1981) 'Feeding behavior of bowhead whales in the southeastern Beaufort Sea', *Abstract, Proc. of 4th Biennial Conference on the Biology of Marine Mammals*, 14–18 Dec. 1981, San Francisco, Calif.

Fraser, F.C. (1974) *Report on Cetacea Stranded on the British Coasts from 1948 to 1966*, British Museum (Natural History), London

Frazer, J.F.D. and Huggett, A. St. G. (1973) 'Specific foetal growth rates of cetaceans', *J. Zool., Lond., 169*(1), 111–26

—— (1974) 'Species variations in the foetal growth rates of eutherian mammals', *J. Zool., Lond., 174*, 481–509

Frazier, J. (1983) 'Records of cetaceans from Kenya', *Afr. J. Ecol.*, *21*(2), 115–17

Frost, S. (ed.) (1978) *Whales and Whaling, Vols. I and II*, Australian Govt. Printing Service, Canberra

Gambell, R. (1968) 'Seasonal cycles and reproduction in sei whales of the Southern Hemisphere', *Discovery Rep.*, *35*, 31–134

—— (1972) 'Sperm whales off Durban', *Discovery Rep.*, *35*, 199–358

—— (1973) 'Some effects of exploitation on reproduction in whales', *J. Reprod. Fert., Suppl.*, *19*, 533–53

—— (1976a) 'World whale stocks', *Mammal Review, 6*, 41–53

—— (1976b) 'Population biology and the management of whales', in Coaker, T.H. (ed.), *Applied Biology, Vol. 1*, Academic Press, New York, NY and London, pp. 247–343

—— (1979) 'The blue whale', *Biologist, 26*(5), 209–15

Gaskin, D.E. (1968) 'The New Zealand Cetacea', *Fish. Res. Bd N.Z. Mar. Dept.* (new series), *1*, 1–92

—— (1972) *Whales, Dolphins and Seals: with Special Reference to the New Zealand Region*, Heinemann, London

—— (1973) 'Sperm whales in the western South Pacific', *N.Z. J. mar. Freshwat. Res.*, *7*, 1–20

—— (1976) 'The evolution, zoogeography and ecology of cetacea', *Oceanogr. Mar. Biol. Ann. Rev.*, *14*, 247–346

—— (1977a) 'Harbor porpoise *Phocoena phocoena* in the western approaches to the Bay of Fundy 1969–75', *Rep. Int. Whal. Commn, 27*, 487–92

—— (1977b) 'Sei and Bryde's whales in waters around New Zealand', *Rep. Int. Whal. Commn (Special Issue 1)*, 50–2

—— (1979) 'Marine mammals', in Thomas, M.L.H. (ed.), *Marine and Coastal Communities of the Quoddy Region*, New Brunswick, Huntsman Marine Laboratory & University of New Brunswick joint publication

—— (1982) *The Ecology of Whales and Dolphins*, Heinemann, London and Exeter

—— (1984) 'The harbour porpoise *Phocoena phocoena* (L.): Regional populations, status, and information on direct and indirect catches', *Rep. Int. Whal. Commn, 27*, 487–92

Gaskin, D.E. and Blair, B.A. (1977) 'Age determination of harbour porpoise, *Phocoena phocoena* (L.), in the western North Atlantic', *Can. J. Zool.*, *55*, 18–30

Gaskin, D.E. and Watson, A.P. (1985) 'The harbor porpoise, *Phocoena phocoena*, in Fish Harbour, New Brunswick, Canada: occupancy, distribution, and movements', *Fish. Bull., U.S.*, *83*(3), 427–42

Gaskin, D.E., Frank, R. and Holdrinet, M. (1983) 'Polychlorinated biphenyls in harbor porpoises *Phocoena phocoena* (L.) from the Bay of Fundy, Canada, and adjacent waters, with some information on chlordane and hexachlorobenzene levels', *Arch. Environ. Contam. Toxicol.*, *12*, 211–19

Gaskin, D.E., Holdrinet, M. and Frank, R. (1971) 'Organochlorine pesticide residues in harbour porpoises from the Bay of Fundy region', *Nature, Lond.*, *233*, 499–500

—— (1976) 'DDT residues in blubber of harbour porpoises, *Phocoena phocoena* (L.) from eastern Canadian waters during the five year period 1969–1973', *FAO of the UN, Scientific Consultation on Marine Mammals, Bergen, Norway, 31 Aug.–9 Sept. 1976, document ACMRR/MM/SC/96*

—— (1982) 'DDT residues in blubber of harbour porpoise, *Phocoena phocoena* (L.) from eastern Canadian waters during the five-year period 1969–1973', *FAO Fish. Ser.*, [*Mammals in the Seas*] 4, 135–43

Gaskin, D.E., Smith, G.J.D. and Watson, A.P. (1975) 'Preliminary study of movements of harbour porpoises (*Phocoena phocoena*) in the Bay of Fundy using radiotelemetry', *Can. J. Zool.*, *53*, 1466–71

Gaskin, D.E., Smith, G.J.D., Watson, A.P., Yasui, W.Y. and Yurick, D.B. (1984) 'Reproduction in the porpoises (Phocoenidae): implications for management', *Rep. Int. Whal. Commn* (special issue 6), 135–48

Gause, G.J. (1934) *The Struggle for Existence*, William and Wilkins, Baltimore, Md.

Geraci, J.R. and St Aubin, D.J. (eds.) (1979) 'Biology of marine mammals: insights through strandings', Marine Mammal Commission Rep. NTIS no. PB-293 890

Geraci, J.R., Testavarde, S.A., St Aubin, D.J. and Loop, T.H. (1978) 'A mass stranding of the Atlantic whitesided dolphin, *Lagenorhynchus acutus*: a study into pathobiology and life', *Marine Mammal Commission Rep.* NTIS no. PB-289 361

Gianuca, N. and Castello, H.P. (1976) 'First record of the southern bottle-nosed whale, *Hyperoodon planifrons* from Brazil', *Sci. Rep. Whales Res. Inst., Tokyo, 28*, 119–26

Gihr, M. and Pilleri, G. (1979) 'Interspecific body length-body weight ratio and body weight-brain weight ratio in cetacea', *Invest. on Cetacea*, 10, 245–53

Gingerich, P.D. and Russell, D.E. (1981) '*Pakicetus inachus*, a new archaeocete (Mammalia, Cetacea) from the early-middle Eocene Kuldana Formation of Kohat (Pakistan)', *Contributions from the Museum of Paleontology, the University of Michigan*, 25(11), 235–46

Gingerich, P.D., Wells, N.A., Russell, D.E. and Shah, S.M.I. (1983) 'Origin of whales in epicontinental remnant seas: new evidence from the Early Eocene of Pakistan', *Science*, 220, 403–6

Giordano, A. (1981) 'Etude des cétacés de Méditerranée française en consitions hivernales et printanieres', Diplome d'Etudes Approfondies d'Oceanologie (DES), unpublished thesis, University of Marseille, Marseille

Glockner, D.A. (1983) 'Determining the sex of humpback whale (*Megaptera novaeangliae*) in their natural environment', in Payne, R. (ed.), *Communication and Behavior of Whales*, AAAS Selected Symp. Ser., Westview Press, Boulder, Co., pp. 447–64

Glockner, D.A. and Venus, S.C. (1983) 'Identification, growth rate, and behavior of humpback whale (*Megaptera novaeangliae*) cows and calves in the waters off Maui, Hawaii 1977–79', in Payne, R. (ed.), *Communication and Behavior of Whales*, AAAS Selected Symp. Ser., Westview Press, Boulder, Co., pp. 223–58

Goodall, R.N.P. (1978) 'Report on the small cetaceans stranded on the coasts of Tierra del Fuego', *Sci. Rep. Whales Res. Inst., Tokyo*, 30, 197–232

Goodall, R.N.P. and Galeazzi, A.R. (1985) 'A review of the food habits of the small cetaceans of the Antarctic and Sub-Antarctic', in Siegfried, W.R., Condy, P.R., and Laws, R.M. (eds.), *Antarctic Nutrient Cycles and Food Webs*, Springer-Verlag, Berlin, pp. 566–72

Gordon, J.C. (1983) 'Photographic studies of sperm whales (*Physeter catodon*)', *Abstract, Proc. of 5th Biennial Conference on the Biology of Marine Mammals*, 27 Nov.–1 Dec. 1983, Boston, Mass.

Gruber, J.A. (1981) Ecology of the Atlantic bottlenosed dolphin (*Tursiops truncatus*) in the Pass Cavallo area of Matagorda Bay, Texas, MSc thesis, Texas A & M University, College Station, TX 77843

Guinee, L.N., Chu, K. and Dorsey, E.M. (1983) 'Changes over time in the songs of known individual humpback whales (*Megaptera novaeangliae*)', in Payne, R. (ed.), *Communication and Behavior of Whales*, AAAS Selected Symp. Ser., Westview Press, Boulder, Co, pp. 59–80

Gulland, J.A. (1981) 'A note on the strategy of the management of marine mammals', *FAO Fish. Ser. (5), [Mammals in the Seas]* 3, 93–102

Gulland, J.A. and Boerema, L.K. (1973) 'Scientific advice on catch levels', *Rep. Int. Whal. Commn*, 23, 200–12

Gurevich, V.S. (1980) 'Worldwide distribution and migration patterns of the white whale (beluga), *Delphinapterus leucas*', *Rep. Int. Whal. Commn*, 30, 465–80

Gurevich, V.S. and Stewart, B.S. (1978) 'Structure of kill of the common dolphin *Delphinus delphis* from eastern tropical Pacific in 1977. Final report for Contract No. 03-78-M02-0101, Southwest Fisheries Center, La Jolla, Calif., pp. 1–19

—— (1979) 'A study of growth and reproduction of the striped dolphin (*Stenella coeruleoalba*)', final report for contract No. 03-78-D27-1079, Southwest Fisheries Center, La Jolla, Calif., pp. 1–19

Gurevich, V., Stewart, B. and Cornell, L.H. (1980) 'The use of tetracycline in age determination of common dolphins, *Delphinus delphis*', *Rep. Int. Whal. Commn* (special issue 3), 165–9

Hain, J.H.W., Carter, G.R., Kraus, S.D., Mayo, C.A. and Winn, H.E. (1982) 'Feeding behavior of the humpback whale, *Megaptera novaeangliae*, in the western North Atlantic', *Fish. Bull., U.S.*, 80, 259–68

Haines, G. (1974) *Sounds Underwater*, David & Charles, Newton Abbot, Devon

Haley, D. (ed.) (1978) *Marine Mammals of Eastern North Pacific and Arctic Waters*, Pacific Search Press, Seattle, Wash.

Hammond, D.D. and Leatherwood, S. (1984) 'Cetaceans live-captured for Ocean Park, Hong Kong, April 1974 – February 1983', *Rep. Int. Whal. Commn*, 34, 491–6

Hammond, P.S. (1986a) 'Line transect sampling of dolphin populations', in Bryden, M.M. and Harrison, R.J. (eds.), *Research on Dolphins*, Clarendon Press, Oxford, pp. 251–80

Hammond, P.S. (1986b) 'Estimating the size of naturally marked whale populations using capture-recapture techniques', *Rep. Int. Whal. Commn* (special issue 8), 253–82

Handcock, J. (1965) 'Killer whales kill and eat a minke whale', *J. Mammal.*, 46, 341–2

Hansen, L.J. (1983) 'Population biology of the coastal bottlenose dolphin (*Tursiops truncatus*) of southern California', MSc thesis, California State University, Sacramento, Calif.

Harris, M.P. (1984) *The Puffin*, T. & A.D. Poyser, Calton, Staffs.

Harrison, R.J. (1969) 'Reproduction and reproductive organs', in Andersen, H.T. (ed.), *The Biology of Marine Mammals*, Academic Press, New York, NY and London, pp. 253–342

—— (1972) 'Reproduction and reproductive organs in *Platanista indi* and *Platanista gangetica*', *Invest. on Cetacea*, 4, 71–82

Harrison, R.J. and Brownell, R.L. Jr. (1971) 'The gonads of the South American dolphins, *Inia geoffrensis*, *Pontoporia blainvillei*, and *Sotalia fluviatilis*', *J. Mammal.*, 52, 413–9

Harrison, R.J. and Ridgway, S.H. (1976) *Deep Diving in Mammals*, Meadowfield Press, Durham, *Zool. Ser. 7*, 1–51

Harrison, R.J. and Thurley, K.W. (1974) 'Structure of the epidermis in *Tursiops, Delphinus, Orcinus* and *Phocoena*', in Harrison, R.J. (ed.), *Functional Anatomy of Marine Mammals, Vol. II*, Academic Press, New York, NY and London, pp. 45–71

Harrison, R.J., Brownell, R.L. Jr. and Boice, R.C. (1972) 'Reproduction and gonadal appearances in some odontocetes', in Harrison, R.J. (ed.), *Functional Anatomy of Marine Mammals, Vol. 1*, Academic Press, New York, NY and London, pp. 361–429

Harrison, R.J., Bryden, M.M., McBrearty, D.A. and Brownell, R.L. Jr (1981) 'The ovaries and reproduction in *Pontoporia blainvillei* (Cetacea: Platanistidae)', *J. Zool., Lond.*, 193, 563–80

Harwood, M.B., McNamara, K.J., Anderson, G.R.V. and Walter, D.G. (1984) 'Incidental catch of small cetaceans in a gillnet fishery in northern Australian waters', *Rep. Int. Whal. Commn*, 34, 555–9

Hay, K. (1980) 'Age determination of the narwhal, *Monodon monoceros* L.', *Rep. Int. Whal. Commn* (special issue 3), 119–32

Heezen, B.C. (1957) 'Whales entangled in deep sea cables', *Deep Sea Research*, 4, 105–15

Herman, L.M. (ed.) (1980a) *Cetacean Behavior*, Wiley Interscience, New York, NY

—— (1980b) 'Cognitive characteristics of dolphins', in Herman, L.M. (ed.), *Cetacean Behavior*, Wiley Interscience, New York, NY, pp. 363–429

Herman, L.M. and Antinoja, R.C. (1977) 'Humpback whales in the Hawaiian breeding waters: population and pod characteristics', *Sci. Rep. Whales Res. Inst., Tokyo*, 29, 59–85

Herman, L.M. and Forestell, P.H. (1985) 'Reporting presence or absence of named objects by a language-trained dolphin', *Neuroscience & Biobehavioral Reviews*, 9, 667–81

Herman, L.M. and Tavolga, W.N. (1980) 'The communication systems of cetaceans', in Herman, L.M. (ed.), *Cetacean Behavior*, Wiley Interscience, New York, NY, pp. 149–209

Herman, L.M., Richards, D.G. and Wolz, J.P. (1984) 'Comprehension of sentences by bottlenosed dolphins', *Cognition*, 16, 129–219

Hertel, H. (1969) 'Hydrodynamics of swimming and wave-riding dolphins', in Andersen, H.T. (ed.), *The Biology of Marine Mammals*, Academic Press, New York, NY and London, pp. 31–63

Hertz, O. and Kapel, F.O. (1986) 'Commercial and subsistence hunting of marine mammals', *Ambio*, 15(3), 144–51

Hiby, A.R. (1982a) 'Using average number of whales in view to estimate population density', *Rep. Int. Whal. Commn*, 32, 563–5

—— (1982b) 'The effect of random whale movement on density estimates obtained from whale sighting surveys', *Rep. Int. Whal. Commn*, 32, 791–3

Hiby, A.R., Martin, A.R. and Fairfield, F. (1984) 'IDCR cruise/aerial survey in the North Atlantic 1982: aerial survey report', *Rep. Int. Whal. Commn*, 34, 633–44

Holden, A.V. (1975) 'The accumulation of oceanic contaminants in marine mammals', *Rapp. P.-v. Réun. Cons. int. Explor. Mer.*, 169, 353–61

Holligan, P.M. (1981) 'Biological implications of fronts on the northwest European continental shelf', *Phil. Trans. R. Soc. Lond.* A, 302, 547–62

Holt, S.J. (1981) 'Maximum sustainable yield and its application to whaling', *FAO Fish. Ser.* (5), [*Mammals in the Seas*] 3, 21–55

Howard, E.D. (ed.) (1983) *Pathobiology of Marine Mammal Diseases, Vols. I and II*, CRC Press, Boca. Raton, Fla.

Hoydal, K. (1985) 'Attempts to use the 274 years' Faroese time series of catches of pilot whales, (*Globicephala melaena*, Traill) to assess the State of the Stock', *ICES document C.M.1985/N*

Hoyt, E. (1984) *Orca: The Whale Called Killer*, Camden House, Camden East, Ontario

Huber, H.R., Ainley, D.G. and Morrell, S.H. (1982) 'Sightings of cetaceans in the Gulf of Farallones, California, 1971–1979', *Calif. Fish Game*, 68(3), 183–90

Hudnall, J. (1981) 'Population estimates, feeding behavior and food source of gray whales, *Eschrichtius robustus*, occupying the Straits of Juan de Fuca, British Columbia', *Abstract, Proc. of 4th Biennial Conference on the Biology of Marine Mammals*, 14–18 Dec. 1981, San Francisco, Calif.

Hui, C.A. (1977) 'Data preparation and analysis for studies on growth and reproduction of *Delphinus* in the eastern tropical Pacific', Rep. on contract PO-01-6-200-11439, Southwest Fisheries Center, La Jolla, Calif. pp. 1–13

—— (1979) 'Undersea topography and distribution of dolphins of the genus *Delphinus* in the Southern Californian Bight', *J. Mammal.*, 60(3), 521–7

Hussenot, E. (1980) 'Le grand dauphin *Tursiops truncatus* en Bretagne: types de frequentation', *Penn ar Bed*, 12(103), 355–80

Ichihara, T. (1959) 'Formation mechanism of ear plug of baleen whale', *Sci. Rep. Whales Res. Inst., Tokyo, 14*, 107–35

—— (1966) 'The pygmy blue whale, *Balaenoptera musculus brevicauda*, a new sub-species from the Antarctic', in Norris, K.S. (ed.), *Whales, Dolphins and Porpoises*, Univ. of Calif. Press, Berkeley & Los Angeles, Calif. pp. 79–113

Irvine, A.B., Wells, R.S. and Scott, D.M. (1982) 'An evaluation of techniques for tagging small odontocete cetaceans', *Fish. Bull., U.S.*, 80, 135–43

IWC (1978) 'Report of the Scientific Committee. 11.1 Sei whales, southern hemisphere', *Rep. Int. Whal. Commn, 28*, 47–54

—— (1982) 'Thirty-Third Report of the International Whaling Commission', IWC, Cambridge

—— (1983) 'Thirty-Fourth Report of the International Whaling Commission', IWC, Cambridge

—— (1984) 'Thirty-Fifth Report of the International Whaling Commission', IWC, Cambridge

Jackson, T.D. (1980) 'Trip report: porpoise population aerial survey of the eastern tropical Pacific Ocean, January 22–April 25, 1979', *Southwest Fisheries Center Admin. Rep. No. LJ-80-1*

Jansen, J. and Jansen, J.K.S. (1969) 'The nervous system of Cetacea', in Andersen, H.T. (ed.), *The Biology of Marine Mammals*, Academic Press, New York, NY, pp. 175–252

Jenkins, J.T. (1921) *A History of the Whale Fisheries*, Witherby, London

Jennings, J.G. and Gandy, W.F. (1980) 'Tracking pelagic dolphins by satellite', in Amlaner, C.J. and Macdonald, D.W. (eds.), *Handbook on Biotelemetry and Radio Tracking*, Pergamon Press, Oxford, pp. 753–5

Jennings, R. (1982) 'Pelagic sightings of Risso's dolphin, *Grampus griseus*, in the Gulf of Mexico and Atlantic Ocean adjacent to Florida', *J. Mammal.*, 63(2), 522–3

Jerison, H.J. (1973) *Evolution of the Brain and Intelligence*, Academic Press, New York, NY

—— (1978) 'Brain and intelligence in whales', in Frost, S. (ed.), *Whales and Whaling. Vol. II*, Australian Govt. Printing Service, Canberra, pp. 161–97

—— (1980) 'The nature of intelligence', paper presented at the IWC Conference on Cetacean Behavior, Intelligence, and the Ethics of Killing Cetaceans, Washington, D.C., 28 Apr–1 May 1980

Joensen, J.P. (1976) 'Pilot whaling in the Faroe Islands', *Ethnologia Scandinavica*, 5, 1–42

Jolly, G.M. (1965) 'Explicit estimates from capture-recapture data with both death and immigration — stochastic model', *Biometrika*, 52, 225–47

Jones, E.C. (1971) '*Isistius brasiliensis*, a squalid shark, the probable cause of crater wounds on fishes and cetaceans', *Fish. Bull., U.S.*, 69, 791–8

Jones, L.L. (1983) 'Incidental take of Dall's porpoise and harbour porpoise by Japanese salmon driftnet fisheries in the western North Pacific', paper presented at the Scientific Committee of the International Whaling Commission, Cambridge, June 1983 (SC/35/SM8)

Jones, M.L. and Swartz, S.L. (1984) 'Demography and phenology of gray whales and evaluation of whale-watching activities in Laguna San Ignacio, Baja California Sur, Mexico', in Jones, M.L., Swartz, S.L. and Leatherwood, S. (eds.) *The Gray Whale Eschrichtius robustus*, Academic Press, Orlando, Fla., pp. 309–74

Jones, M.L., Swartz, S.L. and Leatherwood, S. (eds.) (1984) *The Gray Whale Eschrichtius robustus*, Academic Press, Orlando, Fla.

Jones, R. (1973) 'Population assessments of Antarctic fin and sei whales', *Rep. Int. Whal. Commn, 23*, 215–59

Jones, S. (1982) 'The present status of the Gangetic susu, *Platanista gangetica* (Roxburgh), with comments on the Indus susu, *P. minor* Owen', *FAO Fish. Ser.* (5), [*Mammals in the Seas*] 4, 97–115

Jonsgård, A. (1951) 'Studies on the little piked whale or minke whale (*Balaenoptera acuto-rostrata* Lacépède). Report on Norwegian investigations carried out in the years 1943–1950', *Norsk Hvalf.* 40(5), 5–54

—— (1966) 'Biology of the north Atlantic fin whale, *Balaenoptera physalus* (L) —

Taxonomy, distribution, migration and food', *Hvalrad. Skr.*, *49*, 1–62

Jonsgård, A. and Darling, K. (1977) 'On the biology of the eastern North Atlantic sei whale', *Rep. Int. Whal. Commn* (special issue 1), 124–9

Jonsgård, A. and Lyshoel, P.B. (1970) 'A contribution to the knowledge of the biology of the killer whale *Orcinus orca* (L.), *Nytt. Mag. Zool.*, *1*, 1–48

Jurasz, C.M. and Jurasz, V.P. (1979) 'Feeding modes of the humpback whale, *Megaptera novaeangliae*, in southeast Alaska', *Sci. Rep. Whales Res. Inst., Tokyo*, *31*, 69–83

Kapel, F.O. (1975) 'Preliminary notes on the occurrence and exploitation of smaller cetacea in Greenland', *J. Fish. Res. Bd Can.*, *32*, 1079–82

—— (1977a) 'Catch of belugas, narwhals and harbour porpoises in Greenland, 1954–75, by year, month and region', *Rep. Int. Whal. Commn*, *27*, 507–20

—— (1977b) 'Catch statistics for minke whales, West Greenland, 1954–74', *Rep. Int. Whal. Commn*, *27*, 456–9

—— (1978) 'Catch of minke whales by fishing vessels in West Greenland', *Rep. Int. Whal. Commn*, *28*, 217–26

—— (1979) 'Exploitation of large whales in West Greenland in the 20th century', *Rep. Int. Whal. Commn*, *29*, 197–214.

Kapel, F.O. and Petersen, R. (1982) 'Subsistence hunting: the Greenland case', *Rep. Int. Whal. Commn* (special issue 4), 51–73

Kasuya, T. (1971) 'Consideration of distribution and migration of toothed whales off the Pacific coast of Japan based upon aerial sighting record', *Sci. Rep. Whales Res. Inst., Tokyo*, *23*, 37–60

—— (1972) 'Growth and reproduction of *Stenella coeruleoalba* based on the age determination by means of dentinal growth layers', *Sci. Rep. Whales Res. Inst., Tokyo*, *24*, 57–79

—— (1973) 'Systematic consideration of Recent toothed whales based on the morphology of tympanoperiotic bone', *Sci. Rep. Whales Res. Inst., Tokyo*, *25*, 1–103

—— (1976) 'Reconsideration of life history parameters of the spotted and striped dolphins based on cemental layers', *Sci. Rep. Whales Res. Inst., Tokyo*, *28*, 73–106

—— (1977) 'Age determination and growth of the Baird's beaked whale with a comment on the fetal growth rate', *Sci. Rep. Whales Res. Inst., Tokyo*, *29*, 1–20

—— (1978) 'The life history of Dall's porpoise with special reference to the stock off the Pacific coast of Japan', *Sci. Rep. Whales Res. Inst., Tokyo*, *30*, 1–63

—— (1985a) 'Effect of exploitation on reproductive parameters of the spotted and striped dolphins off the Pacific coast of Japan', *Sci. Rep. Whales Res. Inst., Tokyo*, *36*, 107–38

—— (1985b) 'Fishery-dolphin conflict in the Iki Island area of Japan', in Beddington, J.R., Beverton, R.J.H. and Lavigne, D.M. (eds.), *Marine Mammals and Fisheries*, George Allen and Unwin, London, pp. 253–72

—— (1986) 'Distribution and behavior of Baird's beaked whales off the Pacific coast of Japan', *Sci. Rep. Whales Res. Inst., Tokyo*, *37*, 61–83

Kasuya, T. and Aminul Haque, A.K.M. (1972) 'Some information on distribution and seasonal movement of the Ganges dolphin', *Sci. Rep. Whales Res. Inst., Tokyo*, *24*, 109–15

Kasuya, T. and Brownell, R.L. Jr (1979) 'Age determination, reproduction, and growth of the franciscana dolphin, *Pontoporia blainvillei*', *Sci. Rep. Whales Res. Inst., Tokyo*, *31*, 45–57, Pl.1–7

Kasuya, T. and Kureha, K. (1979) 'The population of finless porpoise in the Inland Sea of Japan', *Sci. Rep. Whales Res. Inst., Tokyo*, *31*, 1–44

Kasuya, T. and Marsh, H. (1984) 'Life history and reproductive biology of the short-finned pilot whale, *Globicephala macrorhynchus*, off the Pacific coast of Japan', *Rep. Int. Whal. Commn* (special issue 6), 259–310

Kasuya, T. and Nishiwaki, M. (1975) 'Recent status of the population of Indus dolphin', *Sci. Rep. Whales Res. Inst., Tokyo*, *27*, 81–94

Kasuya, T., Miyazaki, N. and Dawbin, W.H. (1974) 'Growth and reproduction of *Stenella attenuata* in the Pacific coast of Japan', *Sci. Rep. Whales Res. Inst., Tokyo*, *26*, 157–226

Kato, H. (1983) 'Some considerations on the decline in age at sexual maturity of the Antarctic minke whale', *Rep. Int. Whal. Commn*, *33*, 393–9

Katona, S., Baxter, B., Brazier, O., Kraus, S., Perkins, J.S. and Whitehead, H. (1979) 'Identification of humpback whales by fluke photographs', in Winn, H.E. and Olla, B.L. (eds.), *Behavior of Marine Animals, Vol. 3: Cetaceans*, Plenum Press, New York, NY, pp. 33–44

Katona, S., Harcourt, P.M., Perkins, J.S. and Kraus, S. (1980) *Humpback Whales of the Western North Atlantic: A Catalog of Identified Individuals*, 2nd edn, College of the Atlantic, Bar Harbor, Maine

Kaufman, G. and Wood, K. (1981) 'Effects of boat traffic, air traffic, and military activity on

Hawaiian humpback whales', *Abstract, Proc. of 4th Biennial Conference on the Biology of Marine Mammals*, 14–18 Dec. 1981, San Francisco, Calif.

Kawakami, T. (1980) 'A review of sperm whale food', *Sci. Rep. Whales Res. Inst., Tokyo, 32*, 199–218

Kawamura, A. (1970) 'Food of sei whale taken by Japanese whaling expeditions in the Antarctic season 1967/68', *Sci. Rep. Whal. Res. Inst., Tokyo, 22*, 127–52

—— (1974) 'Food and feeding ecology in the southern sei whale', *Sci. Rep. Whal. Res. Inst., Tokyo, 26*, 25–144

—— (1977) 'On the food of Bryde's whales caught in the South Pacific and Indian oceans', *Sci. Rep. Whales Res. Inst., Tokyo, 29*, 49- 58

—— (1978) 'An interim consideration on a possible interspecific relation in southern baleen whales from the viewpoint of their food habits', *Rep. Int. Whal. Commn, 28*, 411–20

—— (1980a) 'Food habits of the Bryde's whales taken in the South Pacific and Indian oceans', *Sci. Rep. Whales Res. Inst., Tokyo, 32*, 1–23

—— (1980b) 'A review of food of balaenopterid whales', *Sci. Rep. Whales Res. Inst., Tokyo, 32*, 155–197

Kawamura, A. and Satake, Y. (1976) 'Preliminary report on the greographical distribution of the Bryde's whale in the North Pacific with special reference to the structure of the filtering apparatus', *Sci. Rep. Whales Res. Inst., Tokyo, 28*, 1–35

Kayes, R. (1985) 'The decline of porpoises and dolphins in the Southern North Sea: a current status report', Res. Rep. RR-14, Political Ecology Research Group, Oxford

Keller, R.W., Leatherwood, S. and Holt, S.J. (1982) 'Indian Ocean cetacean survey, Seychelle Islands, April through June 1980', *Rep. Int. Whal. Commn, 32*, 503–13

Kellogg, R. (1969) 'Cetothere skeletons from the Miocene Choptank Formation of Maryland and Virginia', *U.S. Natl. Mus. Bull., 294*, 1–40

Kimura, S. (1957) 'The twinning in southern fin whales', *Sci. Rep. Whales Res. Inst., Tokyo, 12*, 103–25

Kinze, C.C. (1985) 'Et ars observationer af Marsvin (*Phocoena phocoena*) hfra danske faergeruter', *Flora og Fauna, 91*(3–4), 21–7

Kleinenberg, S.E. (1958) 'The origin of the Cetacea', *Doklady Akad. Nauk. SSSR, 122*, 950–2

Klinowska, M. (1986) 'The cetacean magnetic sense — evidence from strandings', in Bryden, M.M. and Harrison, R.J. (eds.), *Research on Dolphins*, Clarendon Press, Oxford, pp. 401–32

Klumov, S.K. (1962) 'The right whales in the Pacific Ocean', *Trudy Inst. Okeonol., 58*, 202–97

Koeman, J.H., Peeters, W.H.M., Koudstaal-Hol, C.H.M., Tijoe, P.S. and Goeij, J.J.M. de (1973) 'Mercury-selenium correlations in marine mammals', *Nature, Lond., 245*, 385–6

Koeman, J.H., Peeters, W.H.M., Smit, C.J., Tijoe, P.S. and Goeij, J.J.M. de (1972) 'Persistent chemicals in marine mammals', *TNO-nieuws, 27*, 570–8

Kraus, S.D. (1986) 'A review of the status of right whales (*Eubalaena glacialis*) in the western North Atlantic with a summary plan for research and management', XZ-000 000, National Technical Information Service, Springfield, Va.

Kraus, S. and Katona, S. (1977) *Humpback Whales* (Megaptera novaeangliae) *in the Western North Atlantic: A Catalog of Identified Individuals*, College of the Atlantic, Bar Harbor, Maine

Kraus, S. and Prescott, J.H. (1983) 'The use of callosity patterns and natural markings to determine distribution, abundance and movements of the North Atlantic right whale, *Eubalaena glacialis*', *Abstract, Proc. of 5th Biennial Conference on the Biology of Marine Mammals*, 27 Nov.–1 Dec. 1983, Boston, Mass.

Kroger, R. (1986) 'The decrease of harbour porpoise populations in the Baltic and North Sea', unpublished Final Report to WWF-Sweden and WWF-Denmark, Hamburg

Kruger, L. (1966) 'Specialized features of the cetacean brain', in Norris, K.S. (ed.), *Whales, Dolphins, and Porpoises*, University of California Press, Berkeley & Los Angeles, Calif. pp. 232–54

Kulu, D.D. (1972) 'Evolution and cytogenetics', in Ridgway, S.H. (ed.), *Mammals of the Sea: Biology and Medicine*, Springfield, Ill., pp. 503–27

Lamb, F.B. (1954) 'The fisherman's porpoise', *Natural History, 63*(5), 231–2

Lambertson, R.H. (1986) 'Disease of the common fin whale (*Balaenoptera physalus*): crassicaudiosis of the urinary system', *J. Mammal., 67*, 353- 66

Lang, T.G. and Pryor, K. (1966) 'Hydrodynamic performance of porpoises (*Stenella attenuata*), *Science, 152*, 531–3

Larsen, F. and Kapel, F. (1983) 'Further biological studies of the west Greenland minke

318

whale', *Rep. Int. Whal. Commn*, *33*, 329–32

Laughlin, W.S. and Harper, A.B. (1982) 'Demographic diversity, length of life and Aleut-Eskimo whaling', *Rep. Int. Whal. Commn* (special issue 4), 75–7

Laws, R.M. (1959) 'The foetal growth rates of whales with special reference to the fin whale, *Balaenoptera physalus* Linn.', *Discovery Rep.*, *29*, 281–308

—— (1977a) 'The significance of vertebrates in the Antarctic marine ecosystem', in Llano, G.A. (ed.), *Adaptations within Antarctic Ecosystems*, 3rd Symposium on Antarctic Ecology, Smithsonian Institution, Washington, DC, pp. 411–38

—— (1977b) 'Seals and whales of the southern ocean', *Phil. Trans. R. Soc. Lond. B*, *279*, 81–96

—— (1984) (ed.) *Antarctic Ecology*, Academic Press, London

—— (1985) 'The ecology of the Southern Ocean', *Amer. Scient.*, *73*(1), 26–40

Laws, R.M. and Purves, P.E. (1956) 'The ear plug of the Mysticeti as an indicator of age, with special reference to the North Atlantic fin whale', *Norsk Hval.*, *45*(8), 414–25

Layne, J.N. (1958) 'Observations on freshwater dolphins in the upper Amazon', *J. Mammal.*, *39*, 1–22

—— (1965) 'Observations on marine mammals in Florida waters', *Bull. Fla. State Mus. Biol. Sci.*, *9*, 131–81

Lear, W.H. and Christensen, O. (1975) 'By-catches of harbour porpoises (*Phocoena phocoena*) in salmon driftnets at West Greenland in 1972', *J. Fish. Res. Bd Can.*, *32*, 1223–8

Leatherwood, J.S. (1977) 'Some preliminary impressions on the numbers and social behavior of free-swimming bottlenosed dolphin calves (*Tursiops truncatus*) in the northern Gulf of Mexico', in Ridgway, S.H. and Benirschke, K.W. (eds.), *Breeding Dolphins: Present Status, Suggestions for the Future*, Marine Mammal Commission Report MMC-76/07, Washington, DC, pp. 143–67

Leatherwood, J.S. and Walker, W.A. (1979) 'The northern right whale dolphin *Lissodelphis* radiotelemetry in field studies of cetaceans', in Winn, H.E. and Olla, B.L. (eds.), *Behavior of Marine Animals. Vol. 3: Cetaceans*, Plenum Press, New York, NY, pp. 1–32

Leatherwood, J.S. and Walker, W.A. (1979) 'The northern right whale dolphin *Lissodelphis borealis* Peale in the eastern North Pacific', in Winn, H.E. and Olla, B.S. (eds.), *Behavior of Marine Animals. Vol. 3: Cetaceans*, Plenum Press, New York, NY, pp. 85–141

—— (1982) 'Population biology and ecology of the Pacific white-sided dolphin *Lagenorhynchus obliquidens* in the northeastern Pacific', Southwest Fisheries Center Admin. Rep. LJ-82-18C

Leatherwood, S., Caldwell, D.K., and Winn, H.E. (1976) *Whales, Dolphins, and Porpoises of the Western North Atlantic: A Guide to their Identification*, National Oceanic and Atmospheric Administration Tech. Rep., NMFS Cir. 396, Seattle, Wash.

Leatherwood, S., Reeves, R. and Foster, L. (1983) *Sierra Club Handbook of Whales and Dolphins*, Sierra Club Books, San Francisco, Calif.

Leatherwood, S., Perrin, W.F., Kirby, V.L., Hubbs, C.L. and Dahlheim, M. (1980) 'Distribution and movements of Risso's dolphin, *Grampus griseus* in the eastern north Pacific', *Fish. Bull., U.S.*, *77*(4), 951–63

Leatherwood, S., Reeves, R.R., Perrin, W.F. and Evans, W.E. (1982) *Whales, Dolphins, and Porpoises of the Eastern North Pacific and Arctic Adjacent Waters; A Guide to their Identification*, NOAA Techn. Rep. NMFS Circ. 144.

Leatherwood, S., Reeves, R.R., Bowles, A.E., Stewart, B.S. and Goodrich, K.R. (1984a) 'Distribution, seasonal movements and abundance of Pacific white-sided dolphins in the eastern North Pacific', *Sci. Rep. Whales Res. Inst., Tokyo*, *35*, 129–57

Leatherwood, S., Peters, C.B., Santerre, R., Santerre, M. and Clarke, J.T. (1984b) 'Observations of cetaceans in the northern Indian Ocean sanctuary, November 1980–May 1983', *Rep. Int. Whal. Commn*, *34*, 509–20

Lehman, J.W. and Peterle, T.J. (1971) 'DDT in Cetacea', *Invest. in Cetacea*, *3*, 349–51

Leung, Y.M. (1967) 'An illustrated key to the species of whale lice', *Crustaceana*, *12*, 279–91

Lichter, A. and Hooper, A. (1984) *Guia para el Reconocimiento de Cetáceos en el Mar Argentino*, Fundacion Vida Silvestre Argentina, Buenos Aires, Argentina

Lien, J. (1981) 'Whale collisions with inshore fishing gear in Newfoundland', CAFSAC Working Paper WP 81/99, CAFSAC Marine Mammal Meetings, Halifax, NS, 14–16 Apr. 1981

Lilly, J. (1967) *The Mind of the Dolphin: A Nonhuman Intelligence*, Doubleday, New York, NY

—— (1978) *Communication Between Man and Dolphin*, Crown, New York, NY

Lipps, J.H. and Mitchell, E.D. (1976) 'Trophic model for the adaptive radiations and extinctions of pelagic marine mammals', *Paleobiology 2*, 147–55

Litchfield, C., Greenberg, A.J., Caldwell, D.K., Caldwell, M.C., Sipos, J.C. and Ackman, R.G. (1975) 'Comparative lipid patterns in acoustical and nonacoustical fatty tissues of dolphins, porpoises and toothed whales,' *Comp. Biochem. Physiol.* 50B, 591–7

Ljungblad, D.K., Leatherwood, S. and Dahlheim, M. (1980) 'Sounds recorded in the presence of an adult and calf bowhead whale', *Mar. Fish. Rev.*, *42*, 86–7

Ljungblad, D.K., Moore, S.E. and Van Schoik, D.R. (1986) 'Seasonal patterns of distribution, abundance, migration and behavior of the western Arctic stock of bowhead whales, *Balaena mysticetus*, in Alaskan seas', *Rep. Int. Whal. Commn* (special issue 8), 177–206

Ljungblad, D.K., Thompson, P.O. and Moore, S.E. (1982) 'Underwater sounds recorded from migrating bowhead whales, *Balaena mysticetus*, in 1979', *J. Acoust. Soc. Am.*, *71*, 477–82

Ljungblad, D.K., Wursig, B., Swartz, S.L. and Keene, J.M. (1985) 'Observations on the behavior of bowhead whales (*Balaena mysticetus*) in the presence of operating seismic exploration vessels in the Alaskan Beaufort Sea, OCS Study MMS 85–0076, unpublished Report, Minerals Management Service, Anchorage, Alas.

Lloze, R. (1973) 'Contributions a l'étude anatomique, histologique et biologique de l' *Orcaella brevirostris* (Gray, 1866) du Mekong', Doctoral thesis, Université de Toulouse, Toulouse

Lockyer, C. (1972) 'The age at sexual maturity of the southern fin whale (*Balaenoptera physalus*) using annual layer counts in the ear plug', *J. Cons. int. Explor. mer.*, *34*(2), 276–94

—— (1974) 'Investigation of the ear plug of the southern sei whale, *Balaenoptera borealis*, as a valid means of determining age', *J. Cons. int. Explor. mer.*, *36*(1), 71–81

—— (1978) 'A theoretical approach to the balance between growth and food consumption in fin and sei whales, with special reference to the female reproductive cycle', *Rep. Int. Whal. Commn*, *28*, 243–9

—— (1979) 'Changes in a growth parameter associated with exploitation of southern fin and sei whales', *Rep. Int. Whal. Commn*, *29*, 191–6

—— (1981a) 'Growth and energy budgets of large baleen whales from the southern hemisphere', *FAO Fish. Ser.* (5), [*Mammals in the Seas*] 3, 379–487

—— (1981b) 'Estimates of growth and energy budget for the sperm whale, *Physeter catodon*', *FAO Fish. Ser.* (5), [*Mammals in the Seas*] 3, 489–504

—— (1981c) 'The age at sexual maturity in fin whales off Iceland', *Rep. Int. Whal. Commn*, *31*, 389–93

—— (1984) 'Review of baleen whale (Mysticeti) reproduction and implications for management', *Rep. Int. Whal. Commn* (special issue 6), 27–50

—— (1986) 'Body fat condition in northeast Atlantic fin whales, *Balaenoptera physalus*, and its relationship with reproduction and food resource', *Can. J. Fish. Aquat. Sci.*, *43*(1), 142–7

—— (in press) 'The relationship between body fat, food resource and reproductive energy costs in north Atlantic fin whales (*Balaenoptera physalus*)', *J. Zool., Lond.*, Symposium Series

Lockyer, C.H. and Brown, S.G. (1981) 'The migration of whales', in Aidley, D.J. (ed.), *Animal Migration*, Soc. for Experimental Biology Seminar Ser. 13, Cambridge University Press, Cambridge, pp. 105–37

Lockyer, C.H. and Martin, A.R. (1983) 'The sei whale off western Iceland. II. Age, growth and reproduction', *Rep. Int. Whal. Commn*, *33*, 465–76

Lockyer, C.H., Goodall, R.N.P. and Galeazzi, A.R. (in press) 'Age and body length characteristics of *Cephalorhynchus commersonii* from incidentally caught specimens off Tierra del Fuego', *Rep. Int. Whal. Commn* (special issue 9)

Lockyer, C.H., McConnell, L.C. and Waters, T.D. (1985) 'Body condition in terms of anatomical and biochemical assessment of body fat in North Atlantic fin and sei whales', *Can. J. Zool.*, *63*, 2328–38

Lopez, J.C. and Lopez, D. (1985) 'Killer whales (*Orcinus orcinus*) of Patagonia, and their behaviour of intentional stranding while hunting inshore', *J. Mammal.*, *66*(1), 181–3.

Loughlin, T.R., Fiscus, C.H., Johnson, A.M. and Rugh, D.J. (1982) 'Observations of *Mesoplodon stejnegeri* (Ziphiidae) in the central Aleutian Islands, Alaska', *J. Mammal.*, *63*(4), 697–700

Lowenstein, J.M. (1985) 'Marine mammal evolution: the molecular evidence', *Abstract, Proc. of 6th Biennial Conference on the Biology of Marine Mammals*, 22–26 Nov. 1985, Vancouver, British Columbia

Lowry, L.F. and Frost, K.J. (1984) 'Foods and feeding of bowhead whales in western and northern Alaska', *Sci. Rep. Whales Res. Inst., Tokyo*, *35*, 1–16

Lubbock, B. (1937) *The Arctic Whalers*, Brown, Son and Ferguson, Edinburgh

Lynch, K. and Whitehead, H. (1984) 'Changes in the abundance of large whales off Newfoundland and Labrador, 1976–1983, with special reference to the finback whale', Int. Whal. Commn, Sci. Comm. Doc. SC/36/02

McAlister, W.B. (1981) 'Estimates of fish consumption by marine mammals in the eastern Bering Sea and Aleutian Island area', Draft ref., NMML, NWAFC, NMFS, NOAA, pp.1–29

McBride, A.F. and Hebb, D.O. (1948) 'Behavior of the captive bottlenose dolphin, *Tursiops truncatus*', *J. Comp. Physiol. Psychol.*, *41*, 111–23

McCann, C. (1974) 'Body scarring on cetacea — odontocetes', *Sci. Rep. Whales Res. Inst., Tokyo*, *26*, 145–55

McIntyre, J. (ed.) (1974) *Mind in the Waters*, McClelland & Stewart, Toronto

Mchedlidze, G.A. (1976) [*Basic features of the paleobiological history of cetaceans*], Akademiia Nauk Gruzinskoi SSR. Institut Paleobiologii, "Metsniereba" Press. (Translation under title *General Features of the Paleobiological Evolution of Cetacea*, published 1984 for the Smithsonian Institution Libraries and the National Science Foundation. TT 78–52026. Amerind Publishing Company, New Delhi, India)

Mackintosh, N.A. (1965) *The Stocks of Whales*, Buckland Foundation Fishing News (Books) Ltd, London

—— (1973) 'Distribution of post-larval krill in the Antarctic', *Discovery Rep.*, *36*, 95–156

—— (1974) 'Sizes of krill eaten by whales in the Antarctic', *Discovery Rep.*, *36*, 157–78

Madsen, C.J. and Herman, L.M. (1980) 'Social and ecological correlates of cetacean vision and visual appearance', in Herman, L.M. (ed.), *Cetacean Behavior*, Wiley Interscience, New York, NY, pp. 101–48

Maigret, J. (1977) 'Les mammifères du Senegal II. Les mammifères marins', *Bull. A.A.S.N.S.*, *57*, 13–30

Maigret, J., Trotignon, J. and Duguy, R. (1976) 'Observations de cétacés sur les côtes de Mauritanie (1971–1975)', *Conseil Intern. pour L'Exploration de la Mer C.M. 1976/N:4*, pp. 1–5

Malme, C.I., Miles, P.R., Clark, C.W., Tyack, P. and Bird, J.E. (1983) 'Investigations of the potential effects of underwater noise from petroleum industry activities on migrating gray whale behavior', BBN Rep. No. 5366, Bolt Beranek & Newman Inc., Cambridge, Mass.

—— (1984) 'Investigations of the potential effects of underwater noise from petroleum industry activities on migrating gray whale behavior[.] Phase II: January 1984 migration', BBN Rep. No. 5586, Bolt Beranek & Newman Inc., Cambridge, Mass.

Mansfield, A., Smith, T. and Beck, B. (1975) 'The narwhal, *Monodon monoceros*, in eastern Canadian waters', *J. Fish. Res. Bd Can.*, *32*, 1041–6

Marchessaux, D. (1980) 'A review of the current knowledge of the cetaceans in the Eastern Mediterranean Sea', *Vie Marine*, 2, 59–66

Marchessaux, D. and Duguy, R. (1978) 'Note preliminaire sur les Cétacés de la Méditerranée orientale', XXIe Congrès-Assemblée plénière, Antalya, 24 novembre–2 decembre 1978. Comité des Vertebres marins et Cephalopodes

Marquette, W.M. and Braham, H.W. (1982) 'Gray whale distribution and catch by Alaskan eskimos: a replacement for the bowhead whale?', *Arctic*, *35*(3), 386–94

Marsh, H. and Kasuya, T. (1984) 'Changes in the ovaries of the short-finned pilot whale, *Globicephala macrorhynchus*, with age and reproductive activity', *Rep. Int. Whal. Commn* (special issue 6), 311–36

—— (1986) 'Evidence for reproductive senescence in female cetaceans', *Rep. Int. Whal. Commn* (special issue 8), 57–74

Martin, A.R., (1983) 'The sei whale off western Iceland. 1. Size, distribution and abundance', *Rep. Int. Whal. Commn*, *33*, 457–63

Martin, A.R., Hembree, D., Waters, T.D. and Sigurjonsson, J. (1984) 'IDCR cruise/aerial survey in the north eastern Atlantic', *Rep. Int. Whal. Commn*, *34*, 645–53

Martin, A.R., Katona, S.K., Matilla, D., Hembree, D. and Waters, T.D. (1984) 'Migration of humpback whales between the Caribbean and Iceland', *J. Mammal.*, *65*, 333–6

Martinez, D.R. and Klinghammer, E. (1970) 'The behavior of the whale *Orcinus orca*: A review of the literature', *Z. Tierpsychol.*, *27*, 828–39

Masaki, Y. (1976) 'Biological studies on the North Pacific sei whale', *Bull. Far Seas Fish Res. Lab.*, *14*, 1–104

—— (1978) 'Yearly change in the biological parameters of the Antarctic sei whale', *Rep. Int. Whal. Commn*, 29, 375–96

—— (1979) 'Yearly change of the biological parameters for the Antarctic minke whale', *Rep. Int. Whal. Commn*, 29, 375–96

321

Mate, B.R. (1981) 'Marine mammals', in Maser, C., Mate, B.R., Franklin, J.F. and Dyrness, C.T., *Natural History of Oregon Coast Mammals*, U.S. Department of Agriculture, Forest Service Gen. Tech. Report PNW-133, pp. 372–458

—— (1983) 'Movements and dive characteristics of a satellite monitored humpback whale', *Abstract, Proc. of 5th Biennial Conf. on the ,Biology of Marine Mammals*, 27 Nov.–1 Dec. 1983, Boston, Mass.

—— (1984) 'Tracking whales by satellite', *Abstract, Proc. of 9th Int. Reunion of the Mexican Society for the Study of Marine Mammals*, 29–31 Mar. La Paz, Baja California Sur, Mexico

Mate, B.R. and Greenlaw, C. (1981) 'An acoustic harrassment system to reduce marine mammal-fishery conflicts', *Abstract, Proc. of 4th Biennial Conf. on the Biology of Marine Mammals*, 14–18 Dec. 1981, San Francisco, Calif.

Mate, B.R. and Harvey, J.T. (1984) 'Ocean movements of radio-tagged gray whales', in Jones, M.L., Swartz, S.L. and Leatherwood, S. (eds.), *The Gray Whale* Eschrichtius robustus, Academic Press, New York, NY, pp. 577–89

Mate, B.R., Harvey, J.T., Hobbs, L. and Maiefski, R. (1983) 'A new attachment device for radio-tagging large whales', *J. Wildl. Mgmt.*, 47(3), 868–72

Mattila, D.K., Carlson, C.A., Clapham, C.J. and Mayo, C.A. (1983) 'Resightings of individually identifiable fin whales in the waters of Stellwagen Bank and Cape Cod Bay, Massachusetts', *Abstract, Proc. of 5th Biennial Conf. on the Biology of Marine Mammals*, 27 Nov.–3 Dec. 1983, Boston, Mass.

Maul, G.E. and Sergeant, D.E. (1977) 'New cetacean records from Madeira', *Bocagiana*, 43, 1–8

May, R.M., Beddington, J.R., Clarke, C.W., Holt, S.J. and Laws, R.M. (1979) 'Management of multispecies fisheries', *Science*, 205, 267–77

Mayr, E. (1942) *Systematics and the Origin of Species*, Columbia University Press, New York, NY

Mead, J.G. (1975a) 'A fossil beaked whale (Cetacea: Ziphiidae) from the Miocene of Kenya', *J. Paleontol.*, 49, 745–51

—— (1975b) 'Anatomy of the external nasal passages and facial complex in the Delphinidae (Mammalia: Cetacea)', *Smithsonian Contributions to Zoology*, 207, 1–72

—— (1979) 'An analysis of cetacean strandings along the eastern coast of the United States', in Geraci, J.B. and St Aubin, D.J. (eds.), *Biology of Marine Mammals: Insights through Strandings*, US Marine Mammal Commission Report PB-293 890, pp. 54–68

—— (1981) 'First records of *Mesoplodon hectori* (Ziphiidae) from the northern hemisphere and a description of the adult male', *J. Mammal.*, 62, 430–2

—— (1984) 'Survey of reproductive data for the beaked whales (Ziphiidae)', *Rep. Int. Whal. Commn* (special issue 6), 91–6

Mead, J.G. and Mitchell, E.D. (1984) 'Atlantic gray whales', in Jones, M.L., Swartz, S.L., and Leatherwood, S. (eds.), *The Gray Whale* Eschrichtius robustus, Academic Press, New York, NY, pp. 33–53

—— and Payne, R. (1975) 'A specimen of the Tasman beaked whale from Argentina', *J. Mammal.*, 56, 213–18

Mead, J.G., Odell, D.K., Wells, R.S. and Scott, M.D. (1980) 'Observations on a mass stranding of spinner dolphin, *Stenella longirostris*, from the west coast of Florida', *Fish. Bull., U.S.*, 78, 353–60

Mercer, M.C. (1975) 'Modified Leslie-DeLury population models of the long-finned pilot whale (*Globicephala melaena*) and annual production of the short-finned squid (*Illex illecebrosus*) based upon their interaction at Newfoundland', *J. Fish. Res. Bd Can.*, 32, 1145–52

Mermoz, J.F. (1980) 'Preliminary report on the southern right whale in the south-western Atlantic', *Rep. Int. Whal. Commn*, 30, 183–6

Mikhalev, Yu. A. (1980) 'General regularities in prenatal growth in whales and some aspects of their reproductive biology', *Rep. Int. Whal. Commn*, 30, 249–53

Mitchell, E.D. (1970) 'Pigmentation pattern evolution in delphinid coloration: an essay in adaptive coloration', *Can. J. Zool.*, 48, 717–40.

—— (1975a) *Porpoise, Dolphin and Small Whale Fisheries of the World: Status and Problems*, IUCN monograph no. 3, Morges, Switzerland

—— (ed.) (1975b) 'Review of biology and fisheries for smaller cetaceans', *J. Fish. Res. Bd Can.*, 32, 889–983

—— and Kozicki, V.M. (1975) 'Supplementary information on minke whale (*Balaenoptera acutorostrata*) from Newfoundland fishery', *J. Fish. Res. Bd Can.*, 32, 985–94

—— and Reeves, R.R. (1980) 'The Alaska bowhead problem: a commentary', *Arctic*, 33, 686–723

Miyazaki, N. (1977) 'Growth and reproduction of *Stenella coeruleoalba* off the Pacific coast of Japan', *Sci. Rep. Whales Res. Inst., Tokyo, 29*, 21–48

—— (1980) 'Catch records of cetaceans off the coast of the Kii Peninsula', *Mem. Nat. Sci. Mus., Tokyo, 13*, 69–82

—— (1983) 'Catch statistics of small cetaceans taken in Japanese waters', *Rep. Int. Whal. Commn, 33*, 621–31

—— (1984) 'Further analyses of reproduction in the striped dolphin, *Stenella coeruleoalba*, off the Pacific coast of Japan', *Rep. Int. Whal. Commn (special issue 6)*, 343–53

—— and Nishiwaki, M. (1978) 'School structure of the striped dolphin off the Pacific coast of Japan', *Sci. Rep. Whales Res. Inst., Tokyo, 30*, 65–115

Miyazaki, N. and Wada, S. (1978a) 'Observations of cetacea during whale marking cruise in the western tropical Pacific, 1976', *Sci. Rep. Whales Res. Inst., Tokyo, 30*, 179–96

—— and Wada, S. (1978b) 'Fraser's dolphin, *Lagenodelphis hosei* in the western North Pacific', *Sci. Rep. Whales Res. Inst., Tokyo, 30*, 231–44

Miyazaki, N., Jones, L.L. and Beach, J.R. (1984) 'Some observations on the schools of dalli- and truei-type Dall's porpoises in the northwestern Pacific', *Sci. Rep. Whales Res. Inst., Tokyo, 35*, 93–105

Miyazaki, N., Kasuya, T. and Nishiwaki, M. (1973) 'Food of *Stenella coeruleoalba*', *Sci. Rep. Whales Res. Inst., Tokyo, 25*, 265–75

—— (1974) 'Distribution and migration of two kinds of *Stenella* in the Pacific coast of Japan', *Sci. Rep. Whales Res. Inst., Tokyo, 26*, 65–115

Mizroch, S.A. and York, A.E. (1984) 'Have pregnancy rates of southern hemisphere fin whales, *Balaenoptera physalus*, increased?' *Rep. Int. Whal. Commn* (special issue 6), 401–10

Mobley, J.R. Jr and Herman, L.M. (1985) 'Transcience of social affiliations among humpback whales (*Megaptera novaeangliae*) on the Hawaiian wintering grounds', *Can J. Zool., 63*, 762–72

Mohl, B. and Andersen, S. (1973) 'Echolocation: high-frequency component in the click of the harbour porpoise (*Phocoena phocoena* L.)', *J. Acoust. Soc. Am., 54*, 1368–72

Møhl-Hansen, U. (1954) 'Investigations on reproduction and growth of the porpoise (*Phocaena phocaena* (L.)) from the Baltic', *Vidensk. Medd. Dansk naturh. Foren. Kobenhavn, 116*, 369–96

Montevecchi, W.A., Ricklefs, R.E., Kirkham, I.R. and Gabaldon, D. (1984) 'Growth energetics of nestling northern gannets (*Sula bassana*)', *Auk, 101*, 334–41

Moore, J.C. (1968) 'Relationships among the living genera of beaked whales with classifications, diagnoses and keys', *Fieldiana: Zoology, 53*(4), 209–98

Moore, S.E. and Ljungblad, D.K. (1984) 'Gray whales in the Beaufort, Chukchi, and Bering Seas: distribution and sound production', in Jones, M.L., Swartz, S.L. and Leatherwood, S. (eds.), *The Gray Whale* Eschrichtius robustus, Academic Press, New York, NY, pp. 543–59

Morejohn, G.V. (1979) 'The natural history of Dall's porpoise in the North Pacific Ocean', in Winn, H.E. and Olla, B.L. (eds.), *Behavior of Marine Animals, Vol. 3: Cetaceans*, Plenum Press, New York, NY, pp. 45–84

Morgan, D.W. (1979) 'The vocal and behavioral reactions of the beluga, Delphinapterus leucas, to playback of its sounds', in Winn, H.E. and Olla, B.L. (eds.), *Behavior of Marine Animals, Vol. 3: Cetaceans*, Plenum Press, New York, pp. 311–43

Morgane, P.J. (1974) 'The whale brain: the anatomical basis of intelligence', in McIntyre, J. (ed.), *Mind in the Waters*, McClelland & Stewart, Toronto, pp. 84–93

—— (1978) 'Whale brains and their meaning for intelligence', in Frost, S. (ed.), *Whales and Whaling. Vol. II*, Australian Govt. Printing Service, Canberra, pp. 198–217

Morgane, P.J., Jacobs, M.S. and Galaburda, A. (1986a) 'Evolutionary aspects of cortical organization in the dolphin brain', in Bryden, M.M. and Harrison, R.J. (eds.), *Research on Dolphins*, Clarendon Press, Oxford, pp. 71–98

—— (1986b) 'Evolutionary morphology of the dolphin brain', in Schusterman, R.J., Thomas, J.A. and Wood F.G. (eds.), *Dolphin Cognition and Behaviour: A Comparative Approach*, Lawrence Erlbaum, Hillsdale, NJ, pp. 5–29

Moriarty, F. (1975) *Pollutants and Animals*, George Allen and Unwin, London

Muizon, C. de (1983a) 'Un nouveau Phocoenidae (Cetacea) du Pliocène inférieur du Pérou', *Comptes Rendus des Séances de l'Academie des Sciences Paris, série II, 297*, 85–8

—— (1983b) 'Un Ziphiidae (Cetacea) nouveau du Pliocène inférieur du Pérou', *Comptes Rendus des Séances de l'Académie des Sciences Paris, serie II, 297*, 85–8

Murison, L.D., Murie, D.J., Morin, K.R. and Curiel, J. da S. (1984) 'Foraging of the gray whale along the west coast of Vancouver Island, British Columbia', in Jones, M.L.,

Swartz, S.L. and Leatherwood, S. (eds.), *The Gray Whale* Eschrichtius robustus, Academic Press, New York, NY, pp. 451–63

Murray, J. and Burt, J.R. (1969) 'The composition of fish', *Torry Advisory Note No. 38*, Her Majesty's Stationery Office, UK

Myrick, A.C. Jr (1979a) 'Variation, taphonomy, and adaptation of the Rhabdosteidae (= Eurhinodelphidae) (Odontoceti, Mammalia) from the Calvert Formation of Maryland and Virginia', PhD thesis, University of California, Los Angeles, Calif.

—— (1979b) 'Qualitative adaptive models for pelagic and river dolphins', *Abstract, Proc. of 3rd Biennial Conf. on Marine Mammals*, 7–9 Oct. 1979, Seattle, Wash.

Nachtigall, P.E. (1986) 'Vision, audition and chemoreception in dolphins and other marine mammals', in Schusterman, R.J., Thomas, J.A. and Wood, F.G. (eds.), *Dolphin Cognition and Behaviour: A Comparative Approach*, Lawrence Erlbaum, Hillsdale, NJ, pp. 79–113

Nagorsen, D. (1985) '*Kogia simus*', *Mammalian Species (239)*, 1–3

Natural Environment Research Council (NERC) (1983) *Contaminants in Marine Top Predators*, Natural Environment Research Council Publics. Series C, 23, 1–30

Nemoto, T. (1956) 'On the diatoms of the skin film of whales in the northern Pacific', *Sci. Rep. Whales Res. Inst., Tokyo, 11*, 99–132

—— (1959) 'Food of baleen whales with reference to whale movements', *Sci. Rep. Whales Res. Inst., Tokyo, 14*, 149–290

—— (1962) 'Food of baleen whales collected in recent Japanese Antarctic whaling expeditions', *Sci. Rep. Whales Res. Inst., Tokyo, 16*, 89–103

—— (1964) 'School of baleen whales in the feeding areas', *Sci. Rep. Whales Res. Inst., Tokyo, 18*, 89–110

—— (1970) 'Feeding pattern of baleen whales in the ocean', in Steele, J.H. (ed.), *Marine Food Chains*, Oliver and Boyd, Edinburgh, pp. 241–52

—— (1978) 'Humpback whales observed within the continental shelf waters of the eastern Bering Sea', *Sci. Rep. Whales Res. Inst., Tokyo, 30*, 245–7

Nemoto, T. and Kawamura, A. (1977) 'Characteristics of food habits and distribution of baleen whales with special reference to the abundance of North Pacific sei and Bryde's whales', *Rep. Int. Whal. Commn* (special issue 1), 80–7

Nemoto, T., Best, P.B., Ishimaru, K. and Takano, H. (1980) 'Diatom films on whales in South African waters', *Sci. Rep. Whales Res. Inst., Tokyo, 32*, 97–103

Nerini, M.K. (1984) 'A review of gray whale feeding ecology', in Jones, M.L., Swartz, S.L. and Leatherwood, S. (eds.), *The Gray Whale* Eschrichtius robustus, Academic Press, New York, NY, pp. 423–50

Nerini, M.K. and Oliver, J. (1983) 'Gray whales and the structure of the Bering Sea benthos', *Oecologia, 59*, 224–5

Nerini, M.K., Braham, H.W., Marquette, W.M. and Rugh, D.J. (1984) 'Life history of the bowhead whale, *Balaena mysticetus* (Mammalia: Cetacea)', *J. Zool., Lond., 204*, 443–68

Nielsen, B. (1986) 'The global plan of action for the conservation management and utilization of marine mammals', *Ambio, 15*(3), 134–6.

Nielsen, H.G. (1972) 'Age determination of the harbour porpoise *Phocoena phocoena* (L.) (Cetacea)', *Vidensk. Medd. Dan. Naturhist. Foren. Kobenhavn, 135*, 61–84.

Nishiwaki, M. (1957) 'Age characteristics of ear plugs of whales', *Sci. Rep. Whales Res. Inst., Tokyo, 12*, 23–32

—— (1959) 'Humpback whales in Ryukyuan waters', *Sci. Rep. Whales Res. Inst., Tokyo, 14*, 49–87

—— (1962) 'Aerial photographs showing sperm whales' interesting habits', *Norsk Hval., 51*, 393–8

—— (1967) 'Distribution and migration of marine mammals in the North Pacific area', *Bull. Ocean Res. Inst., Univ. Tokyo, 1*, 1–64

—— (1975) 'Ecological aspects of smaller cetaceans, with emphasis on the striped dolphin (*Stenella coeruleoalba*)', *J. Fish. Res. Bd Can., 32*, 1069–72

Nishiwaki, M. and Handa, C. (1958) 'Killer whales caught in the coastal waters off Japan for recent 10 years', *Sci. Rep. Whales Res. Inst., Tokyo, 13*, 85–96

Nishiwaki, M. and Oguro, N. (1971) 'Baird's beaked whales caught on the coast of Japan in recent 10 years', *Sci. Rep. Whales Res. Inst., Tokyo, 23*, 111–22

—— (1972) 'Catch of the Cuvier's beaked whale off Japan in recent years', *Sci. Rep. Whales Res. Inst., Tokyo, 24*, 35–41

Nishiwaki, M. and Tobayama, T. (1982) 'Morphological study on the hybrid between *Tursiops* and *Pseudorca*', *Sci. Rep. Whales Res. Inst., Tokyo, 34*, 109–21

Norris, K.S. (1967) 'Aggressive behavior in Cetacea', in Clemente, C.C. and Lindsley, D.B. (eds.), *Aggression and Defense: Neural Mechanisms and Social Patterns (Brain Function,*

Vol. V), UCLA Forum Med. Sci. No. 7, University of California Press, Berkeley & Los Angeles, Calif., pp. 225–41

—— (1969) 'The echolocation of marine mammals', in Andersen, H.T. (ed.), *The Biology of Marine Mammals*, Academic Press, New York, NY, pp. 391–423

Norris, K.S. and Dohl, T.P. (1980a) 'The behavior of the Hawaiian spinner porpoise, *Stenella longirostris*', *Fish. Bull., U.S.*, 77, 821–49

—— (1980b) 'The structure and functions of cetacean schools', in Herman, L.M. (ed.), *Cetacean Behavior*, Wiley Interscience, New York, NY, pp. 211–62

Norris, K.S. and Harvey, G.W. (1972) 'A theory for the function of the spermaceti organ of the sperm whale (*Physeter catodon* L.)', in *Animal Orientation and Navigation*, NASA, Washington, DC, pp. 397–417

—— (1974) 'Sound transmission in the porpoise head', *J. Acoust. Soc. Am.*, 56, 659–64

Norris, K.S. and Mohl, B. (1981) 'Do odontocetes debilitate their prey acoustically?', *Abstract, Proc. of 4th Biennial Conf. on the Biology of Marine Mammals*, 14–18 Dec. 1981, San Francisco, Calif.

Norris, K.S. and Prescott, J.H. (1961) 'Observations on Pacific cetaceans of Californian and Mexican waters', *Univ. Calif. Publ. Zool.*, 63, 291–402

Norris, K.S., Dormer, K.J., Pegg, J. and Liese, G.J. (1971) 'The mechanisms of sound production and air recycling in porpoises: a preliminary report', in *Proc. 8th Ann. Conf. Biol. Sonar Diving Mammals, Stanford Research Institute*, Menlo Park, Calif., pp. 113–29

Norris, K.S., Villa-Ramirez, B., Nichols, G., Wursig, B. and Miller, K. (1983) 'Lagoon entrance and other aggregations of gray whales (*Eschrichtius robustus*)', in Payne, R. (ed.), *Communication and Behavior of Whales*, AAAS Selected Symp. Ser., Westview Press, Boulder, Co., pp. 259–93

Northridge, S. (1984) *World Review of Interactions Between Marine Mammals and Fisheries*, FAO Fisheries Technical Paper 251, FAO, Rome

Northridge, S. and Pilleri, G. (1985) 'A review of human impact on small cetaceans', unpublished Report to Greenpeace, London

Odell, D.K., Asper, E.D. and Reynolds, J.E. III (1984) 'Reproductive biology of pygmy sperm whales, *Kogia breviceps*, stranded in Florida', *Rep. Int. Whal. Commn* (special issue 6), 481

Ohsumi, J.S. (1965) 'Reproduction of the sperm whale in the northwest hPacific', *Sci. Rep. Whales Res. Inst., Tokyo*, 19, 1–35

—— (1971) 'Some investigations on the school structure of sperm whale', *Sci. Rep. Whales Res. Inst., Tokyo*, 23, 1–25

—— (1972) 'Examination of the recruitment rate of the Antarctic fin whale stock by use of mathematical models', *Rep. Int. Whal. Commn*, 22, 69–90

—— (1973) 'Revised estimates of recruitment rate in the Antarctic fin whales', *Rep. Int. Whal. Commn*, 23, 192–9

—— (1975) 'Incidental catch of cetaceans with salmon gillnets', *J. Fish. Res. Bd Can.*, 32, 1229–35

—— (1977a) 'Bryde's whales in the pelagic whaling ground of the North Pacific', *Rep. Int. Whal. Commn* (special issue 1), 140–50

—— (1977b) 'A preliminary note on Japanese records on death-times for whales killed by whaling harpoon', *Rep. Int. Whal. Commn*, 27, 204–5

—— (1979) 'Interspecies relationships among some biological parameters in cetaceans and estimation of natural mortality coefficient of the southern hemisphere minke whale', *Rep. Int. Whal. Commn*, 29, 397–406

—— (1980) 'Population study of the Bryde's whale in the southern hemisphere under scientific permit in the three seasons, 1976/77–1978/9', *Rep. Int. Whal. Commn*, 30, 319–31

—— (1986a) 'Yearly change in age and body length at sexual maturity of a fin whale stock in the eastern North Pacific', *Sci. Rep. Whales Res. Inst., Tokyo*, 37, 1–16

—— (1986b) 'Earplug transition phase as an indicator of sexual maturity in female Antarctic minke whales', *Sci. Rep. Whales Res. Inst., Tokyo*, 37, 17–30

Ohsumi, S., Masaki, Y. and Kawamura, A. (1970) 'Stock of the Antarctic minke whale', *Sci. Rep. Whales Res. Inst., Tokyo*, 22, 75–125

Ohsumi, S., Shimadzu, Y. and Doi, T. (1971) 'The seventh memorandum on the results of Japanese stock assessment of whales in the North Pacific', *Rep. Int. Whal. Commn*, 21, 76–89

Oliver, J.S., Slattery, P.N., Silberstein, M.A. and O'Connor, E.F. (1984) 'Gray whale feeding on dense ampeliscid amphipod communities near Bamfield, British Columbia', *Can. J. Zool.*, 62, 41–9

Omura, H. (1950a) 'Diatom infection on blue and fin whales in the Antarctic whaling area V (the Ross Sea Area)', *Sci. Rep. Whales Res. Inst., Tokyo, 4*, 14–26
—— (1950b) 'Whales in the adjacent waters of Japan', *Sci. Rep. Whales Res. Inst., Tokyo, 4*, 27–113
—— (1962) 'Further information on Bryde's whale from the coast of Japan', *Sci. Rep. Whales Res. Inst., Tokyo, 16*, 7–18
—— (1966) 'Bryde's whale in the northwest Pacific', in Norris, K.S. (ed.), *Whales, Dolphins and Porpoises*, Univ. of California Press, Berkeley & Los Angeles, Calif., pp. 70–8
—— (1977) 'Review of the Occurrence of Bryde's whale in the Northwest Pacific', *Rep. Int. Whal. Commn* (special issue 1), 88–91
Omura, H. and Sakiura, H. (1956) 'Studies on the little piked whale from the coast of Japan', *Sci. Rep. Whales Res. Inst., Tokyo, 11*, 1–37
Omura, H., Fujino, K. and Kimura, S. (1955) 'Beaked whale *Berardius bairdi* of Japan, with notes on *Ziphius cavirostris*', *Sci. Rep. Whales Res. Inst., Tokyo, 10*, 89–132, 10pls.
Omura, H., Ohsumi, S., Nemoto, T., Nasu, K. and Kasuya, T. (1969) 'Black right whales in the North Pacific', *Sci. Rep. Whales Res. Inst., Tokyo, 21*, 1–78
Orr, W.N. and Faulhaber, J. (1975) 'A middle Tertiary cetacean from Oregon', *Northwest Science, 49*, 174–81
Osborne, R.W. (1981) 'Social behavior of Puget Sound killer whales; sequencing, budgeting and circadian independence', *Abstract, Proc. of 4th Biennial Conf. on the Biology of Marine Mammals*, 14–18 Dec. 1981, San Francisco, Calif.
O'Shea, T., Brownell, R.L., Jr, Clark, D.R., Jr, Walker, W.A., Gay, M.L. and Lamont, T.G. (1980) 'Organochlorine pollutants in small cetaceans from the Pacific and South Atlantic Oceans, Nov 1968–June 1976', *Pesticides Monitoring Journal*, 14, 35–46
Otterlind, G. (1976) 'The harbour porpoise (*Phocoena phocoena*) endangered in Swedish waters', *Int. Council for Explor. of the Sea*, Doc. C.M. 1976/N:16, 1–7
Patterson, B. and Hamilton, G.R. (1964) 'Repetitive 20 cycle per second biological hydroacoustic signals at Bermuda', in Tavolga, W.N. (ed.), *Marine Bio-Acoustics*, Pergamon Press, New York, NY, pp. 125–45
Payne, K., Tyack, P. and Payne, R. (1983) 'Progressive changes in the songs of humpback whales (*Megaptera novaeangliae*): a detailed analysis of two seasons in Hawaii', in Payne, R. (ed.), *Communication and Behavior of Whales*, AAAS Selected Symp. Ser., Westview Press, Boulder, Co., pp. 9–57
Payne, R. (ed.) (1983) *Communication and Behavior of Whales*, AAAS Series No. 76, Westview Press, Co.
—— (in press) *Behavior of Southern Right Whales* (Eubalaena australis), University of Chicago Press, Chicago, Ill.
Payne, R. and Dorsey, E.M. (1983) 'Sexual dimorphism and aggressive use of callosities in right whales (*Eubalaena australis*)', in Payne, R. (ed.), *Communication and Behavior of Whales*, AAAS Selected Symp. Ser., Westview Press, Boulder, Co., pp. 295–329
Payne, R. and Guinee, L.N. (1983) 'Humpback whale (*Megaptera novaeangliae*) songs as an indicator of "stocks"', in Payne, R. (ed.), *Communication and Behavior of Whales*, AAAS Selected Symp. Ser., Westview Press, Boulder, Co., pp. 333–58
Payne, R. and McVay, S. (1971) 'Songs of humpback whales', *Science, 173*, 587–97
Payne, R. and Payne, K. (1971) 'Underwater sounds of southern right whales', *Zoologica, 56*, 159–65
Payne, R. and Webb, D. (1971) 'Orientation by means of long range acoustic signalling in baleen whales', *Ann. N.Y. Acad. Sci., 188*, 110–41
Payne, R., Brazier, O., Dorsey, E.M., Perkins, J.S., Rowntree, V.J. and Titus, A. (1983) 'External features in southern right whales (*Eubalaena australis*) and their use in identifying individuals', in Payne, R. (ed.), *Communication and Behavior of Whales*, AAAS Selected Symp. Ser., Westview Press, Boulder, Co., pp. 371–445
Peard, J., Calambokidis, J. and Cubbage, J.C. (1983) 'Organochlorine pollutants in marine mammals from the eastern North Pacific, 1972–1981', *Abstract, Proc. of 5th Biennial Conference on the Biology of Marine Mammals*, 27 Nov.–1 Dec. 1983, Boston, Mass.
Peilie, W. (1978) 'Studies on the baleen whales in the Yellow Sea', *Acta Zoologica Sinica, 24*(3), 269–77
—— (1981) 'On the *Balaenoptera edeni*, found in the southeastern coast of China', *Chinese J. Zool., 3*, 43–6
Perkins, J.S. and Beamish, P.C. (1979) 'Net entanglements of baleen whales in the inshore fishery of Newfoundland', *J. Fish. Res. Bd Can., 36*, 521–8
Perrin, W.F. (1975) 'Variation of spotted and spinner porpoise (Genus *Stenella*) in the eastern tropical Pacific and Hawaii', *Bull. Scripps Instit. Oceanogr.*, vol. 21

—— (1985a) 'The former dolphin fishery at St. Helena', *Rep. Int. Whal. Commn*, 35, 423–8

—— (ed.) (1985b) *Newsletter of the Cetacean Specialist Group, No. 1*, IUCN, Feb. 1985

—— (ed.) (1986) *Newsletter of the Cetacean Specialist Group, No. 2*, IUCN, Mar. 1986

Perrin, W.F. and Donovan, G.P. (eds.) (1984) 'Report of the workshop on reproduction of whales, dolphins and porpoises', *Rep. Int. Whal. Commn* (special issue 6), 1–24

Perrin, W.F. and Henderson, J.R. (1984) 'Growth and reproductive rates in two populations of spinner dolphins, *Stenella longirostris*, with different histories of exploitation', *Rep. Int. Whal. Commn* (special issue 6), 417–30

Perrin, W.F. and Myrick, A.C. Jr (eds.) (1980) 'Age determination of toothed whales and sirenians', *Rep. Int. Whal. Commn* (special issue 3), 1–229

Perrin, W.F. and Oliver, C.W. (1982) 'Time/area distribution and composition of the incidental kill of dolphins and small whales in the U.S. purse-seine fishery for tuna in the eastern tropical Pacific, 1979–80', *Rep. Int. Whal. Commn*, 32, 429–44

Perrin, W.F. and Powers, J.E. (1980) 'Role of a nematode in natural mortality of spotted dolphins', *J. Wildl. Mgmt.* 44(4), 960–3

Perrin, W.F. and Reilly, S.B. (1984) 'Reproductive parameters of dolphins and small whales of the family Delphinidae', *Rep. Int. Whal. Commn* (special issue 6), 97–133

Perrin, W.F. and Walker, W.A. (1975) 'The rough-toothed porpoise, *Steno bredanensis*, in the eastern tropical Pacific', *J. Mammal.*, 56, 905–7

Perrin, W.F., Brownell, R.L. Jr and DeMaster, D.P. (eds.) (1984) 'Reproduction in whales, dolphins and porpoises', *Rep. Int. Whal. Commn* (special issue 6), 1–495

Perrin, W.F., Coe, J.M. and Zweifel, J.R. (1976) 'Growth and reproduction of the spotted porpoise, *Stenella attenuata*, in the offshore eastern tropical Pacific', *Fish. Bull., U.S.*, 74, 229–69

Perrin, W.F., Miller, R.B. and Sloan, B.A. (1977) 'Reproductive parameters of the offshore spotted dolphin, a geographical form of *Stenella attenuata*, in the eastern tropical Pacific, 1973–75', *Fish. Bull., U.S.*, 75, 629–33

Perrin, W.F., Mitchell, E.D. and Van Bree, P.J.H. (1978) 'Historical zoogeography of tropical pelagic dolphins', *Abstract II, Congressus Theriologicus Internationalis*, 20–27 June 1978

Perrin, W.F., Mitchell, E.D., Mead, J.G., Caldwell, D.K. and Van Bree, P.J.H. (1981) '*Stenella clymene*, a rediscovered tropical dolphin of the Atlantic', *J. Mammal.*, 62(3), 583–98

Perrin, W.F., Scott, M.D., Walker, G.J. and Cass, V.L. (1985) 'Review of geographical stocks of tropical dolphins (*Stenella* spp. and *Delphinus delphis*) in the eastern Pacific', NOAA Tech. Rep. NMFS 28, US Dept. of Commerce, National Marine Fisheries Service, Seattle, Wash.

Perrin, W.F., Smith, T.D. and Sakawaga, G.T. (1982) 'Status of populations of spotted dolphin, *Stenella attenuata*, and spinner dolphin, *S. longirostris*, in the eastern tropical Pacific', *FAO Fish. Ser. (5), [Mammals in the Seas]* 4, 67–84

Perrin, W.F., Warner, R.R., Fiscus, C.H. and Holts, D.B. (1973) 'Stomach contents of porpoises, *Stenella* spp. and yellow fin tuna, *Thunnus albacares*, in mixed-species aggregation', *Fish. Bull., U.S.*, 71, 1077–92

Perryman, W.L., Scott, M.D. and Hammond, P.S. (1984) 'A technique for estimating reproductive parameters of small cetaceans from vertical aerial photographs', *Rep. Int. Whal. Commn* (special issue 6), 482

Peterlin, A. (1970) 'Molecular model of drag reduction by polymer solutes', *Nature, Lond.*, 227, 598–9

Pike, G.C. and MacAskie, I.B. (1969) 'Marine mammals of British Columbia', *Fish. Res. Bd Can. Bull.*, 171, 1–54

Pilleri, G. (1971) 'On the La Plata dolphin, *Pontoporia blainvillei* off the Uruguayan coast', *Invest. on Cetacea*, 3, 59–67

Pilleri, G. and Busnel, R.-G. (1968) 'Brain/body weight ratios in Delphinidae', *Acta Anat.*, 73, 92–7

Pilleri, G. and Gihr, M. (1974) 'Contribution to the knowledge of the cetaceans of southwest and monsoon Asia (Persian Gulf, Indus Delta, Malabar, Andaman Sea and Gulf of Siam)', *Invest. on Cetacea*, 5, 95–149

Pilleri, G. and Pilleri, O. (1982) 'Cetacean records in the Mediterranean Sea', *Invest. on Cetacea*, 14, 50–63

Pilleri, G., Kraus, C. and Gihr, M. (1971) 'Physical analysis of the sounds emitted by *Platanista indi*', *Invest. on Cetacea*, 3, 22–30

Pilleri, G., Peixun, C., Peilin, L., Renjun, L. and Kejie, L. (1980) 'Distribution, ecology, behavior and conservation of the dolphins of the middle reaches of Changjiang (Yangtze

River) (Wuhan-Yueyang)', *Invest. on Cetacea*, *10*, 87–103

Pilleri, G., Zbinden, K., Gihr, M. and Kraus, C. (1976) 'Sonar clicks, directionality of the emission field and echolocating behaviour of the Indus River dolphin (*Platanista indi* Blyth, 1859)', *Invest. on Cetacea*, *7*, 13–43

Pingree, R.D. and Mardell, G.T. (1981) 'Slope turbulence, internal waves and phytoplankton growth at the Celtic Sea shelf-break', *Phil. Trans. Roy. Soc. Lond. A*, *302*, 663–82

Pingree, R.D., Holligan, P.M. and Mardell, G.T. (1978) 'The effects of vertical stability on phytoplankton distributions in the summer on the northwest European Shelf', *Deep Sea Research*, *25*, 1011–28

Pippard, L. and Malcolm, H. (1978) 'White whales (*Delphinapterus leucas*): observations on their distribution, population and critical habitats in the St Lawrence and Saguenay Rivers', Dept. of Indian and Northern Affairs, and Parks Canada, project C1632, contract 76/190

Pivorunas, A. (1976) 'A mathematical consideration on the function of baleen plates and their fringes', *Sci. Rep. Whales Res. Inst., Tokyo*, *28*, 37–55

—— (1979) 'The feeding mechanisms of baleen whales', *Amer. Sci.*, *67*, 432–40

Popper, A.N. (1980) 'Sound emission and detection by delphinids', in Herman, L.M. (ed.), *Cetacean Behavior*, Wiley Interscience, New York, NY, pp. 1–52

Praderi, R. (1979) 'Considerations on the population of Franciscana', *Rep. Int. Whal. Commn*, *31*, SM4

Price, C. (1981) 'Some economic aspects of marine mammal management policies: the future and the discount rate', *FAO Fish. Ser* (5) [*Mammals in the Seas*] *3*, 57–65

Price, W.S. (1985) 'Whaling in the Caribbean: historical perspective and update', *Rep. Int. Whal. Commn*, *35*, 413–20.

Pryor, K.W., Haag, R. and O'Reilly, J. (1969) 'The creative porpoise: Training for novel behavior', *J. Exp. Anal. Behav.*, *12*, 653–61

Purves, P.E. (1955) 'The wax plug in the external auditory meatus of the Mysticeti', *Discovery Rep.*, *27*, 293–302

—— (1963) 'Locomotion in whales', *Nature, Lond.*, *197*, 334–7

—— (1967a) 'The structure of flukes in relation to laminar flow in cetaceans', *Zeitschrift fur Saugetierkunde*, *34*, 1–8

—— (1967b) 'Anatomical and experimental observations on the cetacean sonar system', in Busnel, R.-G. (ed.), *Animal Sonar Systems: Biology and Bionics*, Laboratoire de Physiologie Acoustique, Jouy-en-Josas, France, pp. 197–270

Purves, P.E. and Mountford, M.D. (1959) 'Ear plug laminations in relation to the age composition of a population of fin whales', *Bull. Brit. Mus. nat. Hist. (Zool.)*, *5*(6), 123–61

Purves, P.E. and Pilleri, G. (1978) 'The functional anatomy and general biology of *Pseudorca crassidens* (OWEN) with a review of the hydrodynamics and acoustics in Cetacea', *Invest. on Cetacea*, *9*, 67–227

—— (1983) *Echolocation in Whales and Dolphins*, Academic Press, London

Racey, P.A. and Nicoll, M.E. (1984) 'Mammals of the Seychelles', in Stoddart, D. (ed.), *Biogeography and Ecology of the Seychelles*, Junk Publ., Leiden, Netherlands, pp. 607–26

Rae, B.B. (1965) 'The food of the common porpoise', *J. Zool. Lond.*, *146*, 114–22

Ralls, K., Brownell, R.L. Jr and Ballou, J. (1980) 'Differential mortality by sex and age in mammals, with specific reference to the sperm whale', *Rep. Int. Whal. Commn* (special issue 2), 233–43

Ray, C.C., Mitchell, E.D., Wartzok, D., Kozicki, V.M. and Maiefski, R. (1978) 'Radio tracking of a fin whale (*Balaenoptera physalus*)', *Science*, *202*, 521–4

Reeves, R.R. (1977) 'The problem of gray whale (*Eschrichtius robustus*) harrassment: At the breeding lagoons and during migration', US NTIS, PB Rep. PB-272 506

—— and Leatherwood, S. (1984) 'Live capture fisheries for cetaceans in U.S. and Canadian waters, 1973–1982', *Rep. Int. Whal. Commn*, *34*, 497–508

Reeves, R.R., Mitchell, E., Mansfield, A. and McLaughlin, M. (1983) 'Distribution and migration of the bowhead whale, *Balaena mysticetus*, in the eastern North American Arctic', *Arctic*, *36*(1), 5–64

Reilly, S.B. (1984a) 'Assessing gray whale abundance: a review', in Jones, M.L., Swartz, S.L. and Leatherwood, S. (eds.) *The Gray Whale*, Eschrichtius robustus, Academic Press, New York, NY, pp. 203–33

—— (1984b) 'Observed and published rates of increase in gray whales, *Eschrichtius robustus*', *Rep. Int. Whal. Commn* (special issue 6), 389–399

Rice, D.W. (1968) 'Stomach contents and feeding behavior of killer whales in the eastern North Pacific', *Norsk Hval.*, *57*, 35–8

—— (1974) 'Whales and whale research in the eastern North Pacific', in Schevill, W.E. (ed.),

The Whale Problem, Harvard University Press, Cambridge, Mass., pp. 170–95

—— (1977) 'Synopsis of biological data on the sei whale and Bryde's whale in the eastern North Pacific', *Rep. Int. Whal. Commn* (special issue 1), 92–7

—— (1978) 'The humpback whale in the North Pacific: distribution, exploitation, and numbers', in Norris, K.S. and Reeves, R.R. (eds.), 'Report on a Workshop on Problems Related to Humpback Whales (*Megaptera novaeangliae*) in Hawaii', Contract Rep., Marine Mammal Commission, pp. 29–44 (avail. from Natl. Tech. Inf. Serv., PB-280 794)

—— (1983) 'Gestation period and fetal growth of the gray whale', *Rep. Int. Whal. Commn*, 33, 539–44

Rice, D.W. and Wolman, A.A. (1971) 'The life history and ecology of the gray whale (*Eschrichtius robustus*)', *Amer. Soc. Mammal., Spec. Publ. 3*, pp. 1–142

Richards, D.G., Wolz, J.P. and Herman, L.M. (1984) 'Vocal mimicry of computer-generated sounds and vocal labeling of objects by a bottlenosed dolphin, *Tursiops truncatus*', *J. Comp. Psychol.*, 98, 10–28

Richardson, W.J., Fraker, M.A., Wursig, B. and Wells, R.S. (1985) 'Behaviour of bowhead whales *Balaena mysticetus* summering in the Beaufort Sea: reactions to industrial activities', *Biol. Conserv.*, 32, 195–230

Richardson, W.J., Wursig, B. and Green, C.R. Jr (1986) 'Reactions of bowhead whales, *Balaena mysticetus*, to seismic exploration in the Canadian Beaufort Sea', *J. Acoust. Soc. Am.*, 79(4), 1117–28

Ridgway, S.H. (1986) 'Dolphin brain size', in Bryden, M.M. and Harrison, J.R. (eds.), *Research on Dolphins*, Clarendon Press, Oxford, pp. 59–70

Ridgway, S.H. and Benirschke, K. (eds.) (1977) *Breeding Dolphins: Present Status, Suggestions for the Future*, US Marine Mammal Commission Report No. MMC-76/07

Ridgway, S.H. and Dailey, M.D. (1972) 'Cerebral and cerebellar involvement of trematode parasites in dolphins and their possible role in stranding', *J. Wildl. Dis.*, 8, 33–43

Ridgway, S.H. and Green, R.F. (1967) 'Evidence for a sexual rhythm in male porpoises, *Lagenorhynchus obliquidens* and *Delphinus delphis bairdi*', *Norsk Hvalf. 1*, 1–18

Robineau, D. (1982) 'Distribution des grands cétacés dans l'ocean Indien occidental', *Actes du VIe Colloque de Mammalogie*, pp. 17–23

Robinson, B.H. and Craddock, J.E. (1983) 'Mesopelagic fishes eaten by Fraser's dolphin, *Lagenodelphis hosei*', *Fish. Bull., U.S.*, 81, 283–9

Robson, F. (1984) *Strandings: Ways to Save Whales*, The Science Press, Johannesburg

Roe, H.S.J. (1967) 'Seasonal formation of laminae in the ear plug of the fin whale', *Discovery Rep.*, 35, 1–30

—— (1969) 'The food and feeding habits of the sperm whales (*Physeter catodon* L.) taken off the west coast of Iceland', *J. Cons. Int. Explor. Mer.*, 33, 93–102

Rorvik, C.J. (1980) 'Whales and whaling off Mozambique', *Rep. Int. Whal. Commn*, 30, 223–5

Rorvik, C.J. and Jonsgard, A. (1981) 'Review of Balaenopterids in the North Atlantic Ocean', *FAO Fish. Ser. (5), [Mammals in the Seas] 3*, 269–86

Ross, G.J.B. (1984) 'The smaller cetaceans of the southeast coast of southern Africa', *Ann. Cape Prov. Mus. Nat. Hist.*, 15(2), 173–410

Ross, G.J.B., Best, P.B. and Donnelly, B.G. (1975) 'New records of the pygmy right whale (*Caperea marginata*) from South Africa, with comments on distribution, migration, appearance and behavior', *J. Fish. Res. Bd Can.*, 32, 1005–17

Ross, D. (1976) *Mechanics of Underwater Noise*, Pergamon Press, Oxford

Rothausen, K. (1968a) 'Die systematische Stellung der europaischen Squalodontidae (Odontoceti, Mamm.)', *Palaontologische Zeitschrift*, 42, 83–104

Rothausen, K. (1968b) 'Die Squalodontidae (Odontoceti, Mamm.) im Oligozan und Miozan Italiens', *Memorie degli Istituti di Geologia e Mineralogia dell'Universita di Padova*, 26, 1–18

Ruud, J.T. (1945) 'Further studies on the structure of the baleen plates and their application to age determination', *Hvalrad. Skr.*, 29, 1–69

Ruud, J.T., Jonsgard, A. and Ottestad, P. (1950) 'Age-studies on blue whales', *Hvalrad. Skr.*, 33, 1–72

Saayman, G.S. and Tayler, C.K. (1971) 'Responses to man of captive and free-ranging cetaceans', *Baralogia: Proc. 1st 2nd South African Symp. Underwater Sci.*, University of Pretoria, pp. 1–9

—— (1973) 'Social organization of inshore dolphins (*Tursiops aduncus* and *Sousa*) in the Indian Ocean', *J. Mammal.*, 54, 993–6

—— (1979) 'The socioecology of humpback dolphins (*Sousa* sp.)', in Winn, H.E. and Olla, B.L. (eds.), *The Behavior of Marine Animals, Vol. 3: Cetaceans*, Plenum Press, New York, NY, pp. 165–226

Saayman, C.S., Tayler, C.K. and Bower, D. (1973) 'Diurnal activity cycles in captive and free-ranging Indian Ocean bottlenose dolphins (*Tursiops aduncus* Ehrenburg)', *Behaviour*, 44, 212–33

Sadove, S. (1982) 'Individual photoidentification of fin whales, *Balaenoptera physalus*', *Marine Mammal Information*, July 1982, p. 40

St Aubin, D.J., Geraci, J.R., Smith, T.G. and Friesen, T.G. (1985) 'How do bottlenose dolphins, *Tursiops truncatus*, react to oil films under different light conditions?', *Can. J. Fish. Aquat. Sci.*, 42, 430–6

Sanpera, C., Aguilar, A., Grau, E., Jover, L. and Mizroch, S.A. (1984) 'Report of the "Ballena 2" whale marking and sighting cruise in the Atlantic waters off Spain', *Rep. Int. Whal. Commn*, 34, 663–6

Sanpera, C., Grau, E., Jover, L., Recasens, E., Aguilar, A., Olmos, M., Collet, A. and Donovan, G.P. (1985) 'Results of the "Ballena 3" fin whale marking and sightings cruises off Spain, 1983', *Rep. Int. Whal. Commn*, 35, 495–7

Saschenbrecker, P.W. (1973) 'Levels of DDT and PCB compounds in North Atlantic fin-back whales', *Can. J. Comp. Med.*, 37, 203–6

Scammon, C.M. (1874) *The Marine Mammals of the North-Western Coast of North America, Described and Illustrated; Together With an Account of the American Whale-Fishery*, Carmany, San Francisco, Calif.; Putnam, New York, NY

Schevill, W.E. and Watkins, W.A. (1962) *Whale and Porpoise Voices*, Woods Hole Oceanographic Institution, Woods Hole, Mass., pp. 1–24, and phonograph record

—— (1966) 'Sound structure and directionality in *Orcinus* (killer whale)', *Zoologica*, 51, 71–6, 6 plates

—— (1972) 'Intense low frequency sounds from an Antarctic minke whale, *Balaenoptera acutorostrata*', *Breviora*, 388, 1–8

Schevill, W.E., Watkins, W.A. and Backus, R.H. (1964) 'The 20 cycle signals and *Balaenoptera* (fin whales)', in Tavolga, W.N. (ed.), *Marine Bio-Acoustics, Vol. 1*, Pergamon Press, New York, NY, pp. 147–52

Schevill, W.E., Watkins, W.A. and Ray, C. (1969) 'Click structure in the porpoise, *Phocoena phocoena*', *J. Mammal.*, 50, 721–8

Scholander, P.F. (1959) 'Wave-riding dolphins: how do they do it?', *Science*, 129, 1085–7

Schultz, W. (1970) 'Uber das vorkommen von walen in der Nordund Ostsee', *Zool. Anz*, 85, 172–264

Scoresby, W. (1820) *An Account of the Arctic Regions with a History and Description of the Northern Whale-Fishery, Vol. 2: The Whale Fishery*, Constable, Edinburgh (reprinted 1969, David and Charles, Newton Abbot, Devon)

Seagars, D.J. (1983) 'Jaw structure and functional mechanics in six delphinids (Cetacea: odontoceti)' *Abstract, Proc. of 5th Biennial Conf. on the Biology of Marine Mammals*, 26 Nov.–1 Dec. 1983, Boston, Mass.

Seaman, G. and Burns, (1981) 'Preliminary results of recent studies of belukhas in Alaskan waters', *Rep. Int. Whal. Commn*, 31, 567–75

Sears, R. (1983) 'The photographic identification of individual blue whales (*Balaenoptera musculus*) in the Gulf of St. Lawrence', *Abstract, Proc. of 5th Biennial Conf. on the Biology of Marine Mammals*, 27 Nov–1 Dec. 1983, Boston, Mass.

Seger, J. and Trivers, R.L. (1983) 'Sex ratios of whales before birth', *Abstract, Proc. of 5th Biennial Conf. on Biology of Marine Mammals*, 27 Nov–1 Dec. 1983, Boston, Mass.

Sergeant, D.E. (1959) 'Age determination in odontocete whales from dentinal growth layers', *Norsk Hvalf.*, 48, 273–88

—— (1962) 'The biology of the pilot or pothead whale *Globicephala melaena* (Traill) in Newfoundland waters', *Bull. Fish. Res. Bd Can.*, 132, 1–84

—— (1969) 'Feeding rates of Cetacea', *Fisk. Dir. Skr. Havunders*, 15, 246–58

—— (1973) 'Biology of white whales (*Delphinapterus leucas*) in Western Hudson Bay', *J. Fish. Res. Bd Can.*, 30, 1065–90

—— (1980) 'Levels of mercury and organochlorine residues in tissues of sea mammals from the St. Lawrence estuary', *Int. Council for Explor. of the Sea*, Doc. CM 1980/E:55

—— (1982) 'Mass strandings of toothed whales (Odontoceti) as 'a population phenomenon', *Sci. Rep. Whales Res. Inst., Tokyo*, 34, 1–47

Sergeant, D.E., Caldwell, D.K. and Caldwell, M.C. (1973) 'Age, growth and maturity of bottlenosed dolphin (*Tursiops truncatus*) from northeast Florida', *J. Fish. Res. Bd Can.*, 30, 1009–11

Sergeant, D.E., St Aubin, D.J. and Geraci, J.R. (1980) 'Life history and northwest Atlantic status of the Atlantic white-sided dolphin, *Lagenorhynchus acutus*', *Cetology*, 37, 1–12

Shane, S.H. (1980) 'Occurrence, movements, and distribution of bottlenose dolphins,

Tursiops truncatus, in southern Texas', *Fish. Bull., U.S.*, 78, 593–601

Shane, S.H., Wells, R.S. and Wursig, B. (1986) 'Ecology, behavior and social organization of the bottlenose dolphin: a review', *Marine Mammal Review*, 2(1), 34–63

Sheldrick, M.C. (1979) 'Cetacean strandings along the coasts of the British Isles 1913–1977', in Geraci, J.R. and St Aubin, D.J. (eds.), *Biology of Marine Mammals: Insights Through Strandings*, US Marine Mammal Commission, Washington, D.C., pp. 35–53

Shirakihara, K. and Tanaka, S. (1983) 'An alternative length-specific model and population assessment for the Western North Pacific sperm whales', *Rep. Int. Whal. Commn*, 33, 731–40

Shirakihara, K., Tanaka, S. and Nakano, T. (1983) 'The revised age-specific model for population assessment of the western North Pacific sperm whales', *Rep. Int. Whal. Commn*, 33, 757–60

Shrestha, T.K. (1982) 'Ecology of Gangetic dolphin *Platanista Gangetica* Roxb. in the Karnali River', in Himalayan Research Group (eds.) *Nepal Himalaya: Geo-ecological Perspectives*, Himalayan Research Group, Kathmandu, Nepal, pp. 111–42

Sielfeld, W. (1983) *Mamíferos Marinos de Chile*, Ed. Univ. of Chile, Santiago

Sigurjonsson, J. (1984) 'Killer whale census off Iceland during October 1982', *Rep. Int. Whal. Commn*, 34, 609–12

—— (1985) Sightings survey in the Irminger Sea and off Iceland in 1983', *Rep. Int. Whal. Commn*, 35, 499–503

Silverman, H.B. and Dunbar, M.J. (1980) 'Aggressive tusk use by the narwhal (*Monodon monoceros* L.)' *Nature, Lond.*, 284, 57–8

Sleptsov, M.M. (1941) '[On the biology of reproduction of the Black Sea dolphin *Delphinus delphis*]', *Zool. Zh.*, 22, 632–53

—— (1955) *Biology of Whales and Whaling in the Far East*, Pitzepromizdat, Moscow (Japanese transl. published by the Whales Res. Inst., Tokyo, 1955)

Slijper, E. (1979) *Whales*, Hutchinson University Press, London, 2nd edn, (first English edn, Hutchinson, 1962)

Smet, W.M.A. de (1974) 'Inventaris van de walvisachtigen (Cetacea) van de Vlaamse kust en de Schelde', *Bull. de l'Institut Royal des Sciences Naturelles de Belgique*, 50, 1–156

—— (1981) 'Evidence of whaling in the North Sea and English Channel during the Middle Ages', *FAO Fish. Ser. (5) [Mammals in the Seas]* 3, 301–10

Smith, G.J.D. and Gaskin, D.E. (1974) 'The diet of harbor porpoises (*Phocoena phocoena* (L.)) in coastal waters of eastern Canada, with special reference to the Bay of Fundy', *Can. J. Zool.*, 52, 777–82

Smith, T.D. (1982) 'Current understanding of the status of small cetacean populations in the Black Sea', *FAO Fish. Ser. (5) [Mammals in the Seas]* 4, 121–30

—— (1983) 'Changes in size of three dolphin (*Stenella* spp.) populations in the eastern tropical Pacific', *Fish. Bull., U.S.*, 81, 1–13

Smithers, R.H.N. (1983) *The Mammals of the Southern African subregion*, University of Pretoria, Pretoria

Soegiarto, A. and Polunin, N. (1982) *The Marine Environment in Indonesia*, University of Cambridge/IUCN, Cambridge

Sokolov, V.E. (1962) '[Determination of the sexual condition of females of the Black Sea dolphin (*Delphinus delphis* L.) from morphological changes in the sexual system]', *Nauchn. Dokl. Vysshei Shkoly. Biol. Nauk*, 1, 38–50

Sokolov, V., Bulina, I. and Rodionov, V. (1969) 'Interaction of dolphin epidermis with flow boundary layer', *Nature, Lond.*, 222, 267–8

Sorensen, P.W., Medved, R.J., Hyman, M.A.M., and Winn, H.E. (1984) 'Distribution and abundance of cetaceans in the vicinity of human activities along the continental shelf of the northwestern Atlantic', *Mar. Environ. Res.*, 12(1), 69–81

Steiner, W.W. (1981) 'Species-specific differences in pure tonal whistle vocalizations of five western North Atlantic dolphin species', *Behav. Ecol. Sociobiol.*, 9, 241–6

Stoddard, J.H. (1968) 'Fat contents of Canadian Atlantic herring', *Fish Res. Bd Can. Tech. Rep.*, 79, 1–23

Stroud, R.K. (1979) 'Causes of death in marine mammals stranded along the Oregon coast', *J. Wildl. Dis.*, 15, 91–8

Swartz, S.L. (1986) 'Gray whale migratory, social and breeding behavior', *Rep. Int. Whal. Commn* (special issue 8), 207–30

Taber, S. and Thomas, P. (1982) 'Calf development and mother-calf spatial relationships in southern right whales', *Anim. Behav.*, 30, 1072–83

Tanaka, S. (1983) 'Dynamics model of male sperm whales for generalized selectivity', *Rep. Int. Whal. Commn*, 33, 723–4

Taruski, A.G. (1979) 'The whistle repertoire of the North Atlantic pilot whale (*Globicephala melaena*) and its relationship to behavior and environment', in Winn, H.E. and Olla, B.L. (eds.), *Behavior of Marine Animals, Vol. 3: Cetaceans*, Plenum Press, New York, NY, pp. 345–68

Taruski, A.G., Olney, C.E. and Winn, H.E. (1975) 'Chlorinated hydrocarbons in cetaceans', *J. Fish. Res. Bd Can.*, *132*, 2205–9

Tavolga, M.C. (1966) 'Behavior of the bottlenose dolphin (*Tursiops truncatus*): Social interactions in a captive colony', in Norris, K.S. (ed.), *Whales, Dolphins, and Porpoises*, University of California Press, Berkeley, Calif., pp.718–30

Tavolga, M.C. and Essapian, F.S. (1957) 'The behavior of the bottlenosed dolphin (*Tursiops truncatus*): Mating, pregnancy, parturition and mother-infant behavior', *Zoologica*, *42*, 11–31

Tayler, C.K. and Saayman, G.S. (1972) 'The social organization and behaviour of dolphins (*Tursiops aduncus*) and baboons (*Papio ursinus*): some comparisons and assessments', *Ann. Cape Prov. Mus. (Nat. Hist.)*, *9*, 11–49

Teixeira, A.M. (1979) 'Marine mammals of the Portuguese coast', *Sonderdruck aus Z. f. Saugetierkunde Bd*, *44*(4), 221–38

Thomas, J.A., Awbrey, F.A. and Fisher, S.R. (1986a) 'Use of acoustic techniques in studying whale behaviours', *Rep. Int. Whal. Commn* (special issue 8), 121–38

Thomas, J.A., Fisher, S.R., Ferm, L.M. and Holt, R.S. (1986b) 'Acoustic detection of cetaceans using a towed array of hydrophones', *Rep. Int. Whal. Commn* (special issue 8), 139–48

Thomas, P. (1986) 'Methodology of behavioural studies of cetaceans; right whale mother-infant behaviour', *Rep. Int. Whal. Commn* (special issue 8), 113–20

Thompson, P.O. and Cummings, W.C. (1969) 'Sound production of the finback whale, *Balaenoptera physalus*, and Eden's whale, *B. edeni*, in the Gulf of California', *Abstract*, *Proc. 6th Ann. Calif. Biol. Sonar and Diving Mammals*, Stanford Research Institute, Calif., p. 109

Thompson, T.J., Winn, H.E. and Perkins, P.J. (1979) 'Mysticete sounds', in Winn, H.E. and Olla, B.L. (eds.), *Behavior of Marine Animals. Vol. 3: Cetaceans*, Plenum Press, New York, NY, pp. 403–31

Tin Thein, U. (1977) 'The Burmese freshwater dolphin', *Mammalia*, *41*(2), 233–4

Tobayama, T., Nishiwaki, M. and Hung, C.Y. (1973) 'Records of the Fraser's Arawak dolphin (*Lagenodelphis hosei*) in the western north Pacific', *Sci. Rep. Whales Res. Inst., Tokyo*, *25*, 251–63

Tomilin, A.G. (1967) *Cetacea*, Israel Program for Scientific Translations, Jerusalem

Tonnessen, J.N. and Johnsen, A.O. (1982) *The History of Modern Whaling*, Hurst, London (English trans. of original Norwegian edn)

Torres, D., Yanez, J. and Cattan, P.F. (1979) 'Mamíferos Marinos de Chile. Antecedentes y situación actual', Biol. Pesq. Stgo. Chile, 11, 49–81

Tower, D.B. (1954) 'Structural and functional organization of mammalian cerebral cortex: the correlation of neurone density with brain size. Cortical neurone density in the fin whale (*Balaenoptera physalus* L.) with a note on the cortical neurone density in the Indian elephant', *J. Comp. Neurol.*, *101*, 19–51

Trivers, R.L. (1972) 'Parental investment and sexual selection', in Campbell, B.G. (ed.), *Sexual Selection and the Descent of Man*, Aldine, Chicago, Ill., pp. 136–79

Tyack, P. (1981) 'Interactions between singing Hawaiian humpback whales and conspecifics nearby', *Behav. Ecol. Sociobiol.*, *8*, 105–16

Tyack, P. and Whitehead, H. (1983) 'Male competition in large groups of wintering humpback whales', *Behaviour*, *83*, 132–54

UNEP (1978) *The Southern Ocean: The Living Resources of the Southern Ocean*, FAO, Rome

Van Utrecht, W.L. (1978) 'Age and growth in *Phocoena phocoena* Linnaeus, 1758 (Cetacea, Odontoceti) from the North Sea', *Bijdr. Dierk.*, *48*, 16–28

—— (1981) 'Comparison of accumulation patterns in layered dentinal tissue of some Odontoceti and corresponding patterns in baleen plates and ear plugs of Balaenopteridae', *Beaufortia*, *31*, 111–22

Van Valen, L. (1968) 'Monophyly or diphyly in the origin of whales', *Evolution*, *22*, 37–41

Viale, D. (1978) 'Evidence of metal pollution in Cetacea of the western Mediterranean', *Ann. Inst. oceanogr., Paris*, *54*, 5–16

Walker, W.A. (1975) 'Review of the live-capture fishery for smaller cetaceans taken in southern California waters for public display, 1966–73', *J. Fish. Res. Bd Can.*, *32*, 1197–211

—— (1981) 'Air sinus parasitism and pathology in free-ranging common dolphins

(*Delphinus delphis*) in the eastern tropical Pacific', SWFC Admin. Rep. LJ-81–23C

Walker, W.A., Leatherwood, S., Goodrich, K.R., Perrin, W.F. and Stroud, R.K. (1986) 'Geographical variation and biology of the Pacific white-sided dolphin, *Lagenorhynchus obliquidens*, in the north-eastern Pacific', in Bryden, M.M. and Harrison, R.J. (eds.), *Research on Dolphins*, Clarendon Press, Oxford, pp. 441–65

Watkins, W.A. (1980) 'Acoustics and the behavior of sperm whales', in Busnel, R.-G. and Fish, J.F. (eds.), *Animal Sonar Systems*, Plenum, New York, NY, pp. 283–90

—— (1981) 'Activities and underwater sounds of fin whales', *Sci. Rep. Whales Res. Inst., Tokyo, 33*, 83–117

Watkins, W.A. and Schevill, W.E. (1976) 'Right whale feeding and baleen rattle', *J. Mammal., 57*, 58–66

—— (1977) 'Sperm whale codas', *J. Acoust. Soc. Am., 62*, 1485–90

—— (1979) 'Aerial observation of feeding behavior in four baleen whales: *Eubalaena glacialis, Balaenoptera borealis, Megaptera novaeangliae*, and *Balaenoptera physalus*', *J. Mammal., 60*, 155–63

—— (1980) 'Characteristic features of the underwater sounds of *Cephalorhynchus commersonii*', *J. Mammal., 61*, 738–9

Watkins, W.A. and Moore, K.E. (1982) 'An underwater acoustic survey for sperm whales (*Physeter catodon*) and other cetaceans in the southeast Caribbean', *Cetology*, no. 46, 1–7

Watkins, W.A. and Wartzok, D. (1985) 'Sensory biophysics of marine mammals', *Marine Mammal Science, 1*, 219–60

Watkins, W.A., Moore, K.E., Wartzok, D. and Johnson, J.H. (1981) Radio tracking of finback (*Balaenoptera physalus*) and humpback (*Megaptera novaeangliae*) in Prince William Sound, Alaska', *Deep Sea Research, 28*, (577–88

Watkins, W.A., Schevill, W.E. and Best, P.B. (1977) 'Underwater sounds of *Cephalorhynchus heavisidii* (Mammalia: Cetacea)', *J. Mammal., 58*, 316–20

Watkins, W.A., Schevill, W.E. and Ray, C. (1971) 'Underwater sounds of *Monodon* (narwhal)', *J. Acoust. Soc. Am., 49*, 595–9

Watson, A.P. (1976) 'The diurnal behaviour of the harbour porpoise (*Phocoena phocoena* L.) in the coastal waters of the Bay of Fundy', MSc thesis, University of Guelph, Ontario

Watson, L. (1981) *Sea Guide to the Whales of the World*, Hutchinson, (London

Webb, N.G. (1978) 'Boat towing by a bottlenose dolphin', *Carnivore, 1*, (122–30

Webb, P.W. (1975) 'Hydrodynamics and energetics of fish propulsion', *Fish. Res. Bd Can. Bull., 190*, 1–158

Wells, R.S., Irvine, A.B., and Scott, M.D. (1980) 'The social ecology of inshore odontocetes', in Herman, L.M. (ed.), *Cetacean Behavior*, Wiley Interscience, New York, NY, pp. 263–318

West, R.M. (1980) 'Middle Eocene large mammal assemblage with Tethyan affinities, Ganda Kas region, Pakistan', *Journal of Paleontology, 54*(3), (508–33

White, M.J. Jr, Jennings, J.J., Fandy, W.F. and Cornell, L.H. (1981) 'An evaluation of tagging, marking, and tattooing techniques for small delphinids', NOAA Tech. Memorandum NMFS. NOAA-TM-NMFS-SWFC-16

Whitehead, H. and Carscadden, J.E. (1985) 'Predicting inshore whale abundance — whales and capelin off the Newfoundland coast', *Can. J. Fish. Aquat. Sci., 42*(5), 976–81

Whitehead, H. and Glass, C. (1985) 'Orcas (killer whales) attack humpback whales', *J. Mammal., 66*(1), 183–5

Whitehead, H. and Gordon, J. (1986) 'Methods of obtaining data for assessing and modelling sperm whale populations which do not depend on catches', *Rep. Int. Whal. Commn* (special issue 8), 149–66

Whitehead, H. and Payne, R. (1981) 'New techniques for assessing populations of right whales without killing them', *FAO Fish. Ser.* (5) [*Mammals in the Seas*] 4, 189–209

Whitmore, F.C. and Sanders, A.E. (1977) 'Review of the Oligocene Cetacea', *Syst. Zool., 25*(4) (for Dec 1976), 304–20

Williamson, G.R. (1975) 'Minke Whales off Brazil', *Sci. Rep. Whales Res. Inst., Tokyo, 27*, 37–59

Wilke, F. and Nicholson, A.J. (1958) 'Food of porpoises in waters off Japan', *J. Mammal., 391*–3

Winn, H.E. and Perkins, P.F. (1976) 'Distribution and sounds of the minke whale, with a review of mysticete sounds', *Cetology, 19*, 1–12

Winn, H.E. and Winn, L.K. (1978) 'The song of the humpback whale, *Megaptera novaeangliae*, in the West Indies', *Mar. Biol. (Berl.), 47*, 97–114

Winn, H.E., Bischoff, W.L. and Taruski, A.G. (1973) 'Cytological sexing of Cetaceans', *Mar. Biol. (Berl.), 23*, 343–6

Winn, H.E., Edel, R.K. and Taruski, A.G. (1975) 'Population estimate of the humpback whale (*Megaptera novaeangliae*) in the West Indies by visual and acoustic techniques', *J. Fish. Res. Bd Can.*, 32, 499–506

Winn, H.E., Perkins, P.J. and Poulter, T.C. (1971) 'Sounds of the humpback whale', *Proc. 7th Ann. Conf. Biol. Sonar and Diving Mammals*, Stanford Res. Inst., Calif., pp. 39–52

Winn, H.E., Thompson, T.J., Cummings, W.C., Hain, J., Hudnall, J., Hays, H. and Steiner, W.W. (1981) 'Song of the humpback whale — population comparisons', *Behav. Ecol. Sociobiol.*, 8, 41–6

Winn, L.K. and Winn, H.E. (1985) *Wings in the Sea. The Humpback Whale*, University of Rhode Island, University Press of New England, Hanover, New Hampshire

Wood, F.G. and Evans, W.E. (1980) 'Adaptiveness and ecology of echolocation in toothed whales', in Busnel, R-G. and Fish, J.F. (eds.), *Animal Sonar Systems*, Plenum Press, New York, NY, pp. 381–425

Wood, F.F. Jr, Caldwell, D.K. and Caldwell, M.C. (1970) 'Behavioral interactions between porpoises and sharks', *Invest. on Cetacea*, 2, 264–77

Wolman, A.A. and Wilson, A.J. (1970) 'Occurrence of pesticides in whales', *Pestic. Monit. J.*, 4, 8–10

Wursig, B. (1978) 'Occurrence and group organization of Atlantic bottlenose porpoises (*Tursiops truncatus*) in an Argentine bay', *Biol. Bull.*, 154, 348–59

—— (1983) 'The question of dolphin awareness approached through studies in nature', *Cetus*, 5, 4–7

—— (1986) 'Delphinid foraging strategies', in Schusterman, R.J., Thomas, J.A. and Wood, F.G. (eds.), *Dolphin Cognition and Behavior: A Comparative Approach*, Lawrence Erlbaum, Hillsdale, N J, pp. 347–59

Wursig, B. and Wursig, M. (1977) 'The photographic determination of group size, composition, and stability of coastal porpoises (*Tursiops truncatus*)', *Science*, 198, 755–6

—— (1979) 'Behavior and ecology of bottlenose porpoises, *Tursiops truncatus*, in the South Atlantic', *Fish. Bull., U.S.*, 77, 399–442

—— (1980) 'Behavior and ecology of dusky porpoises, *Lagenorhynchus obscurus*, in the South Atlantic', *Fish. Bull., U.S.*, 77, 871–90

Wursig, B., Wells, R.S., and Croll, D.A. (1986) 'Behavior of gray whales summering near St. Lawrence Island, Bering Sea', *Can. J. Zool.*, 64, 611–21

Wursig, B., Dorsey, E.M., Fraker, M.A., Payne, R.S., Richardson, W.J. and Wells, R.S. (1984a) 'Behavior of bowhead whales, *Balaena mysticetus*, summering in the Beaufort Sea: surfacing, respiration, and dive characteristics', *Can. J. Zool.*, 62, 1910–21

—— (1984b) 'Behavior of bowhead whales, *Balaena mysticetus*, summering in the Beaufort Sea: A description', *Fish. Bull., U.S.*, 83, 357–77

—— (1986) 'Behaviour of bowhead whales, *Balaena mysticetus*, summering in the Beaufort Sea: A summary', *Rep. Int. Whal. Commn* (special issue 8), 167–76

Wursig, M., Wursig, B. and Mermoz, J.F. (1977) 'Desplazamientos, comportamiento general y un varamiento de la marsopa espinosa, *Phocoena spinipinnis*, en el Golfo san José (Chubut, Argentina)', *Physis*, 36, 71–9

Yablokov, A.V. (1964) 'Convergence or parallelism in the evolution of cetaceans', *Palaeontol. Zh.*, 1, 97–106

Yablokov, A.V. and Bogoslovskaya, L.S. (1984) 'A review of Russian research on the biology and commercial whaling of the gray whale', in Jones, M.L., Swartz, S.L. and Leatherwood, S. (eds.), *The Gray Whale* Eschrichtius robustus, Academic Press, New York, NY, pp. 465–85

Yablokov, A.V., Bel'kovich, V.M. and Borisov, V.I. (1972) *Whales and Dolphins*, Israel Program for Scientific Translations, Jerusalem

Yasui, W.Y. (1980) 'Morphometrics, hydrodynamics and energetics of locomotion for a small cetacean, *Phocoena phocoena* L., MSc thesis, University of Guelph, Ontario

Yasui, W.Y. and Gaskin, D.E. (in press) 'Energy budget of a small cetacean, the harbour porpoise, *Phocoena phocoena* (L.)', *Ophelia*, 26

Yurick, D.B. (1977) 'Populations, subpopulations and zoogeography of the harbour porpoise, *Phocoena phocoena* L.', MSc thesis, University of Guelph, Ontario

Zagaeski, M. (1983) 'Effects of high energy sound on guppies', *Abstract, Proc. of 5th Biennial Conference on the Biology of Marine Mammals*, 27 Nov–1 Dec. 1983, Boston, Mass.

Zhou, K. (1982) 'Classification and phylogeny of the superfamily Platanistoidea, with notes on evidence of the monophyly of the Cetacea', *Sci. Rep. Whales Res. Inst., Tokyo*, 34, 93–108

Zhou, K., Quian, W. and Li, Y. (1977) 'Studies on the distribution of Baiji, *Lipotes vexillifer* Miller', *Acta Zool. Sinica*, 23, 72–9

—— (1979) 'The osteology and the systematic position of the baiji, *Lipotes vexillifer*', *Acta Zool. Sinica*, 25, 58–74

Zhou, K., Pilleri. G., and Li, Y. (1980) 'Observations on baiji (*Lipotes vexillifer*) and finless porpoise (*Neophocoena asiaeorientalis*) in the lower reaches of the Changjiang', *Scientia Sinica*, 23, 786–94

Zhou, K., Li, Y., Nishiwaki, M. and Kataoki, T. (1982) 'A brief report on the observations of the baiji, *Lipotes vexillifer*, in the lower reaches of the Yangtze River between Nanjing and Guichi', *Acta Theriologica Sinica*, 2(2), 253–5

Index